THE COMPLETE WATERCOLOUR ARTIST

The Complete Watercolour Artist

MATERIALS · TECHNIQUES · COLOUR THEORY
COMPOSITION · STYLE · SUBJECT

Edited by Sally Harper

A QUANTUM BOOK

Published by Grange Books
an imprint of Grange Books Plc
The Grange
Kingsnorth Industrial Estate
Hoo, nr. Rochester
Kent ME3 9ND
www.grangebooks.co.uk

Copyright ©MCMXCIV Quintet Publishing Ltd

This edition printed 2001

All rights reserved.

This book is protected by copyright. No part of it may be reproduced, stored in a retrieval system, or transmitted in any form or by any means, without the prior permission in writing of the Publisher, nor be otherwise circulated in any form of binding or cover other than that in which it is published and without a similar condition including this condition being imposed on the subsequent publisher.

1-84013-383-X

QUMCWA

This book is Produced by
Quantum Books Ltd
6 Blundell Street
London N7 9BH

Printed in Singapore by
Star Standard Industries (Pte) Ltd

CONTENTS

Paul Cézanne

Montagne Sainte Victoire

Cézanne's most famous landscape motif is seen in the distance, a shimmering, mirage-like image, floating before our eyes. Here, Cézanne makes extensive use of the untouched white surface of the paper in order both to construct and dissolve the form of the mountain.

Introduction

Of all the painting media, watercolour is perhaps the most idiosyncratic. With watercolour, what is done is done: once applied to paper, a watercolour wash must stay there. But the very unpredictable nature of watercolour painting also brings special satisfaction to the artist. There is a keen pleasure involved in working with watercolour and adapting to it, rather than determining from the outset what the result will be.

The art of watercolour painting has a history that stretches back over 40,000 years. The first known examples were cave paintings, using thick applications of opaque water-based paint. Early Chinese artists, however, used soft-haired brushes and worked on silk and rice paper, whose absorbent surfaces encouraged the use of delicate, transparent washes. With just a few fine strokes, these artists captured a mood of atmospheric space in their landscapes, anticipating by several centuries the work of Western watercolour artists such as Turner and Girtin.

This is the strength of watercolour: its ability to let the texture and tone of the paper mingle with the vivacity of the paint, creating that illusion of light and depth for which many artists strive. True, watercolour may have a mind of its own, but that is all part of the excitement of this intriguing medium.

"I don't do watercolour; it's far too difficult" is a remark often heard from amateur painters, even those who regard themselves as reasonably proficient in other media, such as oils. It cannot be denied that some people find watercolours a little harder to use than oils. This very attractive medium is sometimes unpredictable, but this very unpredictability should be regarded as a virtue, not a drawback. What people really mean when they make this kind of remark is that watercolours cannot be altered over and over again as oils can; a colour or wash, once laid down on the paper, must stay there. To some extent this is true, and it is understandable that people should feel a certain nervousness when approaching a watercolour. But, in fact, many alterations can be made, and often are, as a painting progresses: a wash in a colour that has not come out quite right can be changed dramatically by applying another wash on top of it; areas can be sponged out or worked over; and if the worst comes to the worst the whole painting can be put under running water and washed away.

Watercolour has many virtues, its main attraction for artists being its freshness and translucence, making it ideal for a variety of subjects, especially landscapes and flower paintings. As its name implies, pure watercolour is mixed with water and is transparent, so that it must be applied from light to dark, unlike oil paint or acrylics which are opaque and can be built up from dark to light. Highlights consist of areas of the paper left white or very pale washes surrounded by darker ones. A certain amount of pre-planning is necessary at an early stage to work out where the highlights are to be, but some planning is always needed for painting or drawing, whatever medium is being used.

No one ever quite knows how watercolour will behave, and many watercolour artists find this very unpredictability one of its greatest assets. The medium itself will often begin to "take over" a painting, suggesting ways of creating interesting effects and lending a sparkle and spontaneity to the work. Experience is needed to make the most of the chance effects that occur in watercolour painting. A real feeling for the medium may not be achieved until several attempts

below: John Sell Cotman, *Dolgelly, North Wales.* While on a sketching tour of North Wales in 1802, Cotman made outline pencil drawings from which he would later construct the final watercolour in his studio.

above: In *The Dismasted Brig* by John Sell Cotman, the rain-swept sky has been treated in bold, broad masses, and the swirling movement of the waves has been used to make a geometric pattern of different-sized trangles.

have been abandoned, but there are many ways of using watercolour and with perseverance you will evolve your own style and method. The purely practical advantages of watercolour painting are that you need little expensive equipment, the painting can be done more or less anywhere provided there is enough light, and paints can be cleared up quickly, leaving no mess. Since the paper is relatively cheap, experiments and mistakes are not very expensive.

The Medium

Watercolour, like all paint, is made by mixing pigment with a binding agent, in this case gum arabic, which is soluble in water. There are two types of watercolour, "pure" or "classical" watercolour, which is transparent, and gouache, or "body colour", which is the same pigment made opaque by adding white pigment to the binder. The technique of gouache painting is similar to that of oil or acrylic, since light colour can be laid over dark, and is outside the scope of this book; but gouache is quite frequently used in conjunction with pure watercolour. Its use is a source of constant controversy among watercolourists: some claim that it destroys the character of the medium – its luminosity – and should never be used; others combine the two with considerable success. Nowadays there is a general trend towards mixing different media, and watercolour is often used with pastel, pen and ink, pencils or crayons (see "Techniques"). It can be a useful exercise, when a watercolour has "gone wrong", to draw into it with inks or pastels to see the effects that can be achieved.

The History of Watercolour Painting

It is commonly believed that watercolour was invented by the English landscape painters of the eighteenth century, but this is far from so. Watercolour has been in use in various forms for many centuries. Indeed the ancient Egyptians used a form of it for painting on plaster to decorate their tombs; the great frescoes of Renaissance Italy were painted in a kind of watercolour; it was used by medieval manuscript illuminators, both in its "pure" form and mixed with body colour; the great German artist, Albrecht Dürer (1471–1528), made use of it extensively, and so did many botanical illustrators of the sixteenth century and the Dutch flower painters of the seventeenth century.

It was, even so, in eighteenth-century England that watercolour painting was elevated to the status of a national art. A new interest in landscape painting for its own sake culminated in the work of John Constable (1776–1837), the forerunner of the Impressionists. Landscape had hitherto been purely topographical – a truthful and detailed record of a particular place – but in the hands of artists such as Paul Sandby (1725–1809), John Cozens (1752–97), Thomas Girtin (1775–1802), Francis Towne (1740–1816), John Sell Cotman (1782–1842) and Peter de Wint (1784–1849) it became much more than that. Watercolour was at last

above: John Constable, *Study of Cirrhus Clouds.* English painter John Constable revolutionized the art of watercolour, bringing to it his acute observations of weather, light and atmosphere.

fully exploited and given the recognition that was its due.

Most of these artists worked in watercolour alone, regarding it as the perfect medium for creating the light, airy, atmospheric effects they sought; Constable used watercolour mainly for quick sketches of skies. The greatest watercolourist of all, J.M.W. Turner (1775–1851), achieved his fame as an oil painter, but he produced watercolours of an amazing depth and richness. Quite uninhibited by any "rules", he exploited accidental effects like thumbprints and haphazard blobs of paint, turning them into some of the most magical depictions of light and colour that have ever been seen in paint.

Throughout the nineteenth century the techniques of watercolour continued to be developed and the subject matter became more varied. The poet and artist, William Blake (1757–1827), evolved his own method of conveying his poetic vision in watercolour, as did his follower, Samuel Palmer (1805–81), who used swirls and blocks of opaque colour in his visionary and symbolic landscapes. With the end of the Napoleonic Wars in 1815, travel once again became easier, and the topographical tradition reached new heights in the work of artists like Samuel Prout (1783–1852), a superlative draughtsman who painted the buildings and scenery of western Europe in faithful detail. Travelling further afield, John Frederick Lewis (1805–76) made glowing studies of Middle Eastern scenes, and new techniques, such as the "dragged" wash, were pioneered by Richard Parkes Bonington (1802–28) for both landscape and figure subjects, to be taken further by his friend, the French artist, Eugène Delacroix (1798–1863).

British artists of the twentieth century have not ignored the possibilities of watercolour, its greatest exponents being Graham Sutherland (1903–80) and Paul Nash (1889–1946) and his brother John (b. 1893). It remains a popular medium with both professional artists and amateurs, and new ways are constantly being found of exploring its full potential.

right: Albrecht Dürer, who painted this painting, which has come to be known as *The Great Piece of Turf,* found watercolour a particularly sympathetic medium for detailed studies of nature. We cannot be sure of his precise method, but he probably began by using transparent washes to establish broad areas, such as the large leaves, and then built up intricate details with tiny strokes of opaque paint (or body colour).

Paul Klee, 1918

City of Churches

WATERCOLOUR AND LINE DRAWING

One of the century's most prolific watercolourists, Paul Klee took advantage of the medium's transparency, building images from areas of modulated colour occasionally articulated by animated line drawing.

MATERIALS

"To get the right results, start with the right tools": it's a rule that applies to many undertakings, including watercolour painting. If you are just starting to experiment with watercolour, you may not want to invest a great deal of money in equipment. Certainly, there is no need to rush out and buy an expensive easel and an enormous range of paint colours. It is perfectly acceptable to start small, and purchase equipment when you are sure of precisely what you require. It may be that you never get round to buying that expensive easel: many professional watercolourists work at an ordinary table, with their board supported by a pile of books. All the same, it is just as well not to scrimp in some areas. Good quality paints and brushes will stand the watercolour artist in good stead, and you will not need an enormous range of paints and brushes to start with. Few watercolourists use more than a dozen colours, and most rely on only two or three brushes. The choice of papers available to the watercolour painter can also be daunting. Again, feel free to experiment: buy just a few sheets at a time until you are familiar with the characteristics of different types of paper.

Perhaps the greatest single advantage of watercolour painting is that only a small amount of equipment is needed, equipment which is easy to store. Paints and brushes, although not cheap, last for a long time; indeed brushes should last virtually for ever if looked after. Hand-made paper is expensive, but beginners will find that many satisfactory machine-made papers are available from artist's suppliers.

Paints and Colours

Ready-made watercolour paint is sold in various forms, the commonest being tubes, pans and half-pans. These all contain glycerine and are known as semi-moist colours, unlike the traditional dry cakes, which are still available in some artist's suppliers, but are not much used today. Dry cakes require considerable rubbing with water before the colour is released. It is a slow process, but the paints are therefore economical.

Gouache paints, or designer's colours as they are sometimes called, are normally sold in tubes. These paints, and the cheaper versions of them, poster colours and powder paints, have chalk added to the pigment to thicken it, and are thus opaque, unlike true watercolour. Watercolours themselves can be mixed with Chinese white to make them opaque or semi-opaque, so that they become a softer and more subtle form of gouache.

Success in watercolour painting depends so much on applying layers of transparent, but rich, colour that it is a mistake to buy any but the best-quality paints, known as "artist's quality". There are cheaper paints, sold for "sketching", but since these contain a filler to extend the pigment, the colour is weaker and the paint tends

right: GOUACHE PAINTS These paints are an opaque version of watercolours, which can be used more thickly and sometimes in combination with the transparent colours. Gouache white, in particular, is a useful alternative to Chinese white for adding highlights or thickening paint for certain effects.

right: TUBE PAINTBOX The choice of paintbox needs some thought. Avoid boxes prefitted with a selection of colours. First, you won't know whether they are good-quality paints, and second, you may find yourself stuck with colours you don't need. It is better to buy an empty box that can be filled with colours of your choice, either tubes, pans, or half-pans. The paintbox shown here is designed for tube paints, which you can squeeze into the small sections as needed.

above: PAN PAINTBOX All watercolours contain gum arabic to keep them moist, so don't be put off pans because you think they may dry up. Pans are available in whole and half-sizes. Try a half-pan if you are unsure about a colour. There is a wide range of paintboxes designed to hold pans and half-pans, which can be removed and replaced when used up.

below: TUBES Regular tubes of watercolour are quite small. Some manufacturers make larger sizes, but these are not necessary – it takes a long time to get through even a regular tube. Good-quality paints can be kept indefinitely as long as you screw the caps back after use. If you prefer tubes to pans, you may not need a paintbox; you could use one of the palettes shown on page 23.

Payne's grey and cadmium yellow

Prussian blue and cadmium yellow

Cobalt and cadmium yellow

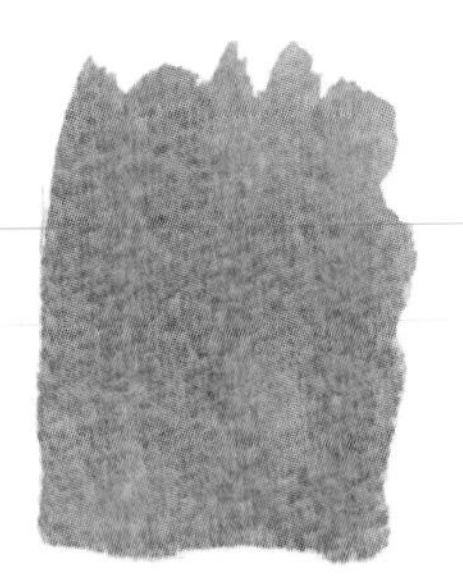

Prussian blue and lemon yellow

Viridian and lemon

Black and cadmium yellow

Cobalt blue and alizarin crimson

Payne's grey and alizarin crimson

Prussian blue and alizarin crimson

Cobalt blue and Payne's grey

Black and Prussian blue

Black and alizarin crimson

Cadmium yellow and cadmium red

Alizarin crimson and cadmium yellow

Lemon yellow and cadmium red

Burnt umber and black

Payne's grey and cadmium red

Burnt umber and cobalt blue

to be chalky and unpredictable.

Whether to use pans, half-pans or tubes is a personal choice. Each type has its advantages and disadvantages. Tubes are excellent for those who work mainly indoors on a fairly large scale, as any quantity of paint can be squeezed out of them on to the palette. Any paint left on the palette after a painting is completed can be used again later, simply by moistening it with a wet brush. Pans and half-pans, which can be bought in sets in their own palette and are easy to carry, are the most popular choice for working out of doors on a small scale. Watercolours can also be bought in concentrated form in bottles, with droppers to transfer the paint to the palette. These are eminently suitable for broad washes which require a large quantity of paint, but they are less easy to mix than the other types.

The choice of colours is also personal, though there are some colours that everyone must have. Nowadays there is such a vast range of colours to choose from that a beginner is justified in feeling somewhat bewildered, but, in fact, only a few are really necessary. One point to bear in mind is that some colours are considerably less permanent than others, which may not be an important consideration for quick sketches and "note-taking", but clearly is for any painting that is intended to be hung or exhibited. A wise course, therefore, is to rule out any colours classified as "fugitive". All the major paint manufacturers have systems of grading permanence.

These appear on the manufacturers' colour charts. The tubes or pans will also bear a code indicating the relative price of each colour, some being more expensive than others according to the cost of the pigment used.

The golden rule when choosing a range of colours, or "palette" as professionals call it, is to keep it as simple as possible. Few watercolourists use more than a dozen colours. For landscape painting, useful additions to the basic palette are sap green, Hooker's green, raw umber and cerulean blue, while monastral blue (called Winsor blue in the Winsor and Newton range) is sometimes recommended instead of Prussian blue. For flower painting the basic range might be enlarged by the addition of cobalt violet and lemon yellow. See the "Colour and Composition" section for more information on colour choice.

Paper

The traditional support – the term used for the surface on which any painting is done – is white or pale-coloured paper, which reflects back through the transparent paint to give the translucent quality so characteristic of watercolours. There are many types of watercolour paper. Each individual will probably need to try several before establishing which one suits his method of working, though sometimes a particular paper may be chosen to create a special effect.

The three main types of machine-made paper are hot-pressed (HP), cold-pressed (CP), which is also rather quaintly known as "not" for "not hot-pressed", and rough. Hot-pressed paper is very smooth and, although suitable for drawing or pen-and-wash, is not a good choice for building up layers of washes in the standard watercolour technique as it becomes clogged very quickly. Cold-pressed paper, which is slightly textured, is the most popular and is suitable for both

below: The range of papers available is vast and can be bewildering even for the experienced artist. In order to find the paper which suits your particular style and immediate needs, buy only a few sheets at a time. The heavier papers are more expensive but can absorb large amounts of water; they do not, therefore, need stretching, which makes them useful for outdoor work. Toned papers provide a convenient middle ground for some subjects, from which to work darks and lights.

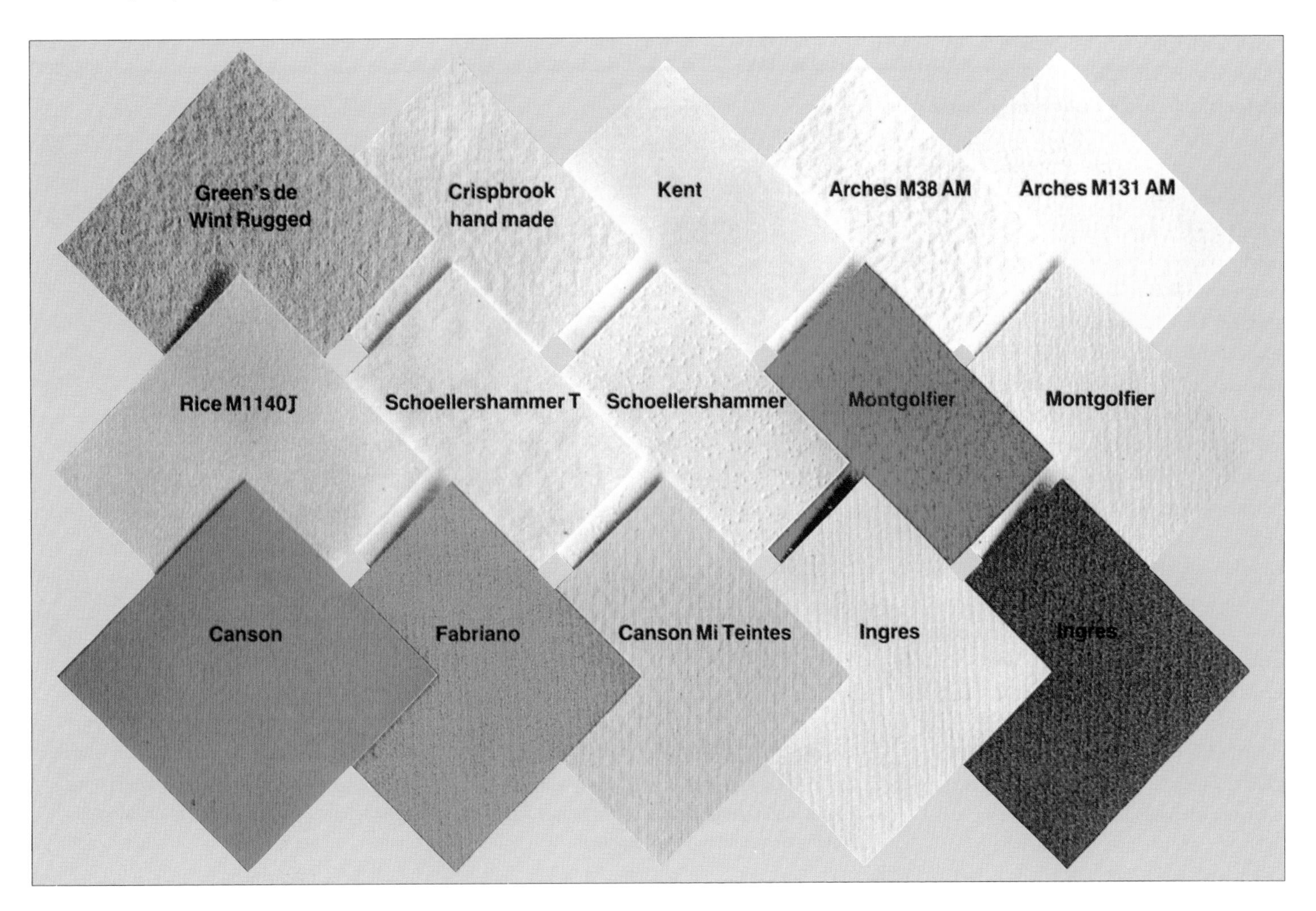

broad washes and fine detail. Rough paper, as its name implies, is much more heavily textured, and the paint will settle in the "troughs" while sliding off the "peaks", giving a speckled effect which can be effective for some subjects but is difficult to exploit successfully. Among the best-known makes of good watercolour papers are Saunders, Fabriano, Arches, Bockingford, Strathmore in the US, Ingres in the UK, and R.W.S. (Royal Watercolour Society), some of which also include hand-made papers.

Hand-made papers are made from pure linen rag and specially treated with size to provide the best possible surface for watercolour work. Such papers are sized on one side only and thus have a right and a wrong side, which can be checked by holding the paper up to the light so that the watermark becomes visible. Many of the better machine-made papers also have a watermark and hence a right and wrong side.

Some papers have surfaces which are tough enough to withstand a great deal of preliminary drawing and rubbing out without damage, but others do not. Bockingford paper, for instance, although excellent in many ways, is quickly damaged by erasing, and the paint will take on a patchy appearance wherever the surface has been spoiled. One of its advantages, however, is that paint can easily be removed by washing out where necesary; the paint, moreover, can be manipulated and moved around in a very free way. Arches paper and Saunders paper are both strong enough to stand up to erasing, but mistakes are difficult to remove from the former, which holds the paint very firmly. Saunders paper is a good choice for beginners: it is strong, stretches well and has a pleasant surface.

Stretching Paper

Watercolour papers vary widely in weight, or thickness, and the lighter ones need to be stretched or they will buckle as soon as wet paint is applied to them. The weight is usually expressed in pounds and refers to the weight of a ream (480 sheets), not to each individual sheet. The thinner papers, ranging from 70 to 140 pounds, must be stretched; any paper weighing 200 pounds or more can be used without this treatment. Watercolour boards can be bought. These have watercolour paper mounted on heavy board, so that the stretching has already been done. They are particularly useful for outdoor work, since no drawing board is needed.

Stretching paper is not difficult, but since the paper must be soaked, it needs to be done at least two hours before you intend to start work. Cut the paper to the size required and wet it well on both sides by laying it in a bath or tray of water. When it is well soaked, hold it up by the corners to drain off the excess water, then lay it right side up on a drawing board and stick down each edge with the gummed brown paper known as gumstrip (do not use masking tape or sellotape). Finally, place a drawing pin in each corner. The paper will dry taut and flat and should not buckle when paint is applied. Occasionally, however, stretching does go wrong and the paper buckles at one corner or tears away from the gumstrip; if that happens, you must repeat the process. Drying can be hastened with a hairdryer, but it is not a good practice to leave the board in front of a fire.

Step by Step: Stretching Paper

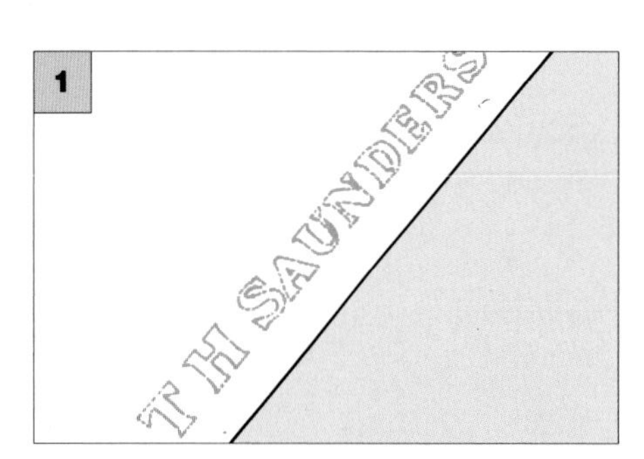

1: First check which is the right side of the paper. Hold it to the light so the watermark appears the right way round.

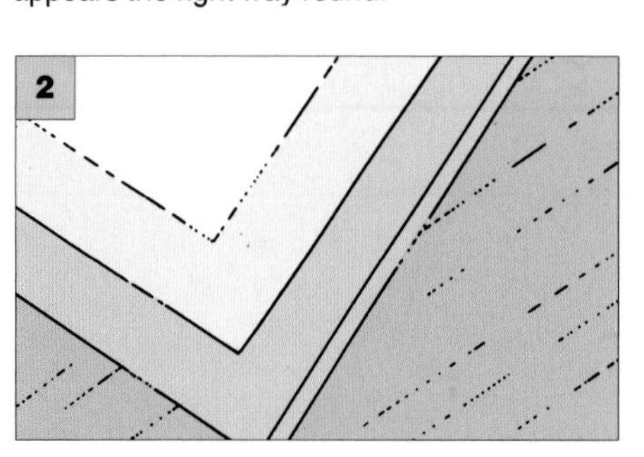

2: Trim the paper to size for the drawing board, leaving a good margin of board so that the gummed tape will adhere.

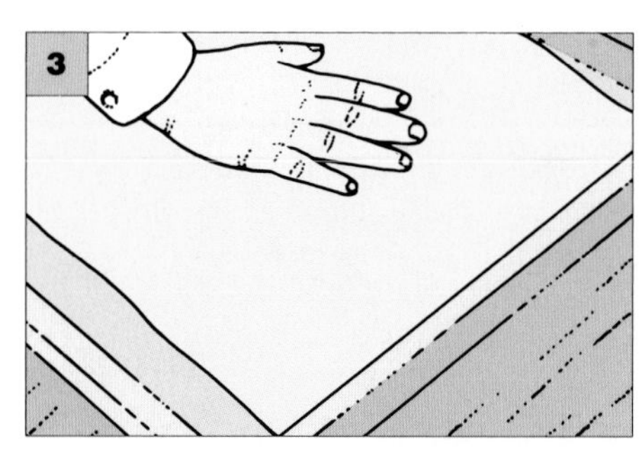

3: Soak the paper in a tray or sink full of clean water. The amount of time needed to soak varies with the type of paper.

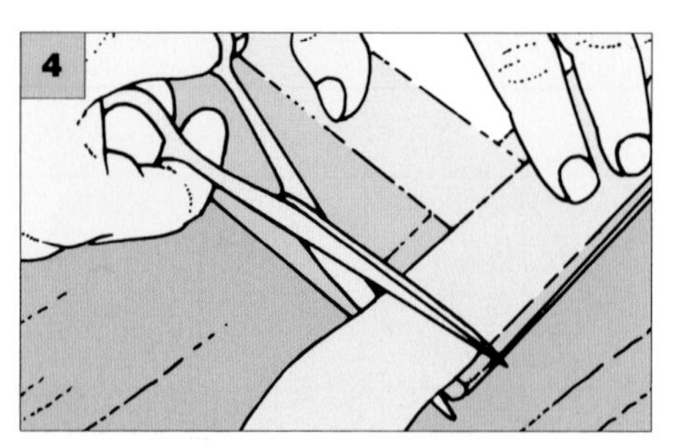

4: Measure out lengths of gummed paper tape to match each side of the drawing board.

BRUSHES

Soft brushes are normally used for watercolour. The best ones are sable, made from the tips of the tail hairs of the small rodent found chiefly in Siberia. Sable brushes are extremely expensive, but if looked after properly they should last a lifetime. Watercolour brushes are also made from squirrel hair (known as "camel hair" for some reason) and ox hair. These are good substitutes for sable, but have less spring. There is now a wide range of synthetic brushes, usually made of nylon or a mixture of nylon and sable, and although they do not hold the paint as well as sable, they are excellent for finer details and are very much cheaper.

Only by experiment will an individual discover which shapes and sizes suit them. It is not necessary to have a great many brushes for watercolour work; for most purposes three or four will be adequate, and many artists use only two. A practical range would be one large chisel-end for laying washes and two or three rounds in different sizes. Some watercolourists use ordinary household brushes for washes, but care must be taken to prevent hairs from falling out as you work.

If you want your brushes to last, it is essential to look after them well. Wash them thoroughly in running water after use – if they are still stained use a little soap. Never leave brushes pointing downwards in a glass of water, as this will bend the hairs out of shape, possibly permanently. If they need to be stored for a length of time in a box or tin make sure that they are absolutely dry; otherwise mildew may form. Store them upright.

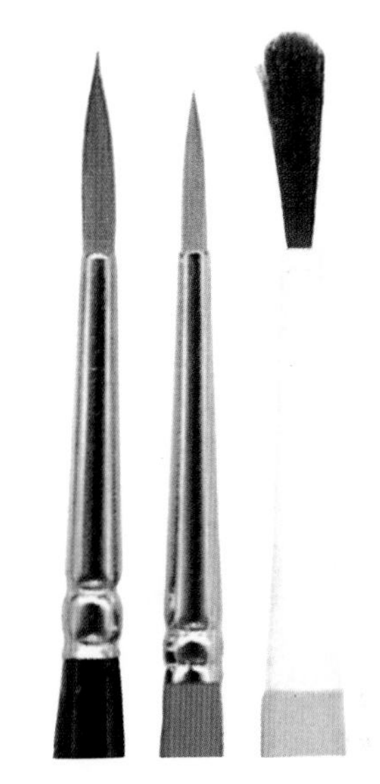

above: The differences between a quality sable brush (left), or synthetic sable (middle), and the kind of cheap brush sometimes provided in watercolour boxes (right), are self evident.

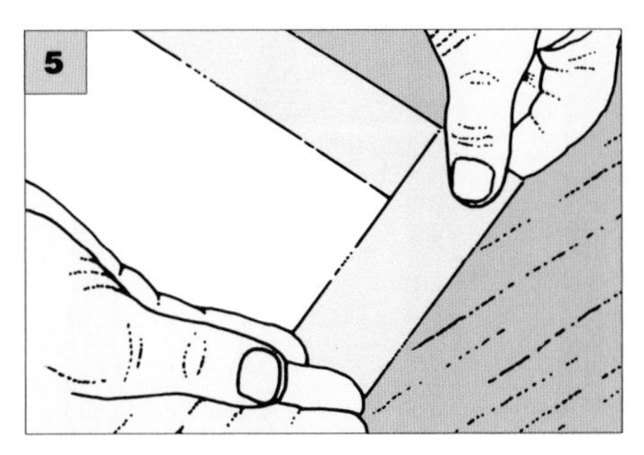

5: Take the paper out of the water and drain it off. Lay it on the board and stick dampened, gummed tape along one side.

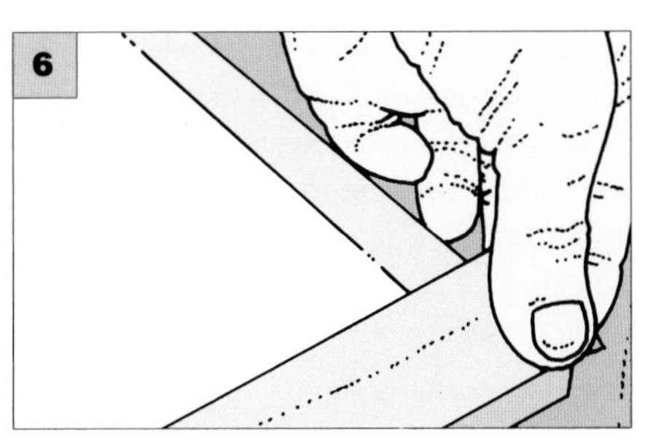

6: Stick gum strip along the opposite side of the paper. Tape the other two sides. Keep the paper quite flat throughout.

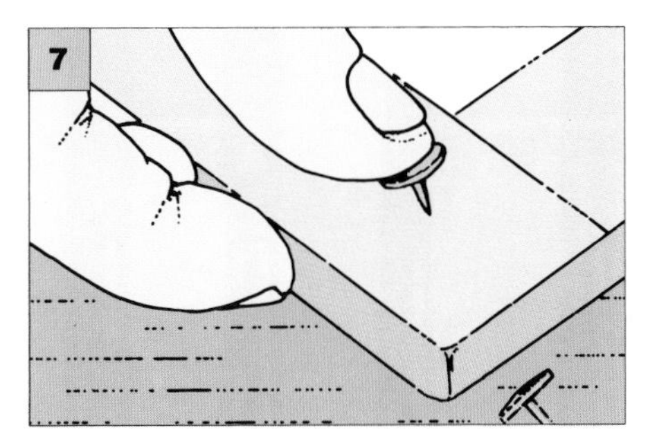

7: To secure the paper, push a drawing pin into the board at each corner. Let the paper dry naturally or it may split.

right: The complete range of sizes available of one make of brush.

right: BRUSHES There are three main shapes of watercolour brush: rounds, flats and mops. All are made in a range of sizes, usually identified by number but sometimes by their actual size (e.g. ½ inch). In most lines, the biggest brush is No. 12 or No. 14, and the smallest is No. 1, No. 0, or even No. 00. The brushes shown here are (from top to bottom): Kolinsky sable round No. 14; mixed hair mop No. 12; ox hair round No. 12; synthetic round No. 11; synthetic flat ¼ inch; goat hair mop No. 6.

Care of Brushes

You will ruin your brushes if you leave the hairs standing in a glass of water. Keep the brushes standing upright in a jar. Or, store them in special cylindrical containers. These are useful for carrying brushes around outdoors, but you must keep the container upright or the tips of the brushes may bend. Make sure that the brushes are dry before storing them in a closed container or mould may develop.

above: Japanese and Chinese brushes are versatile, and are very well suited to fine calligraphic work, but they require some practice and are not recommended for beginners.

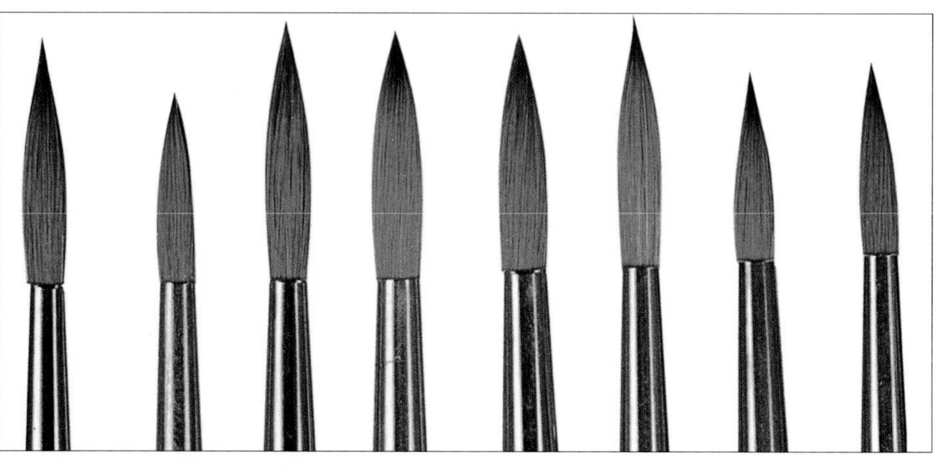

above: Soft sable brushes are the best brushes, but they are very expensive and many synthetic and sable and synthetic mixtures are now available. A beginner should not need more than one flat brush and two or three rounds; specialized brushes such as blenders and fans are used for particular techniques.

above: SPONGES AND COTTON BUDS A small natural sponge is an extremely useful piece of equipment. It can be used for putting on colour, making corrections, and cleaning up. Cotton wool serves much the same purpose, while cotton buds are good for creating small highlights (see page 55).

left: Rinse your brush under running water after each painting session. Use a little soap if traces of dried colour stick to the end near the metal band. Reshape gently with fingers or lips.

EASELS

Watercolours, unlike oils, are best done at close quarters, with the support held nearly horizontal, so that an easel is not really necessary for indoor work. However, an easel can be helpful. It allows you to tilt the work at different angles (many artists prefer to do preliminary drawings with the board held vertical) and to move it around to the best light, which is more difficult with a table. The most important aspects to consider – apart, of course, from price – are stability and the facility for holding the work firmly in a horizontal position.

For outdoor work, the combined seat and easel, which folds and is carried by a handle, is particularly useful. For indoor work, the combination easel, which can be used both as a drawing table and a studio easel, is more convenient. Both are adjustable to any angle from vertical to horizontal. Good easels are not cheap, however, so that it is wise to do without one until you are sure of your requirements; many professional watercolourists work at an ordinary table with their board supported by a book or brick.

below: There are two main types of sketching easel – wooden ones and metal ones. They both weigh about the same, and the height and angle can be adjusted.

Boards, Palettes and Other Equipment

You will need a drawing board, or possibly two boards of different sizes, to support the paper and stretch it where necessary. A piece of plywood or blockboard is perfectly adequate provided the surface is smooth and the wood soft enough to take drawing pins. For outdoor work a piece of hardboard can be used, with the paper clipped to it, though the paper must be heavy enough not to require stretching.

If you buy paints in paintbox form you will already have a palette; if not, you will need one with compartments for mixing paint. Watercolour palettes are made in plastic, metal or ceramic, in a variety of sizes, and some have a thumbhole so that they can be held in the non-painting hand when working out of doors. Water containers are another necessity for outdoor work; there is nothing worse than arriving at your chosen spot to find that you have forgotten the water. Special containers can be bought, but plastic soft-drink bottles can be used to carry the water and any light (unbreakable) container such as a yogurt pot will suffice to put the water in when you reach your destination.

Various other items, though not strictly essential, can be useful and inexpensive aids for watercolour work. Small sponges can be used instead of brushes to apply washes, to sponge out areas and to create soft, smudgy cloud effects; kitchen roll, blotting paper and cotton wool can be used in much the same way. Toothbrushes are useful for spattering paint to create textured effects: to suggest sand or pebbles on a beach, for example. A scalpel, or a razor blade, is often used to scrape away small areas of paint in a highlight area. And both masking tape and masking fluid can serve to block out areas while a wash is laid over the top, leaving a hard-edged area of white paper when removed. The specific uses of such aids and devices are more fully explained in the "Techniques" section.

below: Any plate or dish can be used for mixing watercolour, but there are several specially made palettes on the market. The thumbhole variety is especially useful for outdoor work.

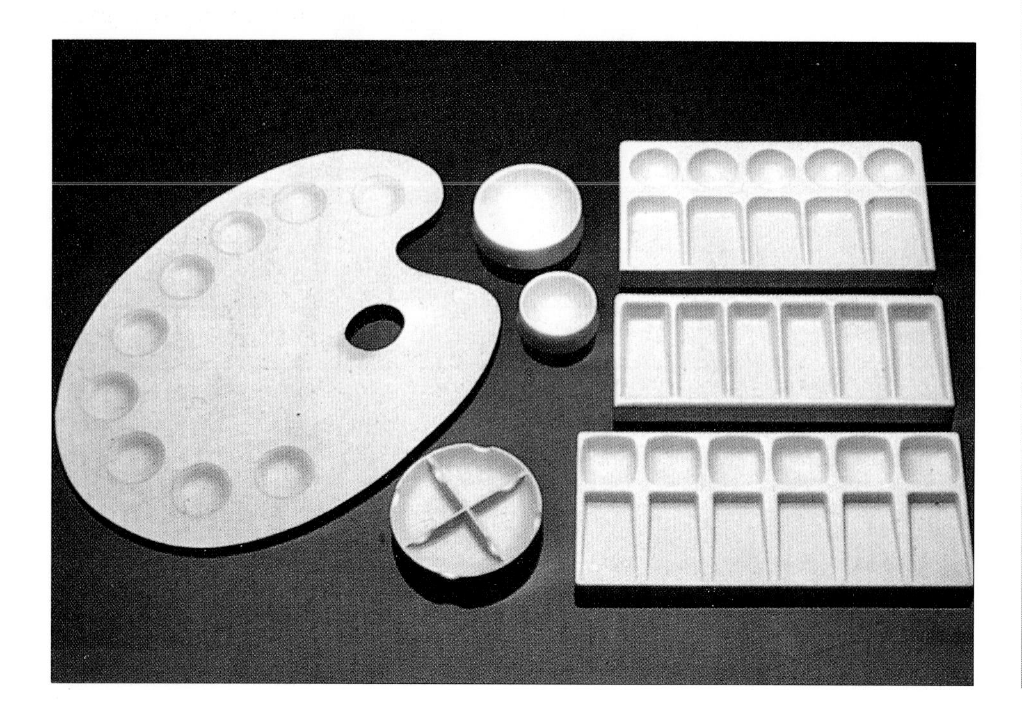

Starter Palette

These colours will provide a perfectly adequate range for most needs. Some artists work with fewer. From top to bottom: cobalt blue, Prussian blue, viridian, yellow ochre, cadmium yellow, lemon yellow, cadmium red, alizarin crimson, burnt umber, Payne's grey and ivory black.

above: PALETTES If you buy pans or half-pans of watercolour and a suitable paintbox (see page 15) you can mix your colours in the box. Although you can mix tube colours in a paintbox (see page 14) many people prefer a palette. Individual palettes, made of china or plastic, are useful for indoor work. You can keep each colour separate, and can stack the palettes after use. The circular palette (top left), also made in plastic or china, is favoured by many artists.

RECESSED WELLS There are many different kinds of palette, but they all have recessed "wells" to hold the colour and divisions to separate one colour from another. The plastic palettes, such as those, are a good all-purpose choice; inexpensive, light, and therefore ideal for outdoor work.

below: Small natural sponges are an invaluable aid to watercolour painting, both for applying paint and for correcting or modifying areas. Rags, kitchen paper and cotton buds should also form part of the basic equipment.

LIGHTING

For indoor work it is vital to organize a good system of lighting. Working by a window with light coming over your left shoulder (or right shoulder if you are left-handed) can be quite satisfactory if the window faces north (or south in the southern hemisphere) and gives an even and relatively unchanging light. It is less so if the window faces the sun, since the light may constantly change from brilliant to murky and may even throw distracting patches of light and shade across your work. An artificial light of the fluorescent "daylight" type will enable you to work in a poorly lit room or corner and to continue working when the light has faded – winter days can seem very short for those dependent on daylight. Such light can be used either instead of natural light or to supplement it, and there is one type with a screw base that can be fitted to the edge of a table or an adjacent shelf.

John Lidzey FRSA

Suburban Interior 1

WATERCOLOUR AND CONTÉ PENCIL

Watercolours can prove the perfect partner to other painting media, including gouache, acrylic, ink and pastels.

Techniques

The two most important characteristics of watercolour are, first, that it is always unpredictable to some extent, even in the hands of experts; and second, that because dark is always laid over light, some planning is needed before starting a painting.

The classic watercolour technique is known as wet-on-dry because each new wash is laid over paint that has already dried. The basis of this technique is the wash, in which a thin skin of paint is laid over the whole paper, or a part of it. That first wash is the moment of decision, because you must then know which areas you wish to "reserve" as white paper.

In this section, the techniques have been grouped roughly in the order you would use them in creating a painting, moving from washes and foundation techniques through brush techniques and colour effects and, lastly, to making changes and corrections.

Approach each method in a spirit of experimentation – it may be worthwhile to set up some practice paper and use it to try out different techniques before launching into a complete composition. Don't be too quick to discard your early efforts, though: it is often possible to rescue apparent mistakes by reworking them using methods such as scumbling or wax resist.

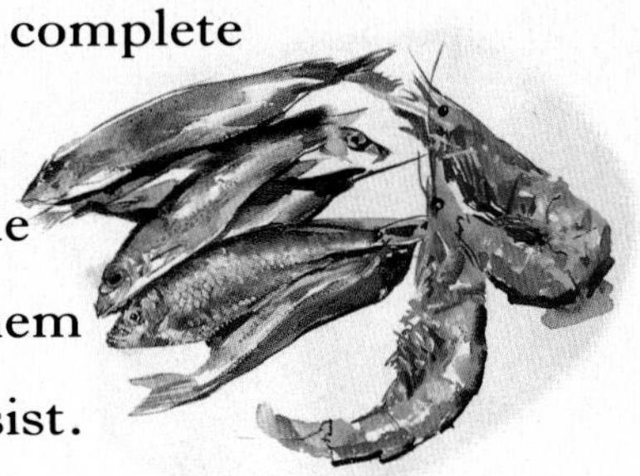

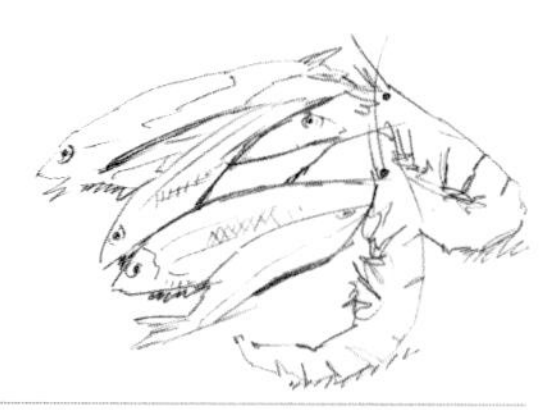

FLAT WASHES

The term "wash" is a rather confusing one, as it implies a relatively broad area of paint applied flatly, but it is also sometimes used by watercolour painters to describe each brush-stroke of fluid paint, however small it may be. Here it refers only to paint laid over an area too large to be covered by one brushstroke.

A flat wash in watercolour, thinned gouache or acrylic can be laid either with a large brush or a sponge (see page 63) and the paper is usually dampened to allow the paint to spread more easily, though this is not essential. Washes must be applied fast with no dithering, so mix up plenty of paint before beginning – you always need more than you think. Tilt the board slightly so that the brushstrokes flow into each other but do not dribble down the paper. Load the brush with paint, sweep it horizontally across the paper, starting at the top of the area, and immediately lay another line below it, working in the opposite direction. Keep the brush loaded for each stroke and continue working in alternate directions until the area is covered.

Sometimes it is necessary to lay a wash around an intricate shape, such as a skyline of roofs or chimneys. In this case the wash must start at the bottom, not at the top, to allow you to paint carefully around the shapes, so you will have to turn the board upside down. If you are dampening the paper first, dampen only up to the edge, as the paint will flow into any wet part of the paper.

–ARTISTS' HINTS–

- When laying a flat wash, never go back over the wet paint because you feel it is uneven or not dark enough, as this will result in "flooding" and leave blobs or patches.
- If the doorbell or telephone rings while you are in the middle of a wash, ignore it; otherwise you will return to a hard edge that is very difficult to remove.
- Leave the wash to dry before working on adjacent areas of the painting. Watercolour dries much paler than it appears when wet, so only when it is dry can you assess its evenness and colour.
- Purists claim that more than three layers of wash spoils the quality – something to keep in mind should you need to strengthen the colour or darken the tone of a wash.
- It is a useful exercise to lay a very flat wash with no ripples or visible differences in colour. Even if you never use such even washes in your painting, it will give you a feeling for the way the paint behaves.

Step by Step: Wash on Dry Paper

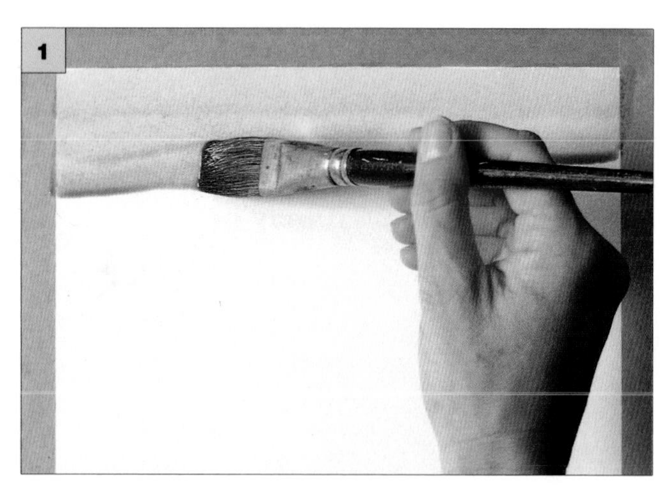

1: The board is tilted at a slight angle, and the paint is taken evenly from one side of the paper to the other.

2: The tilt of the board helps the paint to flow down the paper so that each band of colour runs into the one below.

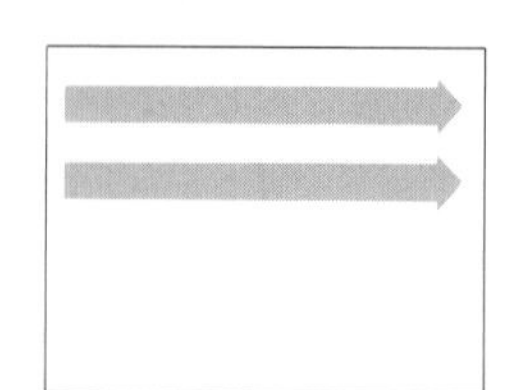

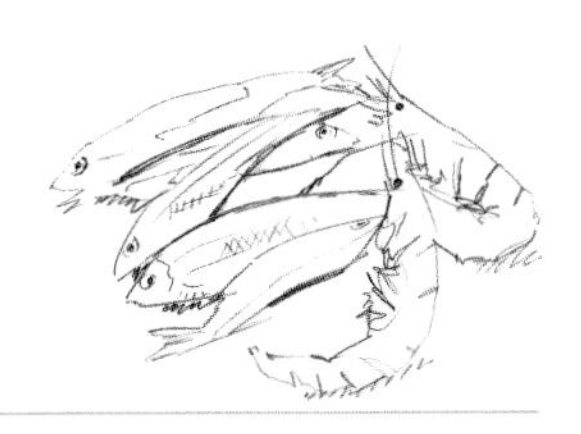

Step by Step: Wash on Damp Paper

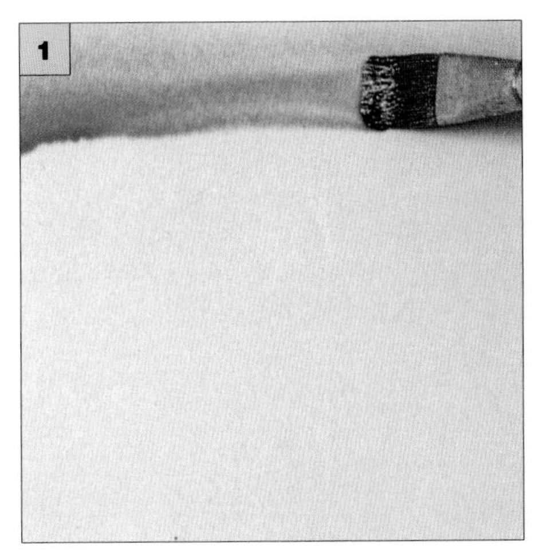

1: Dampening the paper helps the colours to blend, but makes it less easy to control the paint, as it will flow into any damp area. However, you won't achieve neat lines of colour as with the dry-paper method.

2: If runs occur, as you can see here, they will be absorbed into the rest of the wash when further lines of colour are added.

3: Don't be alarmed if your wash looks a little streaky as you lay it. It will probably dry smooth and flat, as this one did.

3: Continue to work in the same direction for each new line of colour, dipping the brush into the paint before each new stroke.

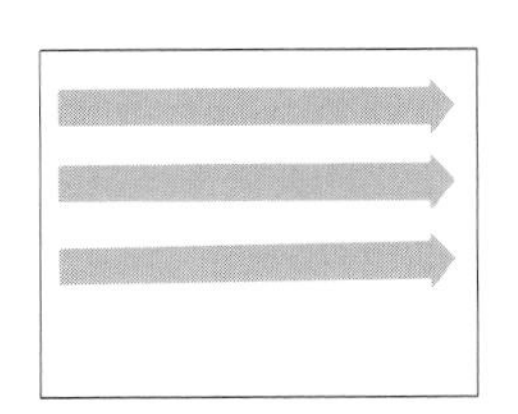

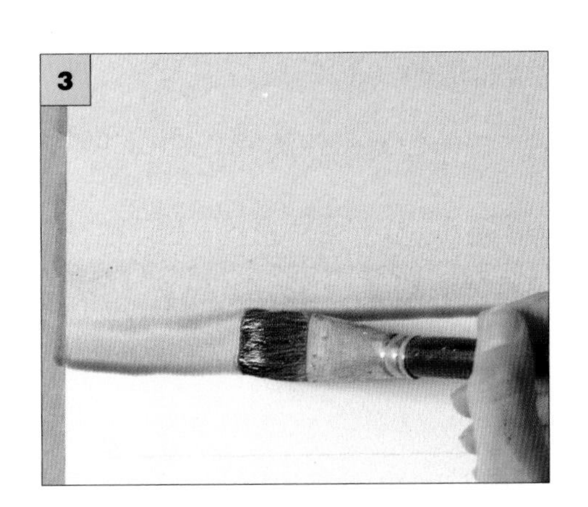

4: If you laid the wash correctly, any slight irregularities will smooth out as the paint dries.

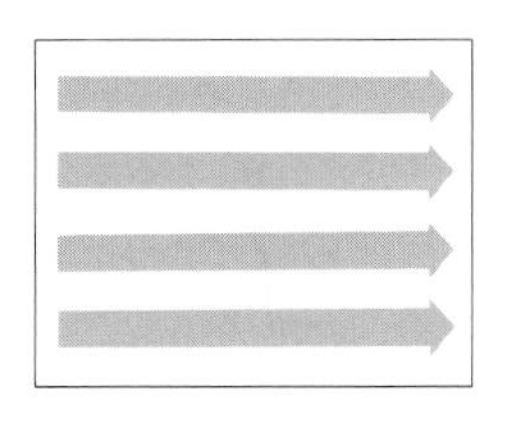

Mixing a Wash

When laying a wash over a large area, as in the examples here, a lot of paint is needed. And it must be thoroughly mixed. Start by putting a generous amount of paint into a palette and keep on adding water and mixing until all the colour dissolves.

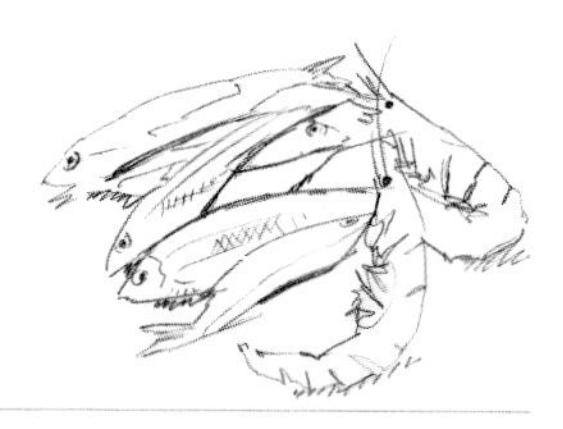

Gradated and Variegated Washes

Colours in nature are seldom perfectly flat and uniform, and it is often necessary to lay a wash that shifts in tone from dark to light or one that contains two or more different colours.

A gradated wash shades from dark to light, and is laid in the same way as a flat wash, the only difference being that more water is added to the pigment for each successive line of paint. It is a little tricky to achieve a really even gradation, as too much water in one line or not enough in another will result in a striped effect. Keep the paint as fluid as possible so that each brushstroke flows into the one below, and never be tempted to work back into the wash if it does not come out as you wished. You may find that a sponge gives better results than a brush, as it is easier to control the amount of water you use.

Variegated washes are those using more than one colour and are much less predictable than flat or gradated ones. However, you can achieve very exciting, if totally unexpected, results by allowing the colours to bleed into one another.

If you intend to paint a sky at sunset, blending from blue at the top to yellows, oranges and reds at the bottom, mix up three or four suitable colours in your palette and then lay them in strips one under the other on dampened paper so that they blend gently into one another.

above: Robert Tilling, *Reservoir Reflections,* watercolour. This lovely painting relies for its effect on the way each colour blends into its neighbour with no hard edges. The artist works with large brushes and very wet paint, tilting his board so that the colours flow down the paper, but controlling them very carefully.

–Artists' Hints–

- Some artists prefer to create gradated washes by beginning with well-watered paint and gradually increasing its strength, rather than the other way round. Try both and see which you prefer.
- For a variegated wash, you may choose to apply the main washes with a sponge, then touch in darker areas with a brush on the still-wet paint.
- Selected areas can be lightened by using a sponge in conjunction with a brush. If you wash the sponge in clean water and squeeze it out you can remove some of the paint laid by brush while it is still wet, thus lightening selected areas – a good technique for skies or distant hills.

right: A slight striping occurs if too much or too little water is added for each new brushstroke, but this can be turned to advantage. Here it suggests the almost transparent layer of misty cloud often seen on a clear, still day.

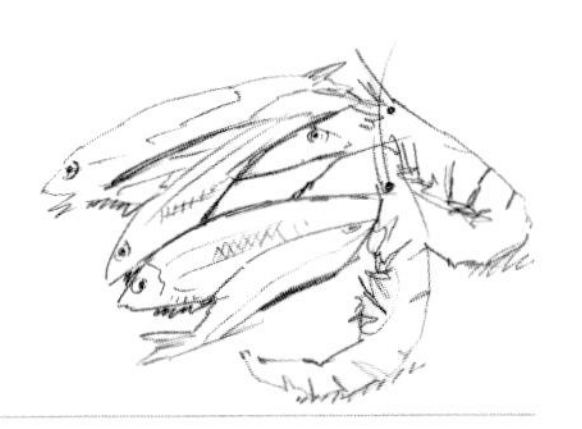

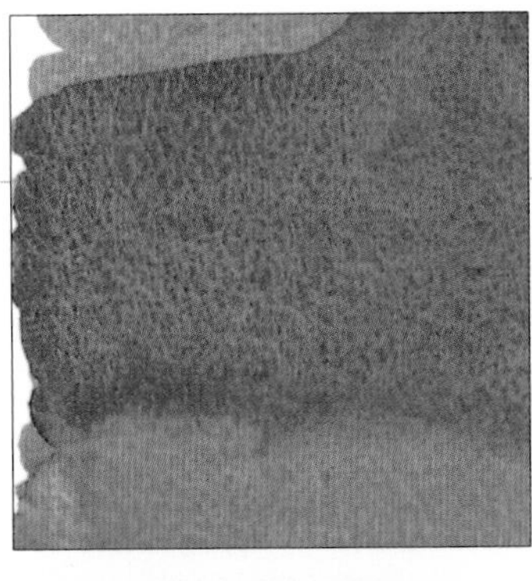

TEXTURES

Watercolour washes can be many things: some simply play the role of a flat backdrop to a visual "drama", while others serve the purpose of providing an underpainting for subsequent work. They can also be an end in themselves, conveying mood and atmosphere by means of a few brushstrokes swept over white paper. In creating a wash, the illusion of texture can be achieved by choosing the right paper and pigments.

One of the best ways to make a wash say more is to use the texture of the paper as an integral part of the painting. Watercolourists who paint mainly in washes choose their supports very carefully, fully aware of the contribution they make to the finished work.

above: The granulation of the pigment that sometimes occurs when a wet wash is applied over a dry one can add extra interest to a painting. It is particularly useful in shadow areas, which can become flat and dull.

Wet or Dry Paper

A wash laid on dampened paper has a soft, diffused quality; the paint goes on very evenly because the first application of water draws the paint down into the troughs of the paper. Working on dry paper gives a much sharper, crisper effect, and some painters find it a more controllable method. If you drag a broad brush, not overloaded with paint, over dry, grainy paper, you will create a lovely, sparkling area of colour, with the raised parts of the paper standing out clearly. The essence of these dragged washes is unevenness as any small areas of white paper left uncovered will enhance the effect. Dry washes can be used alone or over previous wet ones – a combination of the two can be wonderfully expressive.

left and below: Variegated washes need to be applied quickly and with no hesitation, so for both these examples the artist mixed her colours in advance. She worked on well-damped paper with the board at a slight angle. For the sunset, she turned the board upside down to allow her to lay the yellow, red and blue from light to dark, turning it back again to add the streaks of grey over the blue. Once the colours had blended together to create the desired effect, the wash was left to dry flat.

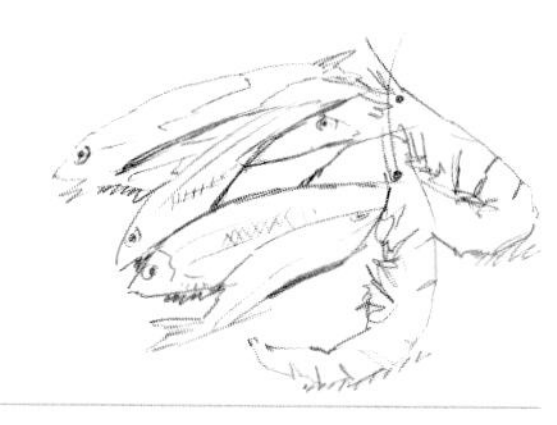

Granulation

Another way to give a touch of something extra to a wash is to use the propensity of certain pigments to precipitate, that is, to separate from the water, when laid on wetly. This causes a slight speckling that is often more suggestive than completely flat colour and can be used to great advantage.

Colours that have this property include cerulean and ultramarine blue, burnt umber, raw umber and yellow ochre (though the characteristics of pigments do vary according to the manufacturer).

The degree of granulation that will occur can only be ascertained by trial and error: some colours will granulate only when laid over a previous wash, and if the paint is mixed with a high proportion of water the process may not occur at all, or be almost imperceptible.

above: Christopher Baker, *Tor Cross, Devon,* 45.7 x 25.4 cm (18 x 10 in), watercolour. The artist has built up his painting mainly in flat washes, but because he has worked on a very heavily textured rag paper they have a lively, broken colour appearance. The sandy beach and the wavelets on the water are created simply by leaving areas of paper unpainted.

–ARTISTS' HINTS–

- Certain pigments have a tendency to separate out when mixed with others in a wash and allowed to dry undisturbed. This separation is caused by the different physical characteristics of the pigments – the earth colours, for example, are coarser by nature than most other colours. As the wash dries, tiny granules of pigment settle on the raised tooth of the paper, giving an area of flat colour with a natural granular texture that can be used to great effect.
- A mixture of burnt sienna and ultramarine creates a very attractive grey, which dries with a subtle granular pattern. This makes it a favourite mixture for painting skies, hinting of the texture within clouds.
- Other colours which granulate when mixed with other colours include yellow ochre, burnt umber, manganese blue, cobalt blue and ultramarine. You could use these colours when painting buildings, allowing the granulation to indicate the pitted texture of stone. Manganese blue is often used for painting the shadows in snow scenes.

below: Charles Knight, *Evening Light, Cotswolds,* 27.3 x 37.5 cm (10¾ x 14¾ in), watercolour and wax crayon. This artist frequently combines watercolour with wax or pencil, or sometimes both. Here areas of the foreground and middle distance have been subtly textured by a light underlay of wax crayon. This can be clearly seen in the detail (right), where an interesting variety of texture has been achieved by allowing wet washes to form backruns on top of the slight striations made by the wax.

below: Colin Paynton, *Welsh Elements VII,* 52.7 x 73.6 cm (20¾ x 29 in), watercolour. Paintings with little colour or tonal contrast can all too easily become monotonous, but the slightly granular paint quality has given this atmospheric composition a lovely touch of sparkle. Paynton has achieved this by working on an absorbent, low-sized paper, normally used for etching.

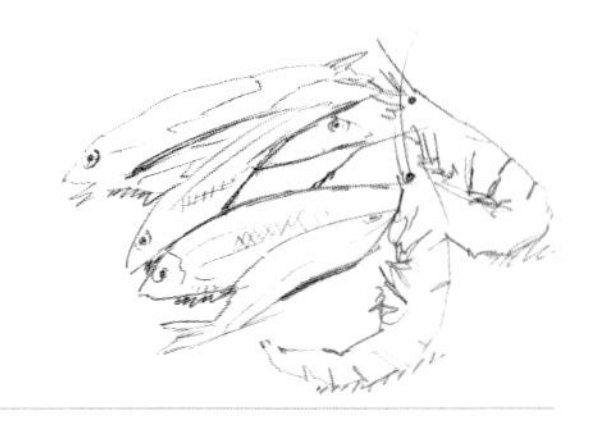

BACKRUNS

These are both a nuisance and a delight to watercolour painters. If you lay a wash and apply more colour into it before it is completely dry, the chances are that the new paint will seep into the old, creating strangely shaped blotches with hard, jagged edges – sometimes alternatively described as "cauliflowers". It does not always happen: the more absorbent or rough-textured papers are less conducive to backruns than the smoother, highly sized ones, and with practice it is possible to avoid them altogether.

There is no remedy for a backrun except to wash off the entire area and start again. However, many watercolour painters use them quite deliberately, both in large areas such as skies or water and small ones such as the petals of flowers, as the effects they create are quite unlike those achieved by conventional brushwork. For example, a realistic approximation of reflections in gently moving water can be achieved by lightly working wet colour or clear water into a still damp wash. The paint or water will flow outwards, giving an area of soft colour with the irregular, jagged outlines so typical of reflections. It takes a little practice to be able to judge exactly how wet or dry the first wash should be, but as a guide, if there is still a sheen on it, it is too wet and the colours will merge together without a backrun, as they do in the wet-in-wet technique.

left: The results of working into a wash before it is thoroughly dry vary widely according to the paper used and the degree of wetness or dryness, but it can look something like this example. Experienced watercolourists learn to make use of such effects, which can often be used descriptively in a painting.

above: Here backruns have been deliberately induced and then blown with a hairdryer so that they form definite patterns. Techniques such as this are particularly useful for amorphous shapes such as clouds, reflections or distant hills.

above: A wash which has "gone wrong" and flooded has been worked in to create a sky effect not previously planned.

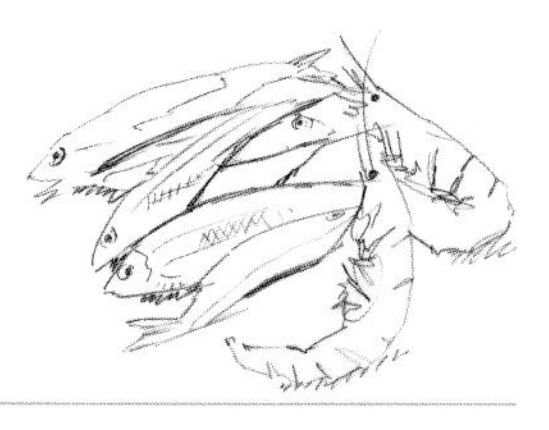

Wet-in-wet

This means exactly what its name implies – applying each new colour without waiting for earlier ones to dry so that they run together with no hard edges. This is a technique that is only partially controllable, but is a very enjoyable and challenging one. Any of the water-based media can be used, providing no opaque pigment is added, but in the case of acrylic, it is helpful to add retarding medium to the paint to prolong the drying time.

The paper must first be well dampened and must not be allowed to dry completely at any time. This means, first, that you must stretch the paper (unless it is a really heavy one of at least 200 pounds) and second, that you must work fast.

Step by Step: Wet-in-wet

1: Having made a preliminary outline drawing on dry paper, the artist damps it thoroughly with a sponge. She is using slightly coloured water to provide a background tint.

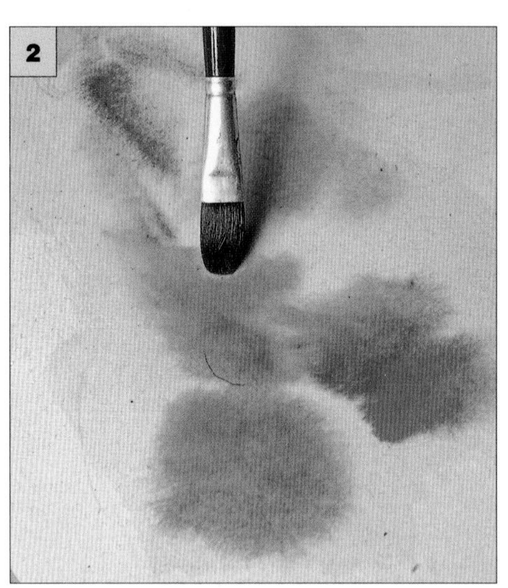

2: Using the point of a large brush, she begins to drop in areas of colour, allowing them to spread and merge.

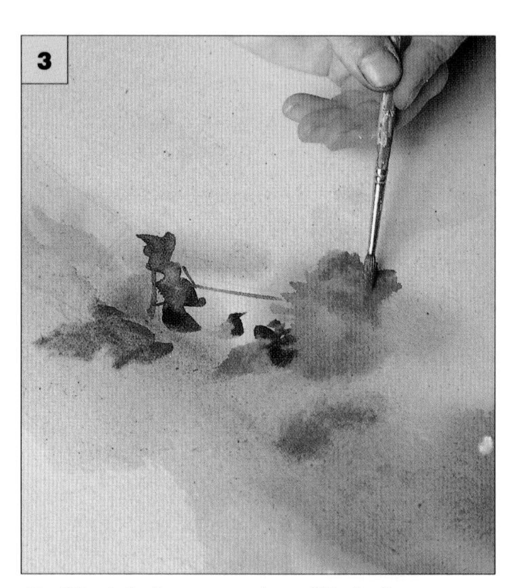

3: She lets the paper dry a little before touching in darker colours, as she wants crisper edges in these areas.

4: As highlights cannot be reserved when working in this way, she has used opaque white in places.

5: She continues to build up, using slightly thickened paint.

6: Touches of soft definition give depth and form to the leaves and flower heads.

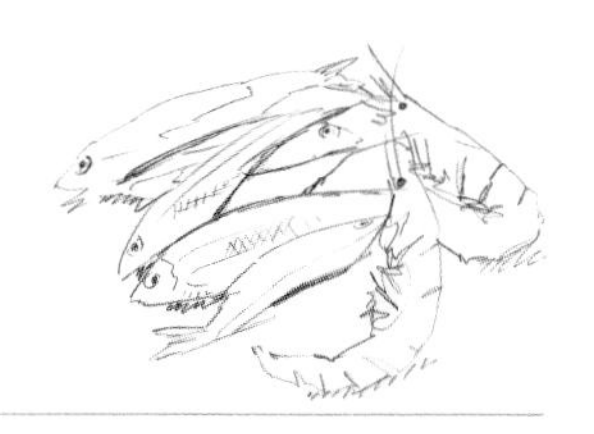

Paradoxically, when you keep all the colours wet, they will not actually mix, although they will bleed into one another. Placing a loaded brush of wet paint on top of a wet wash of a different colour is a little like dropping a pebble into water; the weight of the water in the new brushstroke causes the first colour to draw away.

The danger with painting a whole picture wet-in-wet is that it may look altogether too formless and undefined. The technique is most effective when it is offset by edges and linear definition, so when you feel that you have gone as far as you can, let the painting dry, take a long, hard look at it, and decide where you might need to sharpen it up.

7: The flowers are now complete, but the vase is still no more than a suggestion, with the outline drawing still visible under the pale wash.

8: Having applied a loose, wet wash of darker paint, the artist tilts the board so that the colour flows in the right direction. This is the best way of controlling wet paint and is surprisingly accurate. She is now working wet-in-wet only in the area of the vase, having allowed the surrounding paper to dry so that the wash will not spread beyond the edges.

9: Wet-in-wet is such an enjoyable and seductive technique that it is difficult to know when to stop, and if it is taken too far the whole painting can become woolly and formless. Here, although the general effect is pleasingly soft, there is enough definition and tonal contrast to pull the composition together.

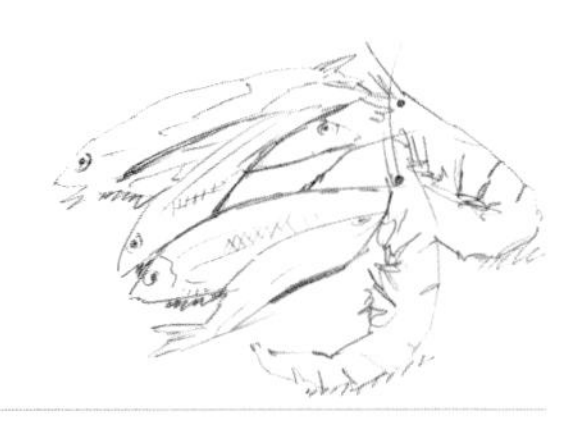

Hard and Soft Edges

A wet watercolour wash laid on dry paper forms a shallow pool of colour which, if left undisturbed, will form hard edges as it dries, rather like a tidemark. This can be alarming to the novice, particularly in the early stages of a painting, but it is one of the many characteristics of the medium that can be used to great advantage. By laying smaller, loose washes over previous dry ones you can build up a fascinating network of fluid, broken lines that not only help to define form and suggest shapes but give a lovely sparkling quality to the work. This is an excellent method for building up rather irregular shapes such as clouds, rocks or ripples on water.

You will not necessarily want to use the same technique in every part of the painting, however. A combination of hard and soft edges describes the subject more successfully and also gives the picture more variety.

above: John Lidzey, *Church Hill, Winchmore Hill*, watercolour on stretched paper.

right: The contrast between hard and soft edges is one of the most exciting features of good watercolours, so it is not advisable to work wet in wet throughout the painting process. The crisp edges shown here were achieved by dropping a fluid but powerful dark blue mixture onto the now dry green wash, giving an ink-blot effect.

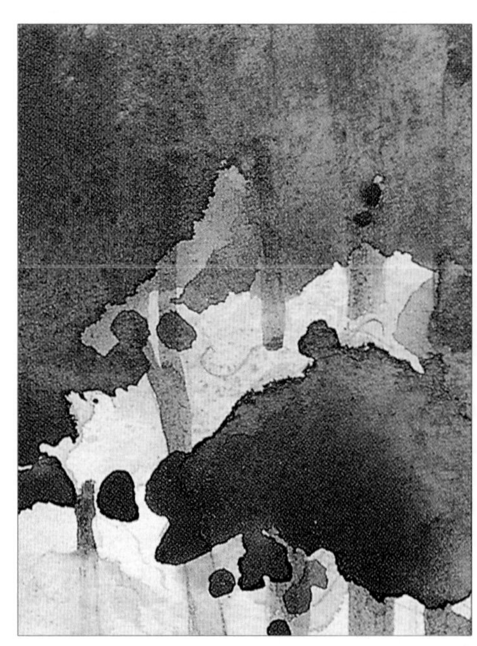

-ARTISTS' HINTS-

- Depending on the wetness of the initial wash and the type of paper used, watercolour can take anything up to 15 minutes to dry thoroughly, so the technique does require a little patience. If the overlay is applied too soon, the colours turn muddy and the definition is lost.
- For flower painting, a combination of wet-in-wet and wet-on-dry passages is most effective. The wet-in-wet washes capture the delicacy of leaves and petals in the initial stages, then further washes applied over the dried underlayer add form and definition.
- The illusion of rippling water can be created using both wet-on-dry and wet-in-wet techniques. The hard and soft edges formed by overlapping wet and dry washes give the shimmering effect of gently moving water.

right: Paul Riley, *Roses and Damsons*, 36.8 x 54.6 cm (14½ x 21½ in), watercolour. Riley also exploits the effects of watercolour to the full, using the pale, delicate colours that we tend to associate with the medium, but with strong, decisive brushwork that gives a taut, linear quality to the painting.

There are several ways of avoiding hard edges. One is to work wet-in-wet by dampening the paper before laying the first wash and then working subsequent colours into it before it dries so that they blend into one another with subtle transitions. A wash on dry paper can be softened and drawn out at the edges by using a sponge, paintbrush or cotton bud dipped in clean water to remove the excess paint. A wash "dragged" or "pulled" over dry paper with either a brush or sponge will also dry without hard edges, since the paint is prevented from forming a pool.

left: This detail shows a carefully controlled use of hard/soft contrast, with the paint blended wet-in-wet in places (notably the bowl of fruit) and allowed to form edges in others. An extra touch of crispness is provided by the little dots and lines made with the point of the brush.

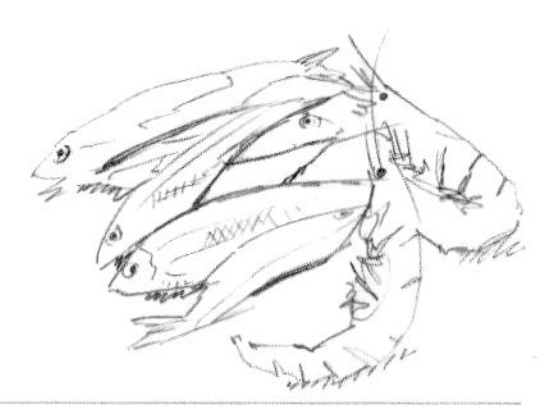

BUILDING UP WATERCOLOUR

Because watercolours are semi-transparent, light colours cannot be laid over dark. Thus, traditional practice is to begin a painting with the lightest tones and build up gradually towards the darker ones by means of successive washes or brushstrokes.

Many, but by no means all, artists start by laying a flat wash all over the paper, leaving uncovered any areas that are to become pure white highlights (known as reserving). This procedure obviously needs some planning, so it is wise to start with a pencil drawing to establish the exact place and shape of the highlights to be reserved. The tone and colour of the preliminary wash also needs to be planned as it must relate to the overall colour key of the finished painting. A deep blue wash laid all over the paper might be the correct colour and intensity for the sky in a landscape, but would not be suitable for a foreground containing pale yellows and ochres. Another variation of the overall wash is to lay one for the sky, allow this to dry, and then put down another one for the land. Both these procedures have the advantage of covering the paper quickly so that you can begin to assess colours and tones without the distraction of pure white paper.

Overpainting

When the first wash or washes are dry, the process of intensifying certain areas begins, done by laying darker washes or individual brushstrokes over the original ones. A watercolour will lose its freshness if there is too much overpainting, so always assess the strength of colour needed for each layer carefully and apply it quickly, with one sweep of the brush, so that it does not disturb the paint below. As each wash is allowed to dry, it will develop hard edges, which usually form a positive feature of watercolour work, adding clarity and crispness.

Some artists find it easier to judge the tone and colour key of the painting if they begin with the darkest area of colour, then go back to the lightest, adding the middle tones last when the two extremes have been established.

Building up a painting in washes is not the only method. Some artists avoid using washes altogether, beginning by putting down small brushstrokes of strong colour all over the paper, sometimes modifying them with washes on top to soften or strengthen certain areas.

Step by Step: Building Up

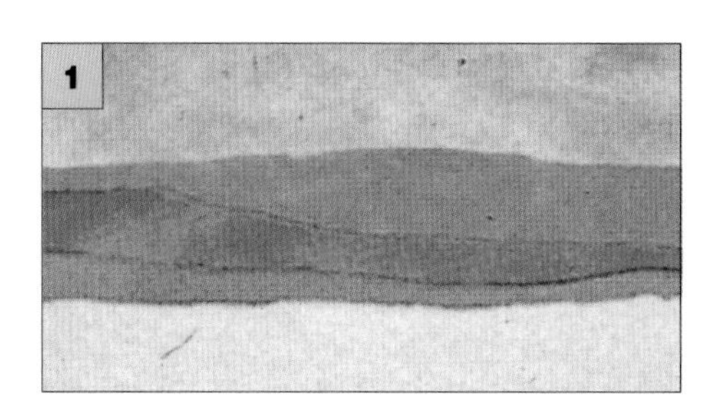

1, 2: Having laid a grey-blue wash over the sky and a slightly darker one for the distant hills, the artist blocks in the details of the middle distance. He leaves these washes to dry and then paints the dark trees in the foreground.

3: The final touch is to lay a green-ochre wash over the area behind the trees. The warm colour creates a sense of recession, as it advances towards the front of the picture, while the cool blues are pushed back.

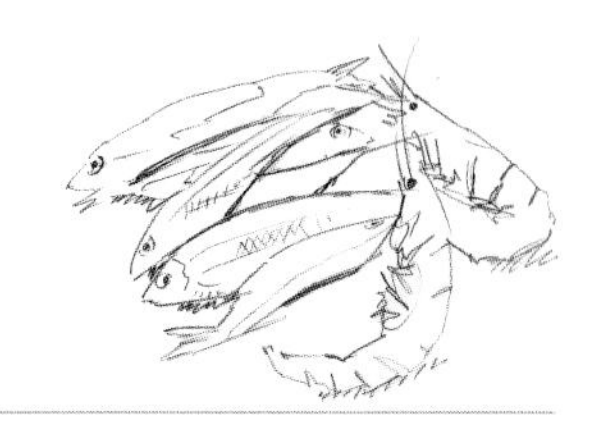

–ARTISTS' HINTS–

- To create a strong and unified image, the tonal values of your painting must be carefully planned. (See "Tonal Values" on page 100.) The contrast of light against dark may prove more effective than setting colour against colour; the latter approach often gives a patchwork effect.
- Plan the tonal pattern of your subject before you start painting. It's a good idea to make a small tonal sketch of the scene you wish to paint, indicating the main areas of light, dark and mid-tone. Remember to group similar tones together into larger shapes – don't scatter small bits of tone all over the painting.
- Use colour to create perspective: foregrounds are often brought forward and emphasized by using warmer colours in the front of the picture.
- In the background of a picture, colours and tones tend to be less distinct, merging into one another in places. In a landscape, objects in the middle and far distance become progressively paler and bluer because the light is filtered through dust and moisture in the atmosphere. Such effects are easier to capture in watercolour than in oil: a pale, flat wash can be put on and then the tiny differences in tone suggested by just a dab or two of barely tinted water.

Gouache and Acrylic

If either of these paints is used thinly, without the addition of white, the procedures are much the same as those for watercolour described on the previous pages. The beauty of acrylic, however, is that no amount of overpainting will stir up earlier paint, because, once dry, it is immovable (a disadvantage of this being that lifting out is impossible). If used opaquely, acrylic can be built up in more or less infinite layers, dark over light or light over dark. Paintings in opaque gouache can, to a certain extent, be built up from dark to light. If the paint is used thick and dry, a light layer will cover a dark one completely, but there is a limit to the number of layers you can apply as this paint continue to be soluble in water even when dry, so that a new application of moist paint will churn up and muddy that underneath. The most satisfactory method is to begin by using the paint thin, increasing its opacity gradually as you work. The building up process is aided by working on a toned ground, which serves the same function as a preliminary wash in watercolour and helps to avoid too many layers of paint.

above: Reading from left to right, this demonstrates the traditional way of building up a watercolour. The sky is the lightest part of the picture, so this is painted first and, while still damp, a light green wash is taken over the whole of the tree and the foreground. Blue-green paint is then applied to the more distant areas of the tree, and a light brown to the branches. The paper is allowed to dry completely before the darkest tones are added. The foliage is given depth by the use of cooler, bluer greens at the back of the tree.

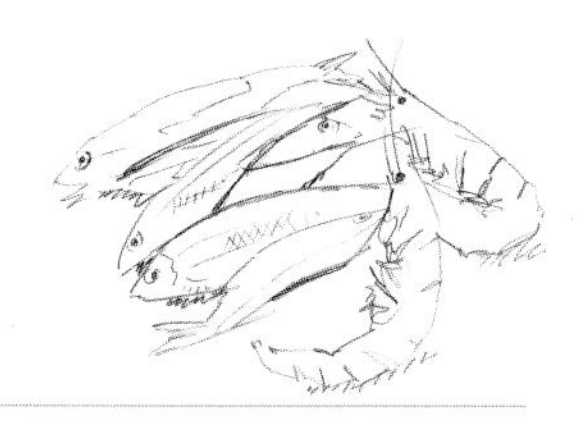

Step by Step: Working in Gouache

1: Working in gouache, the artist begins with the paint well thinned, laying broad washes and allowing runs to occur in places.

2: The prawns are painted less solidly than the fish, as befits their delicate, slender forms, and the opaque paint is restricted to small areas of highlight.

3: Using a strong mixture of gouache, the artist "draws" with the point of the brush on the underbelly of the fish.

When the first washes have dried, she begins to define the detail. The paint is still used as watercolour in most areas, but she intends to build up the textures of the fish more thickly, and has applied a broad stroke of opaque yellow.

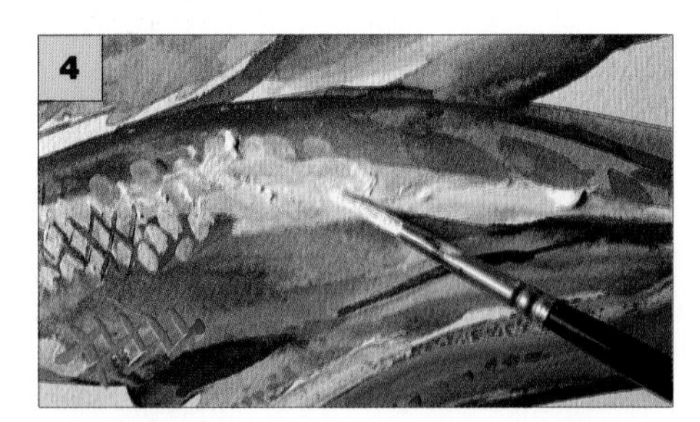

4: Now using really opaque white, she accentuates the silvery highlights. Raised blobs and swirls can be seen where the pigment has been used straight from the tube.

5: The scales of the fish are suggested by a combination of scraping into the paint and working small brushstrokes both wet-in-wet and wet-on-dry.

6: One of the exciting properties of gouache is that it allows a contrast of thick and thin paint, thus providing additional surface interest.

UNDERPAINTING

This involves building up a painting over a monochrome tonal foundation. It is usually associated with oil painting, but the early watercolourists used a modified version of the same technique, particularly for detailed topographical or architectural subjects. You can see the effects of underpainting if you have ever had to wash down a watercolour by dunking it in a bath. Faint shadows of the original will remain, which can often provide a good basis for the next attempt. This kind of "accidental" underpainting highlights the value of a deliberately planned one: establishing the tonal balance of a painting is not always easy, and doing this at the outset avoids having to alter or correct (and possibly overwork) the painting later on.

It is essential to use a pale colour and one that will not interfere with the colours to be placed on top. In a predominantly green landscape, for instance, blue would be a good choice and, since blues tend to stain the paper, a blue wash is less likely to be disturbed by subsequent washes. The paper should be a fairly absorbent one, such as Arches, which allows the undercolour to sink into it. Any areas to be reserved as bright highlights should, of course, be left uncovered so the white paper will show through.

An underpainting for acrylic is much less restricted as it will be permanent when dry and the tonal range can be greater because the later colours can be used opaquely to cover the first one. Underpainting provides a good basis for the technique of glazing, in which colours are built up in successive thin skins.

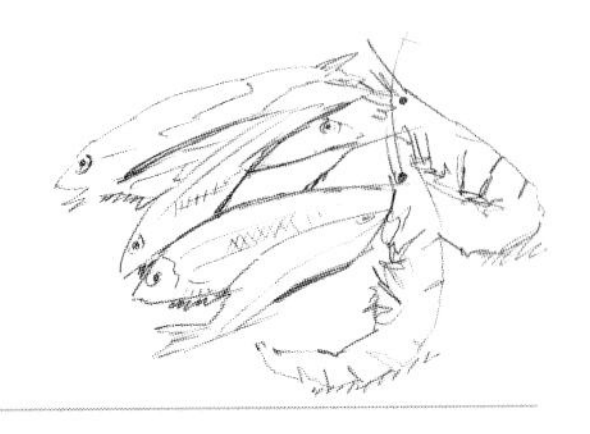

Step by Step: Tonal Underpainting

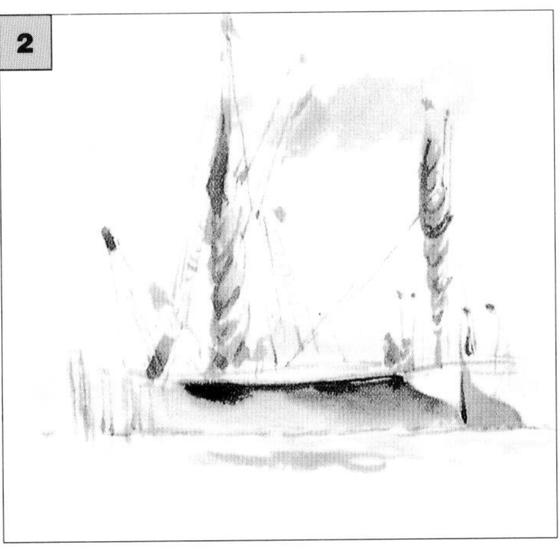

1, 2: A tonal underpainting can provide a better basis than an outline drawing, as pencil lines quickly become obscured. The artist begins with a very light grey, building up to deeper tones in areas that are to remain as dark shadows.

3, 4: The grey chosen for the underpainting is slightly modified by the colours laid over it, but in the shadows it remains virtually unchanged, which highlights the importance of choosing the right colour. Notice that the brightest parts, the stern of the boat and areas of the water, have been left white in the underpainting.

GLAZING

This is a technique that was perfected by the early painters using oils. They would lay thin skins of transparent pigment one over the other to create colours of incredible richness and luminosity. In watercolour painting, overlaying washes is sometimes described as glazing, but this is misleading as it implies a special technique, whereas in fact it is the normal way of working when one is using watercolour paints.

Acrylic paint is perfectly suited to the glazing technique because it dries so fast: each layer must be thoroughly dry before the next one is applied. The effects the technique creates are quite different to those of colour applied opaquely, as light seems to reflect through each layer, almost giving the appearance of being lit from within. The use of a brilliant white ground (acrylic gesso is ideal) on a smooth surface such as hardboard or plain art board further enhances the luminosity.

Special media are sold for acrylic glazing – available in both gloss and matt – and these can be used either alone or in conjunction with water.

A whole painting can be built up layer by layer in this way – as can be seen in some of David Hockney's acrylic paintings – but this is not the only way of using the technique. Thin glazes can also be laid over an area of thick paint (impasto) to great effect. The glaze will tend to slide off the raised areas and sink into the lower ones – a useful technique for suggesting textures, such as that of weathered stone or tree bark. Other ways of conveying rough textures using watercolour include wax resist, spattering and sponge painting. See pages 48, 63 and 71 for more information.

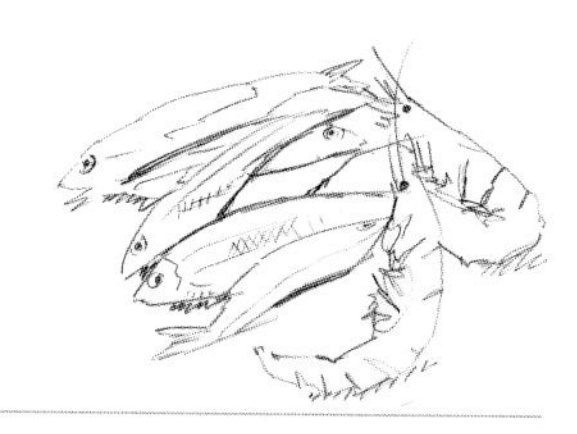

Step by Step: Glazing

1: Working in acrylic on watercolour paper, the artist starts with the paint heavily diluted with water. Acrylic used in this way is virtually indistinguishable from watercolour, but it cannot be removed once dry, a considerable advantage in the glazing technique.

2: A layer of darker colour mixed with special glazing medium has been laid over the orange, and the artist now builds up the highlights with opaque paint.

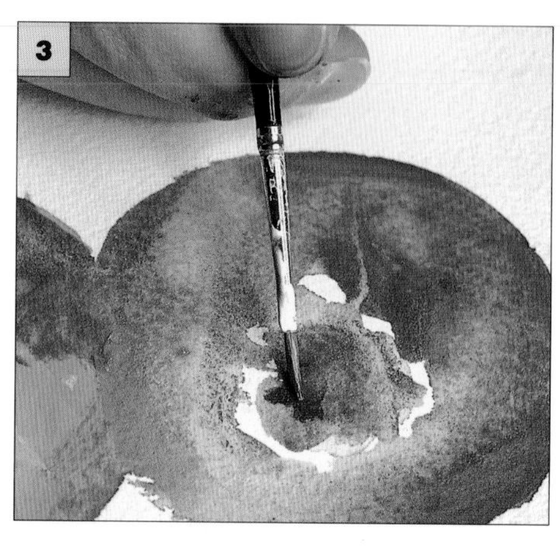

3: Deep-toned glazes are now laid on the apple. The way earlier layers of colour reflect back through subsequent glazes gives a rich, glowing effect.

4: Here the transparent, slightly gluey quality of the paint can be seen. Either water or the special medium can be used for acrylic glazes, but it takes a little practice to achieve the right consistency.

Drawing

Because watercolours cannot be changed radically (except by washing off and beginning again), they need to be planned in advance and it is usual to begin a painting by drawing the subject directly onto the paper. Some artists dispense with this stage, but this is usually because they are familiar with the subject, have painted it before and have a clear idea of how they want the finished painting to look.

There are certain inherent problems with underdrawings for watercolour. One is that the drawn lines are likely to show through the paint in the paler areas. The lines should, therefore, be kept as light as possible and any shading avoided so that the drawing is nothing more than a guideline to remind you which areas should be reserved as highlights and where the first washes should be laid.

Another problem is that on certain papers, such as the popular Bockingford, erasing can scuff the surface, removing parts of the top layer, so that any paint applied to these areas will form unsightly blotches. If you find that you need to erase, use a kneadable putty rubber, applying light pressure.

For a simple land- or seascape your underdrawing will probably consist of no more than a few lines, but a complex subject, such as buildings or a portrait, will need a more elaborate drawing. Then you may find that the squaring up method (see opposite) is helpful, using either a sketch or photograph of the subject.

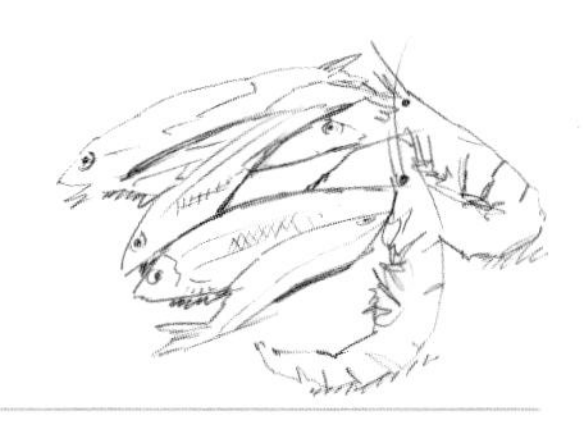

Step by Step: Squaring Up

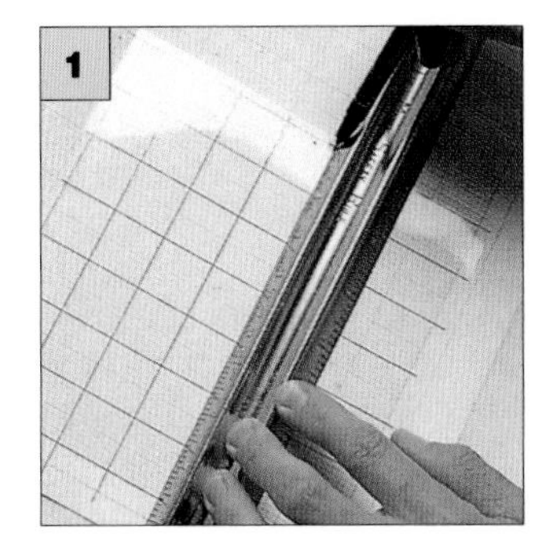

1: The method demonstrated here avoids damaging the original drawing or photograph. A grid is drawn with a felt-tipped pen on a sheet of acetate. The grid is traced from a sheet of graph paper below, which saves time and is very accurate.

2: The next stage is drawing an enlarged version of the grid on to the working paper. Pencil, set square and ruler are needed for this and the pencil lines should be as faint as possible.

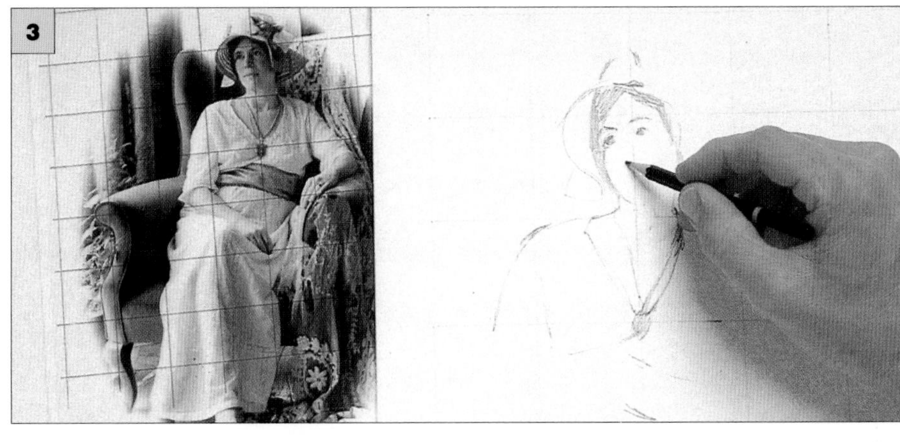

3: The acetate sheet is then placed over the photograph or working drawing, and the image is transferred to the working paper square by square. Do not rush this process as you could place one part of the composition in the wrong square.

One way of avoiding too much drawing and erasing on the paper, which can spoil the surface, is to make a smaller study of the subject first and then to transfer it to the watercolour paper by squaring it up to the size desired. A photograph can be used instead of a drawing, providing you have taken it yourself for this purpose. However, photographs do tend to flatten and distort perspective, and sometimes present an insufficiently clear image, so try to use them only in conjunction with sketches, observation and imagination.

Using a ruler, draw a measured grid over the study or photograph, then draw another grid on the watercolour paper, using light pencil marks. This must have the same number of squares, but if you want to enlarge the drawing, they must obviously be larger. If you use a 2.5 cm (1 in) grid for your original drawing and a 3.8 cm (1½ in) one for the painting, it will be one-and-a-half times the size, and so on. When the grid is complete, look carefully at the drawing, note where each line intersects a grid line and transfer the information from one to the other.

above and right: Having made a preliminary drawing with a very sharp B pencil, the artist lays the first washes. The pencil lines can be erased at this stage, but it is not always necessary as they are unlikely to show in any but the palest areas of the painting.

Brush Drawing

Drawing freely and directly with a brush is enormously satisfying and, like blots, is an excellent way to loosen up your technique. Artists down the centuries have made brush sketches, sometimes using pen marks as well, sometimes not, and the Chinese and Japanese made the technique into a fine art.

Opaque paints are not suitable for brush drawing, as the marks and lines must be fluid – flowing easily from brush to paper. You can use ordinary watercolour, watercolour inks or acrylics thinned with water. Good, springy brushes are also essential.

right: Jacqueline Rizvi, *Family on the Beach,* watercolour and body colour on pale grey paper. Working rapidly on the spot, the artist has used the brush very much as a drawing medium.

right: Christopher Baker, *Rydal Water,* 25.4 x 45.7 cm (10 x 18 in), watercolour. This sketchbook study (on cartridge paper) was initially drawn with a brush and then toughened with a dip-pen where necessary. In the background, the paper was damped to allow the paint to spread, thus maintaining the softness of the forms.

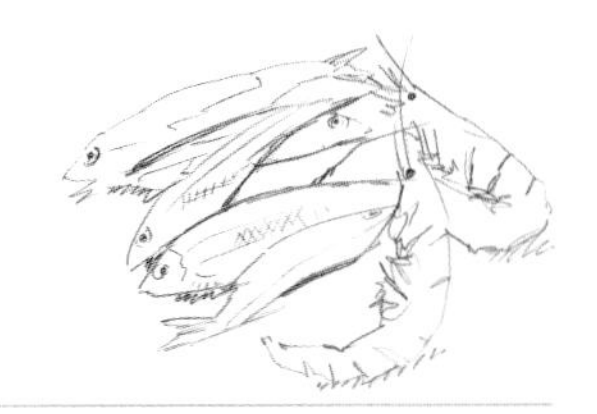

Light pressure with the tip of a medium-sized pointed brush will give precise, delicate lines. A little more pressure and the line will become thicker, so that it is possible to draw a line that is dark and thick in places and very fine in others. More pressure still, bringing the thick part of the brush into contact with the paper, will give a shaped brush mark rather than a line. Thus, by using only one brush you can create a variety of effects and, if you use several brushes, including broad, flat-ended ones, the repertoire is almost endless.

The technique can be combined with others in a painting, and is particularly useful for conveying a feeling of movement, in figures, animals or even landscapes.

–ARTISTS' HINTS–

- You will need to practise to get the consistency of the paint right for dry brush painting – if it is too wet you simply have a rather blotchy wash, so you may need to thicken it with some gouache or Chinese white.
- With a small amount of paint on the brush, experiment by dragging, rolling or even stabbing with it to build up a vocabulary of different marks.
- The most common method for painting fur is to build up the textures by flicks of the brush starting at the "roots" and ending by lifting the brush off the paper to produce a slightly uneven and tapering effect.

left: Christopher Baker, *Beachy Head,* 30.5 x 20.3 cm (12 x 8 in), watercolour, charcoal, pencil and pen. In this study for a large oil painting, Baker has combined expressive brush drawing with the more overtly linear marks of pen and charcoal.

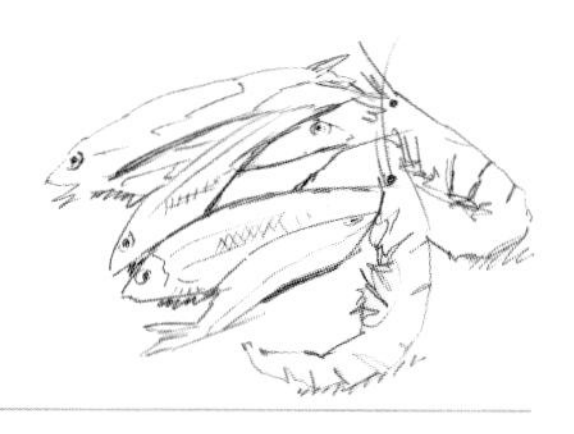

Brush Marks

The marks made by the brush as a contributing factor to a finished painting are exploited most fully in the thick, buttery medium of oil paint. This has often led people to ignore the importance of brush marks in watercolour, but they can play a vital and expressive part in a painting, making all the difference between a lively, dynamic picture and a dull, routine one.

The most obvious example of visible brush marks in watercolour occurs in the technique of stippling. Then the painting is built up entirely with tiny strokes of a pointed brush. However, it is possible to discern the strokes of the brush in most watercolours to a greater or lesser degree. Some artists use a broad, flat brush, allowing it to follow the direction of a form, while others use a pointed one to create a network of lines in different colours and tones. A popular technique for creating the impression of squalls of rain or swirling mist is to work into a wet wash with a dry bristle brush to "stroke" paint in a particular direction, while an exciting impression of foliage can be conveyed by dabbing or flicking paint onto paper using short strokes of a small square-ended brush. Another useful technique for foliage – a notoriously tricky subject – is dry brush, which creates a pleasing feathery texture because the dry paint only partially covers the paper.

left: John Tookey, *Blackwater at Heybridge,* 25.4 x 35.5 cm (10 x 14 in), watercolour. Sweeping strokes of a large, soft brush define the sky and much of the foreground, contrasting with the finer, linear marks for the boats and their reflections.

below left: Donald Pass, *Top of the Hill,* 45.7 x 66 cm (18 x 26 in), watercolour. The excitement and feeling of movement in this painting derives from the highly individual use of directional brushstrokes.

above: Ronald Jesty, *Durdle Door,* approx. 40.6 x 27.9 cm (16 x 11 in), watercolour. This artist always paints wet-on-dry so that his brush marks remain crisp and clear with no blurring of edges. Here he has "drawn" with the brush, making marks of different shapes and sizes to describe the clouds, rock textures and patterns of the water.

below: Juliette Palmer, *Strande Water and Hogweed,* approx. 27.9 x 40.6 cm (11 x 16 in), watercolour. Palmer uses her small brush marks descriptively to build up pattern and texture. Notice the variety of different marks – little leaf-shaped blobs and dots at the top, long strokes for the clumps of rushes, and broader squiggles for the reflections.

Dry Brush

This technique is just what its name implies – painting with the bare minimum of paint on the brush so that the colour only partially covers the paper. It is one of the most often used ways of creating texture and broken colour in a watercolour, particularly for foliage and grass in a landscape or hair and fur textures in a portrait or animal painting. It needs a little practice as, if there is too little paint it will not cover the paper at all, but if there is too much it will simply create a rather blotchy wash.

As a general principle, the technique should not be used all over a painting as this can look dull. Texture-making methods work best in combination with others, such as flat or broken washes.

Opaque gouache and acrylic are also well suited to the dry brush technique. In both cases the paint should be used with only just enough water to make it malleable – or even none at all – and the best effects are obtained with bristle brushes, not soft sable or synthetic-hair brushes (these are, in any case, quickly spoiled by such treatment).

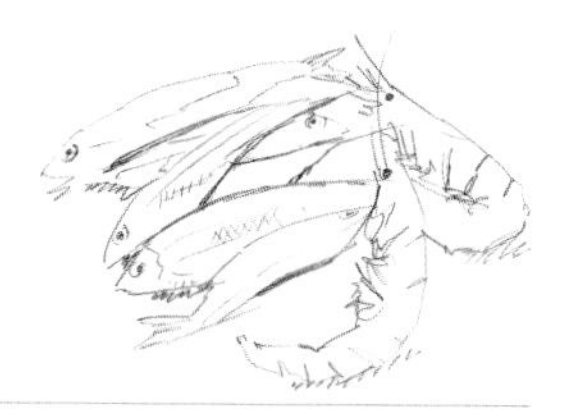

Step by Step: Dry Brushing

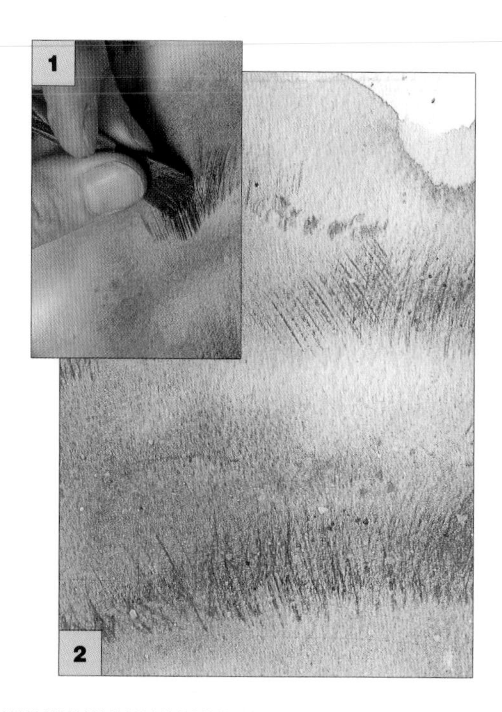

1: The artist uses a square-ended brush, fanning out the hairs slightly with his thumb and forefinger and then dragging it over the paper to create a series of fine, roughly parallel lines. The paint must be fairly dry, so before you begin, flick off the excess or dab the brush lightly on to blotting paper.

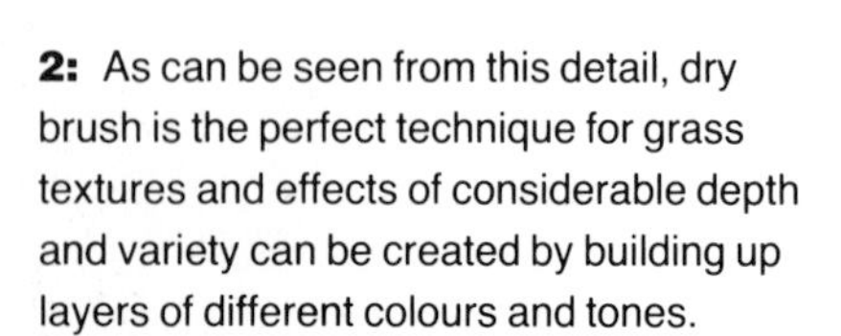

2: As can be seen from this detail, dry brush is the perfect technique for grass textures and effects of considerable depth and variety can be created by building up layers of different colours and tones.

3: It is usually more effective to restrict techniques like this to one area of a painting, as the artist has done here. The dry paint and spiky, linear marks in the foreground stand out well in contrast with the broad, free treatment of the buildings and sky.

above: David Bellamy, *Evening,Pantygasseg*, watercolour. The outer twigs and branches of the trees are suffused by light from the sky. The artist uses a lighter tone for the fine outer branches and merely suggests the twigs using quick drybrush-strokes.

–ARTISTS' HINTS–

- In scumbling, the different colours used mix optically and thus become more resonant, following one of the tenets observed by the Impressionists.
- Use a circular or back-and-forth scrubbing motion when scumbling, so that the paint goes on to the paper from all directions and picks up the texture of the surface.
- Scumbling is effective when used for relatively small areas to provide contrast to flat washes, but if used too extensively in one painting it can become monotonous.
- It is important to build up scumbles thinly, in gradual stages: if the paint is applied too heavily the hazy effect will be lost. Remember that the idea is not to blend the colour but to leave the brush marks showing.

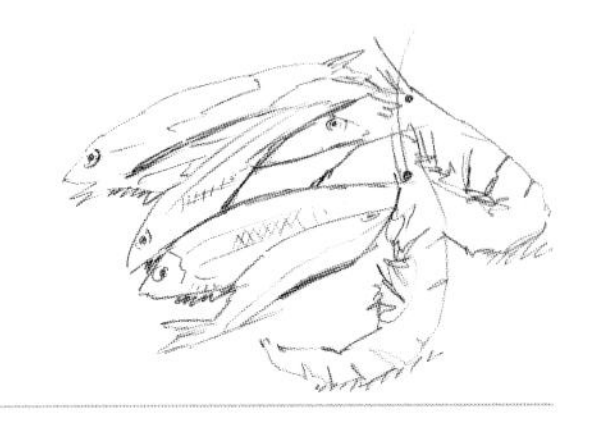

SCUMBLING

This is one of the best known of all techniques for creating texture and broken colour effects, particularly in the opaque media. It involves scrubbing very dry paint unevenly over another layer of dry colour so that the first one shows through, but only partially.

Scumbling can give amazing richness to colours, creating a lovely glowing effect rather akin to that of a semi-transparent fabric with another, solidly coloured one beneath.

There is no standard set of rules for the technique, as it is fundamentally an improvisational one. You can scumble light over dark, dark over light or a vivid colour over a contrasting one, depending on the circumstances, but do not try to use a soft, sable-type brush or the paint will go on too evenly (and you will quickly ruin the brush). A bristle brush is ideal, but other possibilities are stencilling brushes, sponges, crumpled paper or your fingers.

The particular value of the method for gouache is that it enables colours to be overlaid without becoming muddy and dead looking – always a danger with this medium.

Scumbling is less well suited to watercolour, but it is possible to adapt the dry brush method to scumbling, using the paint as thick as possible – even straight out of the tube – and working on rough paper.

right: Hazel Harrison, *Sun and Shadow, Santorini,* 52 x 36.8 cm (20½ x 14½ in), acrylic on smooth art board. Here successive layers have been built up over a pre-tinted yellow ochre ground. In places thick paint has been scumbled over thinner applications, and in others, notably the shadow, transparent colour thinned with acrylic medium has been glazed over opaque paint. The detail shows thin over thick scumbling with a bristle brush.

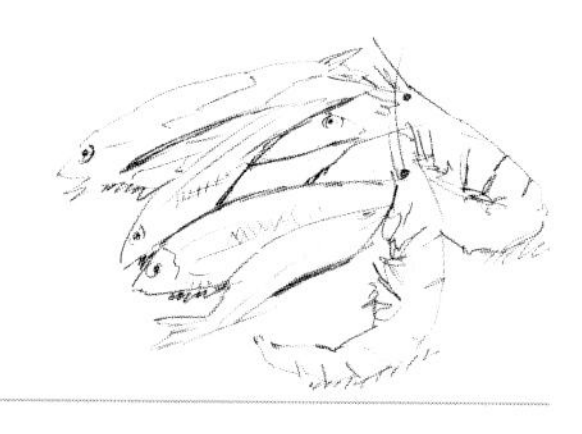

STIPPLING

This is a method of applying paint in a series of separate, small marks made with the point of the brush, so that the whole image consists of tiny dots of different colours. It was and still is a technique favoured by painters of miniatures, and is seldom used for large paintings for obvious reasons. However, for anyone who enjoys small-scale work and the challenge of a slow and deliberate approach, it is an attractive method and can produce lovely results quite unlike those of any other watercolour technique.

The success of stippled paintings relies on the separateness of each dot: the colours and tones should blend together in the viewer's eye rather than physically on the paper. Like all watercolours they are built up from light to dark, with highlights left white or only lightly covered so that the white ground shows through, while dark areas are built up gradually with increasingly dense brush marks. However, it is quite permissible to use body colour to emphasize the smaller highlights and to establish a larger, darker area of colour by laying a preliminary wash.

Step by Step: Stippling

1: The artist has chosen a fairly rough paper to enhance the textural quality of the stippled paint. She begins with an outline drawing and paints carefully and methodically with the point of a sable brush.

2: She continues to build up the tones and colours in the same way. Although she is working on white paper because she likes the sparkling effect of tiny areas of white showing through the dots of colour, it is perfectly permissible to establish a large area of colour by laying a preliminary wash.

The beauty of the technique is that it allows you to use a great variety of colours within one small area – a shadow could consist of a whole spectrum of deep blues, violets, greens and browns. As long as these are all sufficiently close in tone, they will still read as one colour, but a more ambiguous and evocative one than would be produced by a flat wash of, say, dark green.

SPATTERING

Spraying or flicking paint onto the paper, once regarded as unorthodox and "tricksy", is now accepted by most artists as an excellent means of either enlivening an area of flat colour or of suggesting texture.

Spattering is a somewhat unpredictable method and it takes some practice before you can be sure of the effect it will create, so it is wise to try it out on some spare paper before running the risk of spoiling a painting. Any medium can be used, but the paint must not be too thick or it will simply cling to the brush. To make a fine spatter, load a toothbrush with fairly thick paint, hold it horizontally above the paper, bristle side down, and run your forefinger over the bristles. For a coarser effect, use a bristle brush, loaded with paint of the same consistency, and tap it sharply with the handle of another brush.

The main problem with the method is judging the tone and depth of colour of the spattered paint against that of the colour beneath. If you apply dark paint – and thick watercolour will of necessity be quite dark – over a very pale tint it may be too obtrusive. The best effects are created when the tonal values are close together. If you are using the technique to suggest the texture of a pebbled or sandy beach, for which it is ideal, you may need to spatter one pale colour over another. In this case the best implement is a mouth diffuser of the kind sold for spraying fixative. The bristle brush method can also be used for watery paint, but will give much larger drops.

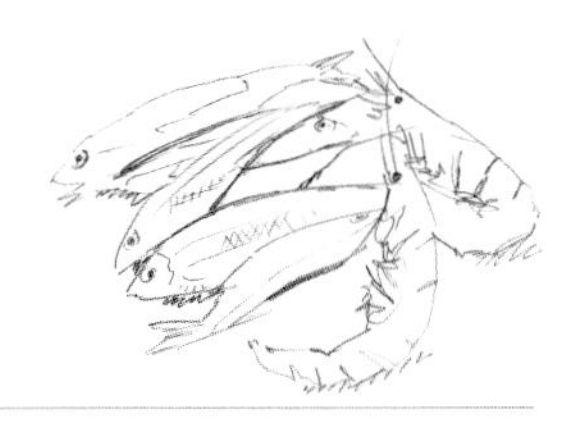

Step by Step: Spattering

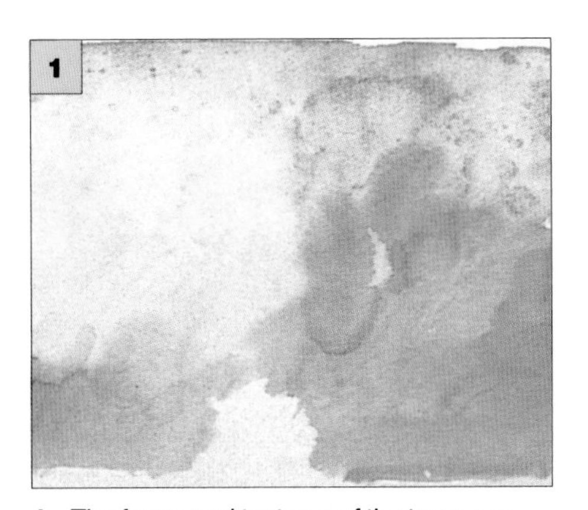

1: The forms and textures of the trees are to be built up by spattering, so the first washes are deliberately uneven, with the paint almost thrown from the brush in the sky area. A white patch is left in the foreground for the path.

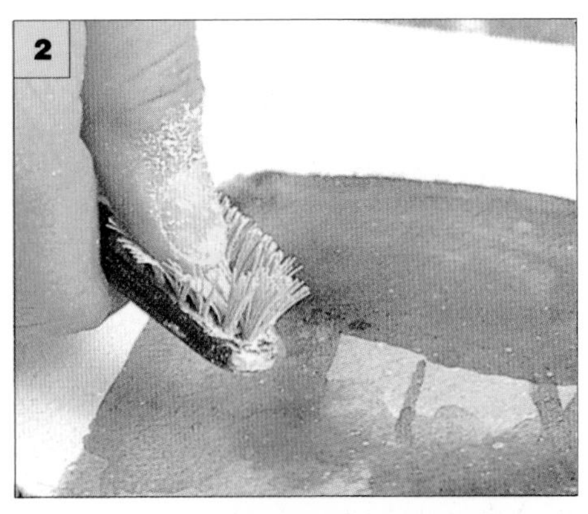

2: A loose newspaper mask protects the top of the picture while paint is spattered on to the trees and foreground. The yellow needs to be thickened if it is not to disappear into the darker colour, so a mixture of watercolour and acrylic is used.

3: At this stage, the artist takes stock of the painting to see where further definition is needed. The trees are still rather pale, but the sky area where the paint has formed a backrun, enhances the composition by echoing the curves below.

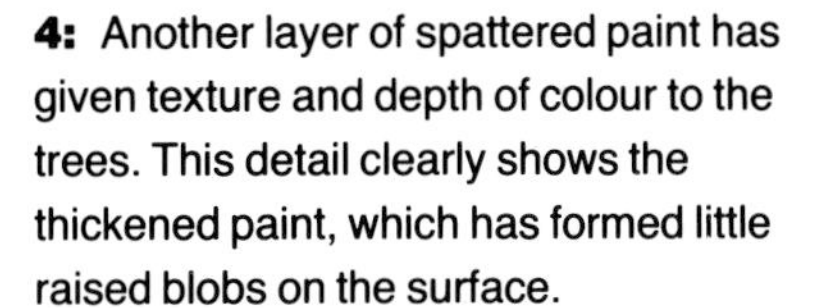

4: Another layer of spattered paint has given texture and depth of colour to the trees. This detail clearly shows the thickened paint, which has formed little raised blobs on the surface.

5: In the final stages, opaque paint is used to sketch in the trunks and branches and the area of path in the foreground, which was too uncompromisingly white, is darkened. The accidental blot in the sky directly above the path will be removed with a knife blade (see page 80).

below: In this example, slightly diluted gouache white was used for spattering. The soft, misty effect of the wave top was produced by taking the wash for the sky and sea right across the paper and lifting out with a tissue. The lower part was dampened when painting the sea, after which the whole wave was again dampened and shadows run in.

above: Moira Huntly RI, RSMA, *Still Life with Teapot and Decanter,* 48 x 38.5 cm (18⅞ x 15⅛ in), watercolour and gouache. Huntly likes to exploit the physical contrast between thin and thick paint, and in some areas has overlaid watercolour with opaque gouache.

left: Robert Dodd, *Bamburgh Castle,* 52 x 71.1 cm (20½ x 28½ in), gouache. This painting is entirely in gouache, used quite thickly, particularly in the foreground. One of the problems with gouache is that the paint becomes dead and muddy-looking if too many layers are built up. Dodd brings up the colours by varnishing them, so that his paint has rather the appearance of acrylic.

Body Colour

This slightly confusing term simply means opaque water-based paint. In the past it was usually applied to Chinese white, either mixed with transparent watercolour in parts of a painting or used straight out of the tube for highlights. Nowadays, however, it is often used as an alternative term for opaque gouache paint.

Some watercolourists avoid the use of body colour altogether, priding themselves on achieving all the highlights in a painting by reserving areas of white paper. There are good reasons for this, as the lovely translucency of watercolour can be destroyed by the addition of body colour, but opaque watercolour is an attractive medium when used sensitively.

Transparent watercolour mixed with either Chinese white or gouache zinc (not flake) white is particularly well suited to creating subtle weather effects in landscapes, such as mist-shrouded hills. It gives a lovely, milky, translucent effect slightly different from that of gouache itself, which has a more chalky, pastel-like quality.

A watercolour that has gone wrong – perhaps become over-worked or too bright in one particular area – can often be saved by overlaying a semi-opaque wash, and untidy highlights can be tidied up and strengthened in the same way.

Toned Ground

For a picture that is planned as an exercise in dark, rich tones and colours it can be an advantage to begin with a pre-tinted ground. It is possible to buy heavy coloured papers for watercolour work, but these have to be sought out; few of the smaller, less specialist art supply shops stock them.

A quick and simple way to pre-tint watercolour paper is to lay an overall wash of thinned acrylic (after stretching the paper if you are doing this). The colour, when dry, will be permanent, so there is no danger of stirring it up with the next layer of paint.

The advantages of toned grounds are two-fold. First, they help you to achieve unity of colour because the ground shows through the applied colours to some extent. Secondly, they allow you to build up deep colours with fewer washes, thus avoiding the risk of muddying.

The main problem with pre-tinting is deciding what colour to use. Some artists like to paint a cool picture, such as a snow scene, on a warm, yellow ochre ground so that the blues, blue-whites and greys are heightened by small amounts of yellow showing through. Others prefer cool grounds for cool paintings and warm grounds for warm ones. You need to think carefully about the overall colour key of the painting and you will probably have to try out one or two ground colours.

above: Jacqueline Rizvi, *Interval at the Globe Theatre,* 30.5 x 27.9 cm (12 x 11 in), watercolour and body colour. This artist uses watercolour mixed with opaque white and builds up very gradually, usually working on a toned paper (the ground for this painting is a light beige-grey). The red of the velvet was brought out in places by laying transparent red watercolour over a slightly opaque crimson and white mixture.

below: Charles Knight, RWS, ROI, *Church Ruins,* 28.6 x 34.9 cm (11¼ x 13¾ in), watercolour with pen on tinted paper. This artist likes to achieve his effects by means of a very free and direct application of paint, with as little overlaying of washes as possible. The cream-coloured paper has been left uncovered on parts of the building.

–Artists' Hints–

- More than one colour can be used for a ground, particularly if you already know where you will want warm and cool tones in the finished picture.
- A warm undertone of burnt sienna will have a vitalizing effect on a cool green landscape.
- A toned ground of acrylic paint will dry in minutes, making it possible to begin the overpainting in the same session.
- It is possible to judge the relative intensity of colour mixtures more effectively when using a toned ground. This is because the pre-tinted ground gives you an idea of how the colours will look when surrounded by other colours, rather than on a brilliant white background.

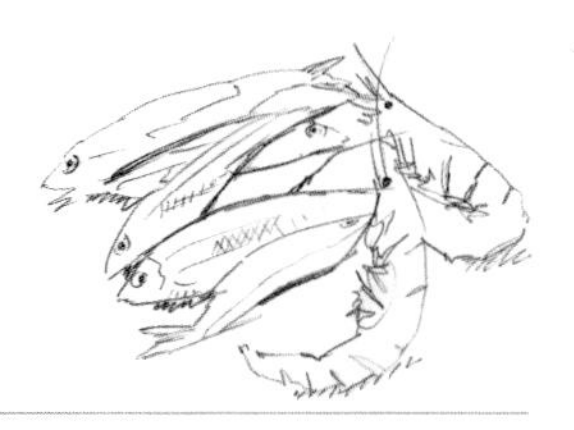

HOW A TONED GROUND WORKS

A toned canvas helps you to judge the relative intensity of your colour mixtures more accurately than a white canvas. This is because the toned canvas gives you an idea of how the colours will look when surrounded by other colours. To demonstrate how a toned ground works, this illustration (below) shows a piece of canvas, of which half is painted with a toned ground of raw umber and half is left white. Small squares of ultramarine and cadmium yellow are applied to each half: observe closely and you will see how much more intense the colours appear on the toned ground than they do on the white canvas.

BLENDING

This means achieving a soft, gradual transition from one colour or tone to another. It is a slightly trickier process with the water-based paints than with oil or pastel, because they dry quickly, but there are various methods that can be used.

One of these is to work wet-in-wet, keeping the whole area damp so that the colours flow into one another. This is a lovely method for amorphous shapes such as clouds, but is less suited to precise effects, such as those you might need in portraits, as you cannot control it sufficiently. You can easily find that a shadow intended to define a nose or cheekbone spreads haphazardly.

To avoid the hard edges formed where a wash ends or meets another wash, brush or sponge the edge lightly with water before it is dry. To convey the roundness of a piece of fruit or the soft contours of a face, use the paint fairly dry, applying it in small strokes rather than broad washes. If unwanted hard edges do form, these can be softened by "painting" along them using a small sponge or cotton bud dipped in a little water.

The best method for blending acrylics is to keep them fluid by adding retarding medium. This enables very subtle effects, as the paint can be moved around on the paper. Opaque gouache colours can be laid over one another to create soft effects, though the danger is that too much overlaying of wet colour stirs up and muddies the earlier layers.

right: The different methods of blending used in watercolour, gouache and acrylic are demonstrated by this comparison of ways of depicting the shadows and tones of an apple.

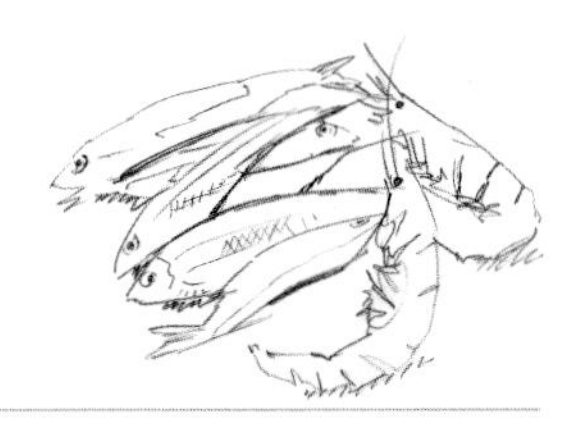

Watercolour

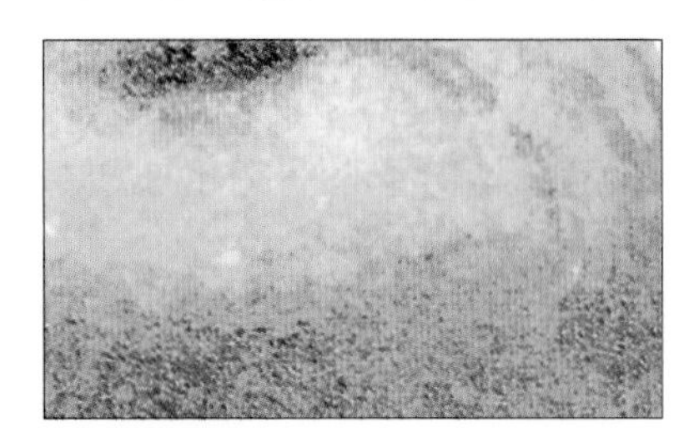

A pale green wash is laid and some darker greens and browns flooded into it while still wet. This is allowed to dry and the tones are built up with small brushstrokes of paint carefully blended together with a moistened brush.

Gouache

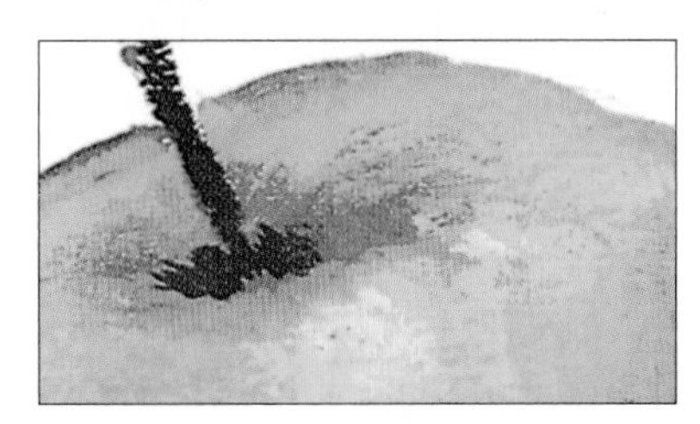

The same technique can be used for thin gouache, but here the paint is used thickly, with the blending done by working very dry paint over the underlayer with a bristle brush. On the top of the apple, light paint has been applied over dark.

Acrylic

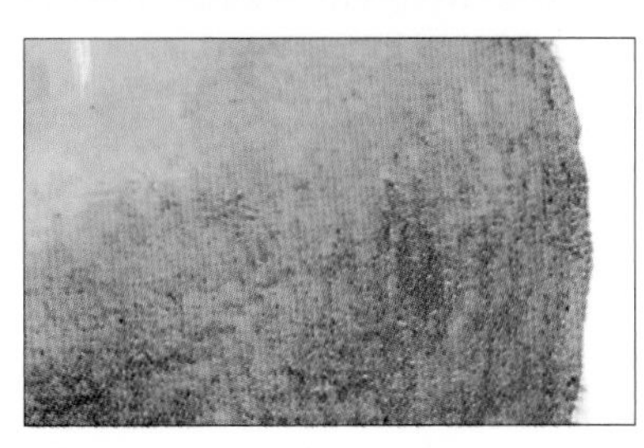

Because acrylic dries so fast it cannot be moved around on the paper as watercolour can, retarding medium has been used to slow the drying time. This also increases the transparency of the paint, so that the brushstrokes used to build up the shadows are clearly visible.

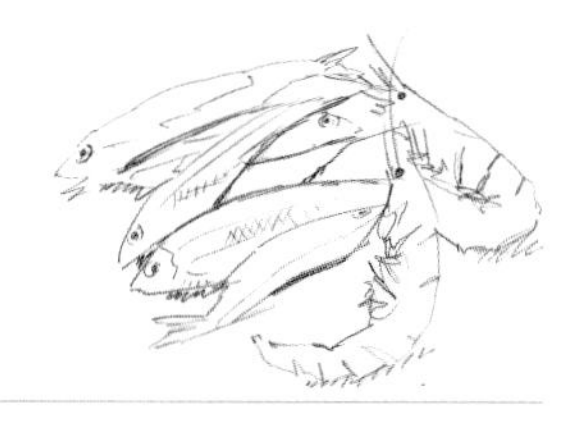

Broken Colour

It is one of the paradoxes of painting that a large area of flat colour seldom appears as colourful, or, indeed, as realistic, as one that is textured or broken up in some way. The Impressionists, working mainly in oils, discovered that they could best describe the fleeting, shimmering effects of light on foliage or grass by placing small dabs of various greens, blues and yellows side by side instead of using just one green for each area. This technique can be adapted very successfully to watercolour, but there are many other ways to break up colour.

If you "drag" a wash over a heavily textured paper, the paint will sink into the troughs, but will not completely cover the raised tooth of the paper – a broken colour effect much exploited by watercolourists. If you then apply drier paint over the original wash – in a different colour or a darker version of the same one – the effect will be even more varied and the painting will have a lively and interesting surface texture.

In gouache and acrylic, broken colour effects are best achieved by applying the paint rather dry with a stiff brush. Acrylic is perfect for this kind of treatment as it is immovable once dry, which means that more or less endless layers can be laid one over the other. This is not true of gouache: although it is opaque, it is also absorbent and so too many new layers will disappear into those below.

below: John McPake, RE, *Frame Tent,* 35.6 x 49.5 cm (14 x 19½ in), watercolour and gouache. The rather sombre colour scheme is enlivened by the loose application of paint, with clearly visible brush marks. McPake has thickened his paint by adding acrylic medium to the water as well as to some of the paint mixtures.

below: Michael Cadman, *Cornish Farm I,* 45.7 x 63.5 cm (18 x 25 in), acrylic and watercolour. Cadman has used no vivid colours, but the way each area is broken up into a multitude of separate "pieces" by the brick-like brushstrokes gives the painting a bright and sparkling quality. He likes acrylic because it holds the marks of the brush well.

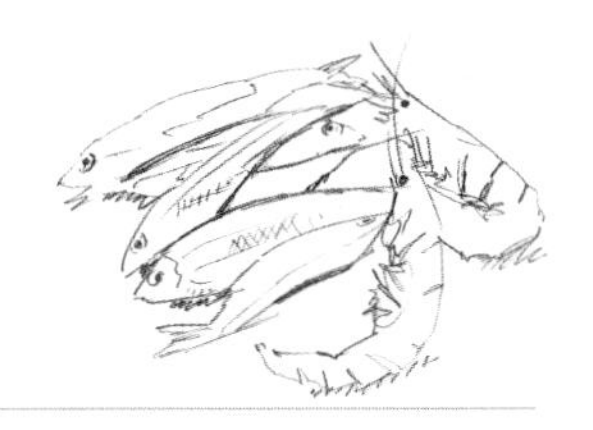

below: Lucy Willis, *Cattle in the Orchard,* 38.1 x 55.9 cm (15 x 22 in), watercolour. Willis works on dry paper, with no preliminary drawing, beginning by making little dots and dashes of colour and then working in turn on different parts of the composition. She keeps her effects fresh and clear by leaving each brushstroke or tiny wash to settle undisturbed except where she wants a soft gradation, in which case she regulates the amount of water carefully to avoid unwanted pools.

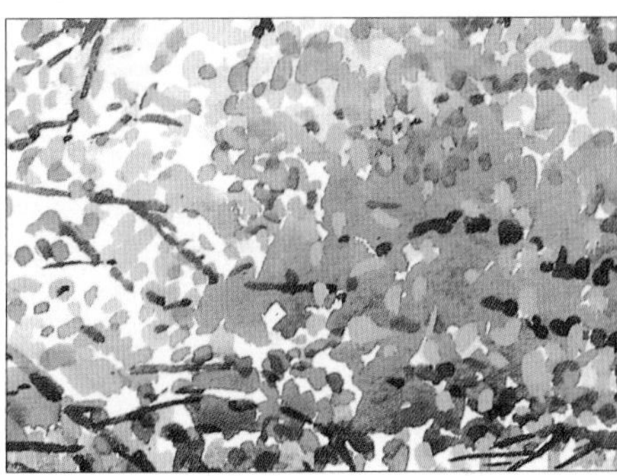

above and right: These two details show the lovely impression of dappled light created by means of small, separate brush marks with areas of white paper left uncovered.

Highlights

The light reflecting off white paper is an integral part of a watercolour painting, giving good watercolours their lovely translucent quality. For this reason the most effective way of creating pure, sparkling highlights is to "reserve" any areas that are to be white by painting around them. This means that when you begin a painting you must have a clear idea of where the highlights are to be, so some advance planning is necessary.

Not all highlights, of course, are pure white: in a painting where all the tones are dark, whites could be over-emphatic. Thus, before the painting has advanced very far you will have to decide whether to reserve areas of an initial pale wash or to build up really dark tones around a later, mid-toned one.

When you lay a wash around an area to be reserved for a highlight, it will dry with a hard edge. This can be very effective, but it is not necessarily what you want. You might, for example, need a softer, more diffused highlight on a rounded object such as a piece of fruit. In such cases, you can achieve a gentler transition by softening the edge with a brush, small sponge or cotton bud dipped in water, so that it blends into the white area.

Small highlights, such as the points of light in eyes or the tiny sparkles seen on water, which are virtually impossible to reserve, can either be achieved by masking or added with thick Chinese white or zinc white gouache paint as a final stage. Highlights can also be made by removing paint.

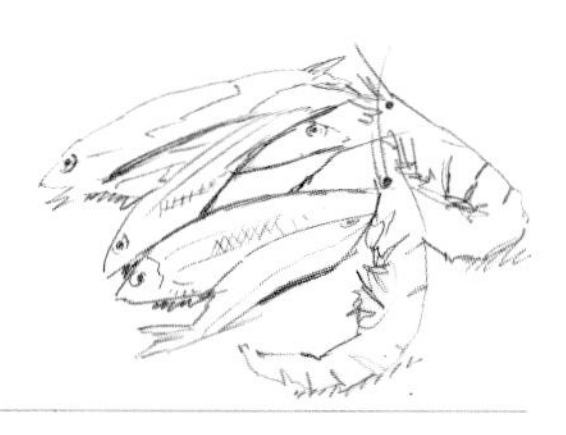

Step by Step: Highlighting

1: The shapes of the fruit are initially left white, their outlines defined by the pale brown wash.

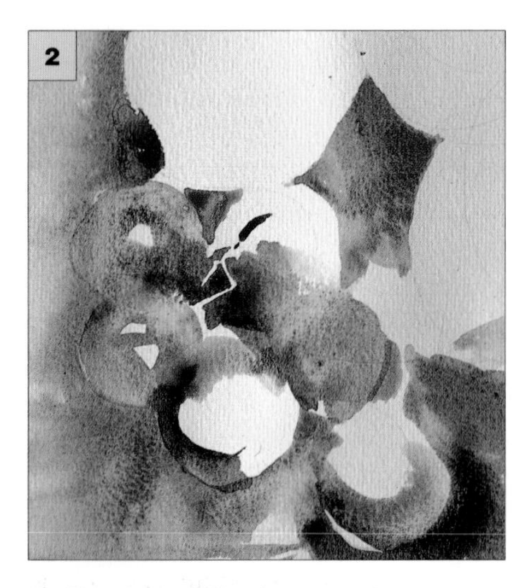

2: Paint is carefully taken around the highlights and darker colour is flooded in wet-in-wet. The paint is kept loose and fluid: hesitant niggling in the early stages can quickly destroy the freshness of the colour.

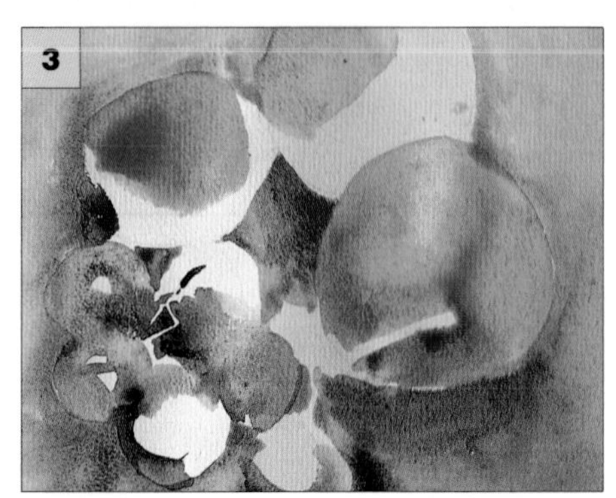

3: Instead of applying a flat wash all over the fruit and then adding darker tones, each area of colour is treated separately, though some washes will overlap at a later stage.

4: With all the paper covered and the main washes in place, the artist decides where further light and dark emphasis is needed.

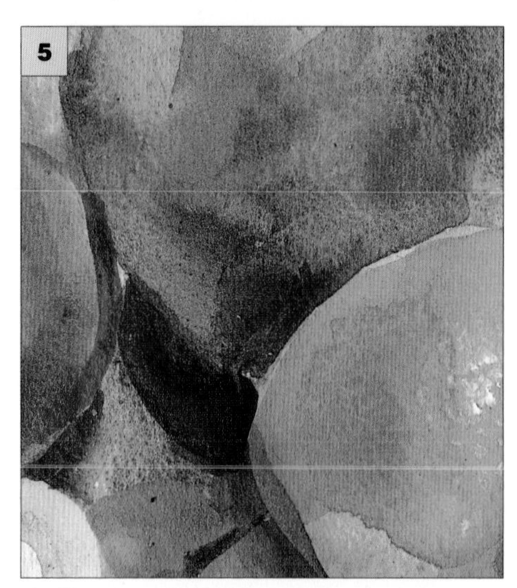

5: She darkens the cast shadows on and below the green apple and uses opaque white to add additional highlights on the fruit at left and right. Those on the orange have been applied lightly with the point of the brush, giving a realistic impression of the slightly pitted texture of the peel. The artist has been conscious of texture throughout, using the granulated quality of the wetly applied paint to add surface interest (see the earlier section on washes).

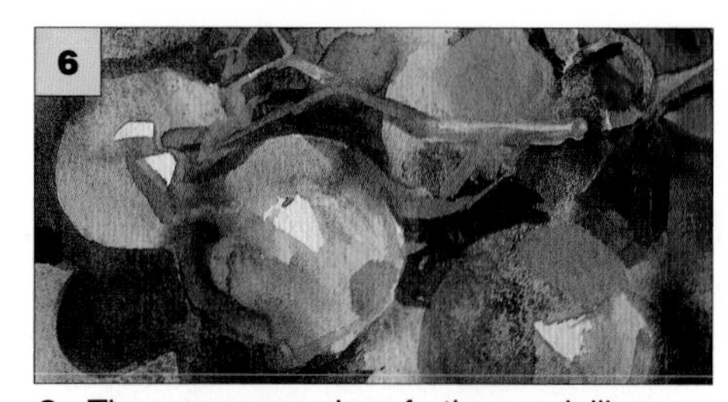

6: The grapes are given further modelling, with the dark paint again kept very wet. The original reserved highlights are not touched again, but the stalks are defined with a combination of opaque paint and reserving.

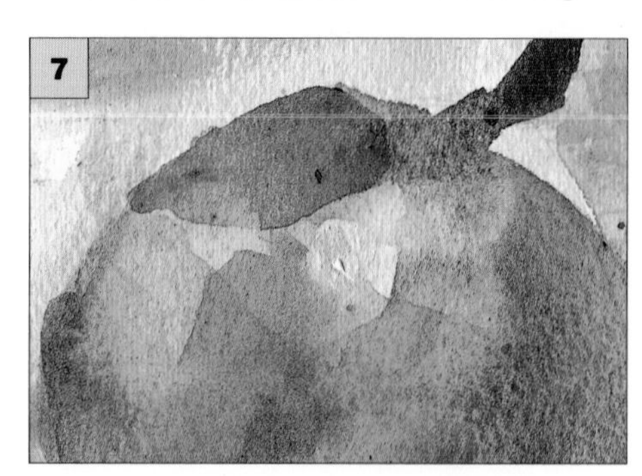

7: The treatment is impressionistic rather than literal, and the patch of dark green at the top of the apple, which could be either a shadow or a leaf, has been added primarily to separate it from the background and emphasize the highlighted areas.

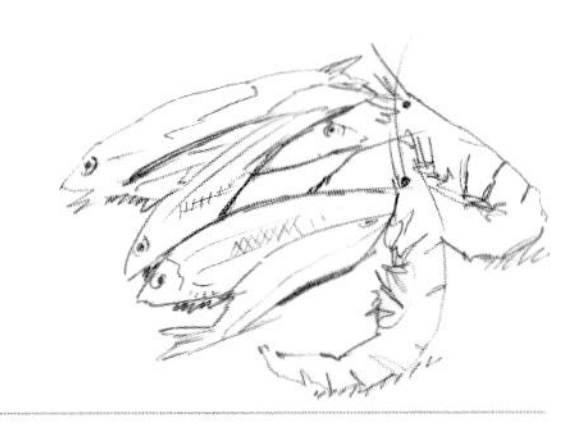

above: In watercolour painting, unpainted paper provides the brightest highlights you could wish for, because it reflects the maximum amount of light. In this lighthouse scene the crisp areas of white paper capture the effect of the intense sunlight on the tower and buildings.

MASKING

Some watercolourists feel a certain disdain for masking methods, regarding them as "cheating" or as being too mechanical. It is true that if over-used they can detract from the quality of spontaneity that we associate with watercolours, but masking is a method that can be used creatively, giving exciting effects that cannot be obtained by using the more classic watercolour techniques.

The two main purposes of masking are to create highlights by reserving certain areas of a painting and to protect one part of a picture while you work on another. If you have planned a painting that relies for its effect on a series of small, intricate highlights, such as a woodland scene with a pattern of leaves and twigs catching the sunlight, or a seascape where the light creates tiny bright points on choppy water, masking fluid can be the answer.

The fluid is available in two types. One has a slight yellow tint, the other is colourless. Both are applied with a brush and, once dry, washes are painted over it. When the painting or the particular area of it is complete, the fluid is removed by gently rubbing with a finger or an eraser. Be warned, however: if the paper is too rough or too smooth it will either be impossible to remove or will spoil the paper – the best surface is a medium one (known as not).

above: Masking fluid is ideal for hard-edged highlights such as the ripples on water. Such effects are difficult to achieve by the classic technique of reserving (see "Highlights" on page 55), as the paint in the darker areas can easily become overworked and the edges lose their crispness and clarity. This is a very direct and satisfying way of working, as the "negative" brushstrokes can be as varied and expressive as the "positive" ones.

below: Masking tape can be very helpful for buildings. It takes the tension out of painting, allowing you to work freely without the danger of spoiling an edge that needs to be straight and crisp.

The beauty of masking fluid is that it is a form of painting in negative – the brushstrokes you use can be as varied in shape as you like, and you can create lovely effects by using thick and thin lines, splodges and little dots. The advantage of the yellow-tinted fluid is that you can see how the brushstrokes look as you apply them, whereas with the white version it is rather a matter of guesswork. The disadvantage is that the yellow patches are always visible as you paint and tend to give a false idea of the colour values.

Sometimes a painting needs to be approached rather carefully and methodically, be dealt with in separate parts, and this is where the second main function of masking comes in. Masking fluid or masking tape (ideal for straight lines) can be used as a temporary stop for certain areas of the painting. Suppose your subject is a light-coloured, intricately shaped building set against a stormy sky or dark foliage, and you want to build up the background with several layers of colour. Covering the whole area of the building with masking fluid or putting strips of masking tape along the edges will allow you to paint freely without the constant worry of paint spilling over to spoil the sharp, clean lines. Once the background is finished, the mask can be removed and the rest of the painting carried out as a separate stage. It may be mechanical, but it is a liberating method for anyone who wishes to have complete control over paint.

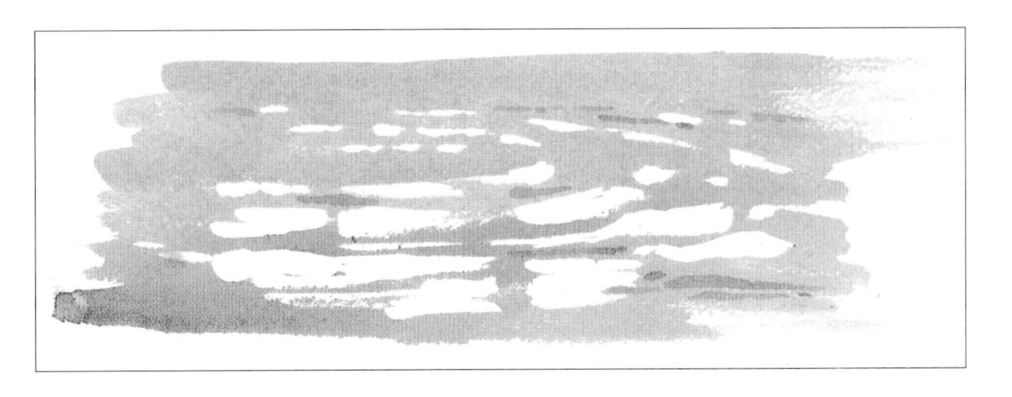

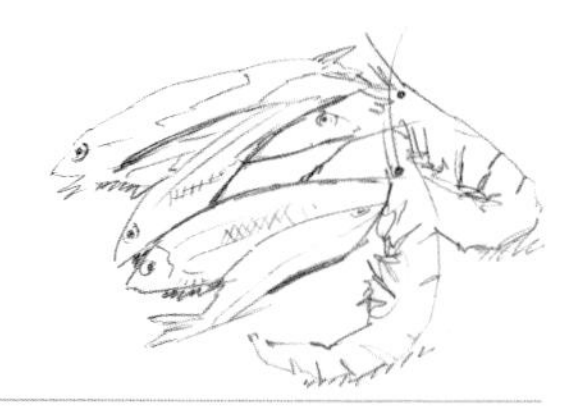

Step by Step: Masking

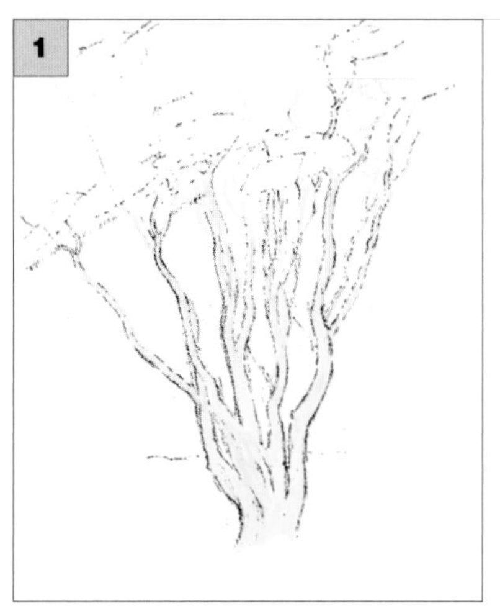

1: The tree trunks are carefully drawn, masking fluid is applied, and then left to dry before any further work is done. The artist is working on Bockingford paper with a not surface, from which the rubbery fluid is easily removed; it is not suitable for use on rough papers as it sinks into the "troughs" and cannot be peeled off.

2: With the fluid protecting the intricate shapes of the trunks and branches, dark washes are built up behind and above without fear of paint splashing onto the pale areas. When the washes are dry, the fluid is removed by rubbing with a finger.

3: The trunks and branches are modelled with darker paint in places and touches of white gouache define the highlights.

Step by Step: Spattering with a Mask

1: The artist uses detail paper to trace the area he wants to mask.

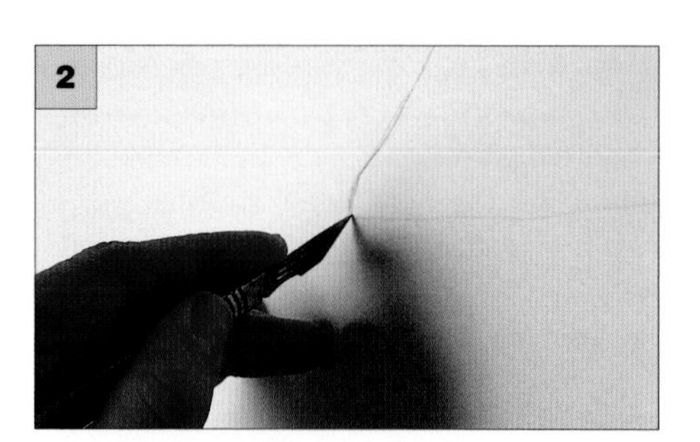

2: He then carefully cuts the mask with the scalpel.

3: The mask is applied and the tree is painted in sap green, mixed with a little gum water to give it extra body and brilliance.

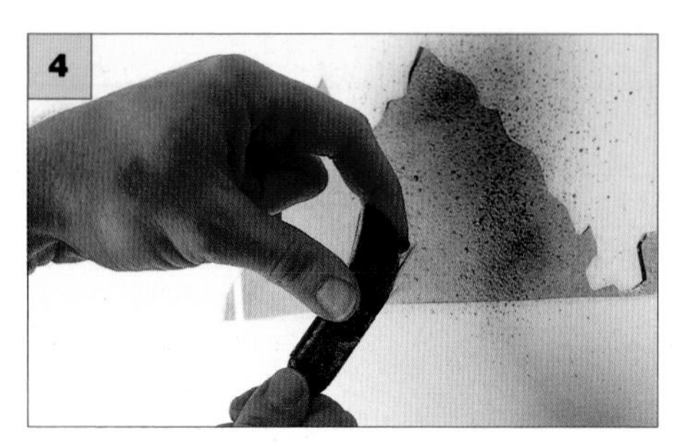

4: More sap green, again mixed with gum water, is spattered on the area with an ordinary household brush.

5: The slightly irregular stippled effect is clear, even before the mask is peeled off.

6: The mask is removed, leaving a sharp, clean outline. The slightly irregular texture is very effective in suggesting foliage.

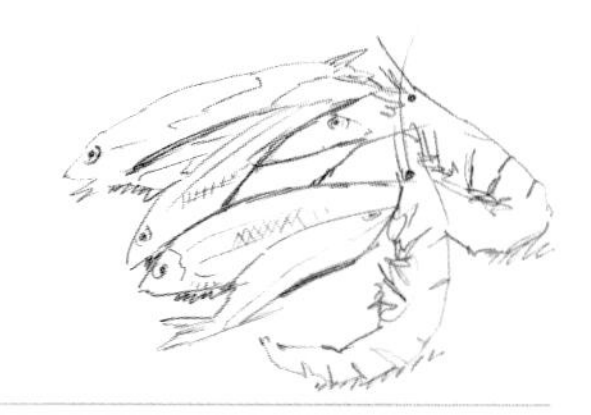

Lifting Out

Removing paint from the paper is not only a correction method, it is a watercolour technique in its own right and can be used to great effect to soften edges, diffuse and modify colour and create those highlights that cannot be reserved. For instance, the effect of streaked wind clouds in a blue sky is quickly and easily created by laying a blue wash and wiping a dry sponge, paintbrush or paper tissue across it while it is still wet. The white tops of cumulus clouds can be suggested by dabbing the wet paint with a sponge or blotting paper.

Paint can also be lifted out when dry by using a dampened sponge or other such tool, but the success of the method depends both on the colour to be lifted and the type of paper used. Certain colours, such as sap green and phthalocyanine blue, act rather like dyes, staining the paper, and can never be removed completely, while some papers absorb the paint, making it hard to move it around.

Bockingford, Saunders and Cotman papers are all excellent for lifting out in this way, so if you become addicted to the technique, choose your paper accordingly. Another useful aid to lifting out is gum arabic. Add it in small quantities to the colour you intend to partially remove.

Large areas of dry paint can be lifted with a dampened sponge, but for smaller ones the most useful tool is a cotton bud. Never apply too much pressure when using a cotton bud, as the plastic may poke through the cotton tip, scratching the surface of the paper.

above: Surprisingly complex sky effects can be obtained by lifting out from wet paint. Here a light ochre wash was laid and allowed to dry, a blue wash was taken over the whole area and the clouds blotted immediately with a crumpled tissue. The paper was then damped and pale grey added in small strokes that were allowed to spread, leaving areas of the original yellow untouched.

below: Here a gradated wash of blue was laid over the whole sky and grey added when still wet. The lighter areas of the clouds and the sun's rays were lifted out with tissue rolled into a point.

above: This dramatic sky has been created very simply, by laying a warm grey gradated wash (see the section on washes) over a dry merged wash of yellow and red. While the grey was still wet, the clouds were lifted out with a piece of tissue formed into a blunt point.

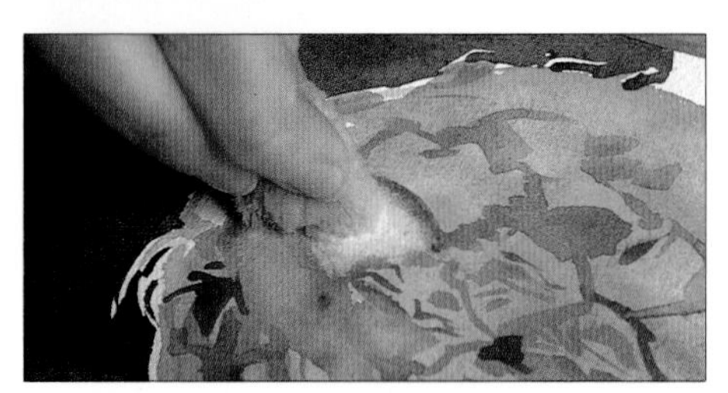

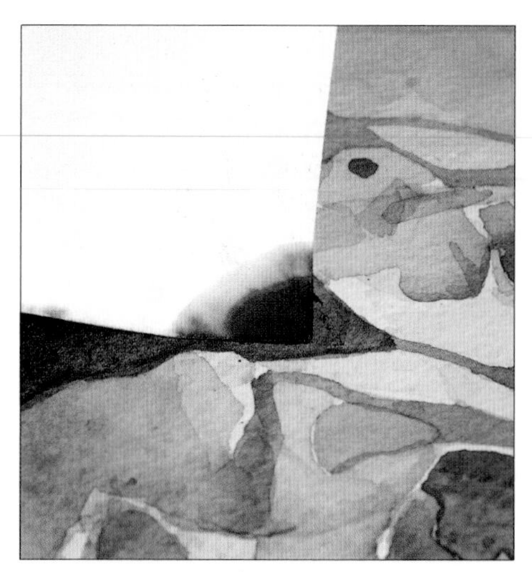

above: With this fruit group nearly complete, the artist has decided to lighten certain areas, using a dampened sponge to coax the paint off the paper. The success of lifting out dry paint depends very much on the paper used (this is Bockingford), but highlights created in this way can be very effective, as they are softer and less obtrusive than reserved areas of white paper.

above: When working with lots of wet washes, tissue is useful for wiping areas that have become too wet, and for controlling the flow of paint. Use a blot-and-lift motion with the tissue – rubbing may damage the surface of the paper. Tissue paper can be used to lift out amorphous shapes in a wet wash – when painting clouds, for example. Use this technique sparingly.

above: Blotting paper is thicker and more absorbent than tissue and, once dry, it can be re-used. If you wish to life out a small, precise area, hold the corner of the blotting paper against the surface until the excess paint is absorbed.

Step by Step: Lifting Out

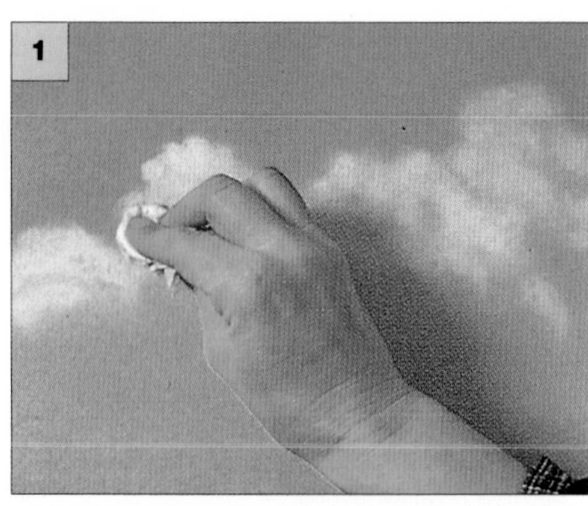

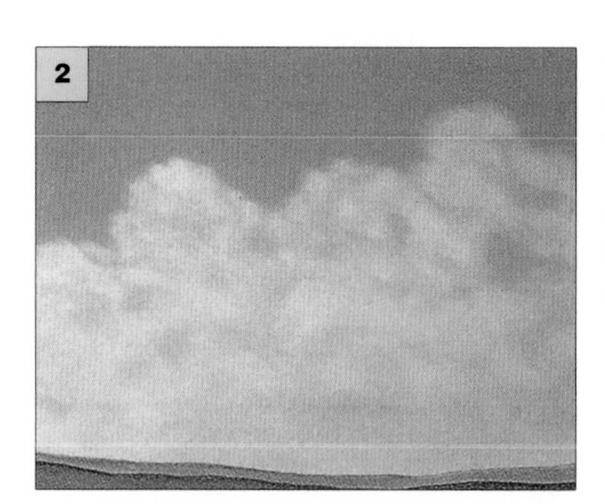

1: With the blue wash still wet, areas are lifted out with a piece of crumpled tissue to give a deliberately uneven effect.

2: Less pressure was used towards the bottom of the sky; clouds are always smaller and less distinct above the horizon.

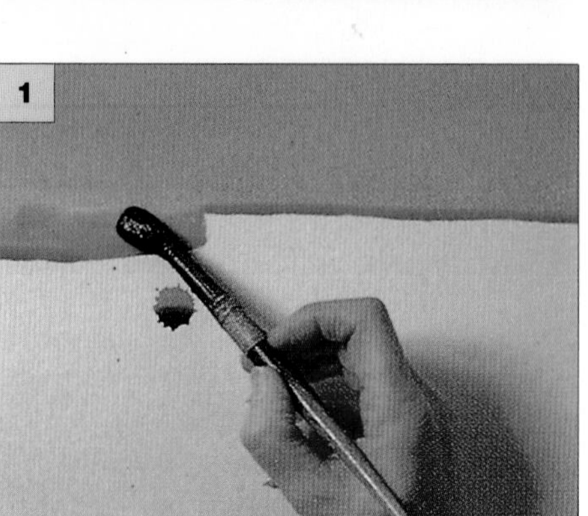

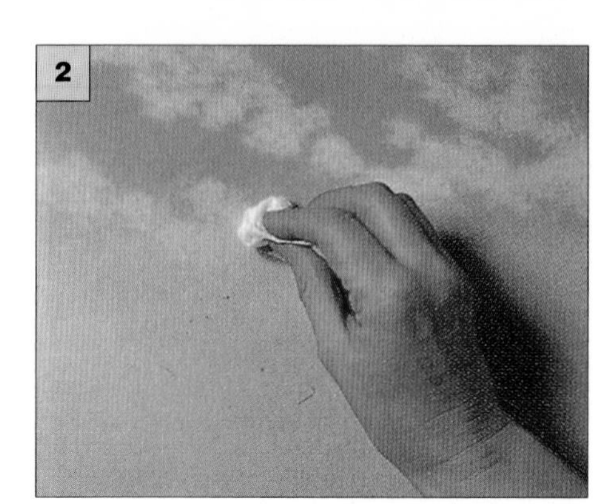

1: In this case two washes have been laid, and the blue is to be lifted out to reveal the dried pink wash below.

2: Again, a small piece of tissue is used to dab into the paint. For broader effects you might try using a sponge, rag or large piece of cotton wool.

above: The results obtained by the salt technique vary according to how close the crystals are to one another and how wet the paint is. Here crystals have been sprinkled into a very wet wash, while in the first example the paint was left to dry a little first.

top: Fascinating effects can be made by scattering salt crystals into wet paint. Elaborate textures can be built up by laying further washes over one salt-scattered area and then repeating the process.

TEXTURES

There are two main kinds of texture in painting: surface texture, in which the paint itself is built up or manipulated in some way to create what is known as surface interest, and imitative texture, in which a certain technique is employed to provide the pictorial equivalent of a texture seen in nature. These naturally overlap to some extent: surface texture is sometimes seen as an end in itself, but in many cases it is a welcome by-product of the attempt to turn the three-dimensional world into a convincing two-dimensional image on the page.

Surface Texture

Since watercolours are applied in thin layers, they cannot be built up to form surface texture, but this can be provided instead by the grain of the paper. There are a great many watercolour papers on the market, some of which – particularly the hand-made varieties – are so rough that they appear almost to be embossed. Rough papers can give wonderfully exciting effects, as the paint will settle unevenly (and not always predictably), breaking up each area of colour and leaving flecks of white showing through. Reserved highlights on rough paper stand out with great brilliance – because the edges are slightly ragged, the white areas appear to be standing proud of the surrounding colours.

Acrylic paints are ideal for creating surface interest because they can be used both thickly and thinly in the same painting, providing a lively contrast. You can vary the brush marks, using fine, delicate strokes in some places and large, sweeping ones in others. You can put on slabs of paint with a knife and you can even mix the paint with sand or sawdust to give it an intriguing grainy look.

Imitative Texture

Several of the best-known techniques for making paint resemble rocks, tree bark, fabrics and so on are described in the sections on brush techniques and alternative techniques, but there are some other tricks of the trade you might like to experiment with. One of these – unconventional but effective – is to mix watercolour paint with soap. The soap thickens the paint without destroying its translucency. Soapy paint stays where you put it instead of flowing outwards, and allows you to use inventive brushwork to describe both textures and forms.

Intriguingly unpredictable effects can be obtained by a variation of the resist technique. If you lay down some turpentine or white spirit on the paper and then paint over it, the paint and the oil will separate to give a marbled appearance. A slightly similar effect can be gained by dropping crystals of sea salt into wet paint. Leave it to dry, brush off the salt, and you will see pale, snowflake shapes where the salt has absorbed the surrounding paint. If the crystals are close together these shapes will run into one another to form a large mottled blob rather resembling weathered rock.

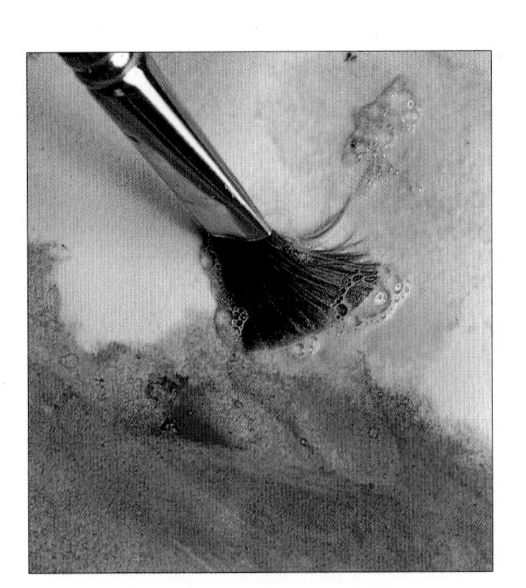

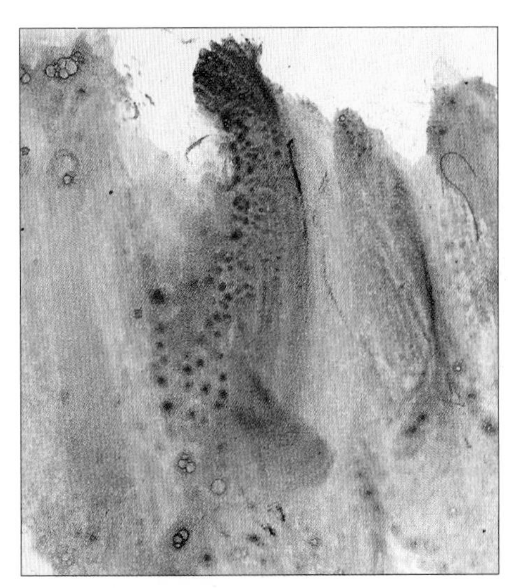

above left and right: Mixing paint with soap has a similar effect to mixing it with gum arabic. It loses much of its fluidity, holding the marks of the brush very well, and thus providing considerable scope for textural painting. The bubbles leave pronounced rings and blobs on the paper when dry. This is a less predictable method than salt scattering, but it is an enjoyable one to experiment with.

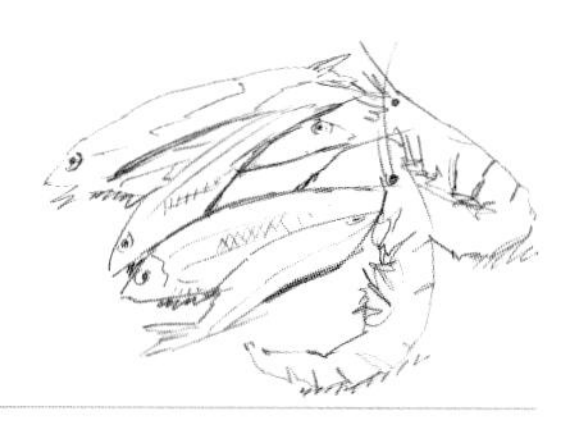

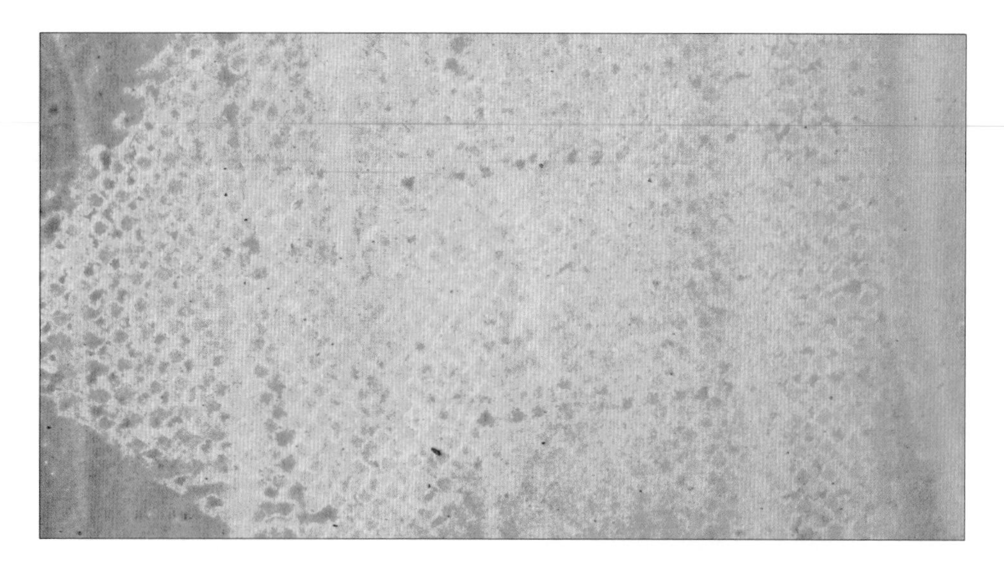

above: This method, known as a "blot-off", is a very direct way of creating texture. It is basically a simple printing technique, involving pressing a textured paper or piece of fabric on to wet paint and then removing it, so that its imprint is left behind. Almost anything can be used for this technique and quite intricate textures can be built up by using several different printing surfaces in one area of a painting.

below left and right: Sgraffito, which means scratching into paint, is another well-known texturing method, here used to give the effect of wood grain. It is not suitable for transparent watercolour, but is excellent for thick gouache or acrylic. Broad areas can be scraped with the side of a knife and fine lines made with a pointed implement. See page 68 for more detail.

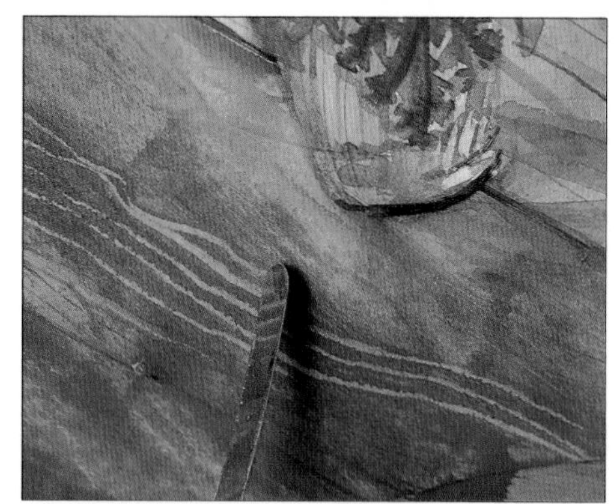

below: This is another version of the method shown above, but here the paint is not lifted off but dabbed on. In this example, the colour was applied with a crumpled piece of paper, but again, more or less anything can be used, and the variety of effects that can be created is almost unlimited.

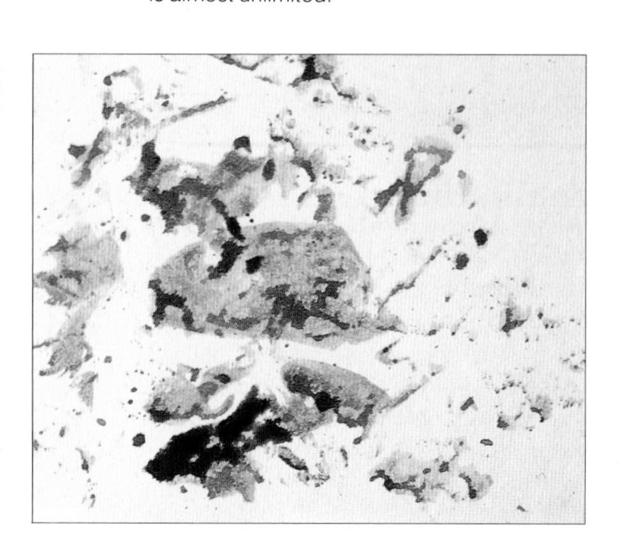

above: Jean Canter, *Autumn Leaves,* 40.6 x 59.7 cm (16 x 23½ in), watercolour. For this painting the artist has combined the wet-on-dry and wet-in-wet methods, beginning by painting each leaf individually on slightly damp paper and allowing the colour to spread. A variety of texturing methods was used on the leaves, including dry brush, stippling and scattering salt into wet paint. The effect of the delicate white veins was achieved by masking, while the darker ones were drawn into wet paint with a cocktail stick.

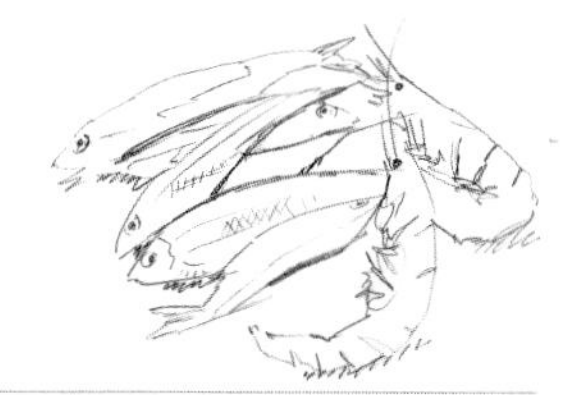

Sponge Painting

Sponges are an essential part of the artist's tool kit. As well as being useful for mopping up unwanted paint, tidying up edges and making corrections, they can be used for applying paint – either alone or in conjunction with brushes.

Laying a flat wash is just as easy (some claim it is easier) with a sponge as it is with a brush. The only thing it cannot do satisfactorily is take a wash around an intricate edge – for which a brush is best – but if you intend to begin a painting with an overall wash of one colour, the sponge is ideal. For a completely even wash, keep the sponge well saturated and squeeze it out gently as you work down the paper. If you want a less regular wash, squeeze some of the paint out so that the sponge is only moistened. This will give a slightly striated effect, which can be effective for skies, seas, the distance in a landscape or hair in a portrait.

Dabbing paint onto paper with a sponge gives an attractive mottled effect quite unlike anything that can be achieved with a brush, particularly if you use the paint reasonably thick. This method is an excellent way in which to describe texture, and you can suggest form at the same time by applying the paint lightly in some areas and densely in others.

–ARTISTS' HINTS–

- Most artists keep two sponges in their painting kit: a synthetic one for laying a flat, even layer of colour in large areas, and a natural sponge for creating patterns and textures.
- Natural sponges are more expensive than artificial ones, but they have the advantage of being smoother and more pliant to work with, and their irregular texture produces more interesting patterns in the paint.

There is no reason why whole paintings should not be worked using this method, but the one thing the sponge cannot do is create fine lines or intricate details, so brushes are usually brought into play for the later stages of a picture when extra definition is needed.

Step by Step: Painting with a Sponge

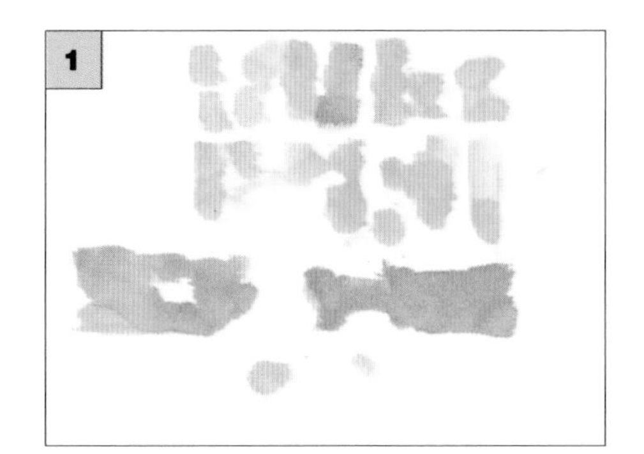

1

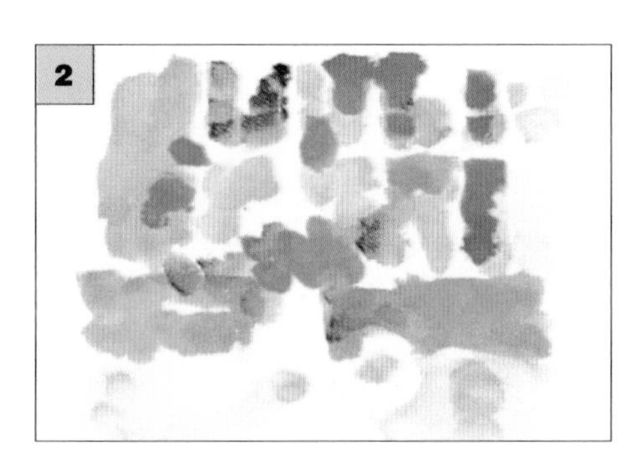

2

1, 2: It is often necessary to employ some system of masking when painting with a sponge, as you cannot take paint around edges as precisely as you can with a brush. The artist has masked the window bars, which are to remain white, by the simple method of holding a ruler against each edge as he works. He does not worry unduly if paint splashes over in places, as he is aiming at a soft, impressionistic overall effect.

3

3: Working carefully, the artist continues to build up the painting, using the paint fairly wet so that each new application merges with the surrounding colours.

4

4: One of the problems with combining sponge painting and brushwork is that the contrast of techniques, if over-emphasized, can destroy the unity of the composition. Although the artist has used conventional brush washes in places, he has kept the paint loose and fluid throughout, blurring the edges of the brush marks on the crockery so that they blend in with the sponge work.

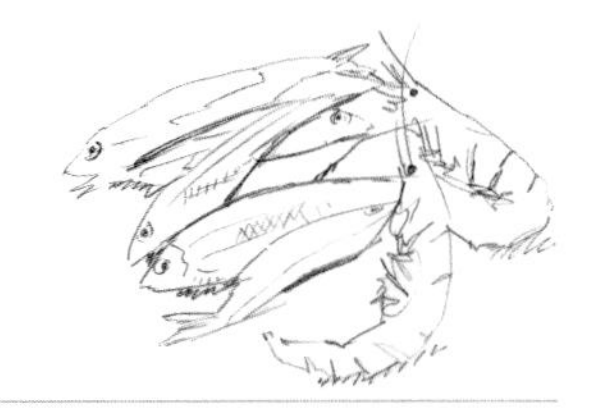

Step by Step:
Stippling with a Sponge

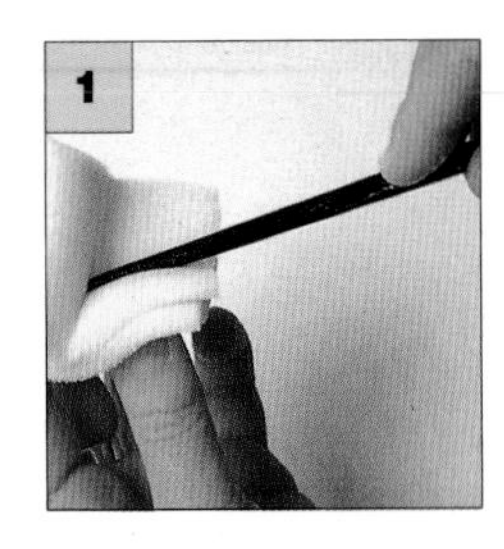

1: You can stipple with a small round sponge – synthetic ones will produce a more regular pattern. For small areas, make a stippling tool by wrapping a piece of sponge or foam rubber round the end of a paintbrush. This will give you greater control over the technique.

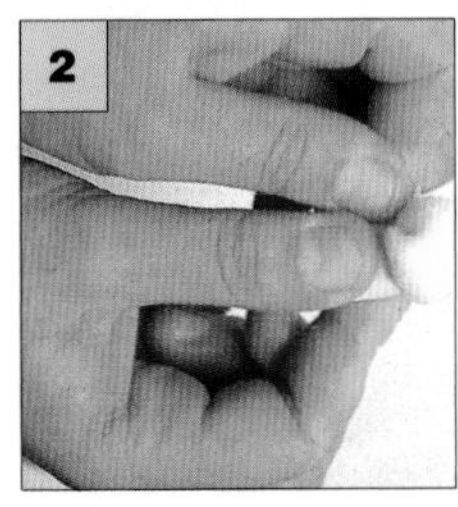

2: Make sure the wad of sponge is thick enough to prevent the sharp point of the brush handle sticking through, and tape it firmly in position.

3: Moisten the sponge and dip it into fairly stiff paint, then apply with a press-and-lift motion – don't scrub.

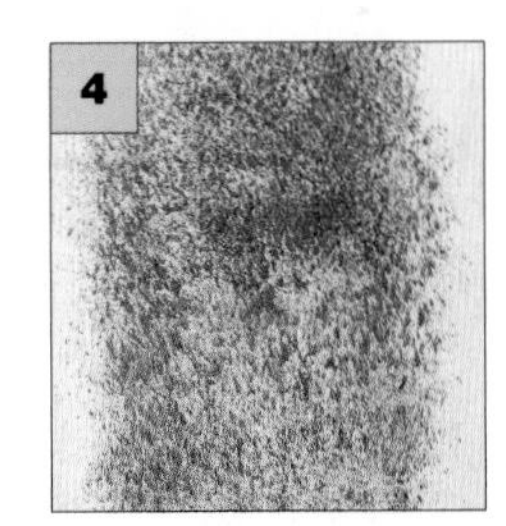

4: Keep dabbing and lifting, overlapping the patterns until you achieve the density and texture that you want. Try dabbing one colour into another, or producing graded tones by altering the density of stipple.

PAINTING FOLIAGE WITH A SPONGE

Painting with a sponge gives you natural-looking foliage effects with great economy of means. Be sure to use a natural sea sponge, though: man-made sponges are too smooth-textured. You'll find large, rough-textured natural sponges in most chemists and hardware stores. Look for a sponge with plenty of rough, ragged edges on its surface; tear it into small pieces and you have a perfect tool for painting foliage and a whole range of other textures.

Try dipping the sponge into several shades of green at one time. Or dab one colour over another to achieve stronger tones in the shadow areas of the foliage. Experiment with the technique on scrap paper – aim to create a range of marks that vary from a solid imprint to a delicate dry brush effect.

To make the sponge pliable, dip it in water then squeeze it dry. If water is left in the sponge it will dilute the pigment and the marks will be blurred. For the same reason, paint for sponging should not be too fluid. Use it straight from the tube, or diluted with just a drop of water.

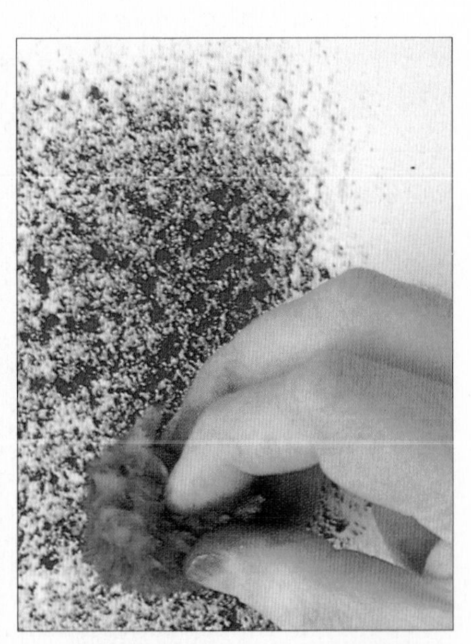

For delicate foliage, use a stippling technique. Tap the finer side of the sponge onto the paper very lightly, using a straight up-and-down motion. One or two taps with the sponge are usually all that's needed – any more and the texture becomes too dense.

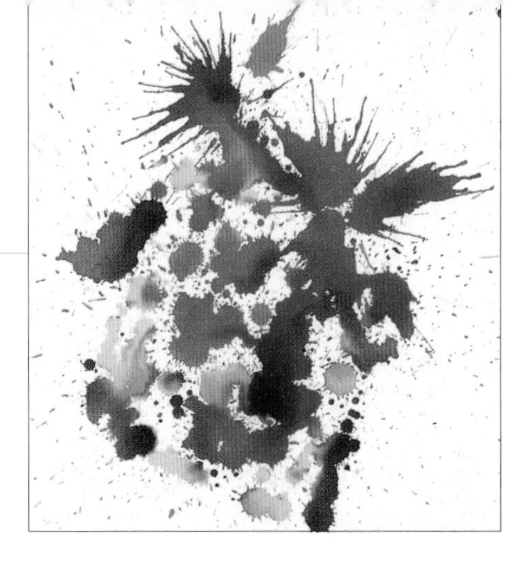

Blots

Blot painting is a technique most often associated with monochrome ink drawing, but since watercolours are available in liquid (ink) form I have included this technique here. The other reason for its inclusion is that it is an excellent way of loosening up technique. Like backruns, blots are never entirely predictable, and the shapes they make will sometimes suggest a painting or a particular treatment of a subject quite unlike the one that was planned. Allowing the painting to evolve in this way can have a liberating effect and may suggest a new way of working in the future.

The shapes the blots make depend on the height from which they are dropped, the consistency of the paint or ink and the angle of the paper. Tilting the board will make the blot run downhill; flicking the paint or ink will give small spatters; wetting the paper will give a diffused, soft-edged blot. A further variation can be provided by dropping a blot on to the paper and then blowing it, which sends tendrils of paint shooting out into various directions. Blots can also be used in a controlled, selective way to suggest the texture of trees, flowers or pebbles in a particular part of a painting.

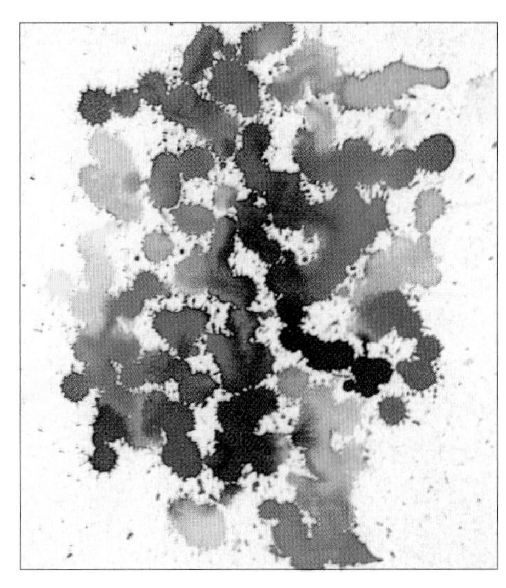

Step by Step: Blown Blots

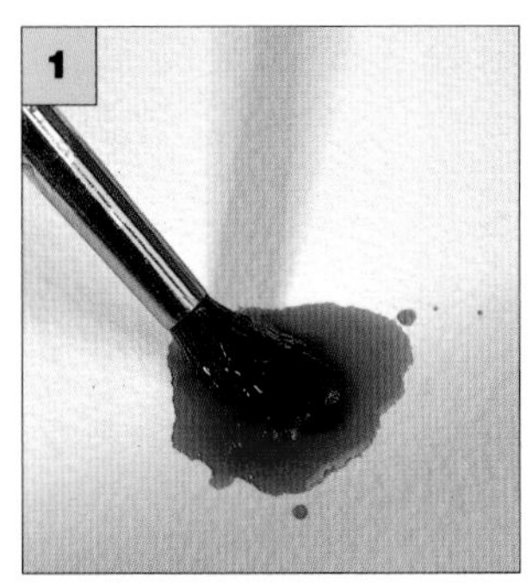

1: The artist splashes a large brushful of yellow ink on to dry watercolour paper to produce a deep pool of colour.

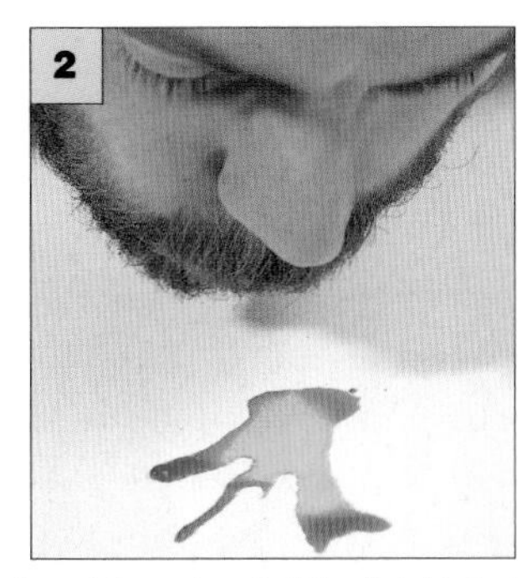

2: He then blows hard at the ink blot at close range. Blow in several directions until the ink takes on an interesting shape.

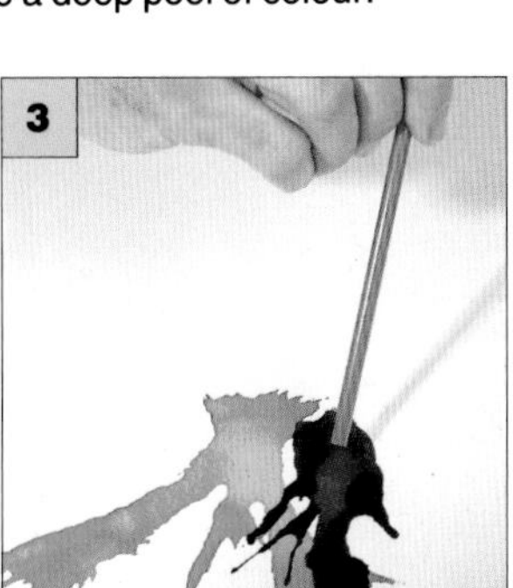

3: When the first colour is dry, a blot of purple ink is applied. Here the artist blows through a straw to create even finer trails of ink. This method allows you more control over the shape and direction of the trails.

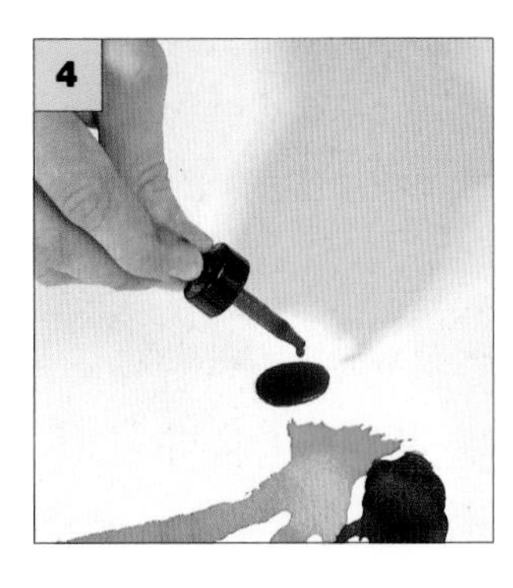

4: A blot of red ink is added, using an eye dropper. Experiment with several different colours, making them overlap partially, or try adding new colours while the previous ones are still wet. Then use your imagination to turn these "accidental" forms into a recognizable image, or develop them with different media.

above: Blot painting is a form of constructive doodling. Because you are freed from the constraints imposed by the need to "make a painting", you can loosen up and enjoy yourself. Sometimes a random effect of coloured blots will suggest an actual subject, and can be developed into a roughly representational treatment, but often, as here, they are simply pleasing as abstract patterns. These examples have been produced by dropping coloured inks on to the paper from different heights. Some of the colours have been used undiluted and some mixed with a little water. The lines and tendrils of ink spreading outwards are the result of blowing the blots, a useful and simple technique for flower and foliage effects.

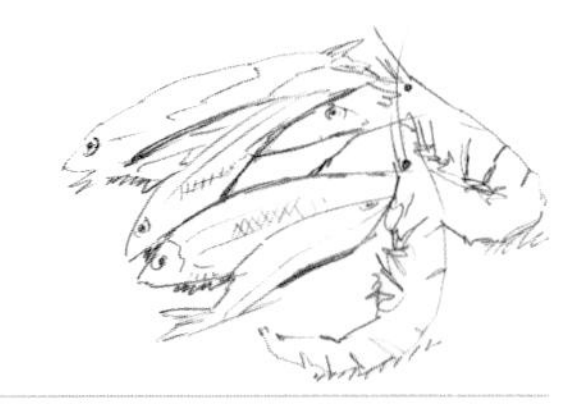

LINE AND WASH

This technique has a long history, and is still much used today, particularly for illustrative work. Before the British watercolourists of the eighteenth century began to exploit the full possibilities of watercolour as a painting medium, it had been used mainly to put pale, flat tints over pen drawings, a practice that itself continued the tradition of the pen and ink-wash drawings often made by artists as preliminary studies for paintings.

The line and wash technique is particularly well suited to small, delicate subjects such as plant drawings or to quick figure studies intended to convey a sense of movement. Rembrandt's sketchbooks are full of monochrome pen and wash drawings, conveying everything he needed to record in a few lines and one or two surely placed tones.

The traditional method is to begin with a pen drawing, leave it to dry and then lay in fluid, light colour with a brush. One of the difficulties of the technique is to integrate the drawing and the colour in such a way that the washes do not look like a "colouring in" exercise, so it is often more satisfactory to develop both line and wash at the same time, beginning with some lines and colour and then adding to and strengthening both as necessary.

You can also start back to front, as it were, laying down the washes first to establish the main tones and then drawing on top, in which case you will need to begin with a light pencil sketch as a guideline.

above: Doreen Osborne, *Ancient Agora, Kos,* 33 x 52 cm (13 x 20½ in), gouache and pen. Osborne has created a strong sense of pattern in her painting, with the bold line drawing in the foreground providing a nice balance to the dark shapes of the trees and mosque roof.

below: Edward Piper, *Bellagio, Lake Como,* 55.9 x 76.2 cm (22 x 30 in), watercolour and pen. Piper achieves a perfect harmony between line and colour by using both with a light and delicate touch. He never attempts to outline areas of colour with line; instead, the washes are allowed to escape their "boundaries" to merge together in places .

-ARTISTS' HINTS-

- In line and wash, you need not restrict yourself to pen drawing – you can use fibre or felt-tipped pens and hard or soft pencils as well or instead, and you can draw in several colours if you like.
- Some artists favour water-soluble ink, which runs in places where colour is laid on top, giving a contrast between crisp and soft edges.
- If you use felt-tipped pens, make sure that the ink colours are light-fast – some fade in quite a short time.
- Line and wash is also most effective when combined with the masking or wax resist methods that are described on pages 56 and 71.

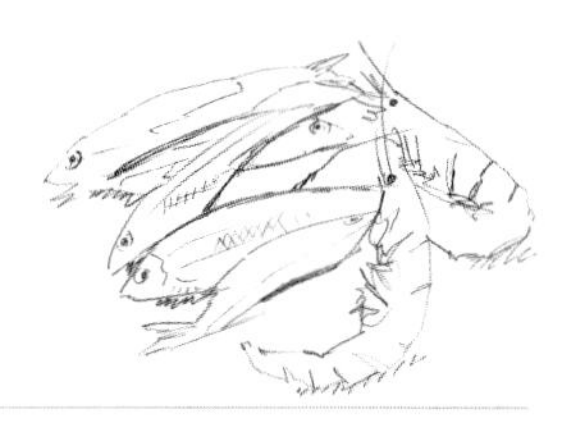

left: Audrey Macleod, *Roses Against a Blue Sky*, 38.1 x 27.9 cm (15 x 11 in), watercolour and pen. This lovely study was done out of doors directly from the subject. The artist has expressed the delicacy of the subject by restricting the definition to the line drawing, using the paint very fluidly so that it does not so much describe the forms as create a soft, diffused halo around them.

Step by Step: Line and Wash

1: A line medium, such as pen or pencil, is the perfect partner for the delicacy of watercolour. Usually the line drawing is done first, as in this case, but there is no hard-and-fast rule.

2: The artist has used a water-soluble pen, so that the lines are softened and spread by the washes laid on top. This prevents the line drawing appearing too hard and clear in contrast to the watercolour.

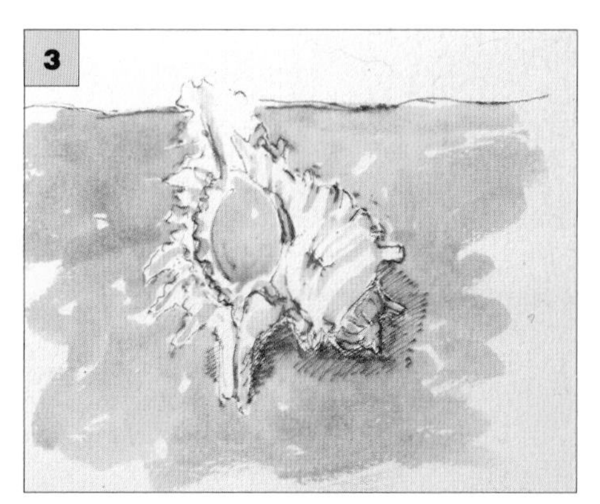

3: The washes on the shell have been kept to a minimum to preserve the delicate effect for which the technique – which is often used for flower drawings – is so well suited.

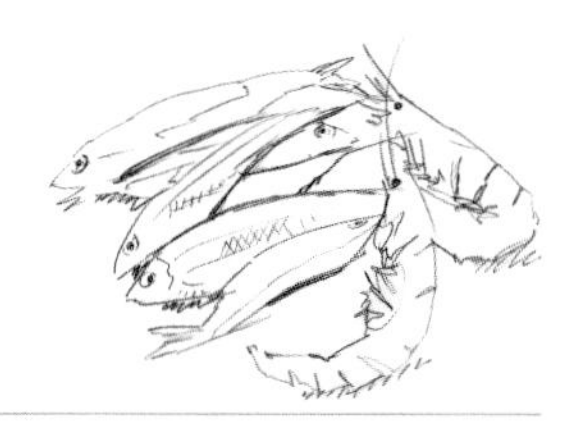

SCRAPING BACK

Sometimes called *sgraffito*, this simply means removing dry paint so that the white paper is revealed. The method is most often used to create the kind of small, fine highlights that cannot be reserved, such as the light catching blades of grass in the foreground of a landscape. It is a more satisfactory method than opaque white applied with a brush, as this tends to look clumsy and, if laid over a dark colour, does not cover it very well.

Scraping is done with a sharp knife, such as a scalpel or craft knife, or with a razor blade. For the finest lines, use the point of the knife, but avoid digging it into the paper. A more diffused highlight over a wider area can be made by scraping gently with the side of the knife or razor blade, which will remove only some of the paint.

below: Large areas of paint can be scraped back with the flat of a knife blade or razor blade. This only removes the raised tooth of the paper, leaving colour still in the "troughs" and creating a mottled, broken-colour effect rather similar to wax resist.

This technique is not successful unless you use a good-quality, reasonably heavy paper – it should be no lighter than 140 pounds. On a flimsier paper you could easily make holes or spoil the surface.

The same method can be used for gouache and acrylic, but only if the surface is one that can withstand this treatment.

below: Cathy Johnson, *Still Pool.* In this painting, colours were flooded onto damp paper to create an impression of perfectly still, brackish water reflecting the green of the forest. Soft, pale reflections were lifted out of the damp wash with a clean brush, and the smooth ripples were scratched out of the wash with a sharp blade just before it dried.

below: The delicate, complex pattern of the frothy water in this painting was created by scraping with a sharp point. The effect, which can be seen clearly in the detail shown here, would be impossible to achieve by any other means. Opaque white gouache or acrylic could be used, but the texture would be less interesting and the lines less fine and crisp.

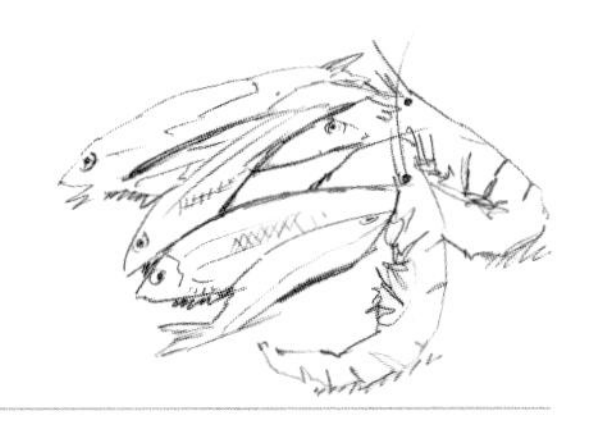

WASH-OFF

This is an unusual and fascinating technique that exploits the properties of Indian ink and gouache. It is not difficult, but it is slow, involving careful planning and a methodical approach.

Basically, the method involves painting a design with thick gouache paint, covering the whole picture surface with waterproof ink and then holding it under running water. This washes off the soluble paint and the ink that covers it, leaving only the ink in the unpainted areas to form a negative image.

First the paper must be stretched – essential, as it has to bear a considerable volume of water. A light wash is then laid over it and left to dry, after which the design is painted on with thick, white gouache paint. White paint must be used, as a colour could stain the paper and destroy the clear, sharp effect. For the same reason the wash should be as pale as possible: its only purpose is to allow the white paint to show up as you apply it.

Once the paint is thoroughly dry, cover the whole picture surface with waterproof ink (make sure it really is waterproof and is clearly marked as such on the bottle). Allow the ink to dry completely before washing it off. The "negative" can either be left as a black-and-white image or it can be worked into with new colours, using gouache, watercolour or acrylic.

Step by Step: Wash-off

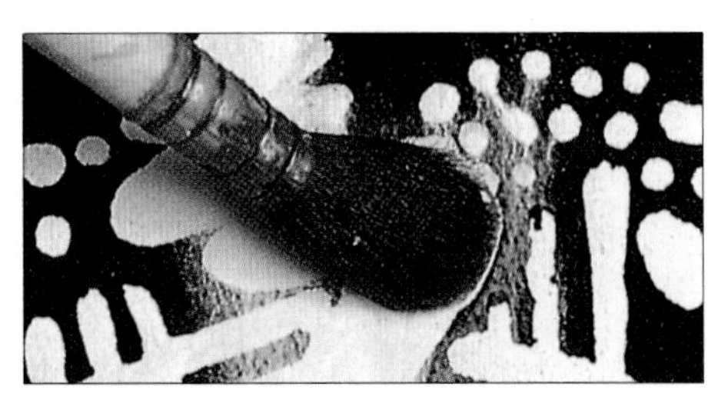

1: In this example, the artist uses a soft brush to remove any excess gouache. The waterproof black ink that was not painted over gouache stays firmly in place, despite repeated washings.

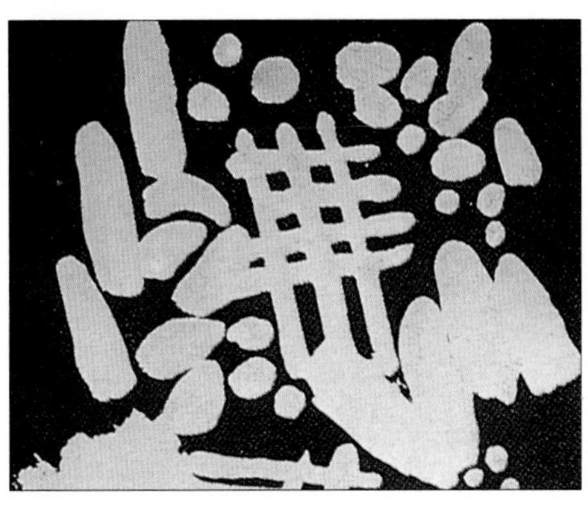

2: The finished effect is a silhouetted image. This can be left as it is, or it can be developed by adding colour to the white parts of the design. For demonstration purposes, the design shown here has deliberately been kept simple. However, the technique is best suited to a more intricate or textural design such as leaves and flowers. Animals, with their fur texture and markings, are another suitable subject.

left: Here, a wash of burnt sienna was laid over a pencil drawing and, when dry, the shapes of the flowers, the vase, and the table were painted over it with white gouache. When the gouache had dried the whole image was covered with waterproof Indian ink. Once this was dry cold water was poured over the paper and within several minutes the ink on the gouache came away, with the gouache. Excess gouache was removed with a paintbrush, still leaving the waterproof black areas on the paper. A thin background wash of Prussian blue was then applied to lift this decorative image out of the purely monochrome.

Step by Step:
Uneven Wash-off

1: Working with a large brush, the artist applies thick gouache paint, having first stained the paper so that she can see what she is doing.

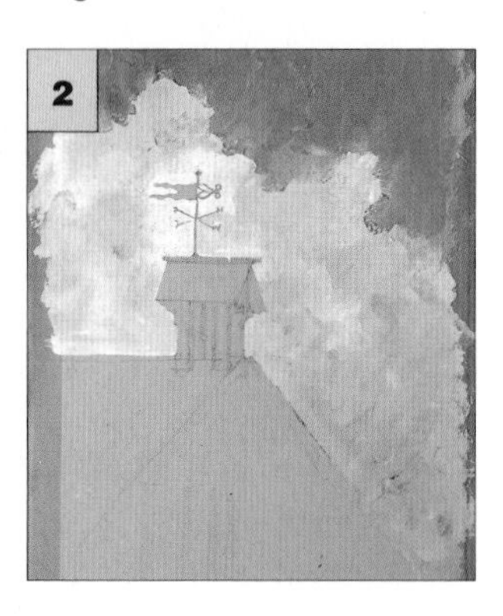

2: She continues to build up the sky which, although to be partially removed in the washing process, will remain as an element of the finished painting.

3: With the gouache painting stage completed, the whole surface is covered with ink. For a complete wash-off, the ink should be applied flat, as in a wash, but in this case the artist intends to leave the paint and the ink to mingle in places, so she applies it deliberately unevenly, in a scrubbing motion.

4: The thicker areas of paint are not completely covered by the ink.

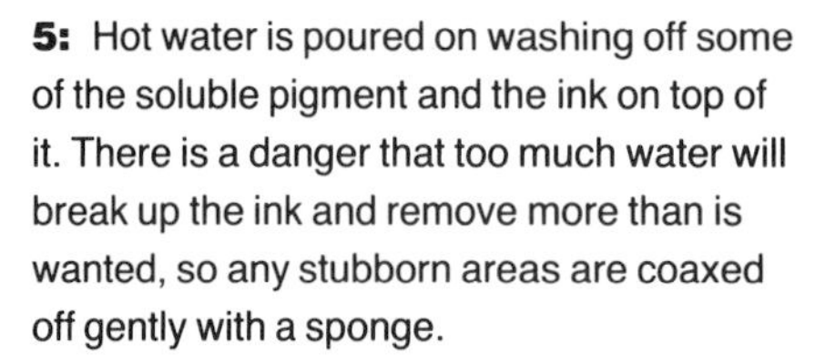

5: Hot water is poured on washing off some of the soluble pigment and the ink on top of it. There is a danger that too much water will break up the ink and remove more than is wanted, so any stubborn areas are coaxed off gently with a sponge.

6: In a complete wash-off, the whole of the sky would have been removed, necessitating repainting, but in this version of the technique, large areas of the original gouache have remained, with the patches of black adding definition and drama.

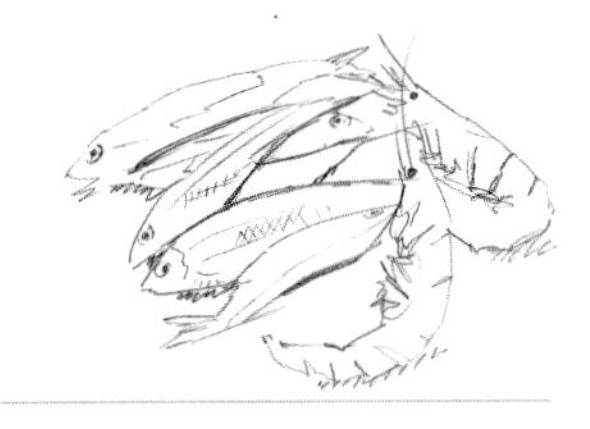

Wax Resist

This, a valuable addition to the watercolourist's repertoire, is a technique based on the antipathy of oil and water, and involves deliberately repelling paint from certain areas of the paper while allowing it to settle in others.

The idea is simple, but can yield quite magical results. If you draw or lightly scribble over paper with wax and then overlay this with watercolour, the paint will slide off the waxed areas. You can use either an ordinary household candle or the type of inexpensive wax crayons produced for children. The British sculptor Henry Moore (1898–1986), also a draughtsman of great imagination and brilliance, used crayons and watercolour for his series of drawings of sleeping figures in the London Underground during the Second World War.

The wax underdrawing can be as simple or as complex as you like. You can suggest a hint of pattern on wallpaper or fabric in a still-life group or portrait by means of a few lines, dots or blobs made with a candle or do something more complex by making quite an intricate drawing using crayons, which are smaller and have good points.

Wax beneath watercolour gives a delightfully unpredictable speckled effect, which varies according to the pressure you apply and the type of paper you use. It is one of the best methods for imitating natural textures, such as those of rocks, cliffs or tree trunks.

below and right: In both these examples, a stick of white wax oil pastel was scribbled over paper with a not surface and watercolour washes were then laid on top. In some areas the paint was left to dry and the process repeated. A more pronounced texture can be gained by working on rough paper.

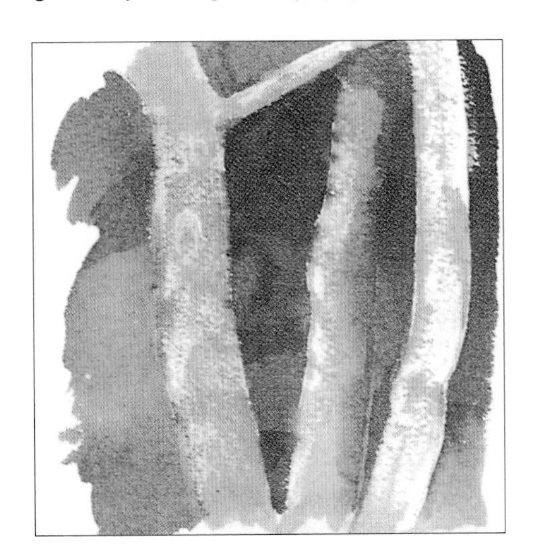

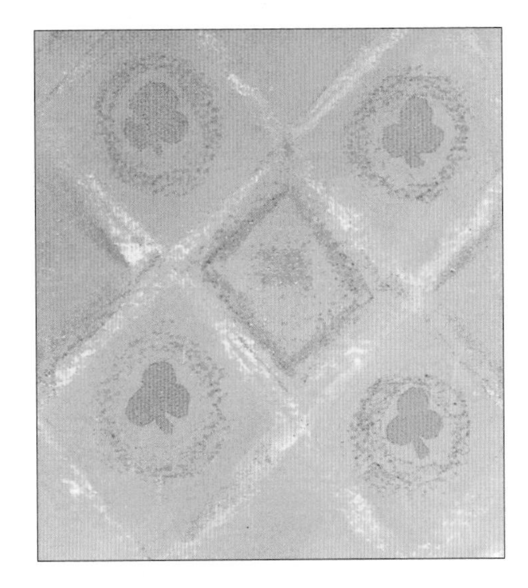

left and below: One of the best ways of learning how combinations of media can be used is by making rough doodles like those shown here, in which coloured wax crayons were overlaid with watercolour.

left: Moira Huntly, RJ, RSMA, *Still Life with Melon Pieces,* 25.5 x 17.9 cm (10 x 7 in), watercolour, wax and wax crayon. The artist has created vibrant colours and lively textures by using candlewax under the paint and wax crayons both under and over it. Rich surfaces can be built up in this way, and further variety can be achieved by scraping into an overlay of wax crayon with a razor blade.

Step by Step: Wax Resist

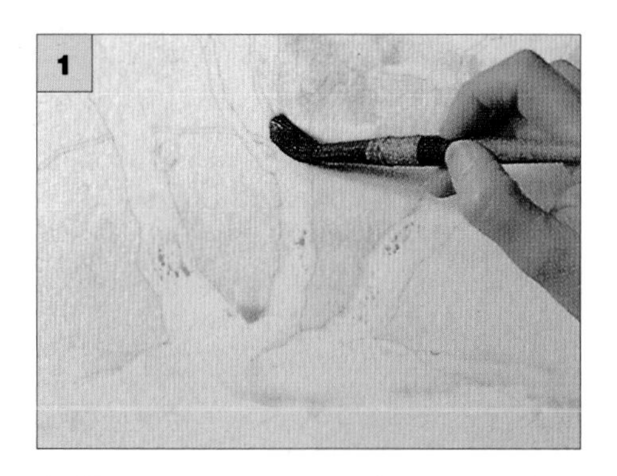

1: Here wax resist is to be used to suggest the texture of tree bark. The artist has scribbled lightly over the tree with a white wax crayon before laying a background wash.

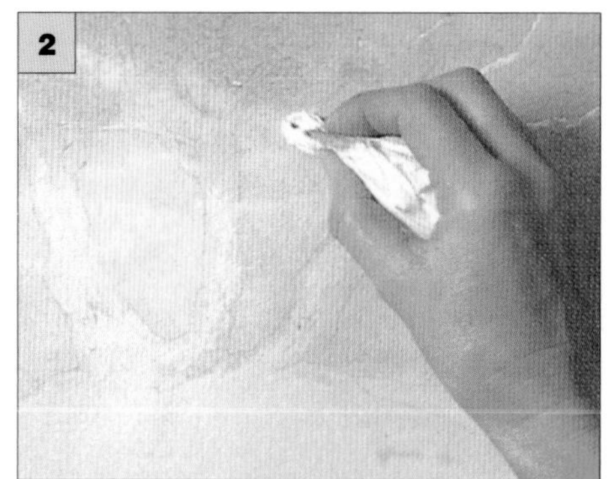

2: Before working further on the tree she lightens parts of the sky by gently dabbing with a tissue.

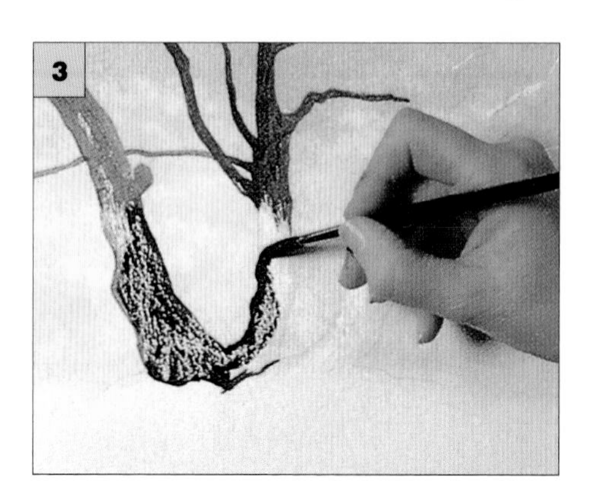

3: The dark paint slides off the waxed areas, leaving a distinct pattern of broken white lines.

4: The effects you achieve with wax resist vary according to the amount of pressure applied and the paper you use. This is a medium (not surface) paper; a rougher one would give a more pronounced speckling, as the wax would adhere only to the raised "peaks" of the paper.

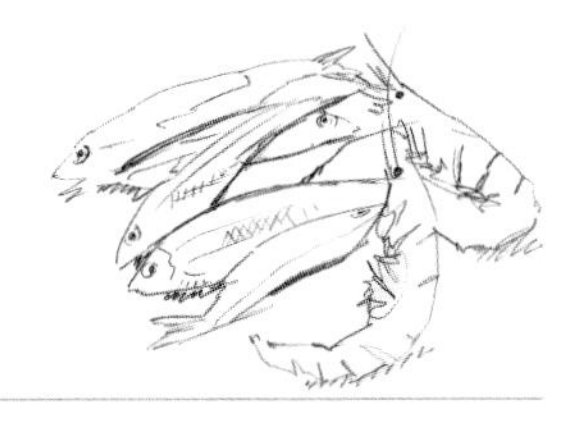

APPLYING WAX RESIST TECHNIQUES

One of the golden rules in painting is "Don't give them too much!" Like a dish that contains too many hot spices, a painting which contains a lot of conflicting details will leave the viewer with a jaded palate. Decide what you want your painting to say, accentuate that, and subordinate any conflicting or competing elements.

In *The Rusty Fence* the image is striking because the artist has kept most of the detail in the foreground and simplified the background. Our attention is focused on the fence and the foreground trees, which register clearly against the soft shapes and tones in the distance.

You may have seen photographs in which the main subject is in sharp focus, with the background deliberately kept out of focus to give a soft, blurred effect. This contrast between sharp and soft adds textural interest to the picture as well as giving emphasis to the main subject. It's not difficult to see how this effect can be achieved with great success in a watercolour painting. Follow Richard Bolton's example, and use crisp details and strong tones in the foreground, or wherever your centre of interest happens to be. Then as you move away from the centre of interest, begin to use softer tones and blurred, wet-in-wet shapes.

In *The Rusty Fence*, see how the contrast between the sharp-focus foreground and the hazy background helps to create the illusion of depth and space in the landscape. It also lends a touch of poetry to the painting, and prevents the objects within it from looking unnaturally hard and brittle.

The trees are painted wet-in-wet to give a pleasing mistiness in the far distance. This also emphasizes the impression of space and depth.

Some middle-ground trees are eliminated to avoid confusion and give emphasis to the foreground trees.

The fence has a pleasing shape, and its weathered texture is given emphasis. The texture is achieved with a combination of wax resist and dry brush strokes. Details, tones and colours are much stronger in the foreground than in the background.

above: Richard Bolton, *The Rusty Fence*.

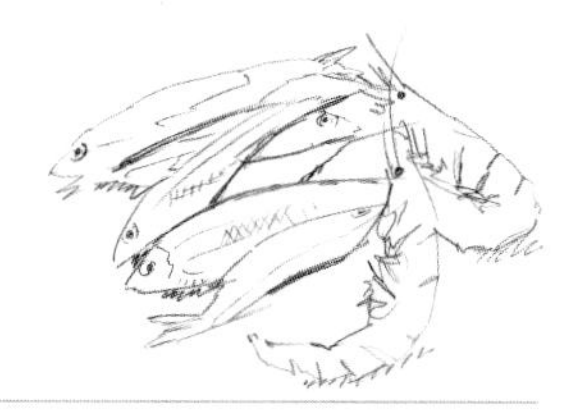

Gum Arabic

This is the medium that, together with gelatine, acts as the binder for watercolour pigment (watercolours also contain glycerine to keep them moist). Gum arabic can be bought in bottled form and is often used as a painting medium. If you add a little gum to your water when mixing paint, it gives it extra body, making it less runny and easier to blend. It is particularly suitable for the kind of painting that is built up in small, separate brushstrokes, as it prevents them flowing into one another.

Its other important property is as a varnish. If a dark area of a painting, such as a very deep shadow, has gone dead through too much overlaying of washes, a light application of gum arabic will revive the colour and give additional richness. It should never be used neat, however, as this could cause cracking. Experience will teach you how much to dilute it when using it as a painting medium, but a general rule of thumb is that there should be considerably more water than gum.

Step by Step: Using Gum Arabic

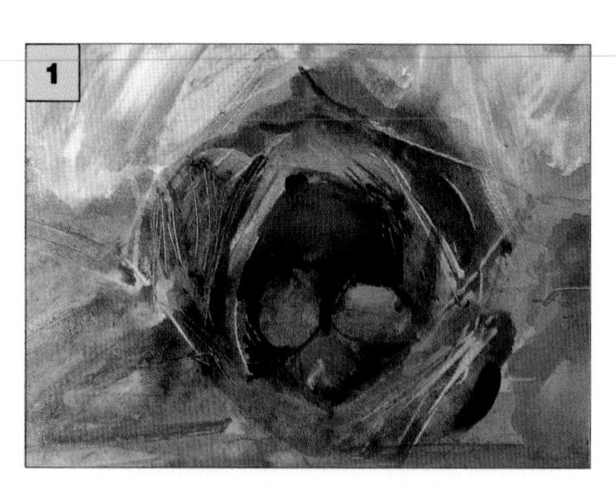

1: Gum arabic can be used with either watercolour or gouache, and here the artist has used a combination of both. Because the gum is soluble in water, it is much easier to lift out areas of paint (see page 59), and here sharp, clear lines have been "drawn" with the point of a brush dipped in water and scratched with the brush handle.

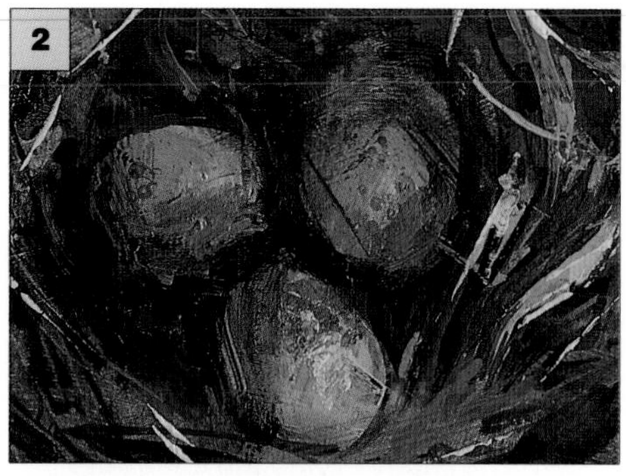

2: Gouache mixed with gum arabic behaves more like opaque acrylic than like watercolour, enabling clear, decisive brush marks and avoiding the matt, dead look the paint sometimes has when too many layers are built up. Here there is considerable overpainting, but the colours have maintained their freshness and sparkle.

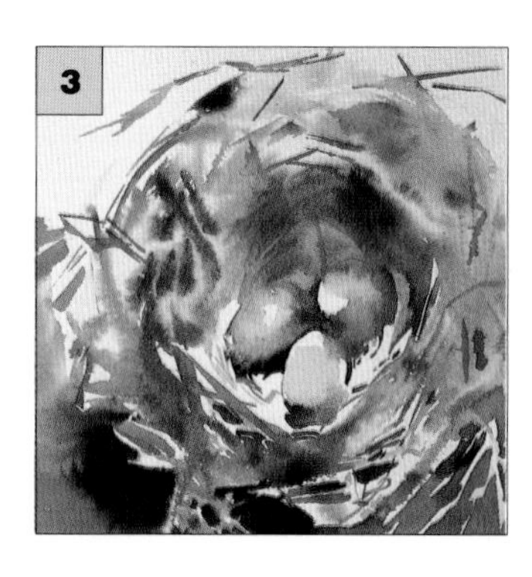

3: This photograph shows the same subject, in this case painted in pure watercolour. Here the colours have merged together softly, but where the gum has been used, distinct brush marks can be seen, and the paint has stayed where it was put.

Step by Step: More Uses for Gum Arabic

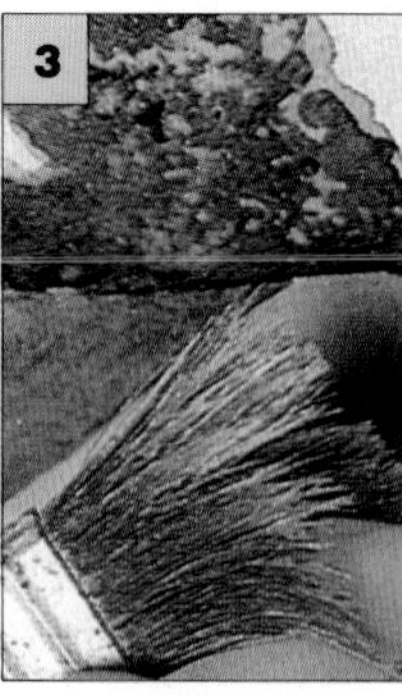

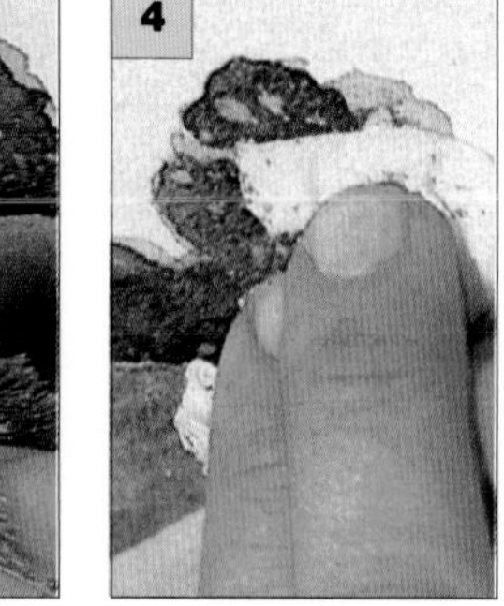

Gum arabic can also be used, as here, as a sort of resist method to create highlights.

1: The tree and hedge are painted in with pure watercolour.

2: A further wash of green is applied, this time mixed with gum water.

3: The area of the central tree is spattered with water, flicked on with a household brush.

4: The central tree is blotted with a rag, so that wherever the water has touched, small areas of paint are lifted off, the gum being soluble in water.

5: The lighter patches of colour give an extra sparkle to the tree, while the addition of the gum arabic imparts richness to the dark green on either side.

above: Michael Cadman, RA, ARCA, *Low Tide, Cornish Harbour,* approx. 50.8 x 35.6 cm (20 x 14 in), watercolour, acrylic and gouache. Cadman regularly mixes the three water-based paints, using them thickly or thinly as the painting demands. Here brushstrokes of transparent colour have been laid over one another, with touches of thick, opaque white on the buildings and water.

Although many artists know that they can create their best effects with pure watercolour, more and more are breaking away from convention, finding that they can create livelier and more expressive paintings by combining several different media.

To some extent, mixing media is a matter of trial and error, and there is now such a diversity of artist's materials that there is no way of prescribing techniques for each one or for each possible combination. However, it can be said that some mixtures are easier to manage than others. Acrylic and watercolour, for example, can be made to blend into one another almost imperceptibly because they have very much the same characteristics, but two or more physically dissimilar media, such as line and wash, will automatically set up a contrast. There is nothing wrong with this – it may even be the point of the exercise – but it can make it difficult to preserve an overall unity.

Watercolour and Acrylic

Acrylic used thinly, diluted with water but no medium or white, behaves in more or less the same way as watercolour. There are two important differences between them, however. One is that acrylic has greater depth of colour so that a first wash can, if desired, be extremely vivid, and the other is that, once dry, the paint cannot be removed. This can be an advantage, as further washes, either in watercolour or acrylic, can be laid over an initial one without disturbing the pigment. The paint need not be applied in thin washes throughout: the combination of shimmering, translucent watercolour and thickly painted areas of acrylic can be very effective, particularly in landscapes with strong foreground interest, where you want to pick out small details like individual flowers (very hard to do in watercolour). It is often possible to save an unsuccessful watercolour by turning to acrylic in the later stages.

Watercolour and Gouache

These are often used together, and many artists scarcely differentiate between them. However, unless both are used thinly it can be a more difficult combination to manage, as gouache paint, once mixed with white to make it opaque, has a matt surface, which can make it look dead and dull beside a watercolour wash.

Step by Step: Painting Gourds

1: One of the most attractive qualities of these gourds is the contrast in textures. As the first stage in building up the pitted surface of the orange gourd, the artist mixes her paint with gum arabic, which makes it settle with a slight bubbling.

2: Still using transparent watercolour, she paints the yellow gourd wet-in-wet, allowing the colours to blend softly together.

3: Opaque gouache is now used for the flat background and some areas of the fruit. The texture of the orange gourd is achieved by further applications of paint mixed with gum arabic. This is blotted with a damp sponge.

4: The finished result shows the pleasing variety of paint quality typical of mixed-media paintings.

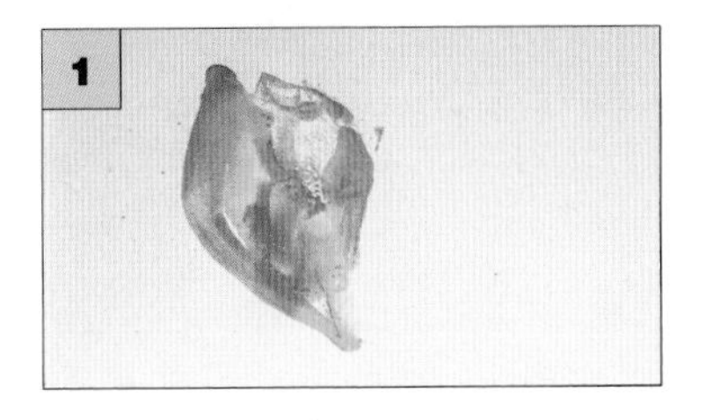

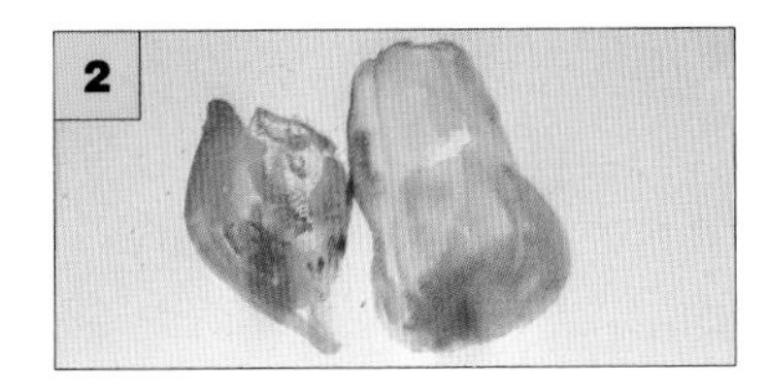

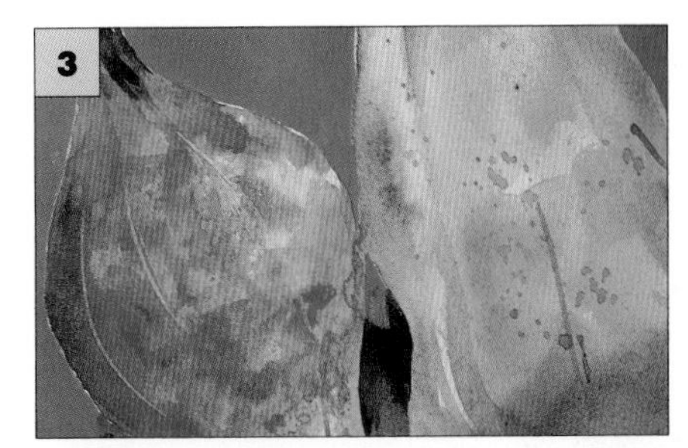

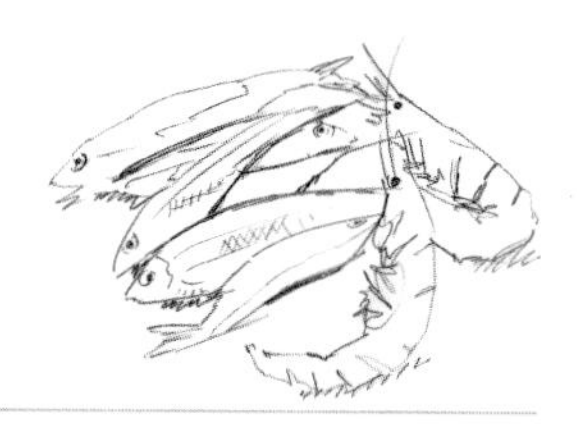

A MIXED MEDIA EXPERIENCE

Rosalind Cuthbert is a British artist who favours mixed-media work. She exhibits widely, with eight solo shows to her credit, and has won several awards. Examples of her work have been bought by various public collections in Britain, including the National Portrait Gallery.

"Mixed media work is a very open-ended thing. If a painting is going badly and you're having to fight it then it's great to know there's another medium you can bring in . . . At some point something magic happens – through this sort of multiplicity of means there comes a kind of integration of the image. That's what interests me about Cubism, painters like Braque, who were interested in combining all kinds of media. There's diversity of textures and colours, but the image is fully integrated."

above: *Still Life with Janus Jug.* A lively picture surface has been created by painting on a textured ground of acrylic medium and pigment with a mixture of watercolour and white ink.

above: *A Walk Around the Garden.* In this poetic and dreamlike painting in watercolour and charcoal, real objects are combined with those drawn from memory and the imagination.

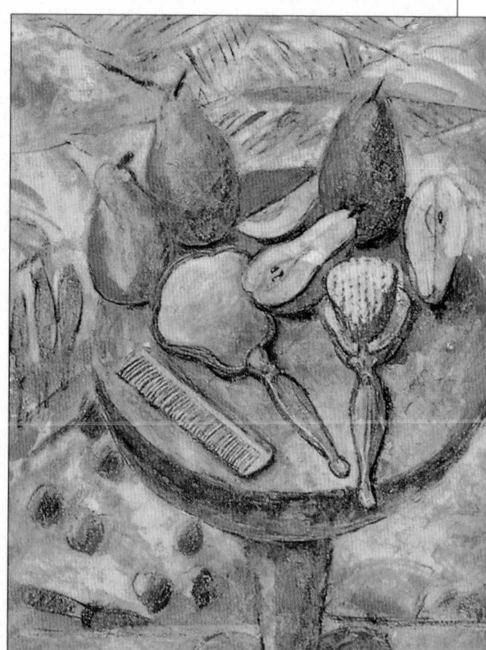

above: *Still Life in Front of a Landscape.* Transparent and opaque watercolour with charcoal have been used here on a ground containing gum arabic.

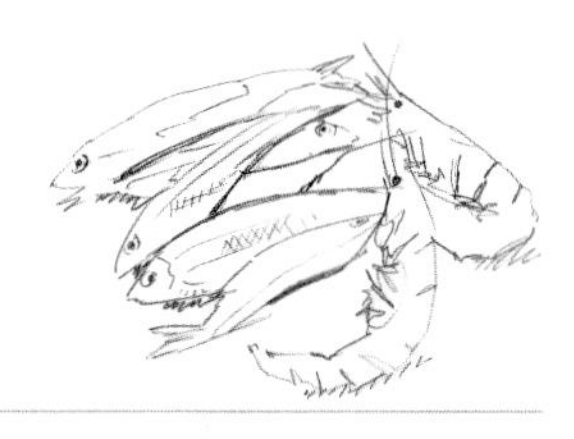

above: A cloudy sky at sunset is particularly striking. Because the sun is lower than the clouds, the undersides of the clouds are brilliantly lit while the tops are thrown into shadow. For the same reason, the brightest clouds are low in the sky, becoming darker farther away from the sun. In this Turneresque sky study the artist has used watercolour and gouache, the former for its transparency and the latter for its brilliance of colour.

First, the background sky colours were brushed in loosely, wet-in-wet with watercolour. Then small strokes and dabs of opaque gouache were touched in for the clouds and allowed to diffuse softly into the still-damp colours beneath. The appearance of bright, luminous colour is achieved by layering warm yellows, oranges and pinks with cool blues and greys which, by contrast, accentuate the warm colours.

Project: Watercolour and Pastel

There are no specific subjects which are particularly suited to mixed media techniques, so you could choose any subject for this project. You might begin by working in pastel over a discarded watercolour painting (watercolour paper is an excellent surface for pastel work). Alternatively, you might arrange a still-life group, choosing some objects which have matt opaque colours and others, like glass and polished metal, which are shiny or transparent.

The usual way to start a watercolour and pastel painting is to lay the watercolour first, but you don't have to work in this way. Try using pastel first and then introducing watercolour later. Unless the watercolour is to be completely overpowered by the pastel, use the paint in strong, positive washes. You should also experiment with using a dry brush technique which produces a broken effect that will combine well with the similar effects created by pastel.

When you have completed your painting, see whether the two media have, in fact, been used in the way you would have predicted. Has the watercolour, for example, been used to describe the transparent or shiny objects, or in practice have you used pastel for some of these?

Paint and Pastel

Soft pastels can be used very successfully with watercolour, and provide an excellent means of adding texture and surface interest to a painting. Sparkling broken colours can be created by overlaying a watercolour wash with light strokes of pastel, particularly if you work on a fairly rough paper.

Oil pastels have a slightly different but equally interesting effect. A light layer of oil pastel laid down under a watercolour wash will repel the water to a greater or lesser degree (some oil pastels are oilier than others) so that it sinks only into the troughs of the paper, resulting in a slightly mottled, granular area of colour.

Gouache and Pastel

These have been used together since the eighteenth century when pastel was at the height of its popularity as an artist's medium. Some mixed-media techniques are based on the dissimilarity of the elements used, which creates its own kind of dynamism, but these two are natural partners, having a similar matt, chalky quality.

below: Ian Sidaway, *Churchyard,* 28.6 x 40.6 cm (11¼ x 16 in), watercolour, pastel and conté pencil. This combination of media has produced a lively contrast of textures. The building and tree are pure watercolour, while the sky and grass are pastel worked over an initial watercolour wash.

Watercolour and Crayons

These are, in effect, mixed media in themselves. When dry they are a drawing medium, but as soon as water is applied to them they become paint, and can be spread with a brush. Very varied effects can be created by using them in a linear manner in some areas of a painting and as paints in others. They can also be combined with traditional watercolours, felt-tipped pens or pen and ink.

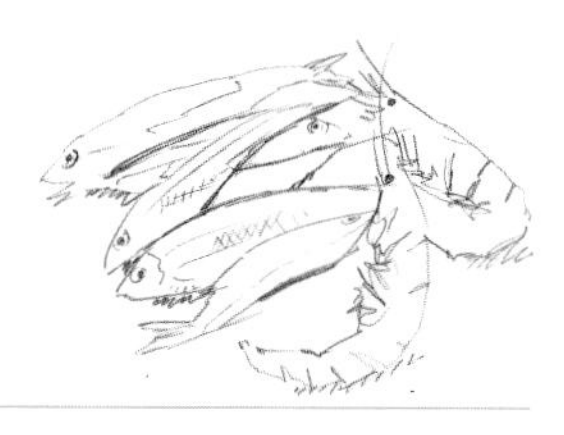

above: Ian Simpson, *From St Martin's, London,* 84 x 58.5 cm (33 x 23 in), acrylic, pencil and charcoal. This was painted on the spot (from a window). It began as a charcoal drawing, which was then fixed, and the painting built up with acrylic, pencil, and more charcoal. Large areas of paper have been deliberately left uncovered.

Pastel with Watercolour Wash

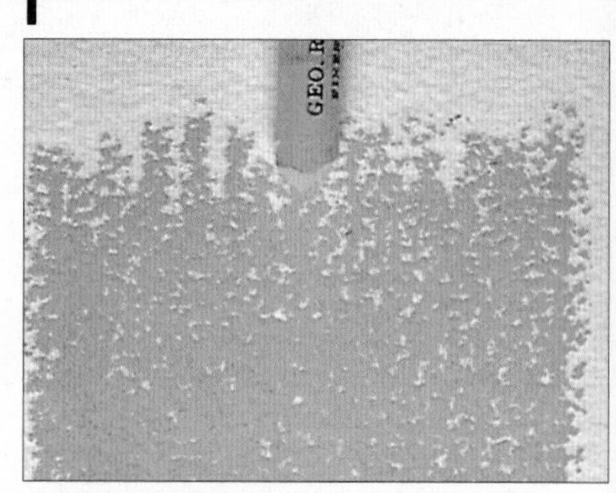

1 The vibrancy of soft pastel colours can be used to enhance the delicate transparency of watercolour washes. Here the artist creates a design with a soft orange pastel.

2 Using a soft watercolour brush, he washes over the pastel with a light toned wash to spread the pastel colour. Any surplus moisture is removed with blotting paper.

3 While the wash is still damp, the artist adds further details with the point of the pastel stick. When the wash dries, more pastel marks and watercolour washes can be added.

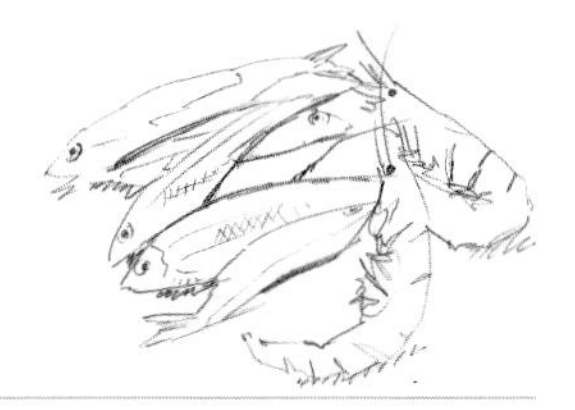

EFFECTS

Oil Pastel with Watercolour Wash

1 Oil pastels produce a slightly different effect because they are more resistant to water than soft pastels are. Here the artist rubs blue oil pastel over rough-textured watercolour paper. The pastel catches the raised tooth of the paper and creates a mottled pattern.

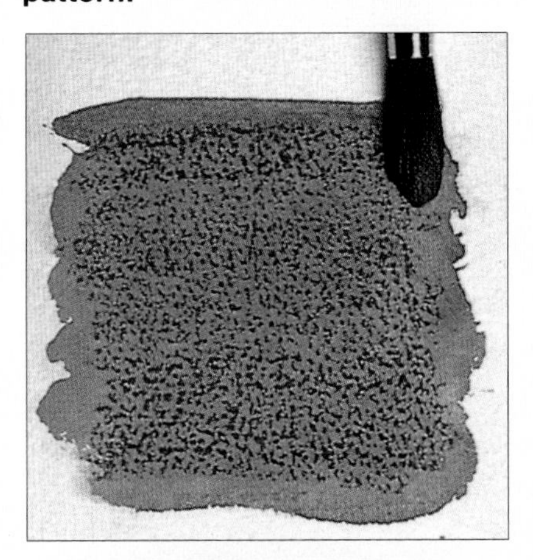

2 A wash of Payne's grey watercolour is applied over the oil pastel. The oil repels the watercolour, which settles into the indents of the paper's texture, which were untouched by the crayon. The wash dries with a granular texture which is effective for depicting stone, rocks and sand.

Acrylic and Oil Crayon

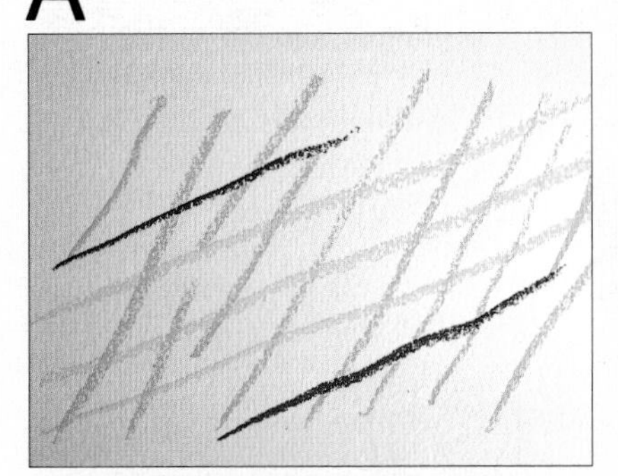

1 The artist begins by drawing a bold design on the canvas with oil crayons. Apply the crayon quite thickly.

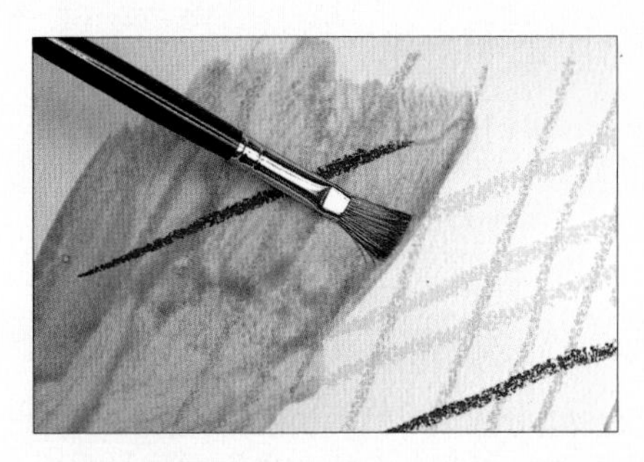

2 Acrylic paint, diluted with plenty of water to a thin, wash-like consistency, is brushed lightly over the crayonned area with a large, soft brush.

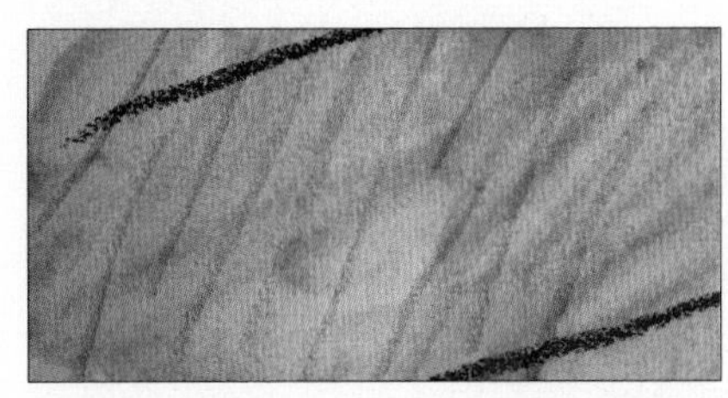

3 The oil crayon resists the watery paint and the design shows up clearly through the coloured wash.

Gouache and Charcoal

1 The artist first applies a thick layer of yellow gouache. When this is completely dry he draws a design onto it with charcoal. Note that if the paint is still wet, the charcoal will not take.

2 Using a No. 4 bristle brush, the artist works into the charcoal drawing with further gouache colours. Interesting variations of tone are achieved by allowing the charcoal to dissolve into the colour in places.

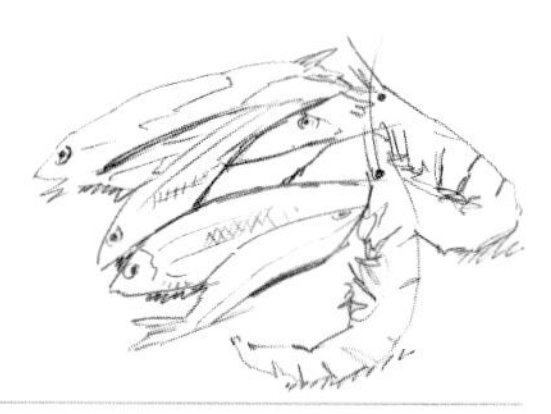

CORRECTIONS

It is a common belief that watercolours cannot be corrected, but, in fact, there are several ways of making changes, correcting or modifying parts of a painting.

If it becomes clear early on that something is badly wrong, simply put the whole thing under cold running water and gently sponge off the paint. For smaller areas, wet a small sponge in clean water and wipe away the offending colour, or for a very tiny area, use a wet brush.

It must be said, though, that some colours are more permanent than others – sap green, for example, is hard to remove totally – and that some papers hold onto the pigment with grim determination. Arches is one of the latter, but both Bockingford and Saunders papers will wash clean very well.

As a painting nears completion, you may find that there are too many hard edges or insufficient highlights. Edges can be softened by the water treatment described above, but here the best implement to use is a dampened cotton bud. Both these and sponges are near-essentials in watercolour painting, as they are ideal for lifting out areas of paint to create soft highlights.

Any specks of dark paint that may have inadvertently flicked onto a white or light-coloured area can be removed with a scalpel blade, but use the side in a gentle scraping motion, as pressure with the point could make holes in the paper.

above: Small blots are easily removed by scraping with a knife or razor blade. Be careful not to apply too much pressure or you could make holes in the paper.

above: If one colour floods into another to create an unwanted effect, the excess can be mopped up with a small sponge or piece of blotting paper.

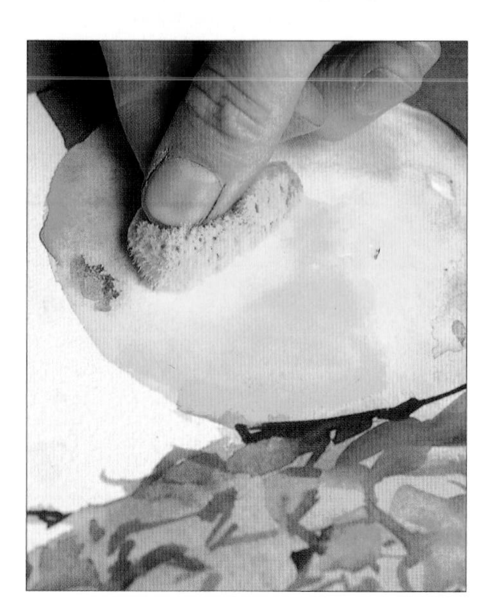

left: Here the artist finds he needs to lighten the colour in this area, so he lifts out some of the paint with a damp sponge.

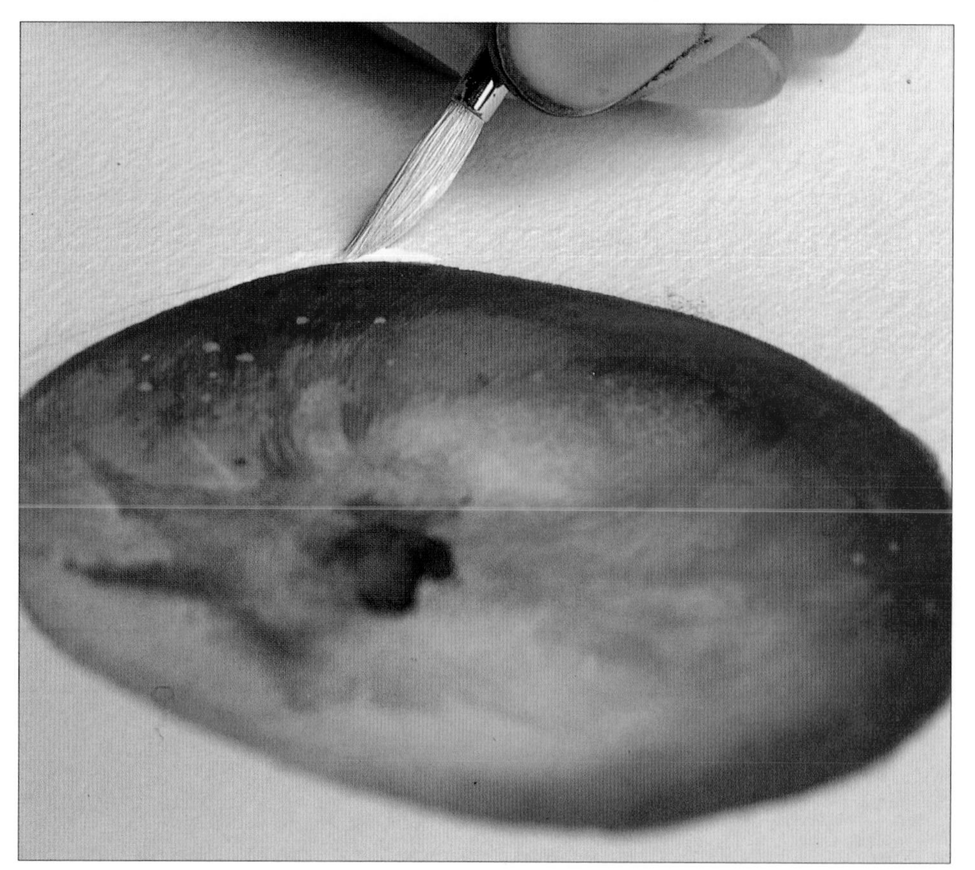

above: Ragged edges can either be tidied up with a knife, as in the first example, or with opaque white gouache paint, as here.

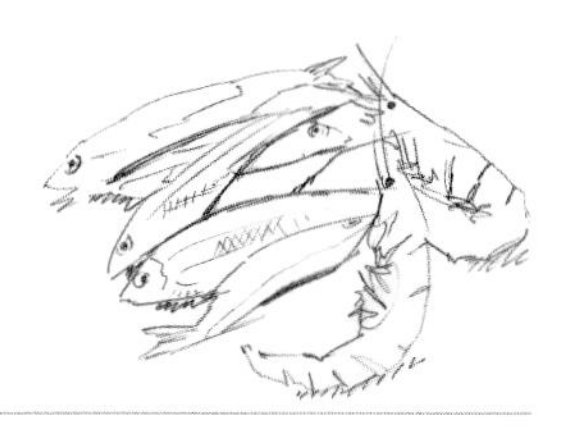

Step by Step: Blotting with a Tissue and a Sponge

1: This illustration shows a detail from a painting of a French vineyard. Having completed the painting, the artist decided that the converging lines of the field in the foreground were too strong in colour and needed softening. To correct this, he first loosens the colour by gently stroking the area with a soft brush and clean water.

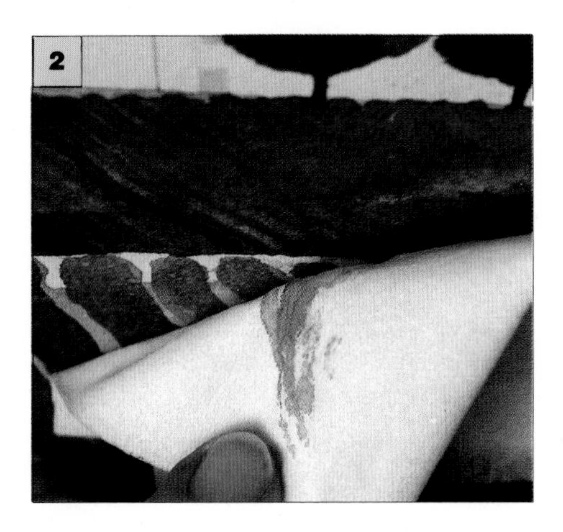

2: After waiting a few moments for the water to be absorbed, the artist lifts off the colour with a piece of tissue.

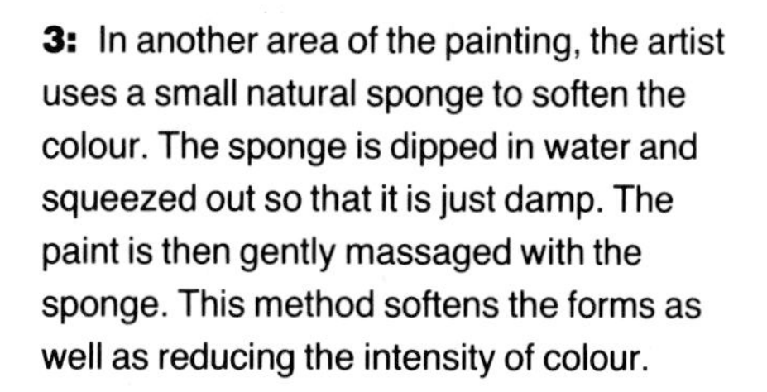

3: In another area of the painting, the artist uses a small natural sponge to soften the colour. The sponge is dipped in water and squeezed out so that it is just damp. The paint is then gently massaged with the sponge. This method softens the forms as well as reducing the intensity of colour.

4: The completed picture. By varying the intensity of colour in the foreground, the artist has introduced greater textural interest and a sense of light into the painting.

COLOUR CHANGES

Newcomers to watercolour often find it difficult to judge the strength and quality of the first colour to be applied. There are two reasons for this: one is that the paint becomes a great deal lighter when dry, the other is that it is hard to judge a colour against pure white paper – the first wash inevitably looks too dark or too bright.

If you find the first colours are wrong, do not despair. Because watercolours are built up in a series of overlaid washes or brushstrokes, the first colour and tone you put down is by no means final: many changes can be made on the paper itself. If a pale yellow wash is covered with a blue one, the colour changes to become green, and the tone darkens because there are now two layers of paint. By the same token, a wash that is too pale is very easily darkened by applying a second wash of the same colour or a slightly darker version of it. Although it is often stated in books about watercolour that light colours cannot be laid over dark ones, this only means that they will not become lighter, but colours can be modified in this way, particularly greens. A green that is too "cool", that is, with too high a proportion of blue, can be changed into a warmer, richer green by laying a strong wash of yellow on top.

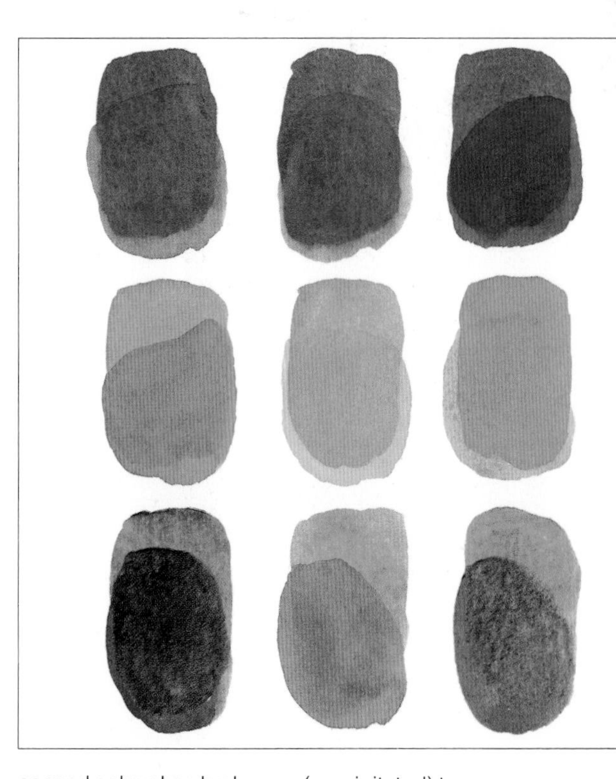

right: It is surprising how radically even quite a strong colour can be altered by overlaying another one. Second and subsequent colours should be applied quickly and surely to avoid stirring up those below. The colours shown here are as follows (left to right). Top row: first colour ultramarine, with Payne's grey, Winsor blue, Winsor violet. Second row: first colour cadmium red, with alizarin crimson, cadmium yellow, raw sienna. Third row: first colour raw umber, with ultramarine, alizarin crimson, viridian green. Notice how in some cases the second colour has broken up (precipitated) to give a granular effect. This can be used to give additional texture and interest to a painting.

Ian Sidaway

Composition with Palm Trees

WATERCOLOUR

This tranquil study demonstrates the possibilities of using just a few colours to create a striking image.

Colour and Composition

Having experimented with the range of techniques used in watercolour painting, it is time to look at the art of composing a picture and putting on paper the colours that are before your eyes (or in your mind). There are questions of selection and balance to be addressed, in order to make a three-dimensional subject come to life in a two-dimensional form.

Many of these principles are common to all painting media, so much of the material in this section does not refer specifically to painting with watercolour. If you are already competent in painting with other media, you may be familiar with the principles explained here; but for those fresh to painting, these guidelines will be particularly valuable in the early stages of constructing a painting.

Having learned these rules, you may wish to break some or all of them. That is one of the elements of creativity. But it is as well to have a firm grasp of the principles of painting so that you are aware of the effects of each decision you make regarding form and colour.

Some people are fortunate enough to have an instinct for good composition and colour use; others have to learn how to create a pleasing scene. If you are one of the latter, don't despair – the simple guidelines in this section will clarify the mysteries of colour and composition.

Deciding how large the picture should be, how the objects you are painting should be grouped together and positioned within the picture area, choosing different elements of line and shape, tone and colour, and applying them in ways that make your painting look right as a whole – all these are the ingredients of composition.

In the following pages, you will be studying themes and styles in painting. But first you need to consider the elements of composition in more detail, as the first step in understanding how you can realize the effects you want to achieve in your finished painting.

SIZE AND SHAPE

The majority of pictures are rectangular or contained by a rectangle. Partly this is just practical – paper is sold in rectangular sheets and it is easier to make a stretcher for canvas or cut a panel for painting in this regular format, than to prepare a painting surface of a different shape. Visually, a rectangle gives a clear-cut, evenly balanced picture area within which you can organize the elements of your painting. Artists can, and do, make paintings that are round, elliptical or irregularly shaped. This may be because the painting is planned for a particular place, but the shape of a painting usually grows out of the demands of an individual subject or approach. Unusual shapes for painting are something that you can consider later if they interest you.

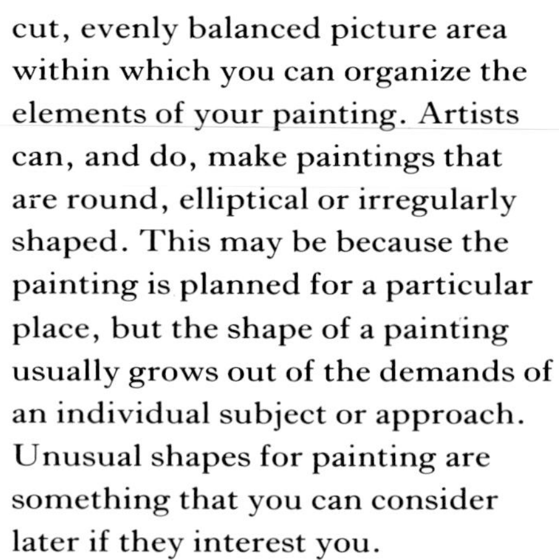

Working with a rectangle, you can choose to make the picture square, or to have a longer dimension from top to bottom, or from side to side. A format in which the upright dimension is longest is often referred to as a portrait shape; one in which the width is longer is called landscape. These terms, however, don't imply a rule for composition – a portrait or figure can occupy a wide canvas, and a landscape can be given vertical emphasis.

When you begin work, you have to choose paper or canvas of appropriate size and, unless you are making a square painting, decide whether you will use it as a portrait or landscape shape. This depends on your choise of subject and what you decide is the best view of it.

Some artists start painting without deciding on the final dimensions of the painting, letting the shape gradually emerge. Alternatively, an unusual format – a long, narrow rectangle, say – may suggest a particular treatment of the subject.

If you work on paper, you don't have to fill the given rectangle. You can trim it or, later on, use a mount to contain the picture area. You can even extend it quite easily if your painting becomes too large for the paper by attaching another piece of paper to it. It is easiest to begin with a format that will work for the painting you have in mind. If you

below: In her watercolour, *Sunday in Central Park,* Carole Katchen achieves a generous sense of space on a small scale by means of both the broad curve travelling diagonally and the set-back position of the figures.

left: Ian Simpson has joined pieces of paper to extend this watercolour study. The irregular panels accentuate the effect of looking through the window panes.

find when you start to develop the composition that something important slips off the edge of the picture, you can adjust your composition by redrawing and overpainting.

When you select a size of paper for your painting, consider it in terms of the actual scale of your subject. A small landscape can be powerful, but you might prefer the spacious feel of a large picture. If you choose a large picture area for a small-scale subject, however, say a still-life or portrait, it may mean that you end up painting the objects larger than life size. This can look strange because objects naturally relate to a personal sense of scale; and when you paint them over life size, you encounter problems in achieving the correct proportions and spatial relationships.

above: The viewpoint of Stephen Crowther's *At the Water's Edge* exploits the strong line of the promenade.

The Dynamics of the Rectangle

Generally, a square is a balanced, self-contained shape; a rectangle with horizontal emphasis is soothing to the eye; and a vertical format is more thrusting and confrontational. However, the impact of a painting is usually more dependent on what you put into it than on its actual shape, although there are exceptions. In an elongated rectangle, the emphasis of the longest side can be a dominant factor. You would find it hard to counteract it completely by the opposing rhythms or directions you create in your composition.

As soon as you put a mark down on your working surface, whether it is a line, a blob or a clearly defined shape, this mark begins to interact with the overall shape of the picture. Firstly, it will seem to come forward from the "background" of the paper. Secondly, it will take your eye to a particular part of the overall rectangular shape. As you add other lines, individual brush strokes or colour areas, they alter the original relationship and react together, forming links or oppositions. These are "abstract" interactions, occurring alongside the pictorial content of your composition, so the framework of your painting has an independent presence of its own.

Dividing the Rectangle

One way of becoming used to controlling the composition of a painting, regardless of its shape, is to think of the main divisions of the picture area as forming a framework of simple shapes. For example, in still-life paintings, you will often see that the group of arranged objects roughly forms a triangle. To create visual interest, a tall object is placed near the back of the group and other objects are spread out sideways across the foreground. The front of the group forms the base of a triangle and the tall object becomes its apex.

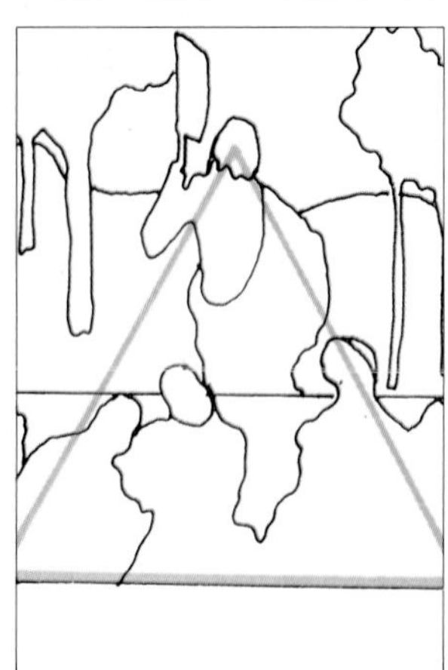

To balance and anchor the triangle, there may be a horizontal line running behind it. This could be the edge of a table, with possibly a vertical line at right angles to it. Once you have discovered the basic structure of the painting, you can also look at its subdivisions – how individual objects are proportioned and whether they overlap each other or have spaces in between.

This kind of scheme can equally apply to a figure group in an architectural setting, for instance, or a clump of trees in a landscape. Artists don't always define a basic framework before starting to paint, or see objects as geometric shapes, but with experience the organization of paintings becomes instinctive. However, when you are learning to plan your compositions, you may find it helpful to practise dividing the picture plane into abstract frameworks using different kinds of shapes and varying their proportions and the dynamics of their lines.

As a rule, it is advisable to avoid placing an emphatic line or shape in a way that divides the picture area in half vertically or horizontally. An even division causes the eye to lose direction. Often an important division falls off-centre and elements on either side of it are composed to create an asymmetrical arrangement. This creates a balance, but avoids the risk that the picture will seem so evenly balanced as to become bland and uninteresting.

left: Painters of the Renaissance usually planned the composition of a painting on a geometric grid structure. This example, by Piero della Francesca, is based on a triangle, a common compositional device which is still much used, as are circles and rectangles. The drawing at the bottom shows how other triangles can be discerned within the main one formed by the figures.

Organizing Pictorial Shape

The central problem in representational painting is recreating a three-dimensional effect on a two-dimensional surface. To do this, you regard the paper as a window, called the picture plane, behind which the spatial arrangement of the picture can be organized in layers, receding in parallel to the picture plane.

Perspective systems are a way of formalizing this layering, allowing you to suggest receding space by means of the principle of convergence. They also allow you to deal with the apparent differences in scale and proportion which will indicate where objects are located within that space. As explained on page 198, the basic guideline for perspective is the supposed horizon line, which corresponds to your eye level. Your viewpoint in relation to the subject is also very important in establishing the framework of a composition. The viewpoint can affect the mood of a painting, as well as its formal structure.

Filling the Shapes

Up to now, the elements of compositions have been discussed in terms of linear frameworks which apply equally to drawing and painting. Sometimes in painting, however, colour and tone are used freely over the underlying framework of the painting. With an Impressionist approach (see page 140) or some kinds of abstract painting (see page 146) the composition can look casual, as the framework of the picture isn't apparent.

If you follow the approach to composition so far defined, once you have achieved a satisfactory structure for your painting, the additional factors of tone and colour are brought into play. Tonal

Project: Thumbnail Sketches

Before starting a painting, spend some time making simple pencil sketches, drawing the basic shapes and directional lines you can see in your subject. Start by making a framework of connecting lines that contain the overall shapes, then start to break down the large areas into small sections, paying attention to the relative height, width and depth of different elements in your subject, the interaction of straight lines and curves, and the links between shapes in different parts of the picture.

When you have made a variety of quick sketches, play around with the size and proportion of the picture. Try drawing a rectangular frame around each sketch to increase the background area or push the edges of the picture closer into the subject, perhaps allowing important shapes to be cut off at the sides, top or bottom of the frame.

1: The picture frame encloses a conventional view with vertical and horizontal stresses evenly balanced.

2: Moving into the subject, the artist makes the vertical stress more central and the background more busy and active.

3: Featured so closely, the tree becomes an abstract shape that divides the background and breaks up the balance.

values are used to create light and shade, enabling you to model three-dimensional form and convey atmosphere. Colour explains the nature of things – local colours are an aid to identification – and can also be expressive. Textures and patterns can add to the description of objects and materials and provide decorative elements in your paintings. But no matter how freely tone, colour, texture and pattern are used, they still function as abstract elements of your composition, and affect the rhythms and dynamics of line and shape.

As you begin to apply tones and colours the balance and emphasis of your composition is altered. You have to orchestrate the abstract elements of the painting and work towards a representation of your subject.

Similarity and Contrast

When looking at a subject for painting you automatically look for ways of organizing the information in your mind, albeit subconsciously. You may look for similarities of shape and colour, and be startled by emphatic contrasts. There is a tendency for the viewer to practise what is known as "visual grouping", bringing together items with common characteristics even when they are spatially separated. You can make your composition more cohesive and harmonious, by providing links between similar objects. Alternatively, you can enhance its dramatic impact, by

left: When drawing a figure from life, measurements and angles need constant checking. By holding up a pencil and moving your thumb up and down on it you can check proportions; angling the pencil to follow the line of the body or limb shows you the precise slope, which can be double-checked by relating it to a vertical, such as a chair leg.

counteracting the viewer's expectations.

Similar colours which link different parts of a painting together can be very valuable. A touch of blue in the foreground of a landscape, for instance, can discretely echo an expanse of blue sky. If you have no such links in a painting – if every area or brushstroke is a new and different colour – the effect is busy and disturbing. Similarly, linking shapes and tones in different parts of the painting gives the viewer related points of contact. A great variety of unrelated elements can make a painting confusing.

USING AND MAKING A VIEWFINDER

Some lucky people have an instinctive "nose" for a good composition – but for most of us, it requires a good deal of practice and experience. When we look at a complex subject like a landscape, it can be difficult to select a balanced composition from the vast array of shapes and colours.

A cardboard viewfinder is a great help in such cases. By moving around the subject and looking through the viewfinder, you can home in on particular sections of the scene and isolate them from the overall view. The edges of the viewfinder act as a kind of picture frame, helping you to see the physical world in terms of how it might appear on a flat rectangle (or square) of paper. By placing a definite border around what you select, you'll find it easier to examine the interplay of shapes and masses, and to judge how the contents of the picture relate to the edges of the frame. You may sometimes find that what appeared at first glance to be a good composition reveals unexpected flaws on closer scrutiny. It is far less frustrating to make this discovery now than when the painting is already under way!

As well as being an aid to linear composition, a viewfinder also enables you to see the subject more clearly in terms of areas of light and dark value – a very important part of composition. And during the course of the painting, the colour of the frame itself also comes in useful. I always make my viewfinders from grey or buff-coloured cardboard; when held up to the subject, this acts as a convenient middle value against which I can judge the relative lightness or darkness of the shapes within it.

Try looking through a viewfinder, not only at landscapes but also at street scenes, figure groups, interiors and familiar objects around the home. You'll begin to discover interesting compositions where you may not have noticed them before.

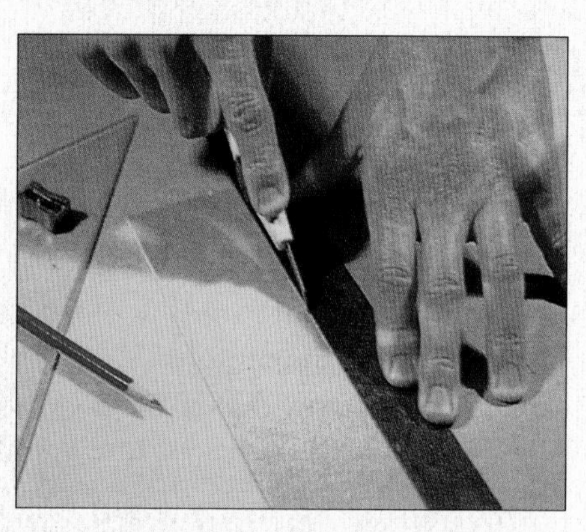

To make a viewfinder all you need is a sheet of grey or buff-coloured card, about 15 cm x 20 cm (6 in x 8 in), a steel ruler, a craft knife and a pencil. Draw a rectangle within the sheet of cardboard, approximately 15 cm x 10 cm (6 in x 4 in). Alternatively, draw a square if this is the format you intend to use. Carefully cut out the window by holding the craft knife against the edge of the steel rule, keeping the edges crisp.

Make sure that the window is centred within the frame, with borders of equal width on all sides.

Close one eye and look through the frame. Move the viewfinder up and down, left and right, toward and away from you, or turn it around to try an upright image, until the subject is framed in a pleasing way. You will notice how seemingly ordinary objects can make effective pictures when they are cleverly positioned and isolated from their surroundings. You will probably find several interesting compositions to explore, all from the same source.

Having found a suitable composition remember to make sure that the dimensions of your paper or canvas are in direct proportion to those of your viewfinder, otherwise the composition won't work.

When organizing contrasts in a painting, bear in mind that the shape and size of an area of colour is as important as its tonal value or intensity. Extreme contrasts of tone and colour – black against white, or one colour against its complementary one – do not work well when they are equal, as they tend to cancel each other out. However, a complete imbalance of shape and size can be highly effective. You can see that, for example, a spot of light set against a huge shadow area, or a tiny stroke of one intense colour on an expanse of its complementary colour, can create a dramatic, vibrant effect.

above: A panoramic view such as this one may appear too daunting to tackle . . . or is it? Using a viewfinder, you could actually make several paintings from this one scene.

above and below: Here the artist has used his viewfinder to isolate three small sections of the scene, each of which makes a satisfying composition in its own right.

Being Selective

Whatever your subject or style of painting, you do not have to include everything you see before you. Part of the process of composing a picture is choosing key elements and discarding unimportant or distracting features. This could mean eliminating whole objects – bushes or parked cars in a landscape, for example. It also means ignoring the kind of detail that is inappropriate to the scale of your painting, or lost over distance – when you see a grassy field from afar, you see only broad areas, not the individual blades of grass, but even if it is near to, you still don't necessarily have to grapple with the details.

When you are deciding what and what not to include, keep in mind the pictorial value of the elements. A telegraph pole may seem superfluous to the content of your landscape, but it could provide a useful vertical emphasis. Think about how each component functions not only as part of the "reality" of the painting, but also in contributing to the composition.

If you find it difficult to decide what to include in your painting, break down your view of the subject into simple, manageable shapes and paint them in flat areas of colour. When you see how they work two-dimensionally, you can move on to selecting more detail from the information in front of you and building up the composition gradually.

The Edges of Paintings

For centuries, the conventions of composition demanded that the "events" of a painting should take place entirely within the picture rectangle. While dynamic lines and shapes might be arranged to lead the eye around the picture, the composition was usually organized in ways that kept the viewer's interest within the painting and no vital element would be cut off at the edges. A figure group might be framed by trees which run off the sides of the painting, for example, but the trees are not important in themselves; they form an archway which concentrates the viewer's attention on the central subject.

With the advent of photography in the mid-nineteenth century, artists discovered that informality could be highly effective in a composition. "Snapshot" images began to appear in paintings where some of the visual information was indistinct and out of focus. Photographs sometimes cut off objects and people in strange ways, and painters began to appreciate how they could use the same kind of effect. They discovered that allowing figures and objects to be cut off by the edges of the picture had the effect of drawing the viewer into the scene. It also created a more complex dynamic effect between the picture area and the shapes within it.

These pictorial devices were first exploited by the Impressionists, and have become widely used in twentieth-century painting. Part of your process of selection in deciding how to frame your subject should include where to place the outer edges of your painting in relation to the subject. It is not essential to include all the objects to be portrayed in their entirety.

left: The structural harmony of Rosalind Cuthbert's watercolour *Barton Rock* is echoed in the gentle colour variations set against patches of deep tone.

VIEWPOINTS

The varying viewpoints that you can take when painting reveal different aspects of the subject's mood and character, as well as presenting alternative ways of composing the picture.

High Viewpoint: **In terms of composition, this is useful – the high view puts a great deal of information clearly on display and reveals how the subject is spatially organized. It can, however, create a detached, even superior impression, especially with human subjects, as it provides an unfamiliar view of people. If you use an imaginary high viewpoint for a townscape or landscape, you will need to work out the formal perspective arrangement.**

Normal Eye Level: **This is your actual experience of objects seen from a normal sitting or standing position. It provides a straightforward view that is easily understood because it is familiar. The information works from front to back of the subject rather than from top to bottom as in a high view, so it is important to organize the depth of your picture effectively.**

Low Viewpoint: **This is an unfamiliar view and can create an unusual composition. Things close to you can seem very large, but the drawback is that they may obscure other interesting features.**

Frontal Viewpoint: **This is a direct view which sometimes seems confrontational. It simplifies spatial concerns, as the objects can usually be clearly indicated receding one behind another, but the resulting painting can appear formal and unsympathetic.**

Oblique Side View: **This viewpoint suggests that you are glancing in on your subject. It can be casual or mysterious in mood, and the way important shapes relate to the picture rectangle can create great dynamism and impact.**

Distant View: **The character of the subject influences the effectiveness of taking a long view. In a landscape, the distant viewpoint can help you to express its spaciousness and variety. If you position a figure or still-life to appear relatively far away, it can enable you to show it in an interesting context, but it may make the main subject seem marginal and insignificant.**

Close-up View: **Homing in on the subject helps you to create a detailed statement. You might paint just a face in close-up, or a huge detailed flower standing in front of an unfocused, small-scale landscape. This kind of view compels the viewer to respond actively to the picture. It can, however, create a feeling of unease.**

below: A view of a tennis court from a window (top) shows an overall perspective that seems normal and acceptable. The higher viewpoint (centre) exaggerates recession and brings the detail of the tree branches into the foreground. From ground level (bottom) the horizontality is emphasized, with the fence becoming the prominent feature.

COMPOSING A FIGURE PAINTING

Posing your Model: If you want to create an impression of character and lifestyle rather than just a figure study, arrange the subject so that the sitter's clothing and the objects in the room say something about your model.

Figure in a Setting: If your subject is posed in a particularly appropriate setting, for example, the sitter's study or greenhouse, think very carefully about the scale of the figure in relation to its surroundings. Do you want the figure to be a dominant element, placed squarely in the foreground and seen large against the background, or to be an integral part of the picture, easily absorbed into the overall view?

Lighting: When painting a figure straightforwardly from life, or making a formal portrait, you need strong light from one direction that helps to reveal form and does not camouflage it by creating strong cast shadows. Soft lighting tends to flatten forms and make the painting lack a feeling of space. Lighting a portrait from above or below can make a dramatic impact.

Viewpoint: Remember that figure paintings usually create associations in the viewer's mind and that he or she is very responsive to the sense of scale. If you choose to take an unusual viewpoint, such as very low, very high, angled sideways or in tight close-up, this tends to produce a more dramatic and atmospheric painting than one which is sight-size with a normal eye level.

left and below: The close-up portrait gives little sense of the model's location, and her character must all be conveyed in her face. The farther view (below) takes in detail of clothing and background that add to the variety of the artist's description and makes a more complete picture.

Format: The format of your painting may be suggested by the subject. A single seated or standing figure usually works best in a portrait format rectangle, whereas a figure group may need the lateral space of a horizontal rectangle to avoid compressing it.

below: Focusing on the head alone creates a confrontational, isolated portrait with tonal drama. The full-figure pose is more calmly neutral.

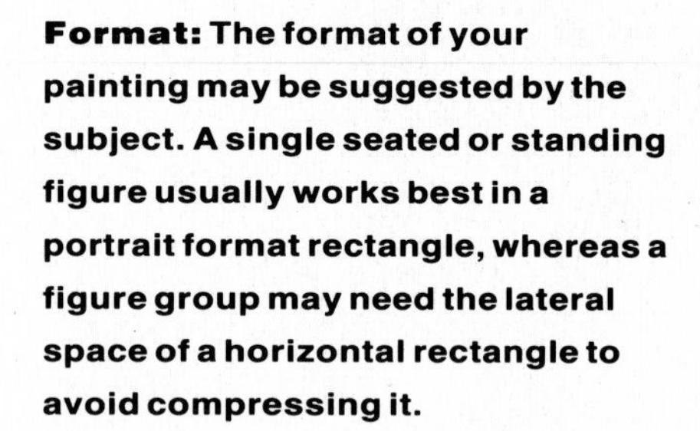

COMPOSING A TOWNSCAPE OR LANDSCAPE

Viewpoint: Move around to get different views of your chosen subject. Consider where you will position the horizon line on your paper or canvas to govern the extent of sky and land seen in your picture. Remember that a low horizon compresses the space given to the landscape, so you need to work out how to layer the view effectively, whereas a high horizon provides a greater ground area in which different features can be located. If you are working at ground level in a town or village, look for views through the buildings and down the streets that will give your composition an interesting structure and sense of space.

above, left and below: Any location offers a number of possible views that vary in terms of basic structure and incidental detail. The panorama (above) of a seaside town gives a strong sense of place through a complex, detailed composition. Focusing interest on the harbour, the artist finds a dramatic bird's-eye view (left) that forms an open, almost abstract image. This contrasts with the picturesque effect of a conventional ground-level view (below) showing the town's local colour.

Focal Points: Look for individual features that will make good points of focus – an imposing old tree, for instance, a colourful façade, or the pattern of a stone wall or wooden fence. Use colour accents provided by flowers, buildings or farm machinery to counterpoint the broader colour areas in an open landscape.

Scale and Format: Decide how much of the view you wish to incorporate in your painting and whether it is best suited to a restful horizontal format or to a rectangle which has a dramatic vertical emphasis.

COMPOSING A STILL-LIFE

Arranging a Group: When you choose objects for a still-life, think about their similarities and differences, and how these can be linked and contrasted within the arrangement. First, position the objects together to form a group and then move them around until you find the most interesting combination of shapes. Consider how the objects overlap, and the spaces between them. Look at your group from different viewpoints before you change things around. From one particular position, it may be excellent.

below: The objects are spread quite evenly across the tabletop, defining the horizontal plane and adding no strong emphasis.

below and right: With the corner of the table leading toward the viewer there is no single directional line to follow. These arrangements make more play of the interaction of shapes.

Found Subjects: Arranged still-lifes can look very contrived, and you may be able to find interesting subjects in your home which require no special arrangement, such as ornaments on a shelf or clothing thrown onto a bed. Visualize these found arrangements as compositions for paintings and move any object you think may look ugly or ambiguous, trying not to lose the informality that initially attracted you to the subject.

Colours and Textures: Decide whether it is the colours and textures, or the variety of the objects that interests you. If you are mainly interested in shape and form, don't include more than one or two patterned objects, as patterns tend to obscure shapes. However, if you want a decorative effect, patterns can enliven the colour and detail.

above: Although the frontal view of the table reinstates the strong horizontal, it is softened and counteracted by the draped cloth and more complex grouping.

above: The high viewpoint separates the still-life from its context and organizes the shapes very formally.

above: The staggered arrangement of objects makes a zigzagging line through the composition that introduces another element to interact with the basic shapes. There is an ordered and logical definition of height and depth.

Backgrounds: A plain background throws three-dimensional form into clear relief; a heavy patterned or textured background can intrude into the still-life group. Where elements of the background form strong directional lines, consider carefully where and how these should link with the objects in the foreground.

right: Ronald Jesty, RBA, *View from Hod Hill.* The eye is always drawn to human figures in a landscape, and their inclusion can turn an ordinary subject into a striking picture. Here the two figures on the right, tiny as they are, form the anchoring point for the whole composition. We look first at them; then, following their gaze, we explore the rolling landscape beyond.

below: Stan Perrott, *The Friendship Sloop,* watercolour. The simplest compositions are often the most dramatic. Here the dark-valued, regular forms of the buildings emphasize the sweeping lines of the little boat. The white mast and boom draw the eye inevitably to the two figures, which themselves form a valuable anchoring point to the composition (cover the figures with your index fingers and you'll see that this is so).

BALANCE AND COUNTERBALANCE

One of the most important goals in composing a painting is achieving visual balance. In other words, the various elements that make up the image – lines, shapes, colours, values and textures – must be arranged with care, so as to create a harmonious result.

Throughout the centuries, artists and critics have put forward innumerable theories about what makes a successful composition. But it was the ancient Greek philosopher, Plato, who expressed most succinctly what good composition is all about. Plato stated quite simply that "composition consists of observing and depicting diversity within unity". By this he meant that a picture should contain enough variety to keep the viewer interested, but that this variety must be restrained and organized if we are to avoid confusion.

Plato's observation sums up, in fact, the dilemma that faces us each time we begin composing a painting. For though the human eye is drawn to stability, order and unity, it is also attracted by freedom, diversity and the element of surprise. The challenge for the artist lies in striking the right balance between these opposite attractions.

The most obvious way to achieve balance is through a symmetrical composition, in which elements of similar value, shape and size are used together in almost equal proportions. Although at times such a structure may serve a concept well, for most purposes too much symmetry results in a rather static and uninspired design, lacking in the element of diversity that Plato talked about.

For most artists, the way to achieve diversity within unity is to create an asymmetrical composition, in which features that are inherently different but of equal interest are arranged so as to counterbalance one another. An

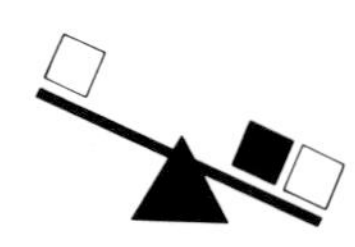

right: In this illustration there is an imbalance between the left and right halves. The mass of the mountains and rocks on the right has great visual weight, with its strong colour and value contrasts, whereas the left half of the picture is virtually empty. The scales demonstrate this imbalance.

left: Here the artist tries to restore equilibrium by lightening the values on the right of the picture and including another foreground rock on the left. This is an improvement, but it's a little too symmetrical: both halves of the picture are virtually identical, and there is no main centre of interest on which the eye can settle.

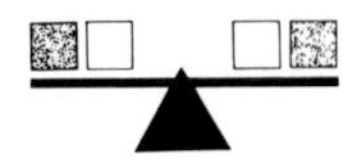

asymmetrical composition succeeds in creating a sense of equilibrium, while at the same time allowing a contrast of shapes, colours and values that lends vitality and interest.

Asymmetrical composition is often compared to a pair of old-fashioned weighing scales, in which a small but heavy metal weight on one side can balance a much larger pile of fruit or vegetables on the other. Think of the shapes and masses within your composition as "weights" to be balanced and counterbalanced until an equilibrium is found. Remember, it is not only size that gives an object visual weight – strong colour, shape, texture or value will attract the eye when used as a contrasting element, even in small amounts. For example, a large area of light value can be counterbalanced by a small area of dark value that has more visual weight; and a large area of cool colour can be offset by a small amount of intense colour that creates a strong focus.

The process of painting a picture is in itself a continual balancing act; one touch of colour applied will alter the relationships already established, while the next restores the balance.

above: This version shows how an asymmetrical composition can create visual interest while, at the same time, retaining balance and unity. The artist has enlarged the distant mountains and included only the foreground rocks on the left. Thus we have a small mass of light value on the left that has enough visual weight to counterbalance the large mass of dark value on the right.

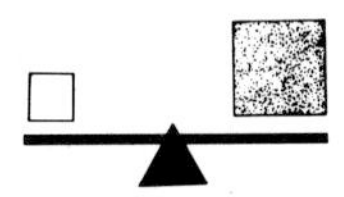

Creating a Centre of Interest

The nineteenth-century English artist and writer John Ruskin was once asked "Does a picture need a focal point?" His reply was firm: "Indeed it does, just as a meal needs a main dish and a speech a main theme, just as a tune needs a note and a man an aim in life . . ."

In other words, a picture should have one strong centre of interest to which the viewer's eye is drawn – the point which contains the message of the picture. Of course, many paintings don't have a centre of interest, but these are usually abstract designs in which the artist sacrifices dramatic interest for the overall unity of pattern or texture. In representational painting, on the other hand, the lack of a centre of interest leads to an incomplete feeling.

When planning the compositional arrangement of the painting, your first question to yourself should be "what do I want to emphasize, and how should I emphasize it?" For example, in a portrait the centre of interest is normally the sitter's face, whose expression conveys his or her personality. In a still-life, the centre of interest might be a jug of flowers, with the other objects playing a supporting role.

There are several devices that the artist can use to bring attention to the centre of interest, such as placing more detail or texture in that area, or more intense colours, or contrasting shapes. But the most dynamic attention-getter is tonal contrast. It is well known that light areas stimulate the nerve endings in the eye and appear to expand, whereas dark areas absorb light and appear to contract. Therefore, by placing the lightest light and the darkest dark adjacent to each other at the centre of interest, you create a visual tension, a "push-pull" sensation that attracts the viewer's eye and holds his or her interest.

left: This seascape has few interesting physical features to hold our interest. But the sea and sky could have been made to look more interesting than they are here; the painting has no obvious focal point, and our eyes dart from one area of the picture to another, unable to settle anywhere in particular.

below: The same scene, but with one marked improvement. Notice how your attention is caught by the light shape of the cliffs against the dark cloud? The artist has placed the lightest and darkest values next to each other, and this sharp contrast makes an arresting focal point. Now the picture has more meaning, and is more satisfying to look at. The dark foreground wave has a part to play, too. It acts as a counterpoint to the centre of interest, while creating a sense of movement that directs our eye toward it.

More often than not, the subject that you want to paint won't have an obvious focal point – it's up to you to create one. This applies particularly to landscapes and seascapes, in which the sheer magnitude of a panoramic view makes it difficult to focus your attention toward a specific point. When you're looking at the real thing your eyes can happily roam at will over the scene without resting on any particular point, and this won't detract from your enjoyment. But it's a quite different matter when you take all that detail, colour and movement and "freeze" it on a small, flat sheet of paper.

One important thing to remember is that there should never be more than one major centre of interest in a painting. If there is more than one dominant area, the message becomes diluted and the picture loses impact. Even if the picture contains multiple subjects, the composition needs to be carefully controlled so that one subject or area commands more attention than the rest. For example, if a landscape scene includes two foreground trees of equal size, they will compete for attention and you may have to deliberately reduce the size of one tree in order to lend more importance to the other.

Directing the Eye

When we look at a picture of any kind we instinctively look for a visual pathway to guide us through the composition and make sense of it. If the elements in the picture aren't connected in a pleasing and rhythmical way, we soon lose interest because the picture has a fragmented, incomplete feeling.

The aim of the artist, then, is to lead the viewer's eye into, around and through the picture in a way that's both stimulating and satisfying. The most obvious way to do this is through directional lines, such as those formed by a road, a fence or a stream as it cuts a swathe through the land. Lines like these can be used to lead the eye from the foreground to the background, or to the centre of interest, but they can look rather clichéd and overdone unless handled with skill.

A mere suggestion or nuance of linear direction is often all that's needed to gently encourage the viewer to explore the composition. Here, once again, contrasts of colour and value can be used to lend rhythm and movement to a composition in a way that is subtle yet compelling.

Directional paths are often created by the nature of the light itself. In a shadowy interior, for example, a shaft of light coming in from a window on the left of the picture will push the eye to the right, producing a momentum that draws the viewer into your work. Think, too, of the patterns caused by sunlight on ripples of water, or of the long shadows cast by trees in the late afternoon.

above: Charles Longbotham, *British Tramp at Sea, Moonlight.* Note how the dark values in the sky and sea set up a swirling, vortex-like rhythm that heightens the tension and drama of the scene.

below: Edward Wesson, *Beached Fishing Boat, Suffolk Estuary.*

Painting and drawing are an extension of the art of seeing; by viewing a familiar object in an unexpected way we often gain new insights not only into the physical world around us but also into ourselves and our own individuality. This intensity of experience inevitably comes through in our paintings and drawings, which take on a greater power and beauty.

Accordingly, the projects and demonstrations in this chapter are designed to develop your awareness of tonal values through close observation and intelligent enquiry. You'll learn how to spot those dynamic shapes of light and shade that lend poetry to even the most ordinary subject; how to make sense of a complex subject by making value sketches; and how a convincing illusion of reality can be achieved by working with a limited range of values.

If all this sounds like hard work – it is. But as any artist will tell you, painstaking observation is as vital to successful picture-making as the knowledge of practical techniques. Added to which, the discovery and understanding of what makes a thing tick is always a rewarding and exciting experience in itself.

What are Tonal Values?

The word "value" simply refers to how light or dark an area is, whatever its colour. Some colours reflect more light than others, which is why we perceive them as being paler in value. For example, navy blue and sky blue are both the same basic colour, but navy blue is dark in value, while sky blue is light in value.

In addition, the value of a colour is changed by the way the light falls on it, so that one colour can show a variety of values. Imagine a man in a navy-blue sweater standing in front of a window so that he is at

right-angles to you. His sweater is all made of the same colour of wool, but you'll notice how its value appears darker at the back than at the front, where the light from the window is striking it.

The idea of tonal values is easy to understand if we look at it in terms of black and white. Every colour (every pure, unmixed colour, that is) has a tonal "value", ranging from white to black and with infinite shades of grey in between. You can test this by looking at a black and white photograph of a painting, or by adjusting the knob of your colour television set until the picture goes black and white. In black and white, a yellow object looks almost white in value; red and green objects are similar in value, appearing as a middle grey; brown and purple appear dark grey.

Now we have defined what values are. But why are they so important in painting? What is all the fuss about? Quite simply, the value framework of a picture – the contrast of light and dark areas – can be compared to the skeleton of the human body, or the foundations of a building. Without this solid framework, the whole thing would collapse. In any painting, we have to be aware of the *weight* of each of the colours we use and how they balance each other; otherwise the picture won't hang together well, nor will it convey a realistic sense of form (think of a black and white photograph that has been overexposed so that everything in it appears the same light grey).

Some artists maintain that the value of a colour is more important than the colour itself. Even a great colourist like Paul Cézanne (1839–1906), who emphasized colour changes to model form, was aware of the significance of the values of the colours he used. We shall see later on in this book how vital is the role played by the interaction of light and dark values – but the first step is to learn how to train your eye to *see* the values of colours and to judge them correctly.

Putting it all Together

Rendering an object or form realistically requires careful observation and an understanding of how tonal values are affected by light. When you're faced with a complex subject such as the human figure, it's easy to become confused by the profusion of lights, halftones and shadows, so that you lose sight of the main value shapes that describe, for example, the rounded form of the head.

The best way to avoid this sort of confusion is to sit down and make a series of pencil sketches that examine the value pattern of your subject – in other words, the main shapes of light and shade that most clearly describe what is going on. Forget for the minute that you're painting a head, or a flower, or a tree, and think purely in terms of patterns of light. Try to adopt this analytical approach from the start, for once you understand the logic of how the light is falling on your subject, it will be much easier to express it in your painting.

above: This still-life contains a wide range of values. The intense colours in the fruit and flowers contrast with the muted colours of the other objects.

above: The same still-life, photographed in black and white, allows us to see the arrangements in terms of light and dark value patterns.

Local values . . .

. . . plus light and shade . . .

. . . combine to create form

Every subject has a "local" value that describes how light or dark its actual colour is. For example, a red apple is darker than a yellow grapefruit, because red absorbs more light than yellow does. But local values are modified by the effects of light and shade, and it is these modifications that describe the form of an object. So in bright sunlight, the highlight on the red apple might be almost as light in value as the yellow grapefruit is, and similarly, the shaded part of the grapefruit may be almost as dark in value as the red apple.

Thus, the full value range of anything you look at is a combination of local value and the pattern of light and shade falling on the subject. Each has influence on the other – as demonstrated in the figure drawings (above). In the first drawing, the artist has blocked in the local values of the model; the local value of the hair is dark, as is the value of the sweater she is wearing. Her face and hands are light, and her skirt is middle in value. The model is lit by a strong overhead light, however, and this creates a definite pattern of light and dark. Now the artist makes a separate drawing, to help him understand the pattern of light and shade falling on the figure. Local values are ignored for the moment.

In the final drawing, we see how the local values and the light and shadow pattern are combined. Remember that the local values will have an influence on the values created by light and shade; notice, for example, that although the same light is striking both the skin and the hair, the highlights on the skin are lighter than those on the hair, because the local value of the hair is darker. Similarly, the shadow side of the hair is darker than the shadow side of the face.

It is this interplay between local values and light and shadow that makes a drawing or painting visually exciting; the underlying local values lend a harmony and cohesiveness to the image, while the pattern of light and shade playing on the surface creates intriguing light/dark rhythms for the eye to explore and enjoy. Remember that a strong, direct light source will create interesting shadows – and therefore interesting value patterns. With flat, indirect light such as you would find on a hazy day or under fluorescent lights, the image is made up of local values only.

Making Value Sketches

Having trained your eye to perceive values, you're now ready to move on to the next stage – using tonal values to create a balanced and unified composition. In nature the range of values from the darkest dark to the lightest light is extremely wide – far wider than we could ever hope to attain in a painting. As artists we are obliged to select from nature only those elements that seem to capture the essential spirit of the subject, and ignore the inconsequential details; in order to give a painting more force, we have to portray what we see in a crystallized form. The problem is that, when faced with a complex subject like a landscape, we "can't see the wood for the trees". So how, when confronted with a profusion of shapes, values and colours, lit by changing light, do we begin this process of selection?

The answer is simple: before you begin painting, make a few pencil sketches of the subject in which you concentrate only on the main shapes and value masses. These sketches are useful firstly because they provide a way of getting familiar with the subject so you feel more confident when starting to paint it, and secondly because you can use them to try out different arrangements of lights and darks until you arrive at the one that seems best. There's an old carpenter's maxim that says "measure twice and cut once". Making preliminary sketches will save you a lot of time and frustration at the painting stage .

Assessing the Values

During the eighteenth century, landscape painters often used a device called a Claude mirror to help them see more clearly the simple pattern of lights, darks and middle values in a landscape. This comprised a piece of darkened mirror glass which, when held up to the subject, reflected the image in a lower key. It also reduced the image in size, enabling the artist to see a large stretch of landscape as it would appear picture-size. The device was named after the French artist Claude Lorrain (1600–82), who is well known for his beautiful tonal landscapes painted in mellow colours.

Today, Claude mirrors are no longer made, but you can achieve a similar effect by looking at the subject through a piece of tinted glass or acetate. This won't, of course, reduce the image in size, but it will cut out most of the colour and detail so you can see a more simplified arrangement of values. Looking at the subject through sunglasses also works well.

When making your value sketch, work quickly and reduce everything to just three values – light, medium and dark (save the white of the paper for the lightest value). Does the finished sketch have a good balance of values? If it doesn't, feel free to arrange and rearrange the proportion and distribution of the light and dark areas, until something "clicks" and you feel happy with the way they hold together. It helps if you can temporarily disregard aspects like colour and identifiable subject matter and look at the sketch as a flat, two-dimensional pattern of light and dark shapes. If this simple light/dark pattern doesn't hold together as a harmonious abstract design, then the painting will most likely fail. What you should strive for is a lively interplay of lights and darks that create a strong movement across the paper. The overall pattern should be simple and cohesive, consisting of a few large, interlocking shapes rather than a lot of small, fragmented ones.

right: A harbour scene like this one makes an attractive painting subject. The only problem here is that the overall value pattern is too busy and scattered.

START WITH FIVE VALUES

When a painting contains too many different colours, it is unsatisfying to look at because the colours end up by cancelling each other out. Exactly the same thing applies with values – too many will cause a painting to look confused and disjointed. Of course we can discern literally dozens of different values in nature – and there is nothing in nature that looks confused or disjointed – but for the purposes of picture-making we need to reduce the number of values we see to just a few, in order to make a clear, uncluttered statement.

One of the most useful lessons you should learn in painting is *how to make less say more*. It's a little like giving a speech – if you include too many irrelevant facts, the listener will very soon become bored, whereas a few considered phrases, well delivered, will make a lasting impression.

Most painters tend to work with around nine to twelve values, but it is possible to create a perfectly good picture with just three to five. In fact, if the whole idea of tonal values leaves you feeling puzzled, a good exercise is to make a few paintings or drawings using only five values: white, a light value, a middle value, a dark value, and black. By doing this, you will train your eye to judge the value of any colour correctly, and you will learn to see things in terms of broad masses instead of getting bogged down in small details.

A value scale like the one below is invaluable in determining the values of the coloured objects you are painting. It gives you something positive to gauge the values of your subject by; you simply give each area of colour a tone value from one to five on the scale, depending on how light or dark it is.

above: By half-closing his eyes, the artist reduces the scene to just three or four values. In this first sketch, he ties similar values together to make larger, stronger shapes.

above: Now he strengthens the areas of darkest value.

-ARTISTS' HINTS-

- On gaining confidence in working with five values, add a further four to your repertoire. These additions will really be half-steps between the original five values, creating an even smoother gradation from black through to white. Nine values will give you greater flexibility and allow you to tackle more complex subjects; they are enough to give your paintings greater subtlety and refinement, while still remaining easy to control.
- Avoid over-emphasizing the lights in a dark area, and the darks in a light area, otherwise you will destroy the illusion of light.
- Always key your light values to the upper end of the value scale, going no darker than a middle value, and your shadow values to the lower end of the scale, going no lighter than a middle value.

Start by drawing a bar 12.5 cm (5 in) long and 2.5 cm (1 in) wide on a sheet of white paper. Divide the bar into 2.5 cm (1 in) squares. Leaving the first square white, take an HB pencil and lightly fill in the other four squares with hatched lines. Exerting the same degree of pressure on the pencil, go over the hatched lines again, this time starting with the third square. Now go over squares four and five again, and finally square five only. So long as you exert the same degree of pressure with the pencil each time, this should give you an even gradation in value from white to black.

It's a little more difficult to create a value scale in paint so that you get an even gradation. If I'm using watercolour I start by mixing up a full-strength solution of ivory black in a jar and then dividing it between four saucers. I keep one saucer "neat", to act as the darkest value. Then, to get my light, middle and dark greys, I add a teaspoon of water to the second saucer, two teaspoons to the third, and three teaspoons to the fourth. For the fifth value, I simply use the white of the paper.

above: Having established the main value masses, he can fine-tune the sketch by adding the middle values and reinforcing the linear design. The attractive layout of the harbour scene remains intact, but the composition is now stronger and more unified. The sketch will serve as the basis for a finished painting, made either on the spot or back at the studio.

below: Use a value scale like these ones to assess the tones in your work.

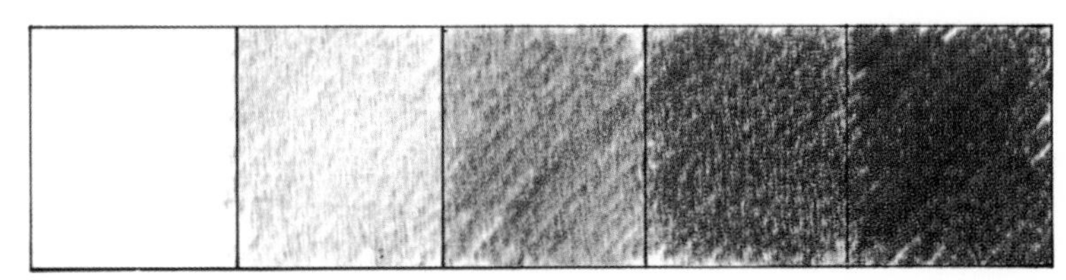

Pencil

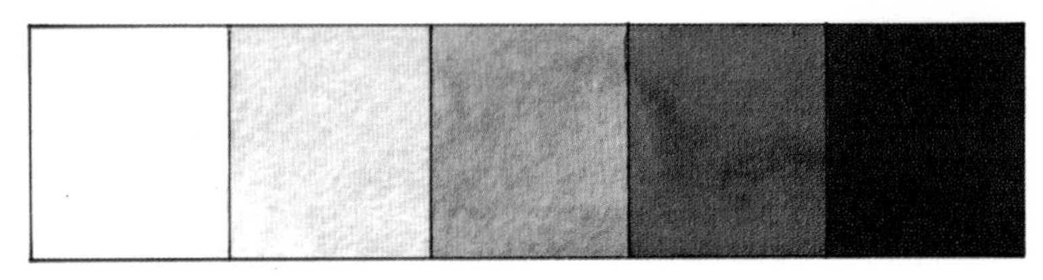

Watercolour

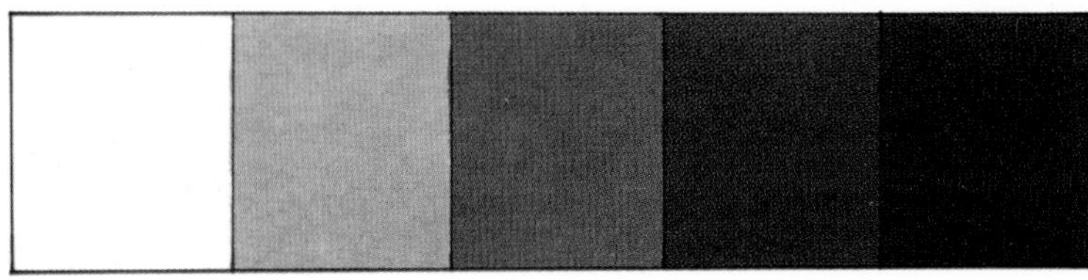

Gouache

Project: Still-life in Five Values

One of the most fascinating aspects of still-life painting is recording the complex interplay of shape and form, value and colour, light and shade – qualities that make each still life unique. The aim of this project is to record those shapes and values as simply and expressively as possible – in other words, to get to the real essentials of the subject.

Set up a simple still-life group similar to the one illustrated. It doesn't matter what you choose to paint, so long as the group includes a range of colours from very pale to very dark. Arrange the objects on a table against a wall, and light them from one side so that you get interesting cast shadows.

Use any medium you like, but stick to just five values. In order to keep the values consistent throughout, it's best to premix them beforehand.

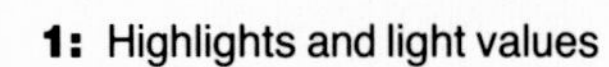

1: Highlights and light values

2: Pale mid-values

3: Dark mid-values

4: Darkest values complete the picture

Self-critique

Did you half-close your eyes to see the value pattern more clearly?

Did you lightly map with pencil the main areas of light and dark?

Did you mix your washes accurately – not too dark and not too light?

Did you keep your shapes simple and your brushwork direct?

Perhaps the greatest challenge in landscape painting is that of creating the illusion of space and depth on a flat piece of paper. The sight of fields, hills and trees stretching away into the hazy distance is a marvellous one, but how can we capture it convincingly in paint?

Simple tricks of linear perspective can work to a certain extent; overlapping one shape in front of another, for example, gives an instant three-dimensional effect, as does the presence of a foreground detail that recedes into the picture, such as a road or fence. But by far the most effective means of improving the quality of depth and distance in a painting is through the use of "aerial perspective". This term, invented by Leonardo da Vinci (1452–1519), describes the phenomenon found in nature whereby dark forms become lighter in the distance but light forms become darker, with the contrasts between values becoming progressively smaller towards the horizon.

This section explains how to use value and colour to reproduce the effects of aerial perspective and so bring your landscapes to life. In addition, you'll find advice on how to choose the best viewpoint so as to emphasize the feeling of depth and recession. Finally, you'll discover ways to capture the subtle nuances of value and colour that lend atmosphere to portraits, still-lifes and indoor scenes.

below: Charles Harrington, *Landscape, Late Afternoon.*

Aerial Perspective

The term "aerial perspective" describes an optical illusion caused by the presence of water vapour and tiny particles of dust in the atmosphere, which act almost like a series of invisible veils strung across the landscape. The farther into the distance we can see, the more "veils" we have to look through, which is why colours and forms appear more hazy and indistinct the closer they are to the horizon.

The effects of aerial perspective are most apparent when there are well-defined planes within the subject, such as a mountain range or a series of cliffs jutting out along a shoreline. They can also be seen clearly when dusk approaches, reducing the forms of the land to almost silhouetted shapes that become lighter in value toward the horizon. This makes it easier to see the changes that occur between the foreground, middle distance and far distance. Let's say, for example, that you're standing on a hill, surveying an undulating landscape of tree-covered fields and hills. As your eye travels from the foreground to the horizon, these are the changes you will notice.

- **Values become altered:** Those objects that are nearest to you are relatively unaffected by atmospheric haze, so you see their values at full strength. In the middle distance, however, some of the strength of the values is lost, due to the intervening atmosphere, and they appear lighter. Way back on the horizon, they are weakest of all, seeming to melt into the pale value of the sky. You will also notice, however, that white objects in the distance become darker, not lighter, in value because they are greyed by the atmosphere.
- **Colours become cooler:** Atmospheric haze has the same effect on colour as it has on value. In the foreground, colours appear bright and warm because they are seen at their fullest intensity. In the middle distance, they lose some of their intensity, become cooler and take on a blue cast. Compare a foreground tree, for instance, with a tree 460 metres (500 yards) away, and notice how the colour of the foliage changes from a warm yellow-green to a cooler blue-green. Farther back still, a tree may not look green at all, but a subdued blue-grey.
- **Detail and contrast are diminished:** Tonal contrasts – say between a light-coloured building and the dark shadow it casts – are sharpest and clearest in the foreground. In the middle distance the intervening haze narrows the range of values and causes contrasts to be less marked, while on the horizon there is often no contrast at all – everything is blurred into one pale value. Similarly, texture and detail become less and less defined the farther you get from the foreground.

So, in order to create the illusion of infinite space and depth in our paintings, all we have to do is to reproduce the effects described above. Strong values and warm colours appear to come forward, whereas weak values and cool colours appear to recede into the distance – and it is the contrast between these values and colours that gives the illusion of distance.

It seems simple, but inexperienced painters often ignore what they see in front of them and put too much colour, detail and clarity into their backgrounds. This is because they have fallen into the familiar trap of painting what they know, instead of what they see: they "know" a tree is supposed to be green, so they paint it green, even though it is miles away on the horizon and actually appears blue. The result is always the same – a flat, unconvincing painting with none of the subtle atmospheric qualities that attracted the artist to the subject in the first place.

above: Juliette Palmer, *Fell and River*, approx. 35.6 x 35.6 cm (14 x 14 in), watercolour. It is interesting to compare this painting with the one on page 176, as both artists work wet-on-dry, but with very different results. Palmer uses countless tiny brushstrokes to build up a variety of textures, giving her paintings an almost embroidered quality. She reserves highlights with great skill and care, for example, the blades of grass and light-against-dark leaves in the right foreground were achieved by painstakingly painting around each shape. The foliage on the more distant trees becomes progressively bluer, with much softer detailing of foliage than is used on the foreground trees.

Choosing the Best Viewpoint

Once you have grasped the principles of aerial perspective, the qualities of depth and atmosphere in your paintings will increase tremendously. However, it is equally important to consider the actual composition of your picture, since this can either enhance the feeling of recession or destroy it.

As we have already seen, the way to achieve depth is to divide your picture into distinct areas in terms of distance – the foreground, middle ground and background – and to keep these areas distinct in value. In this respect, your choice of viewpoint becomes vital; it can make all the difference between a flat, insipid picture and an exciting, effective one.

Let's look first of all at the centre of interest, or focal point – the part of the picture to which the viewer's eye is drawn. This does not necessarily have to be in the forefront of the picture just because it *is* the centre of interest; indeed by placing it in the distance or middle distance, you will encourage the viewer to "step into" the picture and explore the composition, thereby increasing the impression of distance and depth.

The foreground needs careful

above: David Hutter, *Landscape Near Les Baux,* watercolour. In this striking image the artist has chosen a bird's-eye view in which the landscape is rolled out like a map in front of us. Notice how the outer edges of the picture are vignetted; these areas of bare paper seem to pull the eye into the picture and back to the distant mountains.

left: Frederick Walker, *Spring*. Influenced by the Pre-Raphaelites, Walker uses carefully observed and highly wrought detail, picking out the foreground with particular care.

thought, too. It should be the strongest of the three planes in the picture, but not so strong that it sets up a barrier between the viewer and the rest of the composition. For this reason, artists such as Camille Corot (1796–1875) included nothing in the foreground of their pictures that was nearer than 180 or 270 metres (200 or 300 yards) away from their easels. A slight sketchiness in the immediate foreground is often desirable, especially where the values of the landscape are delicate, as in a misty scene.

On the other hand, a prominent object in the foreground can act as a valuable counterpoint to a more distant centre of interest. For example, the overhanging branches of a foreground tree can be used to create a frame within the borders of a picture, through which the viewer looks out across the landscape beyond.

above: Winslow Homer, 1899–1901, *Road in Bermuda*. With dense washes of bold colour, Homer successfully conveyed the intense atmosphere of sunlight, framing the centre of interest with dark foliage.

right: In this lakeside scene, artist Charles Inge was attracted by the elegant shape of the stone bridge in the distance. Unfortunately, the surrounding landscape doesn't contain much in the way of interesting detail and the resulting picture is lacking in depth and atmosphere.

right: Rather than give up, the artist tries another tack. Here he alters his viewpoint, so that now we can see through the arch of the bridge to the hills beyond. He also includes some trees to the left of the picture. This area of strong value helps to bring the foreground forward, in contrast to the pale, recessive values of the background hills. The sky, too, contains a progression of values from dark to light, which increases the feeling of depth still further.

right: Here's another variation of the same scene. The dark shapes in the immediate foreground, and the overhanging branches in the upper right of the picture, create a "frame" through which we look out at the landscape beyond.

So far we've looked at ways of using tonal values to describe the *physical* aspects of what we see – in rendering the character and solidity of objects and the nearness and farness of things, for example. But the *emotional* content of a picture is every bit as important, if not more so. Mood, atmosphere, a certain intangible quality conveyed by the way light falls on a subject – these combine to create "the spell that charges the commonplace with beauty", to quote from the great British photographer Bill Brandt.

Here, once again, tonal values play a major role in creating the mood you want to convey in your pictures. There is a strong connection between the value range in a painting and the mood it conveys; a preponderance of dark values gives a sombre or mysterious atmosphere, whereas light values create a lively or cheerful impression.

The way light and dark values are arranged and distributed can also have an influence on the emotional impact of a painting. For example, dark values in the lower half of the painting convey a feeling of strength and stability; but if the dark values occupy the upper half of the composition, as in a storm scene, the mood alters radically, becoming sombre and threatening.

This section explores the many ways in which tonal values can be organized and used as a means of expression. You'll learn how to key tonal values to convey a particular mood; how to capture the atmospheric effects of light, both indoors and out; how to use light to create mood in portraits; and how to exploit the magic and mystery of shadows in creating powerful and compelling images.

above: Stan Perrott, *Storm from the Sea.*

above: The cottage is outlined against the light part of the sky. Strong tonal contrasts here add impact. Dark, swirling clouds radiate from the centre of the picture in a convincingly dramatic way.

below: The seagulls are painted with masking fluid to preserve the white of the paper before applying the sky wash. When the paint has dried, the fluid is rubbed off to reveal the bird's delicate white shapes.

below: Cobalt blue, Payne's grey and burnt sienna are used for the dark tones of the grass, textured with scumbled brushstrokes using a hog's hair fan brush.

KEYING YOUR VALUES

To express it simply, the term "key" refers to the overall lightness or darkness of a particular painting. A painting of a dimly lit interior, for instance, could be termed "low-key" because it would contain mainly dark values. A depiction of cornfield on a summer day, on the other hand, would be the subject of a "high-key" painting, containing mainly light values.

Where many amateur artists go wrong is in not understanding the importance of using a limited range of values to express a particular mood and to give greater power and directness to their paintings. When a painting contains too many different values, it becomes rather spotty and confused, and furthermore, the emotional message becomes dissipated. It is far better to use a limited range of values – certainly no more than five – and exploit them to the full.

It is possible to draw an analogy between the values in a painting and the notes in a piece of music: they should be used in a controlled range in order to achieve pictorial harmony. To take the analogy a stage further, we can compare the whole range of values of a painting with the key of a piece of music, and the way in that they both create a particular mood.

Music that is composed mainly of high-key notes sounds either light and cheerful or poignant and romantic, depending on the rhythm of the piece. Low-key notes, on the other hand, produce a more sombre, melancholy sound. These high notes and low notes are the equivalent of light and dark values in a painting: light values will create a cheerful and optimistic mood, or a soft and romantic one, whereas dark values will create a sense of drama or mystery.

Look at any successful painting and you'll see immediately that it has a good key – there is a unity, a feeling of strength and solidity that stems from the perfect harmony of values and colours. You'll notice too how the artist has deliberately orchestrated the values to underline the mood he or she wishes to convey. Think of the Impressionists, for example, whose high-key paintings capture perfectly the brilliance of sunshine and the heady warmth of a summer day. At the other end of the scale there are the low-key paintings of the great Dutch masters of the seventeenth century – people such as Rembrandt (1606–69), Vermeer (1632–75) and Pieter de Hooch (b. 1629) – in whose portraits and domestic interiors the tranquil atmosphere is conveyed exquisitely through muted darks offset by a few telling areas of soft light.

So by now you can see that values play a vital role in establishing the overall atmosphere or mood of a picture, no matter what your subject is.

below: Jacqueline Rizvi, *Chinese Cup and Coffee Can,* watercolour. Pale values and high-key colours give this exquisite still-life a delicate, airy feel, in keeping with the nature of the subject.

High-key Paintings

In a high-key painting most of the colours are in the light-to-middle value range, and there are no sharp contrasts of value. This creates a slightly hazy, atmospheric effect that is ideal for expressing qualities such as delicacy, tenderness, softness, fragility or purity.

To create a high-key painting, use pale, gentle colours mixed with a lot of white, and work wet-in-wet so that one colour blends softly into another with no abrupt change in value. To keep the colours lively and luminous, don't overmix them on the palette; it's far better to do as the Impressionists did and use small strokes and dabs of broken colour (see below) which blend in the viewer's eye while still retaining their vibrancy.

Indeed, it was the Impressionists – notably Claude Monet (1840–1926), Edgar Degas (1834–1917), Alfred Sisley (1839–99) and Camille Pissarro (1831–1903) – who were perhaps the greatest exponents of high-key painting. They were fascinated by light and the way it affects the appearance of objects, and their canvases consist almost entirely of high-key colours that capture not only the impression of shimmering light but also the mood of exuberance that everyone experiences when the sun is shining.

So what kind of subjects are suited to the high-key treatment? Let's take a portrait subject to start off with. Suppose you want to paint a portrait of a small child, or a mother nursing her baby, or a pretty young girl. What makes these subjects so attractive is their qualities of youth, innocence, gentleness and grace – qualities that might be lost if you used too many dark values in the painting. Soft, warm, gentle colours, on the other hand, are more in keeping with the emotional spirit of the subject.

Of course I am not presenting this as a rigid rule that cannot be broken, and I have seen mother-and-child portraits executed in dark values that are full of tenderness and feeling. I am simply trying to suggest one way in which you can deliberately orchestrate your values the better to express what you want to say. And in portraiture this is particularly important, since here the emphasis is on the expression of personality. Everything about the painting should be geared to making the viewer aware of the sitter's character.

Landscapes, of course, offer plenty of opportunities for high-key painting. The most obvious examples might be a snow scene on a sunny day; or a river that sparkles with light from the setting sun; or a landscape in autumn, with the sun breaking through a pale mist and clothing everything in a silvery haze. Once again, the trick is to deliberately emphasize the lightness and brightness of the scene – to paint it lighter and brighter than it actually appears if necessary – in order to make a more forceful statement about your emotional response to the fleeting effects of light.

In still-life painting, too, you can create a soft, romantic mood with pale values. Choose pretty, delicate objects – a jar of wild flowers perhaps, or pale china teacups – and arrange them on a windowsill with soft, diffused light coming through the window. Remember to keep the shadows soft, in keeping with the high-key effect.

above: Lucy Willis, *Watching Gulls*, watercolour. In contrast to the romantic mood of Jacqueline Rizvi's still-life, the mood of this high-key painting is one of exuberance.

Middle-key Paintings

The vast majority of paintings fall into the middle-key range, in which neither extreme lights nor extreme darks predominate. When handled skilfully, a painting consisting mainly of middle values creates a subtle and harmonious image with a quiet, contemplative mood. However, while closely related values may be harmonious, a middle-key painting is in danger of emerging flat, bland and lifeless unless it contains some positive contrasts, so try to introduce a few telling lights or rich darks into the scheme to give it more "snap".

Give careful thought also to the choice of colours in a middle-key painting. Since you are sacrificing the dramatic possibilities of *chiaroscuro* (light/dark contrast) it is vital that the image is exciting in terms of colour. By choosing colours that are similar in value but contrasting in temperature or intensity, you will create a picture that is harmonious and vibrant.

above: Trevor Chamberlain, *Hazy Sun and Damp Mist, Boulby Down,* 51.4 x 73 cm (20¼ x 28¾ in), watercolour. This lovely evocation almost makes us feel the damp but warm atmosphere with the sun about to break through. The artist has worked wet-in-wet, controlling the tones and colours with the precision demanded by such a subject.

left: Lucy Willis, *Cat on a Chair,* watercolour. A low-key painting doesn't have to be sombre. In this charming study of a cat on a chair, backlighting throws the subject into near-silhouette and creates interesting positive and negative shapes.

Low-key Paintings

As we have seen, a low-key painting is one that is predominantly dark in value, and such paintings create a very different mood from that of high-key ones. In our subconscious minds, darkness is associated with night, which in turn we associate with mystery, suspense, and emotions such as sadness, fear and loneliness. Dark values can also create a feeling of strength and calm. By choosing your subject carefully and using colours in the mid to dark value range, you can use the psychological effect of darkness and shadow to create exciting, dramatic images.

The example shown above demonstrates the powerful impact low-key paintings can have, both visually and emotionally. The appeal of such paintings lies in their air of mystery, and humans have a strong fascination for the mysterious – as all good film-makers know. After all, doesn't the figure lurking in the shadows strike us with far more terror than seeing the monster face to face?

In the same way, the most memorable paintings are always those that leave just a little to the imagination of the viewer. The portraits that Rembrandt painted are a classic example of this. Rembrandt knew how to use shadow as a veil, softening harsh outlines and creating a subtle atmosphere around the subject. His figures, softly lit, emerge from the shadows and yet seem a part of them. We are mesmerized, and the image continues to haunt us long after we first saw it.

Of course Rembrandt was a great master, and his technical skill with paint was astounding. But don't let that inhibit you: simply study Rembrandt's paintings to absorb the mood they convey, and then see how you can create that mood through your own style of painting.

Never underestimate the value of *the power to suggest*. When we first start painting, we strive to render everything as clearly as possible in the mistaken belief that clarity equals realism. The result, of course, is that the subject ends up looking flat and two-dimensional, more like a cartoon than a painting. With more experience, we learn how to soften an edge here, darken a value there, and skilfully blend one area into another, in the interests of creating a picture that breathes and has life.

Choosing your Subject

As with high-key paintings, it's important that your subject is suited to the low-key approach. A portrait of a child, for example, would not generally be a suitable choice; but portraits of men – particularly older men – benefit from the use of low-key lighting that emphasizes rugged features. Low-key portraits of women work equally well, conveying a sense of mystery and introspection.

A still-life of inanimate objects doesn't necessarily suggest a particular mood; it's up to you to create one. Try placing your still-life against a dark background, lit by a small light source placed to one side of the group. This will create intriguing highlights and shadows, lending a subtle atmosphere and a mood of intimacy.

Outdoors, the low-key mood is more difficult to achieve because you have no control over the lighting. But landscape artists can take advantage of weather effects that create dramatic pictures; even the most ordinary scene is transformed when a storm threatens, or when dusk approaches. Or you could try painting a woodland scene, with shafts of pale sunlight breaking through the gloom.

Mood in Landscapes

In a landscape subject, one of the most important elements to consider is light, because light affects both the values and colours of a picture, and both have a significant effect on mood. Claude Monet put it beautifully when he said: "For me, a landscape does not exist in its own right, since its appearance changes at every moment; but the surrounding atmosphere brings it to life – the air and the light, which vary continually."

Monet became so fascinated by the effects of light and colour that he would happily return again and again to the same scene, painting it at different times of the day and in all seasons. Making a series of paintings of the same subject over a period of time is certainly an exercise worth trying, because it demonstrates how even quite small changes in the lighting can alter the balance of values in a picture, and therefore alter the mood it conveys.

above: Lucy Willis, *Beach Boats,* watercolour. This painting emanates a bracing, seaside atmosphere. A sprinkling of dark values helps to accentuate the crisp, bright light that fills the scene.

left: David Hutter, *Looking Toward Colley Hill,* watercolour. The full drama of rolling storm clouds is captured in this exciting and unusual composition, in which the dark shape formed by the clouds is echoed in the landscape.

left: David Hutter, *Chateau de la Motte,* watercolour. This painting captures the eerie light that occurs when sunlight slices through a gap in storm clouds and spotlights parts of the landscape, creating a dramatic reversal of the normal pattern of dark land against light sky.

For example, a seascape viewed at midday might look flat and uninteresting because the light is very even and there is little contrast in values. But a few hours later, as the sun is going down, the luminous values of the evening sky contrast with the cool blue values of the sea and the land, creating a subtle and evocative image.

The seasons, too, offer splendid opportunities to explore the magic of light on the landscape. In winter, bleakness, silence and isolation can provide strong mood-themes, as when the branches of bare trees create dramatic patterns of light and dark against the sky. Then again, the same scene is transformed by the sparkling light of a bright frosty morning; this time you might choose a limited range of light values with which to capture the bright, high-key mood. A snow-covered landscape on a dull day creates bold patterns of light and dark and there's also an interesting reversal of values as the sky, for once, appears darker than the land, creating a bleak, wintry feeling.

Viewpoint and composition are important elements in creating mood. The brooding atmosphere of an approaching storm is made more dramatic by placing the horizon line very low so as to place emphasis on the sky. On a sunny day you could try positioning your easel so that much of the view is in shadow except for one telling, sunlit spot. This will create a more dramatic and unusual picture than if the subject were evenly lit.

Using Limited Tones

To capture a fleeting mood successfully, it is best to restrict yourself to a limited number of values. Light, by its very nature, is elusive and ever-changing, and often there just isn't time to worry about the finer points – you have to sacrifice details and concentrate on capturing the essentials. With a particularly complex lighting effect, I often make a few simple monochrome sketches in watercolour, using only five values, and these give me enough information about the mood of the scene to be able to create a full-scale painting when I get back to the studio. This method has much to recommend it, in fact, because it forces you to work from memory when recording the details of form and colour. Memory is selective – it "edits out" most of the superfluous details, leaving you with a clear recollection of the elements that most impressed you at first sight. This process of distillation is vital to the success of a picture, because your aim, after all, is to communicate to the viewer the same thrill that you felt – the thrill of the first impression, uncluttered by distracting details.

Even when I make a full-scale painting based on my sketches, I still try to keep to a limited range of values, because the fewer the values, the more forceful the statement. Remember that as an artist you are in control – you're free to use the subject as a starting point, and to try to express your ideas and feelings about it, rather than slavishly copying everything that's in front of you.

right: Ken Howard, *The Grand Canal, September Evening,* watercolour and gouache. This painting captures that magical time of day, just before the sun sinks, when the sky takes on a luminous aspect and the values of the land are reduced to pale, shadowy forms. The sparkling path of sunlight on the water adds a palpable sense of atmosphere and light.

left: Moira Clinch, *The Auvergne*, watercolour. Strong contrasts between warm and cool colour and light and dark values lend a vibrant mood to this sunny landscape in southern France.

Mood in Interiors

Domestic interiors are often not seen as suitable painting subjects by beginners, perhaps because they are so much a part of everyday life that it's easy to take them for granted. This is a pity, since interior scenes offer marvellous opportunities for creating unusual and exciting tonal compositions. Whether illuminated by natural daylight or artificial light, the closed environment of a room is rich with luminous values and soft, deep shadows that create a calm and tranquil atmosphere.

Interiors offer one distinct advantage over landscapes in that you can control both the compositional arrangement of the subject and, to a great extent, the lighting, so as to express what you want to say in your picture. The following are just some of the ideas worth considering:

- A darkened room with an open door in the background that offers a tantalizing glimpse of a scene beyond. The scene might be part of a sunlit landscape, or another room that is brightly lit; this will give you an opportunity to explore the dramatic contrast of light and dark values and warm and cool colours.
- An interior at evening, lit only by a table lamp that sheds a soft pool of light in an otherwise shadowy room. This sets up an intimate, low-key mood.
- Sunlight filtering through thin curtains that bathes the room in diffused light that lends a still, timeless atmosphere.
- To create a mysterious and evocative mood, include a shadowy figure, perhaps sitting at the fireside or reading by a lamp.

Before you begin to paint it's a good idea to make value sketches of the room from different viewpoints, until you find the composition that appeals to you. Observe how and where the light falls. Do the shadows and highlights create interesting patterns? Is the main area of light positioned where you want the centre of interest to be? Is there a lively interplay of shapes and angles formed by the walls, floors, windows and furniture? All these things must be carefully considered; if necessary, rearrange, add or subtract objects until you get the effect you want. This is part of the process of learning to select from what you see in order to amplify what you want your painting to say.

below: Keith Andrew, *Interior, Gwyndy Bach.* Subtle colours and soft mid-tones contribute to the quiet mood of this domestic interior.

above: Lucy Willis, *Hoya in the Window,* watercolour. Another scene, this time with a much more high-key mood. The composition consists of a "frame within a frame". The warm greens of the garden, seen through the window, are surrounded and emphasized by the cool blues of the interior wall. Little slivers of bare white paper activate the painting and give an impression of sparkling light.

Mood in Portraits

Painting a portrait involves much more than simply achieving a likeness. Your painting should also say something about the character and personality of the sitter, an emotional quality that the viewer can empathize with. In this respect, the amount, quality and direction of the light will have an influence on the impression you wish to convey. As in a landscape, lighting affects the values and colours in the subject, which in turn convey a particular atmosphere and sense of place and time. For example, bright sunlight creates strong contrasts that convey energy and light-heartedness, whereas low lighting conveys an air of mystery and introspection.

You can also play two sources of light on the subject: the cool, weak daylight coming in from a window and the stronger, warmer light of a lamp. This creates a range of warm and cool colours that give a special luminosity to the portrait.

So before you start painting a portrait, first decide what kind of mood you wish to convey and arrange the lighting accordingly. Even if you don't have a proper studio, this shouldn't be too difficult; all you need is a couple of lights with adjustable stands.

below: Three-quarter lighting is so called because it falls on about three-quarters of the face. It is demonstrated in David Hutter's *Portrait of Geof Kitching* (below). This is the most popular type of lighting for most subjects, but is especially good for portraits, since not only does it give a strong impression of volume and surface texture, it also creates a satisfying range of tonal variations that give life and vitality to a portrait. If your sitter has strong features or a dynamic personality, use three-quarter lighting to emphasize these qualities.

Consider whether you want to view the sitter from the shadow side or the light side. Facing the sitter's shadow side is best for expressing strong character; facing the light side creates a softer, more subtle effect. It's also worth experimenting with the angle and height of the lamp to see how this affects the shadows and highlights. Watch particularly for the shadow cast by the nose – a strong shadow reaching right down to the mouth can create a rather unattractive effect.

above: David Hutter, *Portrait of Geof Kitching*, watercolour.

right: Side lighting is another type of lighting popular with portrait painters. This time the face is lit directly from one side, leaving the other side in shadow, as in the *Portrait of Andrew Uter* (above right). The strong contrast between light and shadow creates a sense of drama and tension in a low-key portrait, but care must be taken that the effect is not too theatrical. To soften the values slightly on the shadow side, use a white or reflective board to create "fill in" light in the shadow area. This also creates subtle reflected lights in the hair that prevent it from looking "dead"

Experiment with the colours, perhaps using cool ones on the shadow side and warm ones on the lit side to emphasize the contrast, and add highlights on the brow, nose and chin.

below right: Rembrant lighting is a moody, dramatic lighting effect – named after the great Dutch master, who used it in many of his portraits Here a small concentrated light source is positioned to one side so that the light falls at a sharp angle. This creates a spotlight effect, in which the sitter is revealed in dramatic contrast against a dark, shadowy background. Because the angle of the light is so sharp, it casts deep shadows into the eye sockets and plunges the lower part of the face into near-darkness. If handled well, this type of lighting lends a mysterious, enigmatic mood to a portrait, but obviously it is only suitable for some subjects.

The near-silhouette effect created by placing the sitter in front of a soft, diffused light source is known as **contre jour,** which means "against the light". This creates a soft halo of light around the subject, while the facial features are almost lost in shadow. The effect is soft and mysterious, with a wonderful depth and richness of tone. If you're lucky, a small amount of light coming from slightly to one side will illuminate just a few telling edges of the subject – an effect known as "edge light" or "rim light" – adding even greater luminosity to the picture.

For a contre-jour portrait, the sitter should be placed at an angle to a window so that the face is seen in profile or semi-profile. The light should be weak or diffused; if necessary hang a lace curtain at the window to soften the effect of bright sunlight. If the silhouette looks too flat, try placing a reflective board opposite the window to bounce some light back onto the face.

above: David Hutter, *Portrait of Andrew Uter*, watercolour.

left: Rembrandt was a master of lighting effects, as this self-portrait (*Self-portrait with Maulstick, Palette and Brushes, c.*1663, oil on canvas) demonstrates. The figure emerges out of dusk, giving an impressive isolation to the personality of the artist.

above: John Tookey, *Venetian Backstreet,* 29.2 x 21.6 cm (11½ x 8½ in), watercolour and felt-tipped pen. Imagine what this scene would look like under a flat grey drizzle – the buildings would hold no interest for an artist because there be almost no colour or tonal contrast. Tookey has wisely chosen to paint at a time when the sun has turned the right-hand block into a rich gold and cast a decisive slanting shadow across the street. His colour scheme is simple but effective: he has enhanced the yellow by using its complementary, blue-violet, repeated in small patches in several places to unify the composition.

Using Shadows Creatively

As a child I used to love lying in front of the living room fire on winter evenings and watching as the light from the flickering flames sent huge, liquid shadows leaping and dancing around the walls of the room. The shadows of chairs, teacups and potted plants, distorted and elongated, turned into fairies and witches and monsters in my still-fertile imagination.

Film-makers have always known how to use the dramatic potential of shadows to intensify the emotional effect of a scene. We've all gripped our seats while watching a thriller in which someone is being followed down a dimly lit street; we don't get to see the mysterious follower – only his shadow cast on the pavement – and this makes our imagination begin to work overtime. Somehow, being able to see only the shadow heightens the tension and has a far more menacing effect than if the identity of the man were revealed.

The same power of suggestion can be used to great effect in a painting, turning an ordinary image into one that's arresting, mysterious and evocative. Rembrandt achieved powerful dramatic moods through his use of deep, luminous shadows that enveloped most of the subject, just leaving a telling highlight here and there. Salvador Dali (b. 1904) and Giorgio de'Chirico (1888–1978) used very long or distorted shadows to accentuate the timeless, dreamlike atmosphere in their Surrealist paintings. The American painter Edward Hopper (1882–1967) painted people isolated within stark interiors or on deserted streets, and once again cast shadows are used to heighten the sense of loneliness and alienation.

But shadows are not always dramatic or threatening; they can also introduce beauty and poetry to a painting. Most landscape painters prefer to work in the early morning or late afternoon, when the sun is at a low angle to the earth and trees and buildings cast long, descriptive shadows. My own favourite painting time is later afternoon on a sunny day in autumn, when everything is bathed in a soft, golden light and the lengthening shadows lend a magical air of calm and stillness to the scene.

When a cast shadow travels across another object that lies in its path, that object becomes much more interesting to look at. In addition to describing three-dimensional form, the graphic lines of the shadows offer an interesting paradox: unconsciously we shift back and forth between seeing the shadows as a descriptive element and as a purely abstract pattern. In this way our imagination is fuelled and we play an active part in the work.

Carry a sketchbook with you whenever you can and make visual notes of any interesting shadow patterns you come across, such as those cast by a tree, or a wrought-iron gate, or the dappled shadows of trees and plants on a garden path. Indoors you can experiment by moving a lamp around the room, shining it on objects from different heights and angles to see what kind of shadows it creates (adjustable desk lamps are great for this).

The Colours You Will Need

The three primary colours – red, yellow and blue – can be mixed to produce all the other colours, so obviously these must be included in our basic palette. But if we ask in our local art shop for red, yellow and blue paint, we will be asked "Which one?" because there are so many different reds, yellows and blues to choose from. The first ones to buy must be of the brightest, most intense hues because mixing always results in loss of colour intensity.

When I started painting landscapes (in gouache), I used a very limited palette consisting only of cadmium scarlet, lemon yellow, French ultramarine and permanent white. I didn't even use black, relying instead on obtaining the darkest tones by mixing the scarlet with the ultramarine and a touch of yellow. However, I needed colours not obtainable by mixing the three primaries, so I began to extend my palette with violet, magenta and different versions of the primary colours – alizarin crimson, cadmium yellow and cobalt blue. I also added browns (raw umber, burnt umber), yellow ochre and black.

The Blue Paints

If you want to buy only one blue, I would suggest French ultramarine, a strong, rich paint. Other artists might recommend the greener and slightly paler cobalt blue, but ultramarine is that bit brighter and more versatile even though a little less permanent. I always find that it mixes better than cobalt blue and can form a greater range of colours when combined with other paints.

Whichever one you choose at first, make yourself thoroughly familiar with it and then try the other. Later on you could buy a tube of cerulean blue. This is particularly suitable for some skies, but although a lovely rich hue, it has low colouring power. Prussian blue, a very strong greenish blue, is favoured by some painters, as is phthalocyanine blue (or simply phthalo), similiar to Prussian blue, but even more intense and with a higher permanency rating. Proprietary names for it include monestial blue (Rowney) and Winsor blue (Winsor & Newton). Both these blues have high colouring strength and can be mixed with yellows to form very rich but to my mind rather synthetic-looking greens.

The Yellow and Brown Paints

There are two bright yellows which should be included in any palette – cadmium yellow and lemon yellow. Cadmium yellow is the warmer colour, with a hint of orange in it. It mixes with the blues to form warm yellowish greens. Lemon yellow is cooler and paler, and forms blueish greens when mixed with the blues.

Yellow ochre also has a place on most artists' palettes. It is a dark yellow verging on the brown. It has great strength and mixes well when added in small amounts. A similar colour is raw sienna, which is slightly redder than yellow ochre and less powerful, making fine adjustments easier when mixing.

Also available are cadmium yellow pale and cadmium yellow deep, but neither are really necessary, as both can be made, in the first case by mixing cadmium yellow with a little white, and in the second by adding a little ochre. Naples yellow, on the other hand, is a useful colour for obtaining skin tones, although it can be imitated by mixing yellow ochre with white and a tiny proportion of cadmium yellow. Other yellows include aureolin, chrome yellow and chrome lemon. These are less permanent and generally can achieve nothing which cadmium yellow or lemon yellow cannot do.

There are only two browns which I use regularly and which I recommend to start with. The first is raw umber, a versatile, slightly greenish brown ideal for dulling the blues, yellows and greens; it has a fairly low strength so is easy to mix. The second is burnt sienna, a rich reddish brown which has such colouring power that even tiny quantities added to a mixture can alter it drasticaly. Burnt sienna mixed with white forms a warm pink. I often use it to modify blue and white mixtures to obtain sky tones. Another useful, though not essential, brown is burnt umber, which I think of as being the "brownest" of the browns.

The Red Paints

The essential reds are cadmium red, a dense, opaque colour, and alizarin crimson, a deep, powerful, transparent one. Cadmium red is very brilliant, identical in colour to poppies, but it loses its identity quickly on mixing with other colours. Mixed with white, it forms a warm pink, and mixed with blue, a very muddy purple. It is at its best when used straight from the tube, or either darkened with alizarin crimson or lightened with yellow ochre. Mixing it with cadmium yellow gives a brilliant orange, identical to cadmium orange, so it is unnecessary to buy an orange paint. Alizarin crimson is most useful in mixtures. I find I use it constantly – with white to make a cool pink; with blues to counteract their brilliance when painting sky and sea; and combined with yellows and browns to achieve skin tones. (Alizarin is one of the slowest paints to dry on your palette, and areas of painting where it has been used will remain tacky for a long time.)

Occasionally you may find you require even more brilliance than can be given by these two reds, for instance when painting flowers. This subject may call for the use of paints like magenta (a purplish version of alizarin), carmine, the various rose colours (Rowney rose, rose doré, rose madder), geranium and perhaps vermilion. This last, an intense, warm red, is one of the most expensive paints available, and is definitely not essential. The carmine and rose colours must be used with caution as they are less permanent than the other reds.

The Green Paints

A range of greens, including most of those occurring in a natural landscape, can be mixed from yellows with either blues or black, so you may not need to buy any greens initially. However, you will soon find you want some of the brighter greens to cope with the man-made colours of clothing or paintwork and also vegetation in unusual lighting conditions such as sunlit foliage sparkling in a dark forest. Viridian is perhaps the most useful. It is dark and transparent, cool and blueish. When mixed with white, it retains its hue, giving pale, cool greens which cannot be matched by mixing yellow and blue. The opaque counterpart of viridian is called opaque oxide of chromium. Many painters use it a great deal for landscape.

Brighter than these two are colours like chrome green and cadmium green, both pale, yellowish greens which can be good on occasion for foliage. Another useful green is terre verte, a dull green of low colouring power. Straight from the tube, it is often identical to the dark foliage in a landscape, and I use it frequently in mixtures to modify the colours of sky, sea, foliage, flowers, skin – in fact almost anything! However, it is not essential, since an identical green can be mixed from cadmium yellow, lamp black and a little ultramarine. Emerald green in the Winsor & Newton range is an artificial-looking, pale colour which does not mix well, but in some ranges it is an excellent and reliable alternative for viridian.

The Purple and Violet Paints

Purple, like the greens, can be mixed, but only in a low intensity. The brightest violets or purples will have to be taken straight from the tube or mixed together to yield exactly the colour you want. Cobalt violet is excellent, but I find the most useful is Winsor violet which, when mixed with rose madder, alizarin crimson or magenta, together with white, will give almost any violet or purple. It is also extremely useful for modifying the blues of the sky or sea, and for making greys with yellows, browns and greens.

The Black and Grey Paints

I mainly use black for mixing with yellow to make greens, and for this I use lamp black, which is slightly bluer than ivory black. Black will also darken any green, but only small amounts should be used, and it destroys the vitality of other colours, so should be treated with caution. Sometimes, of course, these dark tones can be just what one needs, as when painting the very darkest shadows. In such cases, ivory black is the best one to use, as it's more neutral and a little more transparent. I also use Payne's grey a good deal. This is basically a kind of dilute black which, having relatively less strength, is very useful for modifying blues, browns and greens.

The White Paints

Note that white does not form part of the watercolour palette; the paler tones are achieved by allowing the paper to shine through very thin, dilute washes, while pure white areas in your picture are simply the paper left uncovered. Chinese white, however, a form of zinc white, is useful for adding highlights towards the end of the painting or for correcting small mistakes.

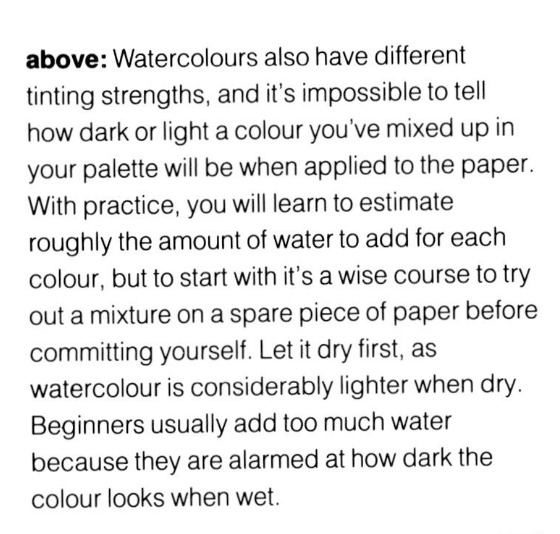

above: Watercolours also have different tinting strengths, and it's impossible to tell how dark or light a colour you've mixed up in your palette will be when applied to the paper. With practice, you will learn to estimate roughly the amount of water to add for each colour, but to start with it's a wise course to try out a mixture on a spare piece of paper before committing yourself. Let it dry first, as watercolour is considerably lighter when dry. Beginners usually add too much water because they are alarmed at how dark the colour looks when wet.

Qualities of Paint

Transparency

One of the most exciting, if unpredictable, qualities of watercolour is its ability to impart colour while allowing underlying layers to remain visible to a greater or lesser degree. Linked to this is the way in which pigments can be diluted with water so that the white of the paper itself dilutes the colour, rather than "polluting" the colour with white, as is the case with opaque paints. Because of the transparency of watercolour, the usual way of working is from light to dark, gradually building up layers. Transparency, however, is relative, and because some pigments are considerably more opaque than others they are categorized as transparent or semi-transparent and semi-opaque.

The amount of water used is a matter of personal preference, but generally a tighter more detailed style uses a higher mix of pigment to water than a looser one. As a rule the more water used the more unpredictable the result. No two mixes will ever contain the same amount of water, and the solution with the higher percentage of water will "run" into the less diluted mix. This "pushes" the pigment creating intriguing, if unpredictable, effects. Tantalizingly, it is seldom possible to recreate them, as they are never exactly the same.

Permanence

Watercolours are graded for permanence, the main categories being extremely permanent, durable, moderately durable and fugitive. Some colours which are durable in strong washes are less durable when applied in thin washes, and other colours fluctuate; they fade in sunlight and recover in the dark.

Mixing Qualities

Some pigments mix very evenly whilst others mix creating granular or interesting mottled effects.

above: The chart shows how both dark and opaque pigments can cover earlier layers of colour when used with very little water (top). The more water used to dilute the pigment the more transparent it becomes (bottom).

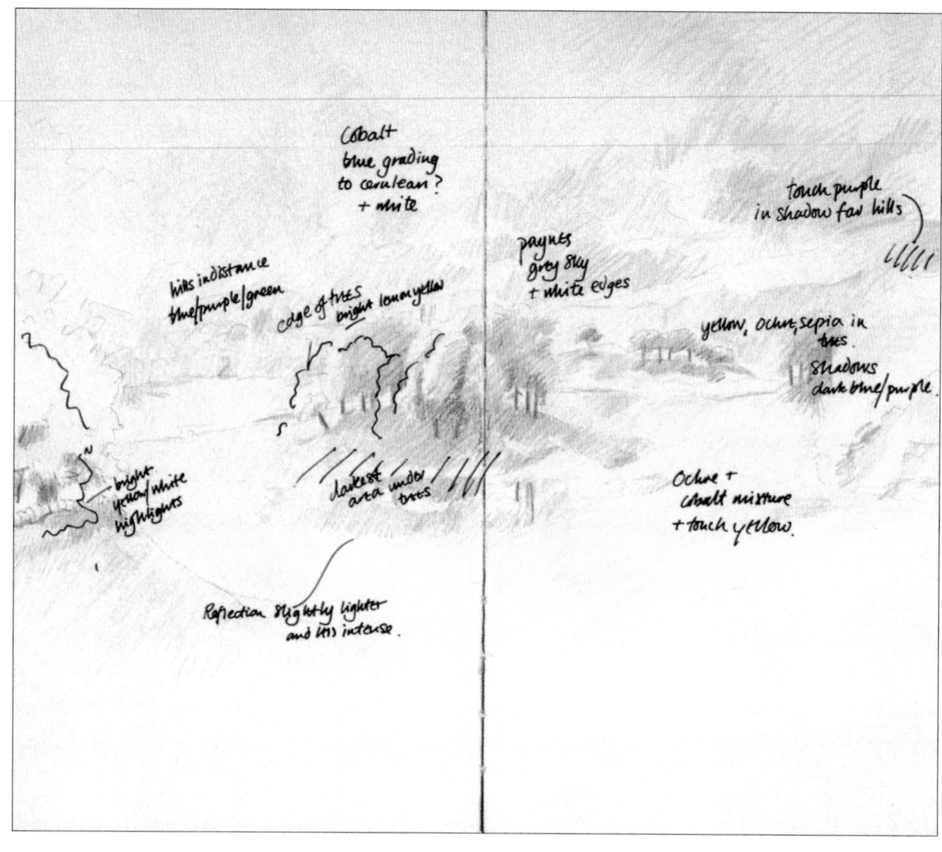

above: Moira Clinch, *Rydal Water,* watercolour, 71 x 50.8 cm (28 x 20 in). This artist works in watercolour, but often uses crayons to record her on-the-spot impressions. "My watercolours are fairly large, and I'm a slow worker, so I usually do the actual painting in the studio, from sketches, notes and sometimes a photograph. Coloured pencils are a handy sketching medium, and I tend to carry them around with me, sometimes making this kind of colour notation in the car if the weather is cold. Here I've put down a general impression of the colours, but as pencils are a cruder medium than watercolour I like to make written notes as well. The most important things to note in this case were the direction and quality of the light, both of which radically affect the choice of colours for the finished painting."

Judging Colour Relationships

Colour relationships can be established by continually comparing your picture to your subject, and marking alterations and modifications until you judge the relationships to be satisfactory. This does require very careful observation which develops with experience. Try to look at the world around you with a painter's eye all the time, thinking which colours you could mix for that yellow-edged cloud or those interesting greenish shadows on the unlit side of someone's face. You'll learn a lot, and you may find being stuck in a traffic jam less frustrating.

A good way of analysing colour changes is to use a piece of card with a 0.6 cm (¼ inch) hole cut in it. Hold this up about a foot from you and look at an area of colour which appears at first sight to be the same all over – an orange, for example, or the cover of a sketchbook. The little square of colour you see, isolated from its neighbours, will look pretty meaningless, but now try moving the card slightly and you will begin to see variations in the colour. You will notice darker shadow areas and slight changes in colour intensity caused by reflected light or the proximity of a different-coloured object. By taking one area of colour out of context you are able to see what is really happening in terms of colour instead of simply what you expect. You don't have to use a piece of card – your fist with a little hole between the fingers will do.

Making Colour Notes

Here we show some systems for making colour notes so that the artist can recreate a scene in the studio. You may remember the general impression of a colour, but no one can recall the subtle variations, so if you're out looking for a likely landscape subject try to jot down some impressions on a rough pencil sketch. This can be done in words, for instance "sky very dark blue-grey, mixture of Payne's grey and ultramarine". If you have paints, pastels, or even crayons with you, make some quick visual notes there and then, trying out various combinations until you are satisfied.

A Personal Palette

Autumn in the Jura, David Hutter, 27.9 x 38.1 cm (11 x 15 in), watercolour. Watercolourists tend to use a more restricted palette than oil painters, and this subtle but colourful picture has been done with only seven colours. The paints have been applied very freely and directly, with some colours mixing wet-in-wet on the paper. In the foreground, a mixture of raw sienna and aureolin was laid down first, and then a second one, of cobalt blue, cerulean and a lighter yellow, was laid on top so that the two flooded together. Notice how the artist has used pencil as another "colour" in places, rather than painting in the outlines of branches with a fine brush.

The Artist's Palette

Cobalt blue

Cerulean blue

Antwerp blue

Aureolin yellow

Raw sienna

Burnt umber

Burnt sienna

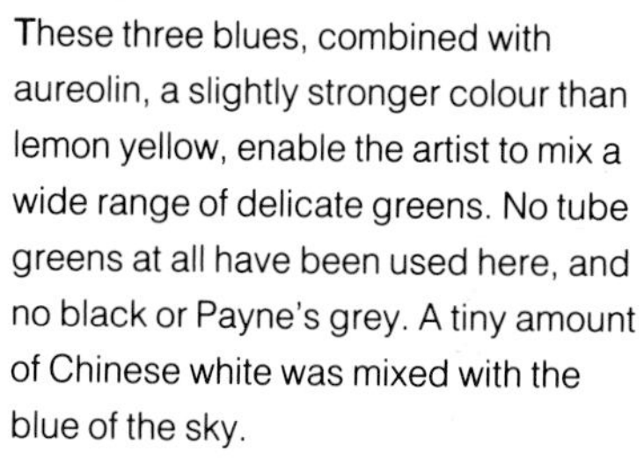

These three blues, combined with aureolin, a slightly stronger colour than lemon yellow, enable the artist to mix a wide range of delicate greens. No tube greens at all have been used here, and no black or Payne's grey. A tiny amount of Chinese white was mixed with the blue of the sky.

Colour Combinations

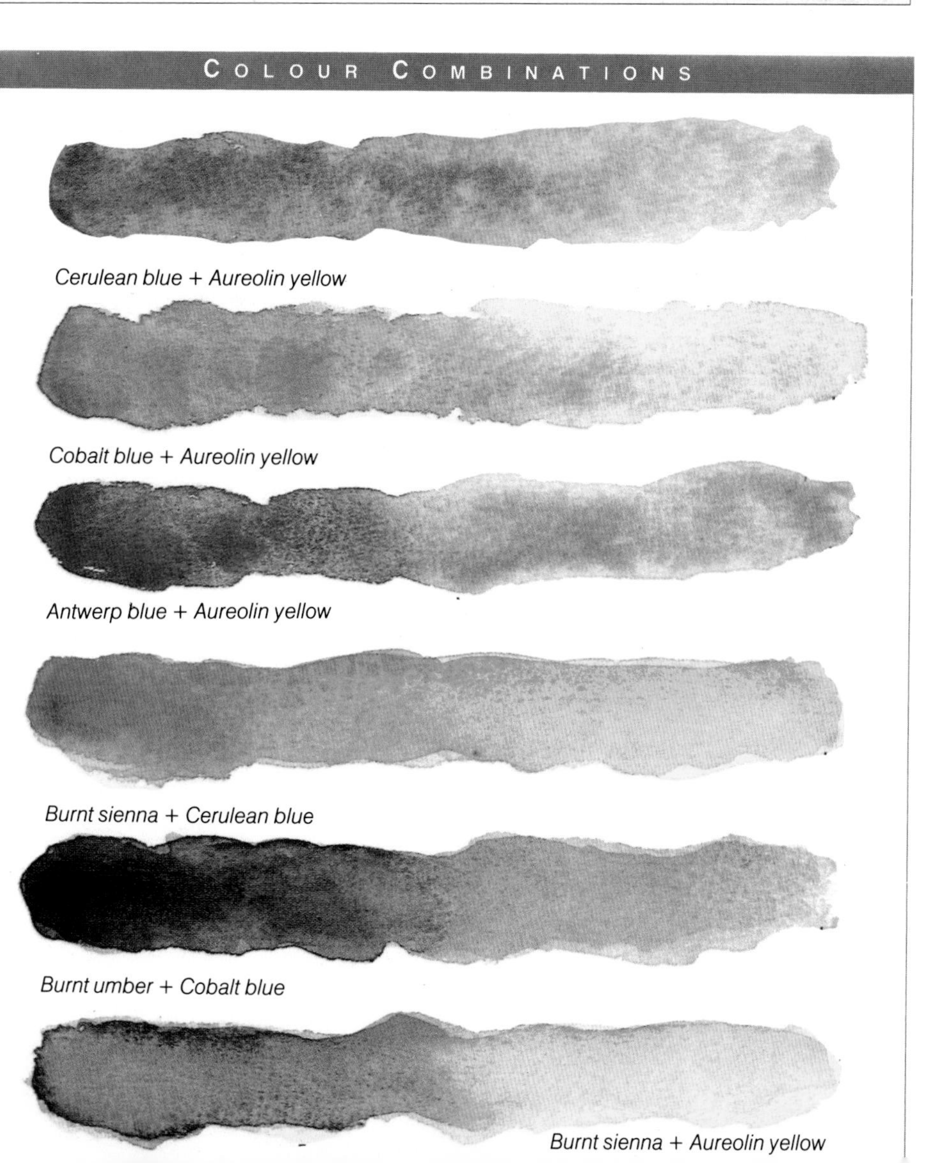

Cerulean blue + Aureolin yellow

Cobalt blue + Aureolin yellow

Antwerp blue + Aureolin yellow

Burnt sienna + Cerulean blue

Burnt umber + Cobalt blue

Burnt sienna + Aureolin yellow

FLOWER COLOURS

Particularly when painting flowers flowers, it is important to keep the colours fresh and vibrant. This can be done by avoiding over-mixing. To achieve greater luminosity for painting delicate petals, the more transparent the paint the better, as the white paper can reflect through it. Instead of using the more opaque cadmium colours, those such as permanent yellow, permanent red or vermilion may be a better choice (though vermilion is very expensive). Ultramarine and cerulean are less transparent than cobalt or phthalo blue. Cerulean is quite surprisingly opaque, and needs to be handled with some caution.

Sometimes flowers are actually less colourful than they seem – it is more a case of what we expect than what we really see. For instance, we all know that daffodils are yellow, but when we set about painting them it comes as a surprise to find that very little yellow paint is needed. A major proportion of the petal turns out to be shades of green and ochre, but a casual glance at a picture of daffodils still shows us the flowers as yellow.

Possible colour mixtures: flowers

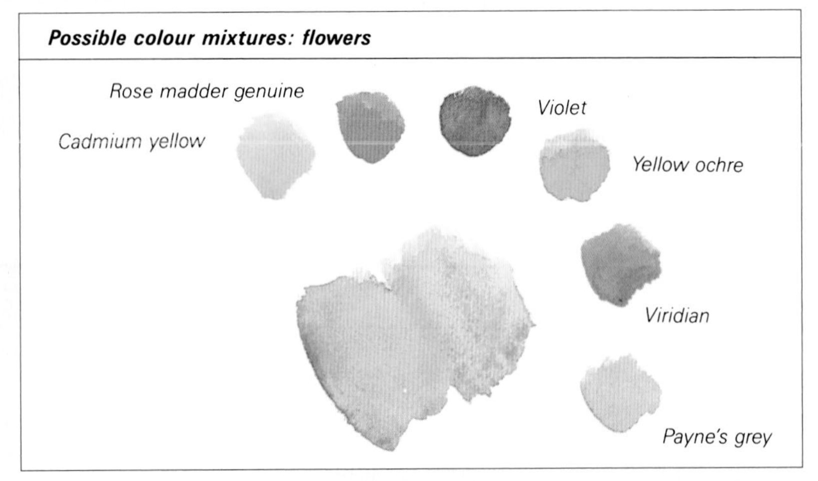

Winter Rose in a Lalique Vase, David Hunter, 30.4 x 25.4 cm (12 x 10 in), watercolour. The vibrant pinks and yellow-greens in this lovely, delicate painting owe much of their richness to the colour of the background, which has been chosen with great care. A neutral but far from characterless grey-brown, it is dark enough to make the flowers and leaves stand out but not so dark they look like paper cut-outs. The flowers themselves are carefully modelled, and the rose shows a considerable range of both tones and colours, from the pale pink highlights at the edges of the petals to the dark blue-red of the shadows.

The Mechanics of Mixing Paints

Oil paints and acrylics, with their thick consistencies, require a relatively large amount of physical effort to mix them. They can be mixed with either a brush or a palette knife. Much of the wear on brushes occurs during this mixing process and for this reason some painters mix paints only with a palette knife. However, I find this an awkward procedure, and always prefer to mix with a bristle brush – although not necessarily the brush I'm using for painting. I try to mix with old, worn brushes, but during the course of a painting often forget to use them, thus slowly ruining my good brushes! Watercolour and gouache are much thinner in consistency so are easier to mix. Only sable or soft-haired brushes are used for these media and mixing is carried out using these brushes. Care should be taken to avoid back-bending of the hairs, as this shortens their life considerably.

As for the palette, it will gradually become covered with your mixtures as the painting progresses, whatever medium you're using, so if you are working indoors try to use a fair-sized palette, as it will take you a longer time before you have to clear spaces for new colours. When I'm painting out of doors, instead of taking a large palette, I usually ensure I have two smaller ones (which both fit into my box), so I can overflow onto the second one if necessary.

The quantity of paint to mix should always be more than you think you'll need. This applies particularly to watercolour washes, which really need a lot of paint. It is infuriating to run out of a mixture which has taken a long time to make. Try to keep your mixture clean. Each colour should be thoroughly mixed – unless you want it otherwise – and not allowed to run into its neighbours. In general, you should avoid mixing colours on the painting itself; although this can be done successfully, it often leads to muddying or an uncontrollable mess.

The tubes or pots of paint themselves must be looked after carefully. It is most important that their caps are screwed on immediately after use. If not, oil paints leak everywhere; acrylics, gouaches and watercolours harden in their tubes. Pastels should be replaced in their correct position in their box, otherwise you'll never find the one you want, especially if you are using a large number.

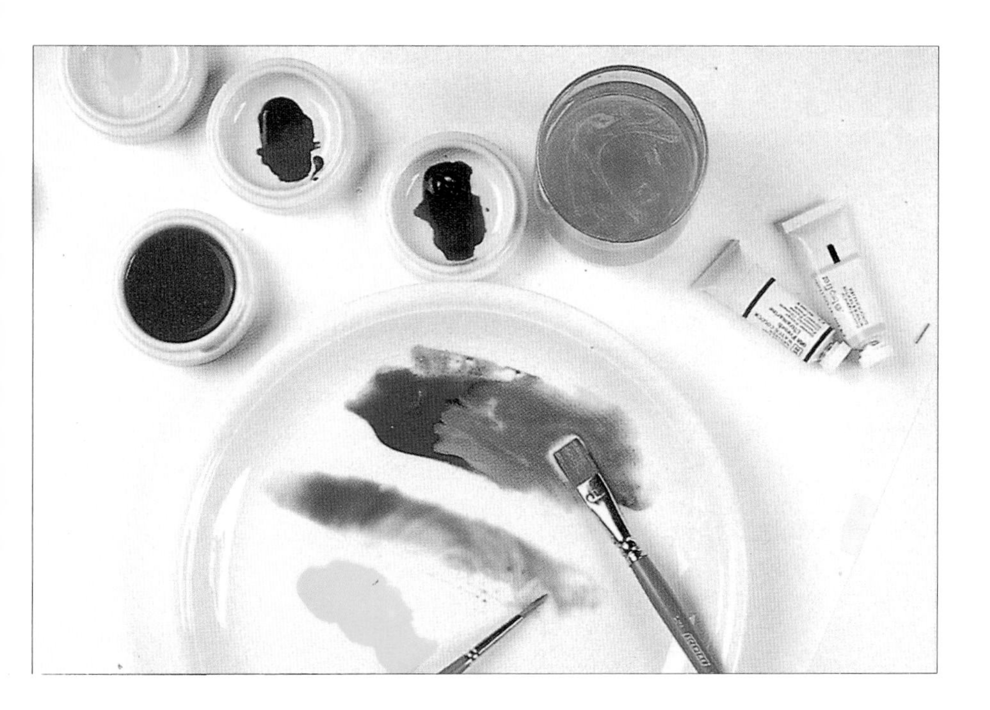

left: Watercolour washes need to be mixed in larger quantities than you think. It is always surprising how fast they are used up. You can use almost any non-absorbent white surface as a palette for watercolour or gouache, including plastic or china crockery. Take care that the colours don't run into each other on the palette (pure tube colours can be put in separate pots) and also that you use a well-cleaned brush each time a new colour is used. In contrast, it is an advantage to keep paint on the brush at the end of a day's painting as the gum binder in watercolour helps the brush to retain its shape. Remember to rinse it clean before using it again.

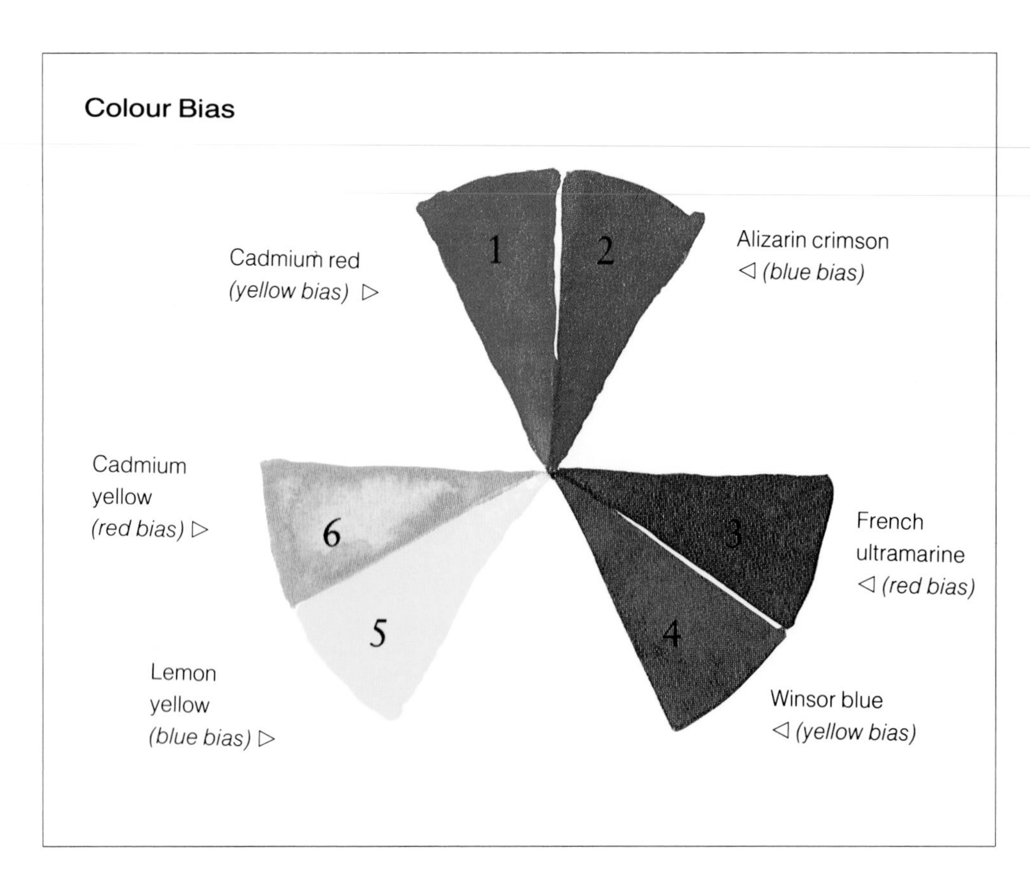

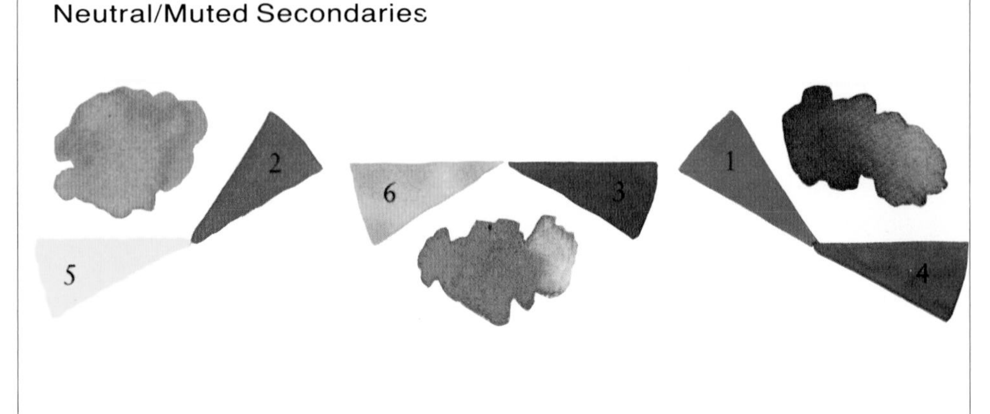

Mixing Secondary Colours

The secondary colours, green, orange and purple, can be bought as various hues in tube or pan form, but generally more colours can be achieved – and it is more fun – if you mix your own.

These pages show how by mixing two primaries together, or by mixing a primary with one of the proprietary secondaries, such as sap green or one of the purples, you can create both intense and muted secondaries.

There are some secondary hues, however, such as viridian and cadmium orange, which cannot be mixed from two primaries as they have an intensity which it is impossible to reproduce.

above left: When colours are placed next to one another you can see the colour bias.

below left: These charts show how the choice of the primary colour affects the mixture. Those closest together on the wheel create intense secondaries, while those furthest apart create neutrals.

Understanding the Mixtures

When mixing secondaries, you will need to know which of the primaries to use, as there are many versions of each one. As you can see from the colour wheel, each one has a bias towards another; for instance, cadmium red veers towards yellow, so it makes sense when trying to achieve an intense secondary to exploit this bias.

Conversely, if you want to mix a neutral secondary or neutral colours, mixing colours that contain the opposite or complementary colour on the colour wheel will give a muted or even muddy result.

Mixing Warm Pigments

The warm colours of burnt sienna, yellow ochre and burnt umber form the basis of Moira Clinch's *La Bougainvillea*. The versatility of a single watercolour pigment is demonstrated by the fact that burnt umber was used to depict both the sombre nature of the gate and the delicate plasterwork of the wall. The only difference between the two is the amount of water used to apply the paint.

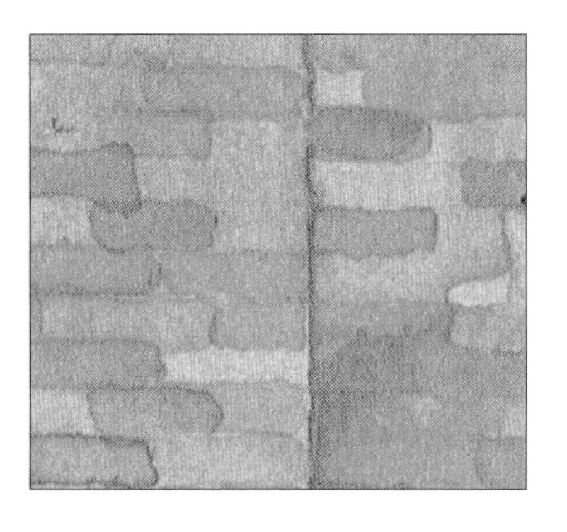

above: A strong diluted flat underwash of burnt sienna was used as the basis for the brickwork. Individual bricks were then overpainted in diluted mixtures of cadmium deep red, raw sienna and yellow ochre.

above: The highlights of the bougainvillea flowers were painted in concentrated rose madder carmine, while shadows were formed by subduing the colour with indigo.

above: The iron gate was painted in a mixture of burnt umber and lamp black, with extra black and indigo for the shadow area.

below: The shadow here was achieved by applying a medium dilution of Payne's grey over very thin dilutions of yellow ochre and raw sienna, and exceptionally thin washes of burnt umber.

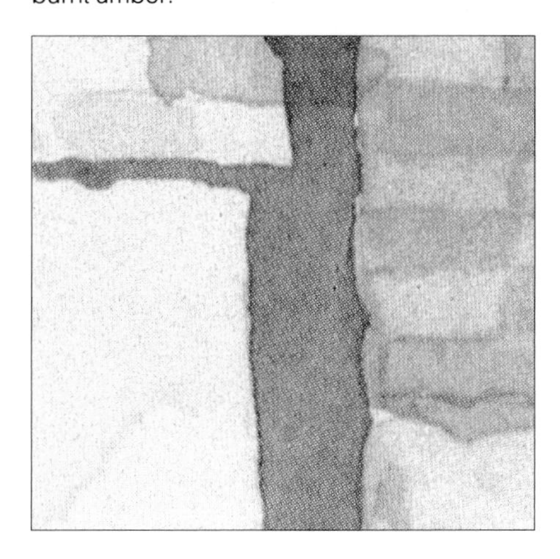

right: Moira Clinch, *Le Bougainvillea,* 48 x 33 cm (19 x 13 in).

above: The distant hills, disappearing into the mist, are painted with thin washes of cobalt and a drop of permanent rose. Cobalt was preferred to cerulean in this case as it is more transparent.

Using Browns and Blues

The gentle, nostalgic atmosphere of David Curtis's painting is emphasized by the use of soft brown tones reminiscent of a sepia photograph. The artist has used washes of raw sienna in various strengths, and this, mixed with the other pigments, creates a muted palette which helps to unify the whole painting. The colour has also been used for the surface of the water, reflecting the brown tones of the fishing boats and the quayside, and merging almost imperceptibly with the soft greys.

above: The sunlit areas of the buildings are painted with mixed washes of raw sienna and permanent rose. Details and cool shadows are defined with thin washes of cobalt, while warmer details have touches of cadmium yellow.

below: A base wash of raw sienna has again been used for the whole quayside, with highlights over-painted with a cadmium yellow wash. The green mossy walls are mixes of raw sienna, cerulean and viridian, and the deep shadow areas are wet-in-wet applications of French ultramarine, used for its transparent quality.

left: Even the red flags, which act as colour highlights, are muted, the cadmium red being subdued by adding a small amount of raw sienna. White highlights sparkle throughout the whole painting. The artist used masking fluid to reserve small areas of white paper, a method which allows the washes to be applied freely.

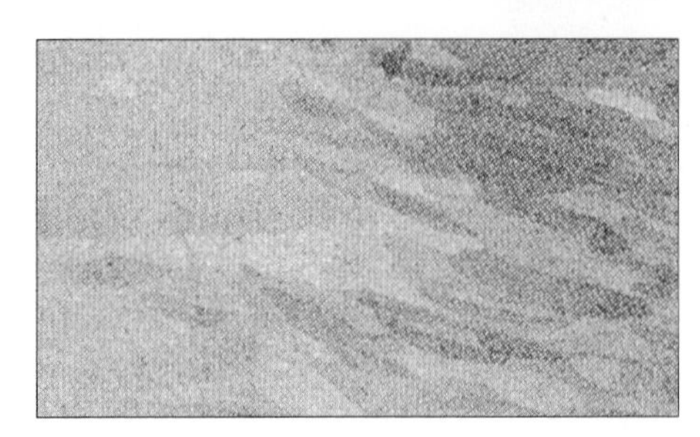

above: To achieve the effect of shimmering water the artist used washes, some being worked wet-in-wet. They consist of mixes of cerulean, cobalt and raw sienna, with delicate touches of viridian and permanent rose.

above: David Curtis, *Red Flag Markers, Whitby*, 53 x 71 cm (21 x 28 in).

Muted Colours

This painting by John Lidzey is taken from a sketchbook, and shows the art of mixing colours very clearly. The artist has used the actual page as a palette on which to mix and drop in the fluid colours. A very limited selection of colours was used to convey a dull winter's day. The cool colours – ultramarine, indigo and Payne's grey – and the spiky, linear pencil drawing emphasizes the bleak atmosphere, but this is cleverly counterbalanced by thin washes and mixes of alizarin crimson and yellow ochre, giving the painting slight touches of warmth.

above: John Lidzey, FRSA, *Fen Cottage,* 20 x 30 cm (8 x 12 in).

above: A thin dilution of yellow ochre formed the base colour of the sky, with thin touches of ultramarine and crimson added to create variety.

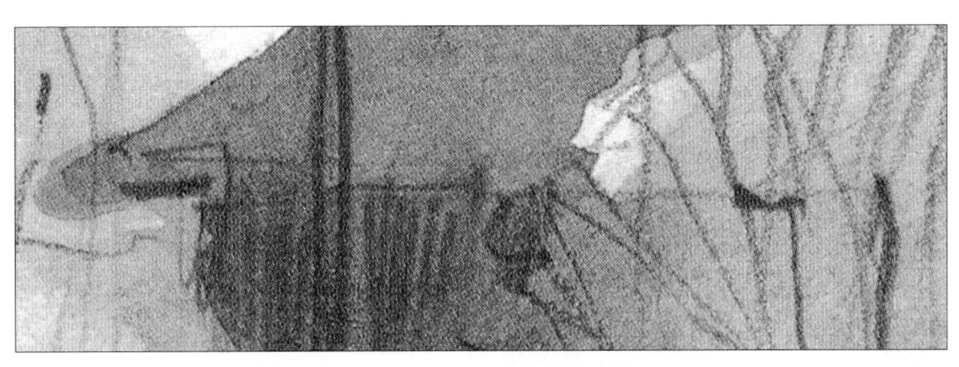

above: The basis of the whole painting can be seen in this detail: the artist has used various mixes of ultramarine, indigo, alizarin crimson and yellow ochre to create the desired cool and warm tones.

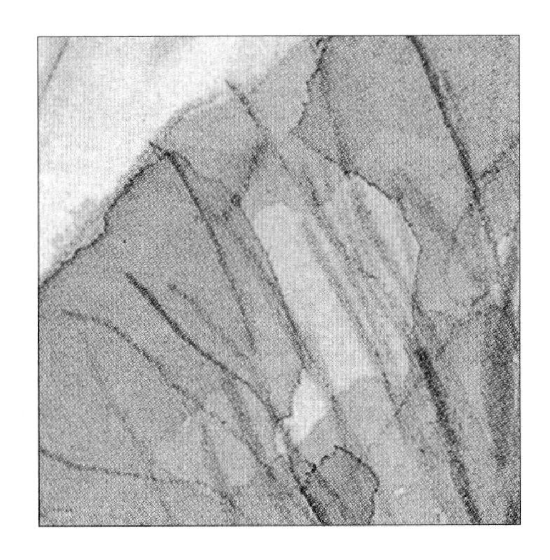

above: The skeleton drawing of the tree is given substance by washes of yellow ochre and ultramarine, with a little alizarin crimson for warmth.

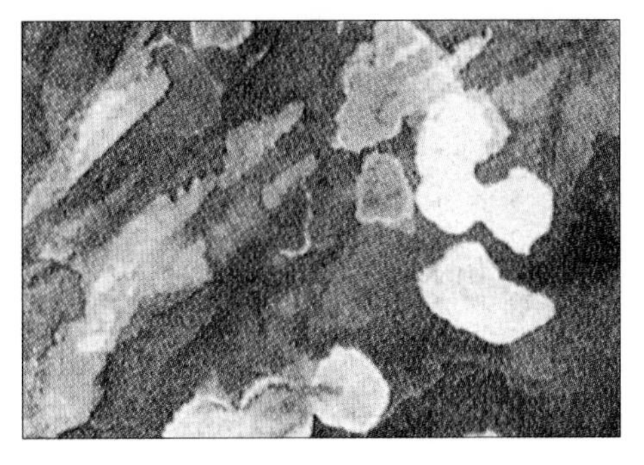

above: Dots and blobs of white gouache were used to depict the blossom on the leafless tree.

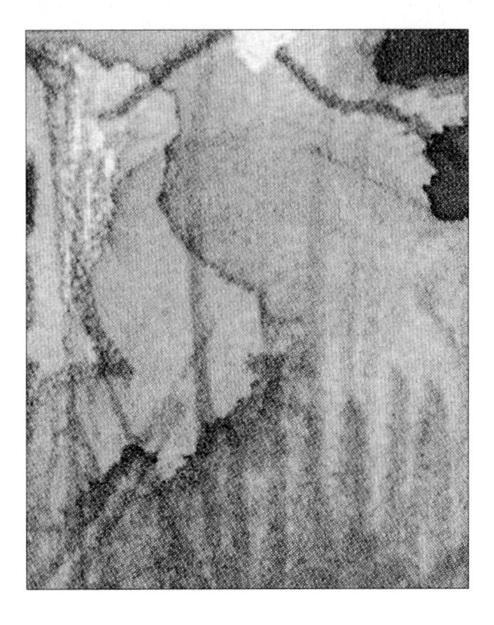

above: The subtle green hues have been achieved by mixes of aureolin yellow and indigo.

Mixing Without Muddying

No other medium can quite match up to the unique freshness and delicacy of watercolour – that is, if you know how to handle watercolour properly. For the beginner it can be very frustrating when colours that sparkle like jewels on the palette end up looking like mud on the paper.

So why do things go wrong? Mostly muddy colour is the result of muddy thinking. In an effort to make something look "real", the inexperienced painter tends to fiddle about on the paper, pushing and prodding the paint and building up dense, chalky layers of colour – as is the case in the still-life painting below.

Compare the rather gloomy aspect of the problem painting to Richard Akerman's *Floral Arrangements IV* (opposite) which is filled with radiant light, colour and excitement. Here the artist has built up his colours with thin, transparent glazes, like delicate layers of tissue paper, so that they retain their freshness and sparkle.

above: This painting illustrates all the key mistakes you need to avoid if you want clear, unmuddied results. There is no white space, the colours are overmixed, dark and dull, and have also been overworked. There is no clarity to the finished painting in contrast to *Floral Arrangements IV*, opposite, by Richard Akerman.

White Space

For some reason, novice painters usually feel compelled to obliterate every inch of the paper with colour, yet more often than not the light-reflecting surface of the paper itself has a positive part to play in the freshness and spontaneity of a watercolour painting. In *Floral Arrangements IV*, for example, areas of untouched paper breathe air and light into the painting and accentuate the delicacy of the colours.

Don't Overmix

When mixing pigments together to create a particular colour, don't be tempted to blend them so thoroughly that they become flat and lifeless. Colours *partly* mixed on the palette, so that the original pigments are still apparent, have a much livelier colour vibration. Try placing the pure, unmixed pigments on damp paper and blending them just slightly so that they fuse together wet-in-wet, as Richard Akerman has done in the background to the flowers.

Keep it Clean

When pure colour is brushed onto white paper and allowed to settle undisturbed, the effect is clear and luminous. So don't prod, poke, dab or scrub your colours once they are on the paper. Be sure of the colour you want before applying it, then brush it on quickly and confidently. Watercolour painting is like playing golf; the fewer strokes you use, the better.

Project: Avoiding Muddy Colours

Floral Arrangements IV by Richard Akerman

Layers of transparent colour applied in thin glazes build up form without looking heavy and overworked. Areas of bare paper reflect light and act as "breathing spaces".

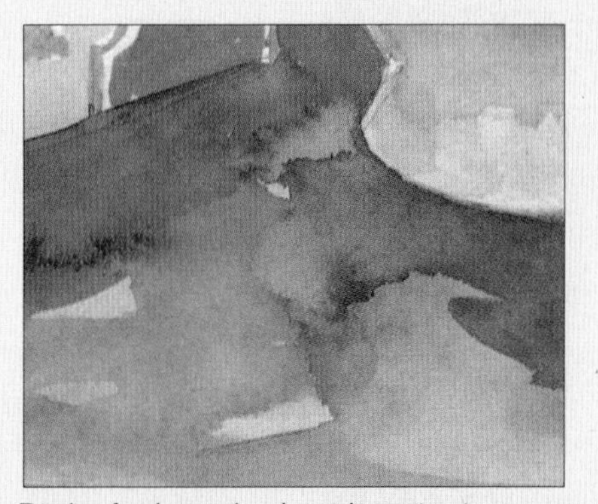

Pools of colour mixed wet-in-wet set up warm/cool colour vibrations.

Mixing too many colours together on the palette creates dense, muddy colour.

Thin, transparent glazes allow light to reflect off the paper and up through the colours, giving them greater clarity and vibrance.

Gustav Klimt

The Kiss

WATERCOLOUR

Klimt is best remembered for his designs for such projects as this mural for Josef Hoffmann's Stoclet Palace, painted in 1909.

STYLE

Before art schools were established, most artists learned to paint in the studios of successful painters. As apprentices they copied their master's work, and once they were sufficiently competent they sometimes even blocked in the master's paintings, leaving perhaps only the finishing touches to the master himself.

The tradition of copying persisted even into the Impressionist era. Pierre-Auguste Renoir (1841–1919), for example, copied the work of the great eighteenth-century masters such as Antoine Watteau (1684–1761) in the Louvre, a task that helped formulate his love of light, luminous colours. In his figure paintings, Cézanne returned constantly to arrangements based on the work of Michelangelo, Rubens and Poussin.

Actual copying continues to be practised by some artists and students today, but it is no longer obligatory. Many modern artists, however, make visual references in their work to paintings they admire, sometimes using the same compositional elements or re-interpreting a particular theme. As you develop your skills as a watercolourist, you will find it useful to study the work of past masters in order to understand and establish your own stylistic preferences.

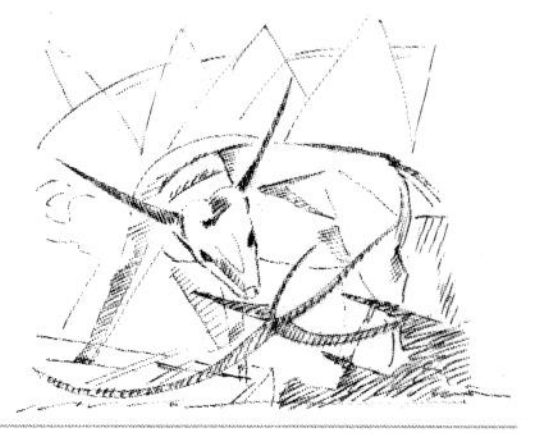

Impressionism set the standards of a new realism that we now take for granted. Despite all the innovation of twentieth-century art, Impressionist paintings still seem fresh and inspirational, and the approaches remain valid for application to contemporary themes. The term "Impressionist" was originally coined as a critical insult, implying that the paintings appeared hasty and unfinished, and that the artists were careless in their perceptions. Yet what we see in the work of Claude Monet, the figurehead of this movement, is a detailed, analytical process of observation and record, which nonetheless results in images that are vital, colourful and celebratory.

The Direct Approach

Of the new concepts developed by Monet and his colleagues, two principles featured importantly. One was the requirement to complete a painting by direct reference to the subject – for example, working outdoors in the landscape, building up an image of the immediate view. Previously, on-the-spot sketches were made which would then be used as reference for a formally constructed studio composition. The other principle was the technique of working directly onto white canvas, often allowing new colours to blend with undried layers below, a method known as working wet into wet. This contradicted the traditional method of developing a painting slowly layer by layer, beginning with a dark or mid-toned ground and proceeding to a monochrome underpainting in which the main forms were modelled in tone alone. When this had dried, colours were introduced, usually in the form of glazes (successive layers of thin paint) and more detailed brushwork.

These concepts were not previously unknown but the Impressionists were the first to adopt them as standard procedures for painting finished works. The immediate impression of the subject became the final image without the imposition of artistic theories and conventions. Essentially, they understood that a painting should reflect the transience of observed realities. They reflected the ways in which solid form and surface detail can appear to change with changing circumstances – above all, the variable effects of natural light. Another significant feature of Impressionism was that it challenged traditional concepts of comparison and drawing. It was no longer considered necessary to have objects precisely defined and clearly distinguished from one another. Paintings did not have to be tidy and distinct in close-up as long as they could be read at a distance.

OTHER ARTISTS TO STUDY

CAMILLE PISSARRO (1830–1903)

PIERRE AUGUST RENOIR (1841–1919)

ALFRED SISLEY (1839–99)

Together with Monet, these artists formed the core of the Impressionist movement, and in their early careers they frequently worked closely together developing new themes and approaches. However, each had an individual and characteristic manner of applying Impressionist principles.

EDGAR DEGAS (1834–1917)

Although he took part in all but one of the Impressionist exhibitions held between 1874 and 1886, Degas departed from some of the main Impressionist principles. Primarily a figure painter, he hardly ever worked outdoors and his paintings often show an emphasis on line and contour, rather than the colour massing of Monet's Impressionism. Technically, his work is very rich and inventive. His approach to composition, much influenced by photography, also broke new ground, with figures posed informally and occasional oblique framing of the image that causes important elements to be cut off by the edge of the picture.

BERTHE MORISOT (1841–95)

MARY CASSATT (1845–1926)

Unusually for the time, two women painters had an active and respected role in the development of the Impressionist style. Their work evolved in parallel with that of their male colleagues, while introducing the extra dimension of notionally "feminine" subjects – both produced beautiful studies of mothers and children, for example. Cassatt worked closely with Degas, while Morisot's paintings proved a strong influence on Edouard Manet (1832–83), persuading him to abandon the use of black paint which had previously been such a powerful element of his compositions.

PIERRE BONNARD (1867–1947)

In the next generation from the original Impressionists, Bonnard developed a personalized treatment of mainly domestic subjects that extracted every spark of light and colour within his view. His vibrant compositions include figure studies of his wife and simple interior settings.

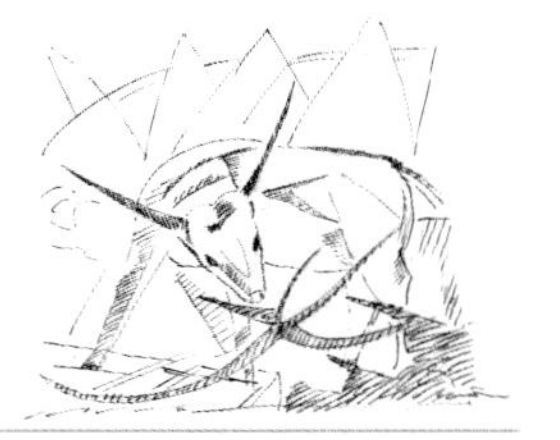

above: Childe Hassam, *The Island Garden,* 1892. Inspired by Claude Monet's Impressionism, Hassam painted the famous garden of his friend Celia Thaxter on the island of Appledore. He captured the flickering effects of air, sunlight and water.

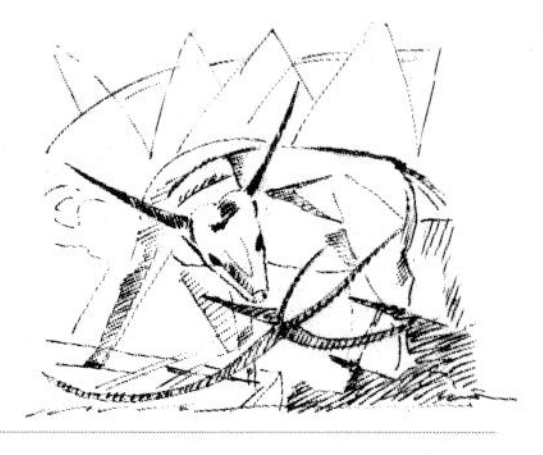

Responding to the Moment

The practical guideline for an Impressionist approach is to free your mind from what you know, or think you know, about your subject and respond directly to the purely visual sensations of colour and light. Monet described it thus: "When you go out to paint, try to forget what objects you have in front of you, a tree, a field. Merely think, here is a little square of blue, here an oblong of pink, here a streak of yellow, and paint it exactly as it looks to you, the exact colour and shape, until it gives you your own naive impression of the scene." This "naive impression" is not simplistic, as the word naive sometimes implies, but it is unique – consisting only of what you saw in that place at that moment. As Monet stressed, your painting records this impression "exactly as it looks to you".

Monet's working method was described in 1888 by the journalist Georges Jeanniot, who accompanied the artist as he went out to paint the landscape near his home. "Once in front of his easel, he draws in a few lines with the charcoal and then attacks the painting directly, handling his long brushes with an astounding agility and an unerring sense of design. He paints with a full brush and uses four or five pure colours; he juxtaposes and superimposes the unmixed paints on the canvas. His landscape is swiftly set down and could, if necessary, be considered complete after only one session ..."

The impression is at the same time a transient and a bold statement, a vivid recreation of innumerable individual perceptions, as described in Monet's instruction quoted above. It frees the artist from the idea that an exceptional painting necessarily requires hours of painstaking work, although we need to guard against the supposition that a first quick impression is naturally the freshest and best. Monet's advice to young artists included the remark that they should not be afraid to paint badly; painting an impression is a process of trial and error, but even the errors contribute to the store of experience in every artist must acquire.

Series Paintings

Monet was preoccupied with the relationship of light and colour from early in his career, and pursued his impressions in the streets of Paris, in the towns and villages along the banks of the River Seine, and on the coastlines of Normandy and Brittany. After his move to Giverny in 1883, where he remained settled for the rest of his long life and constructed the famous water garden that was the subject of his final works, he developed the method of working in series. He focused on a single subject and portrayed it on several different canvases simultaneously, changing the canvas according to changes in the time of day, the quality of light and the weather conditions. *Poplars on the Epte* is one of several series made between 1888 and 1926, which included paintings of haystacks in a field, the cathedral at Rouen, and the garden and waterlily pool at Giverny.

In the series paintings, Monet developed a comprehensive logic of Impressionism that enabled him to record the variations of his motif. Different colour themes and qualities of brushwork describe the range of visual effects produced by the same object or location seen under particular conditions. Although Monet was the supreme landscapist, one can see in his work how the active brushwork and broken colour effects typical of Impressionistic renderings can also be successfully applied to other subjects, including figures and interiors, architectural structures and still-lifes.

Project: Capturing Impressions

An Immediate Impression

To familiarize yourself with basic principles for capturing an impression, choose a subject from the following and try the technical approach suggested below:

- A vase of flowers
- A flowerbed or vegetable garden
- A street scene with brightly painted houses
- A beach with brightly coloured beach huts
- A row of market stalls
- An agricultural landscape, with colourful fields divided by hedges and fences.

Work in oil or acrylic paint, so that you have a range of textural qualities at your command and limit your palette to six colours and white. Don't use black in the projects in this lesson. The Impressionists believed that black did not exist in nature and they excluded it from their palettes. Black is a useful colour but it can sometimes deaden colour mixes.

Keep mixing in the palette to a minimum; instead apply bright, distinct colours to the working surface and allow the hues and tones to mix and merge as you build up the brushstrokes.

Select a few brushes of different sizes – round, filbert or square, hog hair or synthetic bristle – and use the shape of the brush, applied in small strokes of varied directions, to help you create the broken colour effect. Don't lay down great sweeps of a single colour and don't blend the colours too much or they will become muddied.

Series Paintings

Choose a view from your window and make three or more paintings recording the scene at different times of day, or on different days under conditions varying if possible from bright sunlight to clear, cool light, to a rainy or misty atmosphere. Observe carefully how the atmospherics affect local colour and the clarity of shapes and forms.

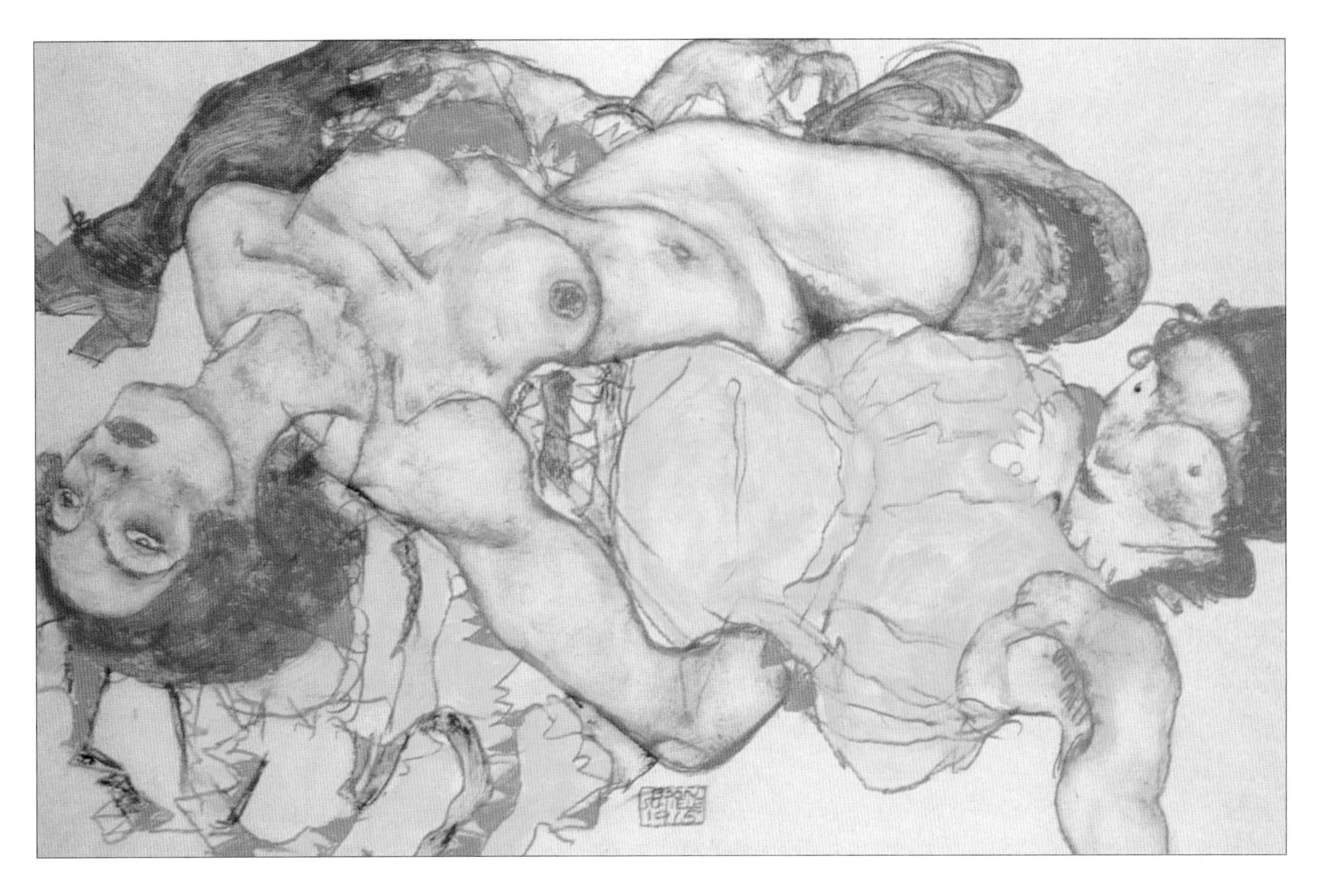

above: Egon Schiele, *Women Upside Down*, 1915. Heightened colour and expressionistic distortion of form are characteristic features of Egon Schiele's anguished portraits of Viennese society.

Expressionist painting goes beyond appearances, using devices of technique and composition to develop mood and atmosphere. By distorting or exaggerating particular aspects of the subject, the artist directs the viewer's response towards the emotive qualities of the picture. The picture is drawn subjectively rather than objectively. An Expressionist painting is not necessarily "unreal", and it need not be threatening, but it has to challenge our normal perceptions of reality.

Composition and Stylization

Distortion and stylization are characteristic features of the Expressionist approach. As in the Schiele painting, the impression of space and distance can be heightened through exaggerated perspective. In landscape, architectural and interior subjects, selective composition and distortion of the subject can create a particular mood. Paintings from the figure commonly use a method similar to caricature. The characteristic features of faces and bodies are exaggerated, even to the point of deformity, as a means of emphasizing the narrative point of the image or its associations. It can also be helpful to simplify detail, so that a person or object is reduced to those essential ingredients that still make it recognizable. But Expressionism does not always aim to provoke or disturb. Sometimes Expressionist devices are used to create lyrical, appealing visions of alternative realities.

Colours as Expression

The colours of *Women Upside Down* are intense and hectic, with dominant high-key tones that create an unnatural brightness.

A startling feature of the painting is the dominant yellow, used as the theme colour in several Expressionist works. Although yellow has some pleasant associations, particularly with sunlight, it is not always easy on the eye and a large expanse of brilliant yellow can have a disturbing effect. The particular hue and tone of the main colour in this painting make it solid and suffocating.

Expressive use of colour always involves a subjective element, but there are also predictable interactions between colours that

can be exploited to create a particular mood. Deliberate contrasts of hue or tone can introduce discordant notes to a composition, underpinning the portrayal of a violent event or uneasy atmosphere. Conversely, colour harmonies and carefully related tones can help to evoke calm and pleasant emotions.

Expressive Mark-Making

A typical feature both of van Gogh's work and of later Expressionist painting is the extremely vigorous brushwork. The masses of heavy directional strokes construct form and texture with exaggerated emphasis.

Drawing with the brush is used as a means of expressing mood and atmosphere. Outlining individual shapes draws attention to features that have been distorted or exaggerated. Areas of colour composed of interactive brush marks – dots, dashes, ticks and scribbles – allow flat surfaces and simple planes to take on an expressive character. Coherent form can still emerge from this mass of strokes.

OTHER ARTISTS TO STUDY

JAMES ENSOR (1860–1949)

To convey his pessimistic view of humankind, the Belgian artist Ensor transformed ordinary people into a gallery of nightmarish, macabre figures, some even wearing grotesque masks. Often his paintings have a strong narrative background, while others express emotions and atmospheres through figurative imagery.

EDVARD MUNCH (1863–1944)

There is nothing veiled about Munch's highly charged emotional Expressionism, as demonstrated by the titles of some of his most famous works, such as *The Scream,* 1893, *The Kiss,* 1892, *Jealousy,* 1895 and *Self Portrait in Hell,* 1895. The shapes, colours and textures bridge a gap between reality and a privately conceived world.

above: Edvard Munch, *The Empty Cross,* 1889–1901. A set of work on the theme of the cross relate closely in style to *The Scream,* an example of his highly charged early work.

EMIL NOLDE (1867–1956)

Nolde's paintings cover a range of subjects from biblical themes to simple studies of flowers and landscapes, with moods varying from menacing to benign. His watercolours, particularly, demonstrate a wonderfully expressive use of pure colour.

ERNST LUDWIG KIRCHNER (1880–1938)

Kirchner's imagery is heavily stylized, and often semi-abstract. Both the subject matter and his technique, which uses strong colour and gestural brushwork, are typical of the Expressionist approach in painting.

FRANCIS BACON (1910–92)

Bacon developed a highly personalized form of Expressionism in which violent distortions of form and space feature prominently. His colours are rarely harsh or garish in the manner of earlier Expressionist works, but even the colour harmonies somehow contribute to the disturbing effect of his paintings.

EGON SCHIELE (1890–1918)

Alienation and eroticism were potent elements in Schiele's work. In this he was influenced by the culture of *fin de siècle* Vienna, centre of developments in psychoanalysis. In his work, Schiele brought into the open previously hidden currents of sexuality. Schiele used watercolour essentially as an adjunct to line work.

above: Franz Marc, *Taureau Rouge.* A founder member of the Blue Rider group, Franc Marc experimented with the expressiveness of colour and Cubist-inspired rhythmic harmonies in watercolours of his favourite animal subjects.

Project: Experiments in Expressionism

Expressing Character
Using a photograph as reference, make a brush drawing of an animal or a bird intended to express its character – the power and aggression of a beast of prey, for example, the sinister quality of a vulture or the timidity of a deer or rabbit. Use a limited, non-naturalistic colour range appropriate to the mood of your subject and avoid the temptation to make a simple likeness. Instead, pay attention to the variety of brush marks you can use to describe the creature expressively.

A Sense of Place
Choose an interior or exterior view – one not containing too much distracting detail – and make several colour sketches investigating the "sense of place" through varying moods. Select specific features of the scene as the basis of each composition, then interpret the shapes and develop the colour scheme in a manner appropriate to the chosen theme. Try using pastel or watercolour to lay in the colours freely.

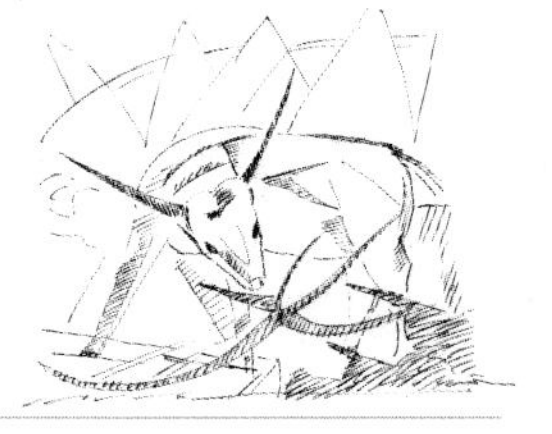

below: Stuart Davis, *Abstraction,* 1937. This study for his *Swing Landscape Mural* contains all the elements of Davis's distinctive style and illustrates how watercolour is sometimes used in a supporting role for large-scale projects.

For some people, the word "abstract" automatically signals that a painting will be difficult to understand and possibly uninteresting to look at. Abstraction frequently evokes an unsympathetic, even hostile reaction, because it seems to reject our common experiences of seeing the world around us.

It is true that an abstract work is one artist's unique response to particular themes and methods, and in that respect it is not as readily accessible to the casual viewer as, say, a recognizable still-life or figure painting. But it is also true that such a work contains the kind of perceptions that are common to us all. For example, an abstract painting can be a two-dimensional rendering of three-dimensional space and form; or it may obey particular conventions of composition and division of the picture plane. It is also composed of the same materials as other paintings, and therefore represents similar preoccupations with technique and surface values.

The idea that figurative and abstract approaches are worlds apart is absolutely false. But this is not helped by some artists and critics who have felt it necessary to create a kind of competition between them, and to claim one approach as being more universally valid than another. In fact, since abstraction became a common, even for a while dominant, form of painting in the middle of the twentieth century, the two apparently different disciplines have usefully exchanged developments of style, concept and technique, so stimulating both areas of image-making.

If you are one of the people who has felt excluded from abstract art, this is most likely because you have not been given the means to relate it to things you do know and understand about painting. This section on abstraction may leave you knowing a bit more.

Sources of Abstract Imagery

There are two basic methods of developing an abstract style. One is to use objects and images from the real world as reference points from which you evolve a personalized, "abstracted" interpretation. The other is to employ purely formal pictorial elements and material qualities such as non-referential shapes and colour relationships and surface effects directly relating to the material properties of the chosen medium. The second approach is investigated on pages 148–151.

Abstracting from nature we can take to mean deriving abstract imagery from things actually seen. Landscape is a frequently used resource for this kind of approach, perhaps because its enormous scale enables us to look at it in broad terms and disregard incidental detail that cannot be clearly identified at a distance. But this basic method can equally well be applied to other themes like figures, natural and man-made objects, indoor and outdoor environments, and actual events.

To describe this process of abstract analysis in the most simple terms, we can take possible examples and relate them to figurative interpretations. For instance, a landscape of fields, hedgerows and distant hills can be seen as a series of rhythmic shapes, each of which has a dominant colour; an abstract painting of such a view might look something like the image that a figurative painter would achieve while blocking in the landscape in the early stages of the painting – broad contours and colour areas not yet broken up by the particular detail of individual features. In the same way, a face can be seen as an elliptical shape coloured an overall uniform pink. Arms and legs can be interpreted as

basically cylindrical forms and clothing as separate areas of bold colour and pattern.

Often, in any subject, you can identify linked and repeated shapes and forms that give a sense of unity to your interpretation. The same type of linkage can be made within the range of hues and tones that you see, so that you can discover a pattern of similarity and contrast. Abstraction means initially breaking down what you see before you into simple, sometimes very obvious visual elements. You can then start to examine the detail, as you would in a representational painting, and see what other information you are provided with that enables you to reinterpret and elaborate your basic image.

OTHER ARTISTS TO STUDY

NICOLAS DE STAEL (1914–55)

Strong shapes and heavy impasto together with brilliant colour theme variations evoke the lights and textures of landscape and townscape.

GRAHAM SUTHERLAND (1903–80)

In work based on the landscape and its individual features, Sutherland evolved a fascinating range of semi-abstract pictorial equivalents to natural forms and environments.

WILLEM DE KOONING (b. 1904)

Working alongside the purely abstract modes of his fellow artists in the New York School of the 1940s and 1950s, De Kooning focused the human figure as a source of abstraction in his well-known *Woman* series. Other works show explicit references to landscape origins.

STUART DAVIS (1894–1964)

Davis' work exhibits a refreshing variation on the abstracting from nature theme, utilizing man-made forms and graphic imagery to develop a decorative abstract style.

above: Milton Avery, *Road to the Sea, c.*1938. Using watercolour washes over a charcoal drawing, Milton Avery abstracted his subject to form an interesting series of shapes and textures while taking care to retain its identity.

HOW FAR DOES IT GO?

So far, we have examined a fairly simplistic approach that opens the door to abstraction but does not wholly bridge the gap between what an artist sees and what goes on the canvas or paper. This is because at some point a new conceptual leap may occur that eliminates some of the links between observed and interpreted realities.

For instance, if you were working on an abstracted landscape, you might see a sudden shaft of sunlight falling on a grassy field, which might then become a slash of bright yellow on your painting. As you step back and see the effect on your image, it may occur to you to give the yellow a different hue or tone, or to turn the slashed brush mark into a distinct, hard-edged shape. Alternatively, you might suddenly decide that every area that had previously represented green grass should be painted bright red, to completely change the character of the painting. Or you might create a broad pattern corresponding to the linear texture of the blades of grass, not necessarily in naturalistic colours. As such ideas develop, you gradually remove the particular associations that would enable an uninvolved viewer to relate elements of your painting directly to those of the original subject.

If you are interested in abstraction and have not previously understood it very well, try looking at abstract paintings in these terms and imagining what might have been the inspiration for specific shapes and colours. But keep in mind that in abstract art there is also an emphasis on the material, surface qualities of the painting, and it is often more directly influential than in figurative works.

above: Roy Sparkes, *Doris Tysterman,* watercolour and pencils. Some natural forms have very strong, characteristic shapes that can be isolated and rearranged. Abstraction is frequently involved with the pure sensations of colour and texture available from a particular medium or mixed-media approach. A natural subject such as flowers can suggest ways of unleashing these properties freely, but from a basis of observed reality.

Project: Abstract Starting Points

Collage from a Landscape or Still-life

Choose a landscape theme – a view that is familiar to you – or set up a simple still-life, and create an abstracted colour study using cut and torn pieces of coloured paper collaged to your base paper. Try to deal with distinctive, strong shapes, eliminating small-scale detail. Don't worry about making the shapes too precise, and you can allow the paper pieces to overlap and modify each other. You can make changes simply by gluing pieces over each other.

A Painted Abstraction

Repeat the project above, but using paint to create the colour areas. Apply the paint in different ways to vary the surface qualities within the different shapes. For instance, use heavy impasto contrasted with patches of transparent colour glazing; or opaque, flat colour next to active, broken brushwork.

Drawing with Colour

Using a similar subject, make a colour drawing with brush and paint, following the contours of shapes and including some detail elements, such as interesting textures on the surface of the objects you are looking at. Try using a bright-coloured piece of paper for your painting in this project, so that you have to select your paint colours boldly to make sure they have an impact.

In abstract painting which makes no reference to the real world, it is the basic ingredients of colour, composition and execution that, in effect, become the subject of the work. Some artists, like Piet Mondrian (1872–1944), arrived at a form of pure abstraction by working their way through figurative styles and processes of abstracting from nature. Others, particularly in the late twentieth century when so many more examples of abstract work have been produced, seen and commented upon, have moved very quickly into this way of thinking and working early in their careers.

It may be impossible to eliminate completely all references to the normal range of human visual experiences, and sometimes a viewer may feel that, for example, a landscape reference can be seen in a particular painting that purports to be wholly abstract. This is because we tend to see marks on canvas or paper as suggesting space and form, and when we are looking for references to real situations or objects, we may claim to identify what seem to us reasonable associations. However, this is unconnected with the artist's intentions; when working in a purely abstract mode, the artist is dealing with shapes and forms, colours and textures in terms of what they actually are, not what they represent.

Compositional Elements

As in any form of image-making, the abstract artist deals with basic elements of pictorial construction – line, mass, colour, tonality, surface texture and pattern, shape, contour, spatial depth and apparent volume. If the painted image is not to refer to anything known, the important question seems to be, where do you start? What prompts the artist first to put down a line rather than a block of colour? Why position the line in one place rather than another? What should be the next mark, and why? It is because such questions cannot usually be answered precisely, or by reference to something else, that many people find it difficult to become interested in abstract art. The logic of an abstract painting seems too personal and inaccessible.

The artist makes positive and negative responses in producing an abstract work. Its logic can lie in what the painting is supposed to do, and in what it should not do. Mondrian is a good example to study because his geometric grids and limited colour range are so apparently restrictive and severe. His intention was to create "dynamic equilibrium", a sense of movement and tension in an image that also had absolute balance.

Mondrian chose the right-angle as a pure and constant factor – it is a fixed and balanced relationship between two lines. When using this to construct squares and rectangles, however, he still had a great deal of scope to vary the proportions and interactions of these simple geometric shapes. In limiting his colour range to the three primaries and the neutral colours of red, yellow, blue, black, white and grey he had a palette which incorporated absolute qualities of hue and tone. As these were applied to the geometric grid, they further influenced the tensions and balances in the painting.

What these paintings are not supposed to do is to create an impression of three-dimensional space, or refer to external reality. In this sense, Mondrian challenges both himself and the viewer to discard received notions of pictorial space. We might tend to relate a grid structure to architectural

below: Wassily Kandinsky, *Painting with White Form*, 1913. The looseness and ease with which Kandinsky used watercolour contributed to the abstract appearance of transitional works that still contained landscape elements.

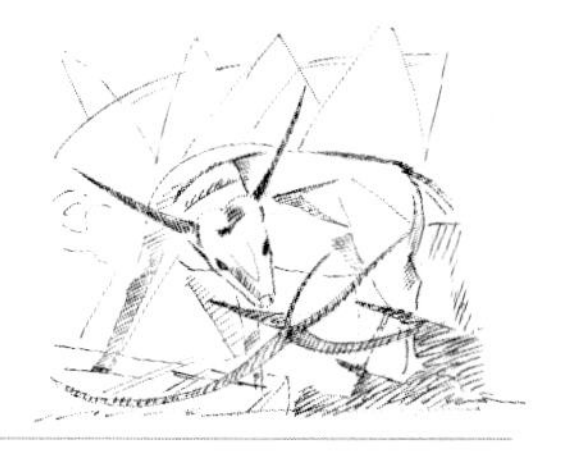

frameworks. The use of black and white usually implies light and shadow, a means of modelling three-dimensional form. But Mondrian's paintings lie flat on the picture plane, and neither the colour nor the construction suggest any element of real space and form. This requires careful judgement of the proportions of the shapes and the extent of the colour areas, and their interactions. Painterly features are also eliminated – the colour is flat and opaque, the marks made by the brush are virtually invisible.

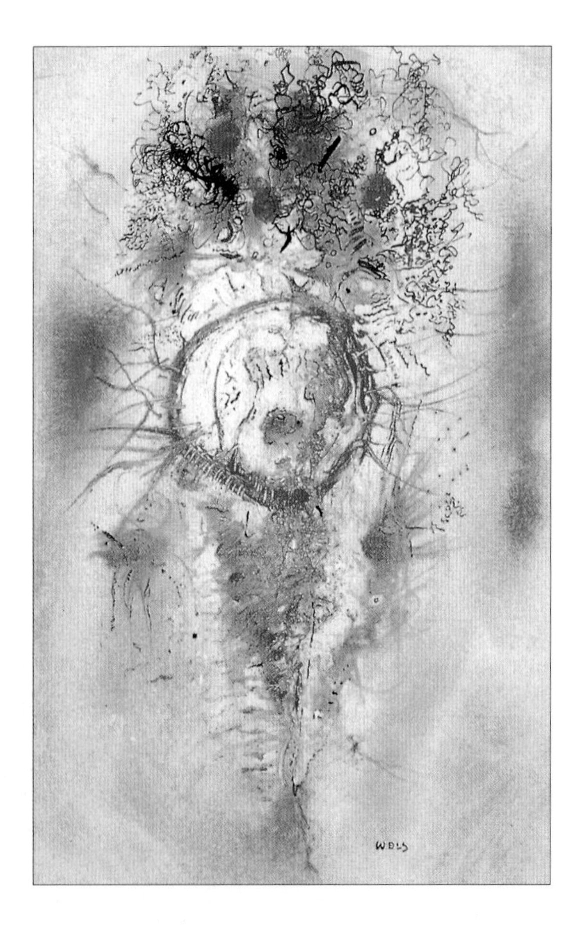

above: Wols, *c.*1950, *Composition.* In Europe, watercolour was used by abstract artists working in a style called Tachisme.

OTHER ARTISTS TO STUDY

WASSILY KANDINSKY (1866–1944)

An influential figure in the development of abstract art, Kandinsky is credited with having produced the first completely abstract painting, a watercolour painted in 1912. He developed a free style of abstraction through series works under the titles *Composition, Improvisation* and *Impression.*

KASIMIR MALEVICH (1878–1935)

Like Kandinsky, Malevich was a pioneer of abstraction, but in the movement known as Suprematism he produced what were among the earliest hard-edged abstracts (predating Mondrian), using strictly geometric shapes and limited colour.

MARK ROTHKO (1903–70)

In large works consisting of rectangles, borders and stripes with heavily brushed, painterly textures, Rothko was a pioneer of the style of abstract work that came to be known as "colour field painting".

JACKSON POLLOCK (1912–56)

The leading figure of the New York School of Abstract Expressionism, Pollock developed the famous "drip painting" method of spattering and pouring the paint onto large canvases laid on the floor. It is sometimes assumed that this meant the work was allowed to evolve almost randomly, but the effects are, in fact, highly controlled and expertly manipulated.

MORRIS LOUIS (1912–62)

Louis developed the form of abstraction in which paint was laid as "stains" and "veils", poured onto unprimed canvases to produce loose runs and broad waterfalls of shimmering colour.

FRANK STELLA (b. 1936)

Stella was a leading figure of hard-edged abstraction in the 1960s, with austere stripe paintings in closely controlled colours. He later moved into a more active, Expressionist style of work, creating paintings that were actually three-dimensional reliefs covered with brilliant patterns and textures.

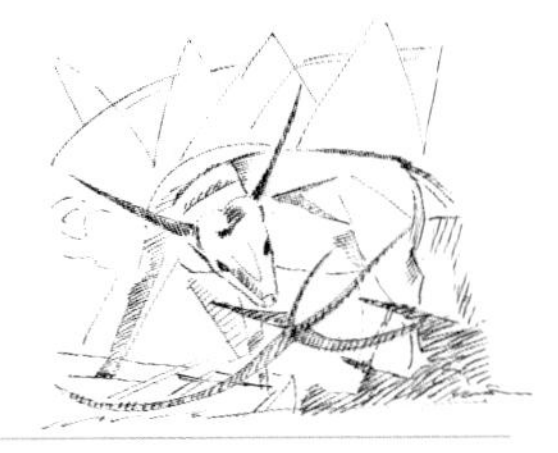

The Range of Abstraction

Mondrian aimed at, and achieved, what he described as "an expression of pure reality", but as you can see from looking through any book on modern art, straight lines and limited colour are by no means the only ingredients of abstract art. It is interesting to compare Mondrian's work with that of the German-born American painter Hans Hoffman (1880–1966), some of whose paintings also conform to a grid-like structure and contain very strong colours and tones. Yet Hoffman's work is vigorous, free and gestural, the colours and textures of the paint are rich and varied. A suggestion of three-dimensionality sometimes occurs when shapes overlap and colours seem to advance or recede but, as with Mondrian, the image exists on the surface of the canvas and is self-referential – the viewer is not led into an illusory pictorial space.

Looking at abstract painting in terms of simple definitions, there are distinctly different styles. In hard-edged abstraction, shapes are sharply defined although not necessarily geometric, and colour interactions are usually strictly controlled. Another style is gestural painting, which is visually busier and more complex, with vigorous brushmarks, splashes, spots and dribbles. There are also more decorative forms of abstraction, in which the picture surface appears heavily patterned. There are other categories, and works by individual artists who draw on all of these conventions.

You may find that it is easiest to develop an approach to pure abstraction by beginning with abstracting from nature. As you work through particular images, you will become gradually more interested in what is happening on your canvas or paper, and you may forget about the actual source. You can start to deal directly with colour interactions; relationships of line and mass; textural contrasts; or developing a composition that suggests space while also emphasizing the flatness of the picture surface. Try to pin down your intentions and ask yourself if the painting is really working in terms of what you tried to do. But beware – it is more tempting to let yourself get away with unsatisfactory solutions in abstract than in representational work, as you have no external points of reference by which to judge what the picture should look like.

You will realize that many of the preoccupations involved are the same as those you had to apply to figurative work, but at some point your subject becomes the painting itself and your own instinct, technical skill and experience will enable you to carry it through.

Project: Techniques in Abstraction

Geometric Abstraction

Choose a single kind of geometric shape such as a square, circle, ellipse or triangle and use it as the basis of a brush drawing, repeating the shape in different sizes and positions, which you then fill with colours. Think carefully about whether you are trying to create a sense of space or keep the picture absolutely flat, and also about why you are choosing certain kinds of colours and what they contribute to the structure of the painting.

Gestural Abstraction

Using watercolour, start by making very free marks on your canvas or paper, initially using lines to create rhythm and direction, then adding broad areas of colour and texture to develop the image. As you progress, study the surface qualities and colour interactions that emerge and make deliberate decisions to enhance those that work successfully and to adjust those that do not.

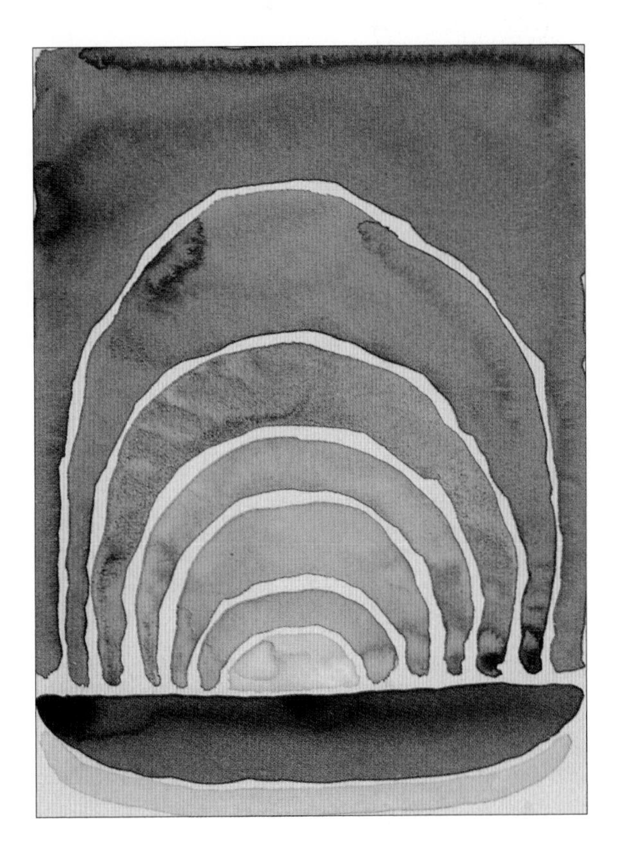

right: Georgia O'Keefe, 1917, *Light Coming on the Plains 1.* With an almost oriental economy, Georgia O'Keefe used watercolour to evoke the American landscape.

J.M.W. Turner

Great Falls of Reichenbach

WATERCOLOUR

This magnificent view of Alpine scenery, painted for exhibition in 1804, reveals Turner's use of watercolour for the expression of a vast and solemn romantic theme.

Subject

As the previous section demonstrated so clearly, painting techniques are no more than vehicles for the expression of ideas. In this section, we will look specifically at how watercolour can be harnessed to depict a personal vision. The explanations and step-by-step demonstrations are grouped according to theme, ranging from still-life and plants and flowers through to animals and portrait and figure work.

For the newcomer to painting, it is worthwhile to work through these themes in order. Still-life offers the luxury of a subject that doesn't move and which can be easily arranged into a pleasing composition, then rearranged and re-lit to suit the artist. People and animals present particular challenges as living subjects; although they can be particularly satisfying to paint, they are at the same time more demanding.

A wide variety of different techniques and approaches is shown in each of the subject areas, together with some explanations of the particular difficulties associated with certain themes. Someone who has never dared to attempt to portray the effects of changing light may see the perfect method for the first time here and say, "so that's how it's done. I could do that too." You probably can.

Still-life, as its name implies, simply means a composition of objects which are not moving and which are incapable of doing so, usually arranged on a table; the French rather depressingly called it "dead life" (*nature morte*).

The subjects can be whatever you like, but traditionally the objects in a still-life group are in some way associated with each other – a vase of flowers with fruit, a selection of vegetables with cooking vessels or implements, and sometimes dead fish, game or fowl with a goblet of water, perhaps, or a bunch of parsley. (Culinary still-lifes are less popular nowadays, possibly because they run the risk of looking like the cover of a cookery book.) Good paintings can be made from quite homely subjects. Vincent van Gogh (1853–90) made a wonderful and moving still-life from nothing but a pile of books on a table.

Most artists have painted still-lifes at one time or another, and several, notably Jan Vermeer (1632–75), included them in their figure paintings. In the seventeenth century a group of Dutch artists became obsessed with still-life to the exclusion of all other subjects, and vied with one another to produce ever more lavish portrayals of table-tops gleaming with edible produce, rare porcelain and golden goblets. In many of these, tiny insects are visible among the foliage, blood drips from the mouths of freshly killed hares or rabbits, and bunches of grapes shine with tiny droplets of moisture, every object painted with breathtaking skill.

Because the subject of a still-life painting can be entirely controlled by the artist, as can its arrangement and lighting, still-lifes present an unusual opportunity for exploring ideas and experimenting with colour and composition. The greatest master of the still-life, Paul Cézanne (1839–1906), found that the form allowed him to concentrate on such fundamental problems as form and space and the paradox of transferring the three-dimensional world to a two-dimensional surface.

The ability to control the subject of a still-life means that you can take as much time as you like to work out the composition, and you can practise painting techniques at leisure, trying out new ones as you feel inspired. Oddly, watercolour was seldom used in the past for still-lifes other than flower paintings, but it is now becoming extremely popular.

below: Cézanne used still-life to explore the relationships of forms and their interaction on various spatial planes. He usually worked in oils, but *Still Life with Chairs, Bottles and Apple* shows his use of watercolour.

above: Angela Gair, *Still Life on a Windowsill,* watercolour and pastel. The whole scene has been freely rendered to give the feeling of dappled light. This is a high-key painting, in which the effect of lightness and gaiety is enhanced by the use of consistently light values and bright colours, with the minimum of contrast. The artist has made extensive use of hatched strokes, both to build up areas of tone and to activate the picture surface by leading the eye through and around the composition.

"Found Groups"

Many still-life paintings are the result of carefully planned arrangements. Paul Cézanne reputedly spent days setting up his groups of fruit and vegetables before so much as lifting his brush. Sometimes, though, you may just happen to see a subject, such as plates and cups on a table or a few vegetables lying on a piece of newspaper, that seems perfect in itself, or needs only small adjustments to make it so. These "found" groups have a particular charm of their own, hinting at impermanence and the routines of everyday life – the vegetables will shortly be made into soup, and the crockery will be washed and put back into the cupboard.

Found groups obviously have to be painted more quickly than arranged ones, but this is in some ways an advantage, since you want to achieve a spontaneous, unposed effect. So make your technique express this also and paint freely, putting down broad impressions of shapes, colour and light.

Alternatively, you can use the idea of the found group as the basis for a more deliberate set-up, placing the objects in a more convenient place for painting or one where they have better light. Be careful, however, not to destroy the essence of the subject by over-planning and including too many extra elements.

above: John Lidzey FRSA, *Oil Lamp,* 24.1 x 15.2 cm (9½ x 6 in), watercolour. This, a page from the artist's sketchbook, is the quintessential "found" still-life, painted rapidly and freely with no overworking. Heavily sized paper, such as the cartridge paper used for sketchbooks, has a non-absorbent surface which causes the paint to mix freely but unevenly. Lidzey has exploited this effect to the full. Using plenty of water, he allowed the paint to flood onto the paper, controlling it with damp cotton wool. He used only three colours, ultramarine, yellow ochre and burnt sienna, but encouraged them to run into one another and mix, treating the paper almost like a palette.

left: Martin Taylor, *Still Life with Pumpkin,* 23 x 33 cm (9 x 13 in), watercolour. We are not all fortunate enough to have such a perfect still-life setting as this old stone outhouse. But neither does Martin Taylor – he happened on this arrangement of fruit and vegetables quite by chance during a trip to Italy, and promptly settled down to paint it. The picture's most striking feature is the way he has built up the rough textures of the stone and contrasted them with the smooth ones of the fruit and vegetables, which glow out like beacons from their neutral-coloured surroundings.

right: Carolyne Moran, *Kitchen Table with Basket and Vegetables,* 36.8 x 54.6 cm (14½ x 21½ in), gouache. This painting gives a powerful impression of spontaneity and immediacy, partly through the sense of movement created by the spilling vegetables, but equally through the manner of painting. Although the drawing is accurate – chairs, basket and vegetables all make sense in terms of structure and proportion – there is no unnecessary detail. The light coming through the cane of the basket is described deftly but with no niggling, and the brushwork throughout the painting is vigorous and expressive. On the left-hand wall, the artist has allowed her brush to follow the sweeping lines of the upright chair struts, and on the table she has smeared still-wet paint with her fingers to simulate the grain of the wood.

Themes

A successful still-life is seldom, if ever, a random collection of objects – there should always be some kind of theme. One of the most popular types of still-life is the culinary one, where fruit, vegetables and kitchen equipment are grouped together. Attractive in themselves, they also are related in subject, so that the viewer is not worried by the discordant notes of objects that seem not to belong. Another kind of theme is the "literary" one. Some still-lifes tell a story about the personal interests of the artist. The best-known examples of such still-lifes are those of Vincent Van Gogh (1853–90), whose paintings of his room at Arles and his moving portrayals of his own work-soiled boots are almost a form of pictorial biography, telling us as much about the artist as about the objects themselves. This approach to painting makes a lot of sense – most people possess some objects that have particular value because they evoke memories, so what better than to make them the starting point for a personal still-life.

You can also take colours and shapes as the theme, choosing objects that seem to be linked visually or set up exciting contrasts. Visual themes need very careful handling at the painting stage – if the objects are widely dissimilar in kind you may have to treat them in a semi-abstract way, allowing them to hide their identity behind their general forms or outlines.

left: Michael Emmett, *By the Cottage Door,* 36.8 x 41.9 cm (14½ x 16½ in), watercolour. This delightful outdoor group is an example of a still-life with a narrative content: we can see that someone, perhaps the painter's wife, has been sitting in the sun preparing fruit and vegetables, but has now abandoned her task. This adds an extra dimension to the picture, inviting us to participate in the domestic scene, but the implied story plays only a secondary role; once drawn in we can admire the carefully planned composition and the artist's technical skill. He has painted mainly wet-on-dry, building up subtle but varied colours by means of successive overlapping washes, and the effect of dappled sunlight by the door has been cleverly suggested by the spattering technique.

right: Martin Taylor, *Grapes and Bread*, 23 x 33 cm (9 x 13 in), watercolour and acrylic. Foodstuffs have always been a popular still-life theme, and this lovely, simple little group is very much in the Dutch tradition of minute observation and truth to the realities of everyday life. Painted in Italy at the end of a holiday, it had an extra significance for the artist, the grapes (wine) and bread symbolizing the Italian way of life as well as suggesting a "last supper".

STILL-LIFE ARTISTS TO STUDY

JEAN-BAPTISTE-SIMÉON CHARDIN (1699–1779)

Chardin's still-lifes are regarded as classics of the genre – precise, detailed statements typically composed of quite ordinary objects, such as basic foodstuffs or the props in his own studio. The coloration and brushwork are subtle and delicate.

DUTCH STILL-LIFE PAINTERS OF THE SEVENTEENTH CENTURY

The elaboration of detail and sensitivity to colour variations in the complex Dutch still-lifes demonstrate how intensely any small-scale subject can be analyzed – from books and musical instruments to food and flowers. Few of these artists – such as Ambrosius Bosschaert (1573–1621), Pieter Claesz (1597–1661) and Jan Davidsz de Heem (1606–83) – are as well known individually as are other seventeenth-century artists such as Vermeer (1632–75) and Rembrandt, but their work is widely appreciated and sets an exceptional standard for acute observation and realism.

Project: Approaches to Still-life

Objects with Associations

Make a painting based on objects that have special appeal to you because they convey memories and associations – sea shells and stones from a favourite place, for instance, or books and ornaments in your home. Again, don't over-complicate the painting by including too many objects, or too many items that have complex forms. As well as paying attention to the purely visual qualities of the arrangement, try to identify the special characteristics of each object that make it important to you.

Objects in the Landscape

Go sketching outdoors, using watercolours as your medium. Avoid making broad, impressionistic landscape views; instead, focus on individual elements, such as a patch of flowers or a tree or shrub with fascinating form and colour, and try to translate your subject with a high degree of accurately observed detail.

Everyday Objects

Devise a compact still-life group using just a few similar objects with simple, distinct shapes – natural forms such as fruits and vegetables or artificial objects such as plain-coloured cups and dishes. Keep the composition simple and set out to make an accurate, detailed painting conveying shape and form, texture, local colour and modelling with light and shade. Don't just rely on black and white for the highlights and shadows; try to see the variations of hue and intensity of colour created by the lighting.

left: Moira Huntly RJ, RSMA, *Still Life with African Artefact,* 49.5 x 35.5 cm (19½ x 14 in), watercolour and gouache. Here the main theme is colour and shape; if you look at the painting through half-closed eyes you can see an abstract pattern, perfectly balanced and carefully controlled. One of the surest ways to tie all the elements in a still-life together is to repeat colours and shapes from one area to another, and there could be few better examples than this painting. Every colour in the foreground has its echo in the background or foreground, while the zigzag patterns on the tablecloth are picked up again in the top left-hand corner.

BACKGROUNDS

One of the commonest mistakes in still-life painting is to treat the background as unimportant. It is easy to feel that only the objects really matter and that the spaces behind and between them are areas that just need to be filled in somehow. All the elements in a painting should work together, however, and backgrounds, although they may play a secondary role, require as much consideration as the placing of the objects.

The kind of background you choose for an arranged group will depend entirely on the kind of picture you plan. A plain white or off-white wall could provide a good foil for a group of elegantly shaped objects, such as glass bottles or tall vases, because the dominant theme in this case would be shape rather than colour, but a group you have chosen because it allows you to exploit colour and pattern would be better served by a bright background, perhaps with some pattern itself.

The most important thing to remember is that the background colour or colours must be in tune with the overall colour key of the painting. You can stress the relationship of foreground to background when you begin to paint, tying the two areas of the picture together by repeating colours from one to another. For example, if your group has a predominance of browns and blues, try to introduce one of these colours into the background also. It is usually better in any case not to paint it completely flat.

above: Geraldine Girvan, *Victoria Day*, 48.3 x 53 cm (19 x 20⅞ in), gouache. Here the background is as busy and eventful as the foreground, as befits a painting in which colour and pattern are the dominant themes. Notice how the artist has echoed the shapes of the blue fish (bottom right) in the patterned wallpaper above.

above: Ronald Jesty RBA, *Plums in a Dish*, 28 x 22.9 cm (11 x 9 in), watercolour. This artist likes to exploit unusual viewpoints in his still-life paintings, and in this example he has chosen to paint his subject from above. This not only neatly solves the problem of a separate background and foreground, it also allows him to make the most of the elegant shape of the metal platter.

-ARTISTS' HINTS-

- A plain background throws three-dimensional form into clear relief; a heavily patterned or textured background can intrude into the still-life group.
- Where elements of the background form strong directional lines, consider carefully where and how these should link with the objects in the foreground.
- If you use drapery as a background to a still-life, try to make the folds look natural and uncontrived.
- If the tone of the background is too similar to that of the objects in front of it, the finished painting will look monotonous and lack "punch". It is useful to have several lengths of fabric on hand, in both light and dark colours, and to try out different ones with your still-life group in order to compare their effects.

above: Shirley Felts, *Still Life with Apples*, 40.6 x 30.5 cm (16 x 12 in), watercolour. For this lovely painting, delicate but strong, the artist has chosen a plain brown background that picks up the colour of the tabletop. But she has not painted it flat: there are several different colours and tones in the "brown", including a deep blue, and she has given movement and drama to it by the use of brushstrokes that follow the direction of the spiky leaves. Her technique is interesting. She builds up her rich colours and softly modelled forms gradually by laying wash over wash, but avoids tired and muddy paint by repeated soaking of the paper. Highlights are lifted out while the paper is wet, and the shadows are deepened later.

Setting Up a Still-Life

There are no specific problems in painting a still-life or flower piece once it has been set up. The real challenge is arranging it, and this may take some time – plonking an assortment of objects down on a table will not give you a good painting. The wisest rule to follow at first is to keep the composition simple. The more objects you have the more difficult it is to arrange them in a harmonious way. It is also best to have a theme of some kind: if the various objects are too different in kind they will look uneasy together.

Start with something you like, a bowl of fruit on a patterned tablecloth, perhaps, or a pot plant, and keep arranging and re-arranging until you are satisfied that you have achieved a good balance of shapes and colours. Drapery is often used to balance and complement the main subject, and it is useful to have a selection of fabrics or tablecloths on hand for this purpose. Many artists make small sketches or diagrams to work out whether a vertical line is needed in the background, or a table-top shown as a diagonal in the foreground. Finally, when you are fairly sure that the arrangement will do, look at it through a viewing frame to assess how well it will fill the space allotted to it. (See page 88 for an explanation of viewing frames.) Move the frame around so that you can assess several possibilities. Often you may find that allowing one of the objects to run out of the picture actually helps the composition.

Lighting is also very important. It defines the forms, heightens the colours and casts shadows which can become a vital component in the composition. If you are working by natural light other than a north (in the northern hemisphere) light, it will, of course, change as the day wears on. This may not matter very much so long as you decide where the shadows are to be at the outset and do not keep trying to change them; but often it is more satisfactory to use artificial light. This solution sometimes brings its own problem, however, since if you are painting flowers or fruit they will wilt more quickly.

above: William Henry Hunt produced charming portraits as well as *genre* subjects, using his paint rather dry to depict colours and textures with great accuracy. *Plums* is an unusual approach to still-life, as it has an outdoor setting but it was almost certainly done in the studio from preliminary sketches.

Flower arrangements are among the most popular of all still-life subjects. Indeed, they are often regarded as a separate branch of painting. In purely practical terms, however, they are a type of still-life, posing the same problems as well as sharing the major advantage of being a captive subject.

With any group of objects set up as a painting subject the main problem is arrangement, and hence the composition of the painting itself. Flowers in a vase, for example, do not always make a shape that fills a rectangle very well; so it is sometimes necessary to add other elements, such as a plate, some fruit or background drapery. Here the composition is simple but very effective: the table-top, with its checked cloth, provides foreground interest to balance the pattern formed by the flowers themselves against the plain background. It also adds to the impression of solidity and its intersecting diagonal lines provide a pleasing contrast with the curved shapes. Interestingly, the tablecloth was added as an afterthought, when the artist had already painted the flower and pot; without it the character of the painting would have been quite different. When arranging a still-life or flower piece it is helpful to make a few advance sketches, as alterations cannot always be made as easily as they were here.

1: A careful outline drawing was made of the flowers and pot, and then the flowers were panted in with a mixture of cadmium red and purple lake. Particular attention was paid to the arrangement of the spaces created by the flowers against the background.

2: The mid-to-light tones of the leaves in the centre were laid on quite freely, sharper definition being reserved for those at the sides, to form a clear, sharp outline. The colours – emerald green, sap green, Payne's grey and a touch of raw sienna – were put on wet and allowed to mix on the paper.

3: The leaves and flowers were darkened in places and a first wash was then laid on the pot. Here, too, the colours were applied wet and moved around on the paper until the artist was satisfied with the way they had blended together.

4: A very pale wash was put on the underside of the dish, leaving the rim white to stand out against the checks. The blue used was chosen to echo the blue on the pot, and the shadow was added later.

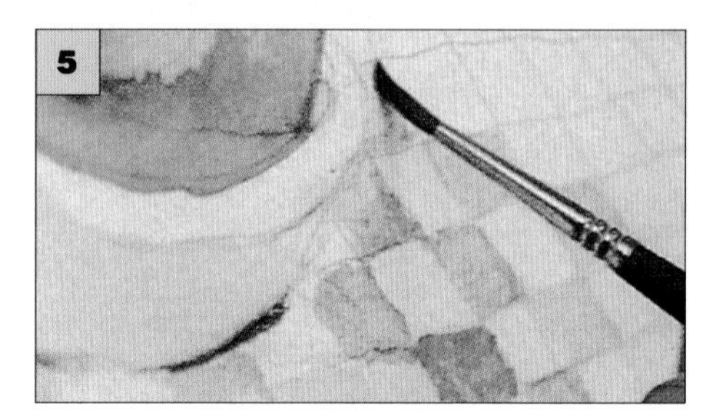

5: Here the artist is using the tip of a sable brush to paint the blue checks. Although they were painted carefully, and varied in size and colour to suggest recession, the artist has not attempted to produce perfectly straight or regular lines, which would have looked mechanical and monotonous.

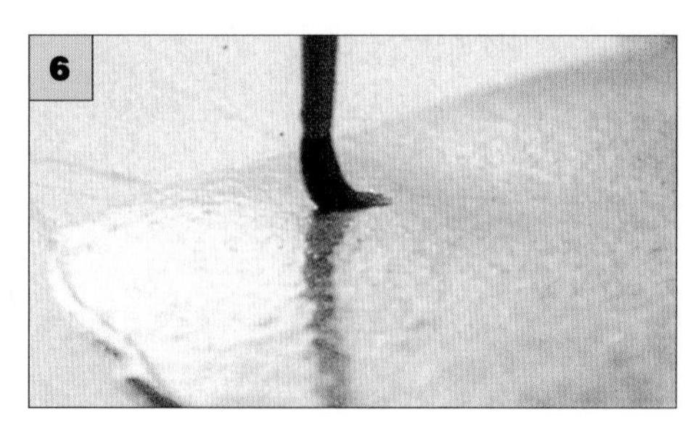

6: The wet-into-wet technique was used for painting the pot, giving it a lively appearance suggestive of light and texture. Widely varying colours were applied with plenty of water and blended into one another. If the paint is too wet, or blends in the wrong way, it can be dabbed off with a sponge or tissue.

Materials Used

SUPPORT: pre-stretched watercolour paper with a not surface, measuring 30 x 40 cm (12 x 16 in).

COLOURS: cadmium red, alizarin crimson, raw sienna, purple lake, emerald green, sap green, lemon yellow, ultramarine, cobalt blue and Payne's grey.

BRUSHES: Nos. 7 and 3 sable.

Step by Step: Persimmon and Plums

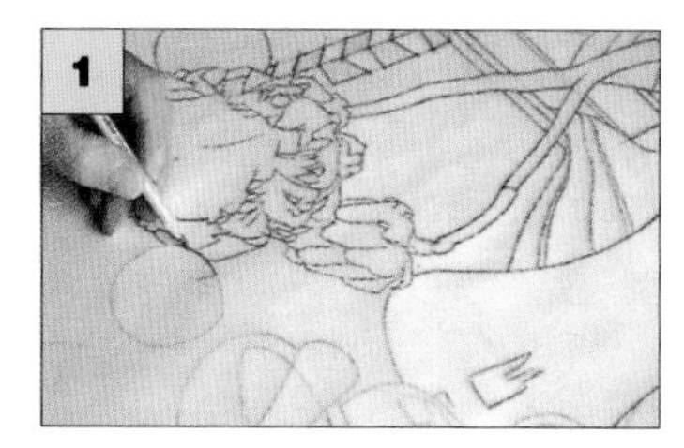

1: Ronald Jesty is an artist who likes to exercise full control over his medium, and he works almost exclusively wet-on-dry. This painting has been planned very carefully, and is built up in a series of separate stages. Here he is transferring a full-scale drawing to the paper by drawing over a tracing.

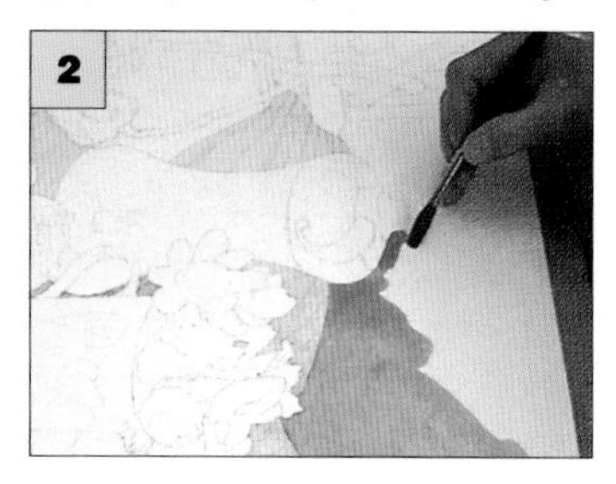

2: He begins with several small, neutral-coloured washes and then paints the golden-brown background. Notice that he has turned the board sideways to make it easier to take the paint around the edges of the bottle.

3: It is important to establish the colour key early on, so once the background is complete he puts down a pale pinkish grey for the table-top and areas of vivid red for the petals of the anemones. Without the background it would have been difficult to assess the strength of colour needed for these. The next stages are the persimmon and the mug that holds the flowers, close in tone and colour but with clearly perceptible differences. None of these areas of colour is completely flat: the modelling on the persimmon and the jug begins immediately, with darker, cooler colours in the shadow areas, linked to the blue-grey of the pestle and mortar.

4: The flowers and fruit are now virtually complete, with the dark rich colours built up in a series of small, overlapping washes to leave highlights of varying intensity. The light blue-grey of the vase on the left represents the colour and tone to be reserved for highlights.

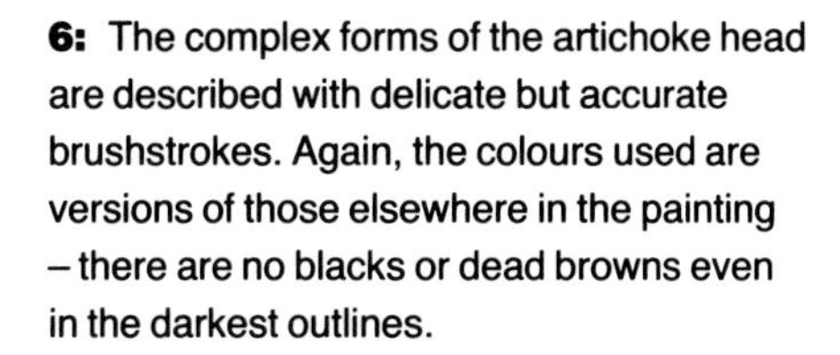

6: The complex forms of the artichoke head are described with delicate but accurate brushstrokes. Again, the colours used are versions of those elsewhere in the painting – there are no blacks or dead browns even in the darkest outlines.

7: With the deep blues and purples of the jug now complete, the painting has a sure and definite focal point. Although the whole picture is eventful and there are some

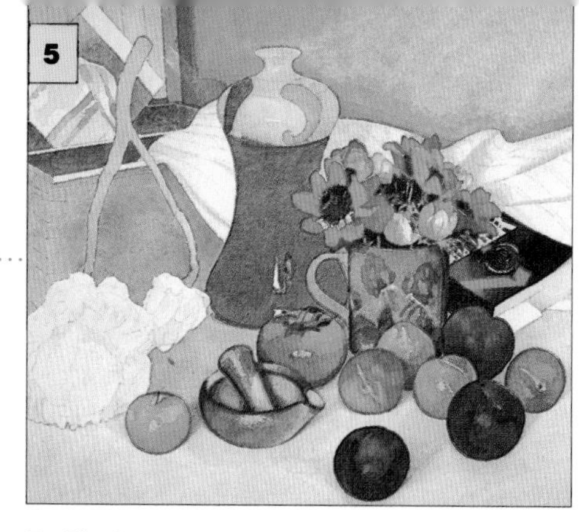

5: The box on the left is painted in a colour that picks up that of the persimmons and yellow plums. Although the painting is vivid and colourful, the colours are deliberately orchestrated to give an overall strength and unity to the composition. A further wash is laid on the blue vase to stand as the mid-toned highlights when the darkest tones have been added.

delightful touches, such as the book title we cannot quite read and the sketch on the left, our attention is drawn to the centre by the strong, dark tones and glowing colours. It is not easy to achieve this intensity in watercolour without muddying the paint by overworking, and this is why Jesty plans so thoroughly. He overlays washes to a considerable extent, but avoids overworking by using barely diluted paint from the outset where the tones are to be dark.

INDOOR ARRANGEMENTS

The great advantage of painting cut flowers indoors is that you can control the set-up and work more or less at your leisure – at any rate until the blooms fade and die. The main problem is that flowers can look over-arranged, destroying the natural, living quality that is the subject's greatest charm. Always try to make them look as natural as possible, allowing some to overlap others, and placing them at different heights, with some of the heads turned away from and others towards you, as they would appear when growing in a garden.

Give equally careful thought to the overall colour scheme – of the flowers themselves, the vase you put them in and the background. Too great a mixture of colours can lead to a muddled painting that has no sense of unity because each hue is fighting for attention with its neighbour.

The best flower paintings are often those with one predominant colour, such as white, blue or yellow, with those in the background and foreground orchestrated to provide just the right element of contrast.

left: Shirley Felts, *Chrysanthemums with Chinese Vase,* 73.7 x 53.3 cm (29 x 21 in), watercolour. One of the considerations in arranging a flower group must be the characteristics of the flowers themselves. A bloom with strong and dramatic shapes, such as a lily, could look exciting on its own or in a small group, but multi-flowered chrysanthemums are best treated as a mass, as here, because that is how they grow. The group is nevertheless very carefully arranged, with a slight asymmetry, and the leaves trailed over the vase on the left to add foreground interest. The little touches of red in the smaller group provide the perfect touch of contrast to the delicate white and green colour scheme.

left: Mary Tempest, *Tiger Lilies,* 50.8 x 40.6 cm (20 x 16 in), gouache. The marvellously vivid colour scheme of this painting has been planned with great care, with the bright yellows and violets repeated throughout. These two colours are complementaries, colours which enhance one another when used together. Tempest has also brought in the other two main complementaries, red and green, so that the whole painting positively vibrates. Although she has placed the vase of flowers centrally, she has avoided a static look by firstly arranging the flowers so that they reach up on the left, following the curve of the jug, and secondly by choosing an irregular shape in the foreground.

left: Muriel Pemberton, *Bright Garden Bouquet,* 45.7 x 62.9 cm (18 x 24¾ in), watercolour, body colour, ink and pastel. Here the off-centre placing of the vase and the way the flowers lean to the left gives a rhythm to the composition, leading the viewer's eye around it from one area to another. Pemberton's technique is equally lively and varied. She makes no preliminary drawing, but begins painting at once, working on the background and flowers at the same time, and building up texture and depth of colour with successive layers of paint, pastel and ink. In some places she applies thin washes over thick, while in others transparent watercolour is allowed to show through opaque paint, creating a fragile, translucent effect.

left: Ronald Jesty, RBA, *Sweet Peas in a Tumbler,* 30.5 x 20.3 cm (12 x 8 in), watercolour. Jesty's compositions are always bold, and often surprising, as this one is. We are so conditioned by the idea of "proper" settings for flower pieces and still-lifes that the idea of placing a vase of flowers on a newspaper seems almost heretical. But it works perfectly, with the newspaper images providing just the right combination of geometric shapes and dark tones to balance the forms and colours of the sweet peas.

below: Carolyne Moran, *Hydrangeas in a Blue and White Jug,* 26.7 x 26.7 cm (10½ x 10½ in), gouache. Here the flowers occupy an uncompromisingly central position, with the rounded shapes of the blooms and vase dominating the picture, but counterpointed by the rectangles formed by the background window frame. Interestingly, we do not immediately perceive this painting as square because the verticals give it an upward thrust. The artist has made cunning use of intersecting diagonals in the foreground to break up the predominantly geometric grid, and has linked the flowers to the background by using the same blue under the windowsill. There is considerable overpainting on the flower heads, as they kept changing colour while the artist worked – one of the flower painter's occupational hazards.

Composition

A group of flowers tastefully arranged in an attractive vase always looks enticing – that, after all, is the point of putting them there – but it may not make a painting in itself. Placing a vase of flowers in the centre of the picture, with no background or foreground interest, is not usually the best way to make the most of the subject – though there are some notable exceptions to this rule. So you will have to think about what other elements you might include to make the composition more interesting without detracting from the main subject.

One of the most-used compositional devices is that of placing the vase asymmetrically and painting from an angle so that the back of the table-top forms a diagonal instead of a horizontal line. Diagonals are a powerful weapon in the artist's armoury, as they help to lead the eye in to the centre of the picture, while horizontal lines do the opposite.

One of the difficulties with flower groups is that the vase leaves a blank space at the bottom of the picture area. This can sometimes be dealt with by using a cast shadow as part of the composition, or you can scatter one or two blooms or petals beneath or to one side of the vase, thus creating a relationship between foreground and focal point.

left: Mary Tempest, *Anemones,* 76.2 x 55.9 cm (30 x 22 in), gouache. This bold, highly patterned composition, with the emphasis on carefully distributed areas of bright colour, is somewhat reminiscent of Henri Matisse. Although the painting is predominantly two-dimensional, there is a considerable degree of modelling in the fruit, jug and flowers, which ensures their place as the focal point of the painting. Tempest uses gouache almost like oil paint and for this painting she has mixed it with an impasto medium (Aquapasto) in order to build it up thickly.

right: Geraldine Girvan, *Studio Mantelpiece,* 57 x 66 cm (22⅜ x 26 in), gouache. Girvan has used a combination of diagonals and verticals to lead the eye into and around the picture. Our eye follows the line of the mantelpiece, but instead of going out of the frame on the left it is led upwards by the side of the picture frame and then downwards through the tall flowers to the glowing heart of the picture – the daffodils. She has avoided isolating this area of bright yellow by using a slightly muted version of it in the reflection behind and has further unified the composition by repeating the reds from one area to another.

Single Specimens

The most obvious example of flowers and plants treated singly rather than as part of a group are botanical paintings. Botanical studies have been made since pre-Renaissance times and are still an important branch of specialized illustration. Many of the best of these drawings and paintings are fine works of art, but their primary aim is to record precise information about a particular species. For the botanical illustrator, pictorial charms are secondary bonuses, but artists, who are more concerned with these than with scientific accuracy, can exploit them in a freer, more painterly way.

However, this is an area where careful drawing and observation is needed. You may be able to get away with imprecise drawing for a broad impression of a flower group, but a subject that is to stand on its own must be convincingly rendered. Looking at illustrated books and photographs can help you to acquire background knowledge of flower and leaf shapes, but it goes without saying that you will also need to draw from life – constantly.

Most flowers can be simplified into basic shapes, such as circles or bells. These, like everything else, are affected by perspective, so that a circle turned away from you becomes an ellipse. It is much easier to draw flowers if you establish these main shapes before describing each petal or stamen.

top: Jean Canter SGFA, *Corn Marigolds,* 24.1 x 33 cm (9½ x 13 in), oval, watercolour with a little white gouache. The oval format chosen for this delightful study gives it a rather Victorian flavour. The artist has created a strong feeling of life and movement, with the sinuously curving stems and leaves seeming to grow outward towards the boundary of the frame.

above: Sharon Beeden, *Apples and Plums,* 25.8 x 25 cm (10 x 10 in), watercolour. This artist is a professional botanical illustrator and the painting was one of a series for a book. Its subject was the introduction of fruit, vegetables and herbs to Britain through the centuries and before she could begin her work, Beeden had to carry out time-consuming research to find old varieties from various periods of history. Each of these specimens was drawn from life, the blossoms being redrawn from sketchbook studies done earlier in the year. The composition was worked out on tracing paper and then transferred to the working paper.

Natural Habitat

Oddly, the term "flower painting" makes us think of cut flowers rather than growing ones, perhaps because most of the paintings of this genre that we see in art galleries are of arranged rather than outdoor subjects. Flowers, however, are at their best in their natural surroundings, and painting them outdoors, whether they are wild specimens in woods, hedgerows or city wastelands or cultivated blooms in gardens, is both rewarding and enjoyable.

It can, however, present more problems than painting arranged groups indoors, because you cannot control the background or the lighting, and you may have to adopt a ruthlessly selective approach to achieve a satisfactory composition.

You will also have a changing light source to contend with. As the sun moves across the sky the colours and tones can change dramatically, and a leaf or flower head that was previously obscured by shadow will suddenly be spot-lit so that you can no longer ignore its presence. The best way to deal with this problem, if you think a painting may take more than a few hours to complete, is to work in two or three separate sessions at the same time of day or to make several quick studies that you can then combine into a painting in the studio.

below: Audrey Macleod, *Rhododendrons in Dulwich Park,* approx. 27.9 x 40.6 cm (11 x 16 in), watercolour and pen drawing. Macleod has used the shapes and forms of the plants to create a composition with a strong two-dimensional pattern quality. To express the delicacy of the subject, she has given careful consideration to the medium, exploiting the line and wash technique to set up an effective hard/soft contrast and retaining the transparency of the paint by touching the colour in lightly to the edges of the forms. She has also washed down some areas to soften the colour, an effect which can be seen behind and below the central bloom. In contrast, the delicate pen lines, made with watered-down mauve and grey inks, stand out with crisp clarity.

right: Norma Jameson RBA, ROI, *Waterlilies,* 30.5 x 40.6 cm (12 x 16 in), gouache and watercolour on cartridge paper. Jameson works partly from life and partly from transparencies and says that the former gives the necessary element of spontaneity to her work while the photographic studies provide the equally necessary time for consideration. For specific flower forms, she takes numerous slides, from different angles and positions and in close-up, using the camera like a sketchbook and then distilling what interests her most when she begins to paint.

NARCISSI IN SUNLIGHT

Most of us have experienced the frustration of setting out to capture the elusive beauty of flowers, only to be disappointed with our ham-fisted attempts! Flowers are so attractive, it's hard to resist the urge to paint them in every detail – and this is where the problems start. As the still-life above demonstrates, beginners often fall into the familiar trap of trying to create a photographic impression of the flowers, which inevitably leads to an overworked image. In this example, the flowers look hard and brittle instead of soft and delicate, and the colours are muddy instead of bright and fresh.

Another fault in this painting is in the arrangement of the flowers, which is too formal and contrived: the blooms look as if they are standing to attention. Also, the two red tulips add a discordant colour note – as does the rather gloomy background, which gives the painting a claustrophobic feel.

Painting flowers well requires close observation to detail and constant practice. However, the most essential thing is knowing how to interpret creatively the particular *character* of the flowers you have chosen to paint – whether they be huge exotic lilies or tiny, dainty snowdrops.

Setting up: Try to keep the arrangement of your flowers simple and informal. Stylized or symmetrical groupings tend to look stiff and unnatural in a painting. Arrange the blooms so that they overlap each other, and include profile and back views of some of them. This adds variety of shape as well as accentuating the three-dimensional impression. In Lucy Willis's painting *Narcissi in Sunlight* (right) the flowers are not "arranged" but allowed to fan out naturally and gracefully, just as they would do when growing out of the earth.

A vase full of multi-coloured flowers is not always a good idea, because the colours fight each other and destroy any impression of delicacy. It's far better to choose flowers of the same colour, or a harmonious arrangement of closely related colours.

Mixing colours: Freshness and clarity of colour are essential in flower painting, so be sure that you are familiar with your pigments and how they mix together. Flowers may be colourful, but you don't need a vast array of pigments in order to paint them.

right: Flower forms are built up from light to dark with glazes of warm and cool colour. Areas of white paper provide "breathing spaces". Flowers viewed from the back can be just as interesting as those viewed from the front.

far right: Spontaneous brushstrokes and lost and found edges give a sense of natural, living forms.

above: Lucy Willis, *Narcissi in Sunlight.*

left: Cast shadows add design interest and help to anchor the vase of flowers to the table-top.

Watercolour has always been closely associated with landscape and seascape painting, and even with today's proliferation of new media for the artist there is still none more able to render the transient and atmospheric qualities of countryside, sea and sky.

THE ENGLISH WATERCOLOUR TRADITION

In England, the country which more than any other can claim to have founded the great tradition of landscape painting in watercolour, landscape was not really considered a suitable subject in its own right until the late eighteenth century. The formal, classical landscapes of the French artists, Claude Lorraine (1600–82) and Nicolas Poussin (1594–1665), were much admired by artists and discerning collectors, as were the realistic landscapes of artists of the Dutch school such as Jacob van Ruisdael (1629–82), but the general public in the main wanted portraits and historical subjects. The great English portrait painter, Thomas Gainsborough (1727–88), had a deep love of his native landscape and regarded it as his true subject, but in order to earn a living he painted many more portraits than landscapes.

The two artists who elevated landscape and seascape to the status of fine art were Constable and Turner. Their influence on painting, not only in Great Britain but all over the world, was immeasurable. By the early nineteenth century landscape had arrived, and at the same time watercolour, a medium hitherto used for quick sketches and for colouring maps and prints, had become the chief medium for many landscape artists. Constable used watercolour as his predecessors had, as a rapid means of recording impressions, but Turner used it in a new and daring way and exploited its potential fully to express his feelings about light and colour.

At much the same time John Sell Cotman, the co-founder of the school of painting known as the Norwich School after its other founder, John Crome (1768–1821), who lived in that town, was producing some of the finest watercolour landscapes ever seen before or since. These paintings by the artists of the English watercolour school have never been surpassed; they became an inspiration to artists everywhere, and remain so today.

below: Thomas Girtin was a pioneer of watercolour painting much admired by his contemporary, Turner. He worked with only five colours – black, monastral blue, yellow ochre, burnt sienna and light red – to create subtle evocations of atmosphere. *The White House, Chelsea,* shows both his fine sense of composition and his mastery of tone and colour. In the darker areas, washes have been laid one over another with great skill. The focal point, the house, is slightly off-centre and has been left as white paper, appearing almost as if floodlit.

above: Thomas Girtin, *Landscape With a Church Beside a River*. A friend and contemporary of Turner, Thomas Girtin specialized in watercolour and in his short life revolutionized landscape painting in that medium.

above: A watercolour of stones at Avebury. The cool tones express the clarity of daylight and the calm grandeur of this ancient monument.

Practical Hints for Outdoor Painting

Once landscape had become an "official" subject for painters, working out of doors directly from nature became increasingly common, the more so after the French Impressionists set the example. It is not now so popular. Photographers queueing up to record a beauty spot are a more usual sight than artists doing so. It is, however, an excellent discipline, which forces you to look hard at a subject and make rapid decisions about how to treat it and lends immediacy and spontaneity to the work itself.

Watercolour is a light and portable medium, ideally suited to outdoor work, but on-the-spot painting, whatever the medium, always presents problems. Chief among them is the weather. You may have to contend with blazing heat which dries the paint as soon as it is laid down, freezing winds which numb your hands, sudden showers which blotch your best efforts or wash them away altogether, and changing light which confuses you and makes you doubt your initial drawing and composition. If the weather looks unpredictable, take extra clothes (a pair of old gloves with the fingers cut off the painting hand are a help in winter), a plastic bag or carrier large enough to hold your board in case of rain, and anything else you can think of for your comfort, such as a thermos of tea or coffee and a radio. If the sun is bright try to sit in a shaded place; otherwise the light will bounce back at you off the white paper, which makes it difficult or sometimes impossible to see what you are doing. If you are embarrassed by the comments of passers-by, a personal stereo serves as an efficient insulation device. Some people also find it an aid to concentration, though others do not. Always take sufficient water and receptacles to put it in, and restrict your palettte to as few colours as possible.

Choose a subject that genuinely interests you rather than one you feel you "ought" to paint, even if it is only a back garden or local park. If you are familiar with a particular area you will probably already have a subject, or several subjects, in mind. On holiday in an unfamiliar place, try to assess a subject in advance by carrying out a preliminary reconaissance rather than dashing straight out with your paints. Finally, try to work as quickly as you can without rushing, so that the first important stages of the painting are complete before the light changes. If necessary make a start on one day and complete the work on another. Seascapes are especially difficult, since the colour of the sea can change drastically – from dark indigo to bright blue-green, for example – in a matter of minutes. It is often advisable to make several quick colour sketches and then work indoors from them.

below: Francis Towne, *The Source of the Arveiron with Mont Blanc in the Background,* 1781. In this work Towne reveals his full power as a draughtsman of genius. The colour is as abstract as the form, imposed upon nature according to the dictates of the composition. Towne was a true forerunner of Cézanne and those European artists whose work was revolutionized by the Japanese print.

Trees and Foliage

Trees, whether covered in a luxurious blanket of green in summer, glowing with warm reds and yellows in autumn or stark and bare in winter, are among the most enticing of all landscape features. Unfortunately, they are not the easiest of subjects to paint, particularly when foliage obscures their basic structure and makes its own complex patterns of light and shade.

To paint a tree in leaf successfully it is usually necessary to simplify it to some extent. Start by establishing the broad shape of the tree, noting its dominant characteristics, such as the width of the trunk in relation to the height and spread of the branches. Avoid becoming bogged down in detail, defining individual shapes in a manner that does not detract from the main mass. If you try to give equal weight and importance to every separate clump of foliage you will create a jumpy, fragmented effect. Look at the subject with your eyes half closed and you will see that some parts of the tree, those in shadow or further away from you, will read as one broad colour area, while the sunlit parts and those nearer to you will show sharp contrasts of tone and colour.

A useful technique for highlighting areas where you want to avoid hard lines is that of lifting out, while sponge painting is a good way of suggesting the lively broken-colour effect of foliage. Dry brush is another favoured technique, well suited to winter trees with their delicate, hazy patterns created by clusters of tiny twigs.

below: Charles Knight RWS, ROI, *Rickmansworth Canal,* 27.9 x 38.1 cm (11 x 15 in), watercolour and pencil on tinted paper. Knight's expressive landscapes are reminiscent of the work of English eighteenth-century watercolourists and, like them, he owes his deceptively simple-looking effects to a thorough knowledge of the medium and a willingness to experiment with it. He has used a variety of techniques, including dry brush, brush drawing and wax resist on the trees, but these technical "tricks" never dominate.

left: Ronald Jesty RBA, *Torteval, Guernsey,* 33 x 15.2 cm (13 x 16 in), watercolour. Jesty also paints wet-on-dry, but individual brushstrokes are only visible in the foreground. He has set up an exciting contrast by using very flat paint for the large, strong shapes in the background and delicate brush drawing for the slender, spiky grasses. The unusual tall, thin format stresses the vertical emphasis of the composition.

left: Moira Clinch, *Lakeland Tree,* 33 x 45.7 cm (13 x 18 in), watercolour. In this painting, Clinch has used a combination of wet-in-wet and wet-on-dry, which gives excitement and variety to her paint surface. She has also suggested texture on the large tree trunk by exploiting the granular effect caused by overlaying washes. She has cleverly prevented the eye being taken out of the picture with the swing of the large branch on the right by blurring the paint, so that we focus on the crisply delineated area in the centre.

right: Robert Dodd, *Amberley and Kithurst Hill, Sussex,* 52 x 71.1 cm (20½ x 28 in), gouache. Dodd has given drama to his quiet subject by the use of bold tonal contrasts and inventive exploitation of texture. He has used his gouache quite thickly, building up areas such as the ploughed field in the foreground by masking and sponging. The more flatly applied paint used for the background and sky allows the textures to stand out strongly by contrast.

below: Martin Taylor, *Castello-in-Chianti,* 26 x 35 cm (10¼ x 13¾ in), watercolour and acrylic. Using acrylic white to give body to his watercolour, Taylor builds up his colours and textures gradually, using tiny brushstrokes to create a shimmering quality, and working on one part of the painting at a time.

below: Donald Pass, *Frosty Morning, Autumn,* 67.3 x 85 cm (26½ x 33½ in), watercolour. Pass has an unusual watercolour style, using his paints almost like a drawing medium. He makes no preparatory drawing, and begins by laying broad washes of light colour. He then builds up each area with a succession of directional or linear brush marks. It is easy to imagine how this subject might have become dull, but the brushwork, as well as being effective in terms of pure description, creates marvellous movement: we can almost feel the light wind bending the grass and sending the clouds scudding across the sky.

Fields and Hills

Mountains always make dramatic subjects, their powerful presence needing only the minimum of help from the painter, but quieter country – flat or with gentle contours – can easily become dull and featureless in a painting. It is seldom enough just to paint what you see, so you may have to think of ways of enhancing a subject by exaggerating certain features, stepping up the colours or tonal contrasts, introducing textural interest or using your brushwork more inventively. Interestingly, there have been artists throughout history who have believed that they have been painting exactly what they have seen, but they never really were – consciously or unconsciously improving on nature is part of the process.

Part of the problem with this kind of landscape is that, although it is often beautiful and atmospheric, much of its appeal comes from the way it surrounds and envelops you. Once you begin to home in on the one small part of it you can fit onto a piece of paper, you often wonder what you found so exciting – a feeling well known to anyone who takes photographs. So take a leaf from the photographer's book and use a viewfinder – a rectangle cut in a piece of cardboard is all you need. With this, you can isolate various parts of the scene and choose the best. If it is still less interesting than you hoped, add some elements from another area, such as a clump of trees or a ploughed field, and consider emphasizing something in the foreground.

Rocks and Mountains

Mountains are a gift to the painter – they form marvellously exciting shapes, their colours are constantly changing and, best of all, unless you happen to be sitting on one, they are far enough away to be seen as broad shapes without too much worrying detail.

Distant mountains can be depicted using flat or semi-flat washes with details such as individual outcrops lightly indicated on those nearer to hand. For atmospheric effects, such as mist or light cloud blending sky and mountain tops together, try working wet-in-wet or mixing watercolour with opaque white.

Nearby rocks and cliffs call for a rather different approach, since their most exciting qualities are their hard, sharp edges and their textures – even the rounded, sea-weathered boulders seen on some seashores are pitted and uneven in surface and are far from soft to the touch. One of the best techniques for creating edge qualities is the wet-on-dry method, where successive small washes are laid over one another (if you become tired of waiting for them to dry, use a hairdryer to speed up the process). Texture can be built up in a number of ways. The wax resist, scumbling or salt spatter methods are all excellent.

below: Michael Chaplin RE, ARWS, *Welsh Cliffs,* 45.7 x 53.3 cm (18 x 21 in), watercolour with some body colour. Very light pen lines accentuate the directional brushstrokes used for the sharp verticals of the cliff face, and texture has been suggested in places by sandpapering washes, a technique that works particularly well on the rough paper the artist has used. The addition of body colour (opaque white) to the paint has produced subtle colours and given a suitably chalky appearance to the cliffs.

above: Ronald Jesty RBA, *Portland Lighthouse,* 25.4 x 25.4 cm (10 x 10 in), watercolour. Jesty has worked wet-on-dry, using flat washes of varying sizes to describe the crisp, hard-edged quality of the rocks. He has created texture on some of the foreground surfaces by "drawing" with an upright brush to produce dots and other small marks, and has cleverly unified the painting by echoing the small cloud shapes in the light patches on the foreground rock. This was painted in the studio from a pen sketch. Advance planning is a prerequisite for Jesty's very deliberate way of painting, and he works out his compositions and the distribution of lights and darks carefully beforehand.

Step by Step: Distant Hills

This painting relies for its effect on the use of linear shapes arranged in such a way as to create an atmosphere of gentle harmony. The colour range is very limited, almost monochromatic, and the minimum of detail, even in the foreground, gives the elegantly uncluttered and stylized look characteristic of many Chinese paintings.

One of the artist's main concerns was to indicate the spaciousness and recession of the landscape. He used two methods to do this. The first was aerial perspective, the term used for the way that the features of a landscape become less distinct as they recede, with the colours becoming paler and cooler. Tonal contrasts are greater in the foreground, where the colours are strong and warm. The second method was to allow the tree on the right to go out of the frame at the top, thus clearly indicating that the group of trees is on the picture plane (the front of the painting).

The painting provides an excellent example of the "classical" approach to watercolour, in which the paint is laid on in a series of thin washes, allowing the brilliance of the white paper to reflect back through them. Unusually, an HP (hot-pressed) paper was used instead of the more popular not, or cold-pressed, but this artist finds that the smoother paper suits his style, and he mixes a little gum arabic with the water to give extra body and adherence. Each wash, once laid down, has been left without any further paint being laid on top, and the painting was worked from the top downward, with the foreground trees painted over the washes for the sky and hills. It was done in the studio from a sketch and the drawing on the support was restricted to a few lines drawn with an HB pencil.

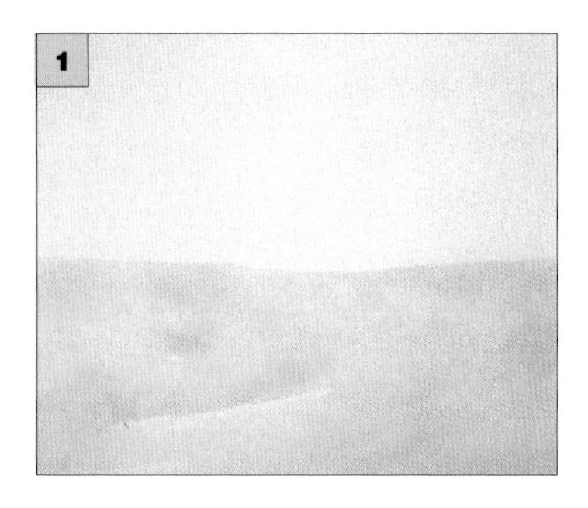

1: The wash for the sky, put on with a No. 10 squirrel brush, was deliberately laid slightly unevenly to suggest a pale blue sky with a light cloud cover.

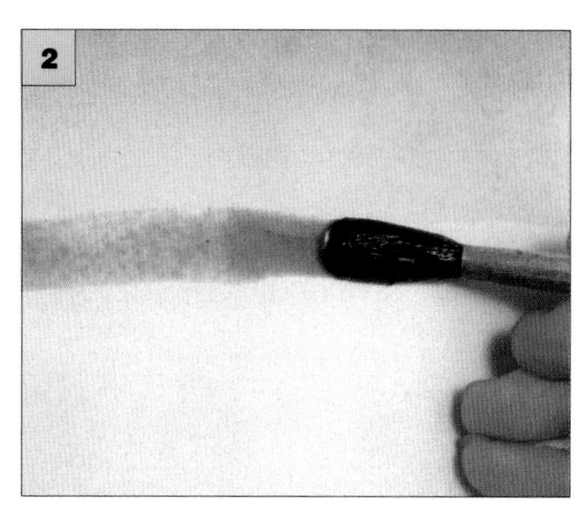

2: As soon as the wash for the sky was dry, the same squirrel brush was used to put on a darker shade, with Payne's grey added to the cobalt blue, to the area of the far hills.

3: The second wash had to be darker than that for the sky but not too dark, as the artist knew that he would have to increase the tonal contrasts in the middle distance to suggest its relative nearness to the picture plane.

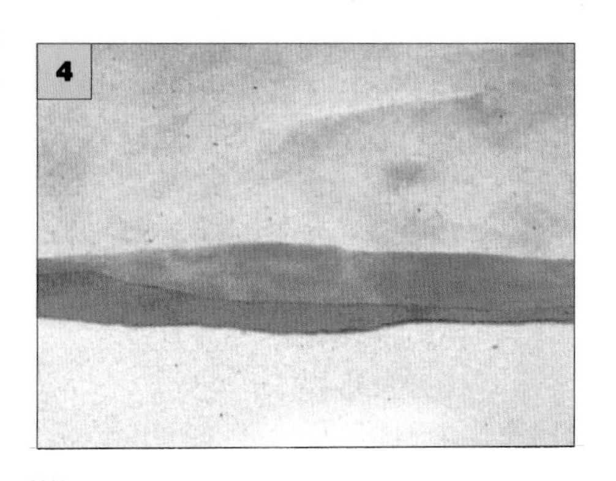

4, 5: As each wash has to be allowed to dry before putting on the next, in this particular technique, a hairdryer is sometimes used to hasten the process. The third and fourth washes, darker shades of the second, were laid on next, leaving the whole of the foreground and middle distance still untouched.

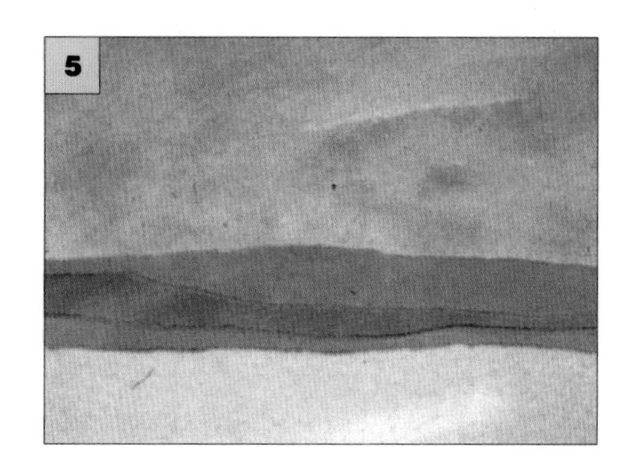

6: The tone of the darker area of the middle distance had to be very carefully calculated to make it appear to be in front of the far hills. This wash has been put on slightly thicker in places to suggest the shapes of the trees.

7: The trees in the foreground were worked on next, the darker paint being taken over the background and sky washes. This overlapping device is most successful when the colours are similar; overlapping two quite different colours, for instance red-brown tree-trunks over a bright green middle distance, would give a third colour, which could provide a jarring element if not planned.

8, 9: At this stage both the background and foreground were complete, but the area between the two was still unpainted. Because warm colours tend to advance and cool ones recede, the artist laid a warm greenish wash over this area to make it come forward toward the picture plane.

MATERIALS USED

SUPPORT: pre-stretched watercolour paper with an HP surface, measuring 35 x 53 cm (14 x 21½ in).

COLOURS: cobalt blue, Payne's grey, raw umber and sap green.

BRUSHES: a No. 10 squirrel and a No. 4 sable.

ADDITIONAL EQUIPMENT: a selection of ceramic palettes for mixing the paint; a little gum arabic for mixing with the water.

Step by Step: Old Harry and His Wife

A large variety of different techniques has been used to create the deceptively simple effect of this painting. The subject is bold and dramatic, and its drama has been emphasized by the juxtaposition of large, solid shapes. The tonal contrasts between the rocks and the sea are distinct enough for the rocks to stand out as light against dark, but not so great as to spoil the delicate balance. Greater contrasts might have looked overstated.

Seascapes can be tricky subjects. It is difficult to decide whether to treat the sea as a flat area or to try to show the movement of the water by "filling in" every wave and ripple. Also, when painting outdoors, you will see the colours constantly changing, which can give rise to uncertainty about the best approach. Here the sea has been treated fairly flat, with just enough unevenness and broken texture to suggest water; the sky hints at clouds, nothing more. The artist did not have to contend with changing colours and lights, since the painting was done in the studio. He used a photograph as his main reference for the shapes and was thus free to decide on a colour scheme without external distraction. The light falling on the rock, which the photograph features very vividly, has been given a minor role in the painting, as the artist was more concerned with the texture of the rock, which is echoed in the ripping reflection below.

Masking fluid provided the ideal way of dealing with the rock. The brightly lit areas were covered with the fluid, so that the shadow areas could be built up without the paints encroaching on the highlights. In places the dry brush technique was used, together with spattering. Both techniques are excellent for suggesting texture, though they should always be used sparingly.

Materials Used

SUPPORT: pre-stretched watercolour paper with a not surface, measuring 54 x 75 cm (21 x 30 in).

COLOURS: Payne's grey, ultramarine, cobalt blue, sap green, lemon yellow, yellow ochre and raw umber, plus a little white gouache.

BRUSHES AND OTHER EQUIPMENT: a selection of large and small soft brushes, a broad bristle brush, gum arabic, masking fluid and masking tape.

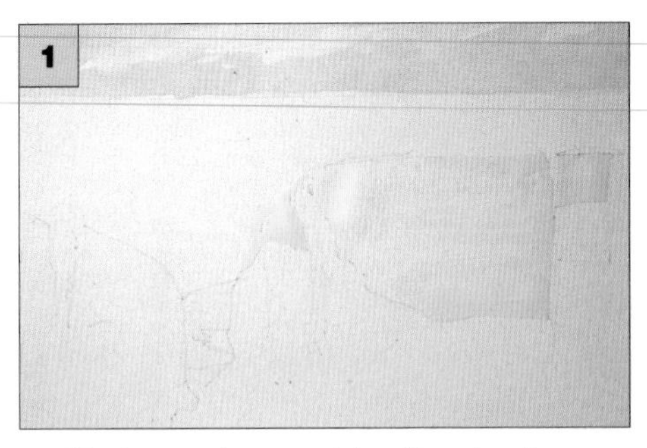

1: Having made a careful outline drawing of the main shapes, the artist blocked out the brightest areas of the rocks with masking fluid. This method highlights the importance of an accurate drawing, since the artist has to know from the outset exactly where to place the masking fluid. When the masking fluid was dry, a broken wash was laid over the sky area and then a darker one for the line of distant cliffs.

2: The sea was laid in with a soft brush and a dilute wash of Payne's grey. This wash was deliberately kept loose and fluid, and the paint was moved around to create different tones.

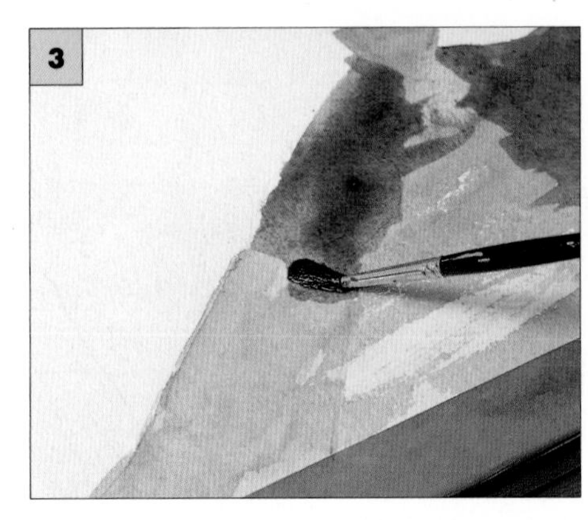

3: Here the artist is using a darker tone of Payne's grey, mixed with ultramarine, a warm blue, to darken the sea in places.

4: At this stage the entire surface has been covered and the masking fluid, yellowish in colour, is still on. A pale wash of lemon yellow was laid on the reflection area and greyish washes put over the darker parts of the rocks.

5: Using diluted black paint the artist works the darkest shadows between the rocks and at the bottom of the central rock.

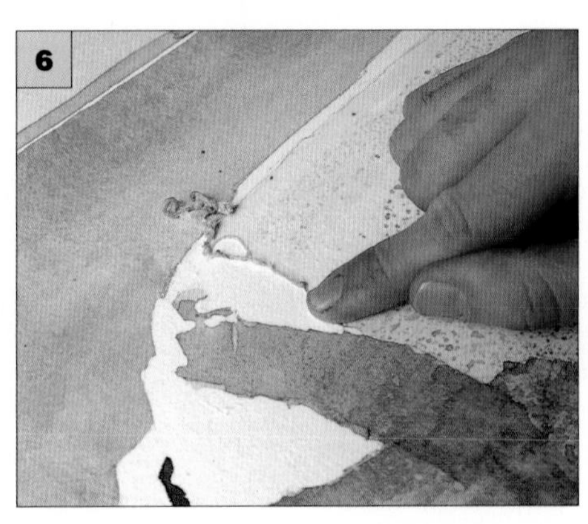

6: Once the dark tones have been put on, the masking fluid is removed by rubbing gently with the finger. Masking fluid is not suitable for use on rough paper, as it sinks into the hollows and cannot be removed.

7: The grassy tops of the cliffs are now painted sap green with a fine brush. Note how the artist darkens the colour at the edge to produce a crisp line of shadow.

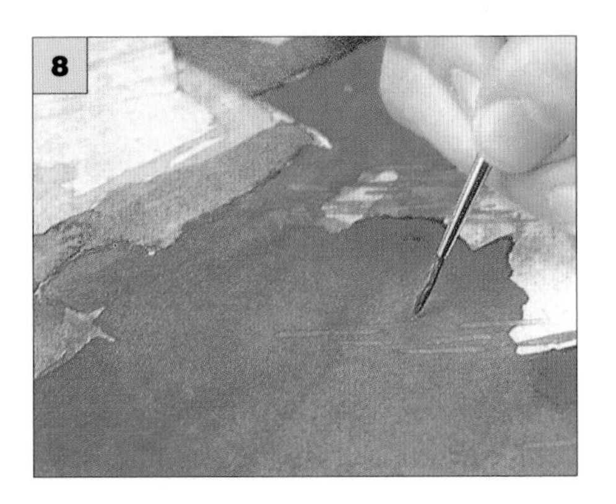

8: Another technique used for this painting was to cover an area already painted with gummed water, leave it to dry, and then gently work into it with a brush dipped in clear water to give small areas of lighter tone.

9: Here the artist is using a broad bristle brush to spatter paint on to the surface. Surrounding areas were masked off first. This is an effective texture-creating technique, but care must be taken to mix a colour which is only slightly darker than that underneath; otherwise you will create a spotted, rather than an unobtrusively textured, effect.

10: As a final touch, the line of wavelets at the bottom of the rocks is added with opaque white paint, which is allowed to mix a little with the blue to give the broken effect of foamy water.

Painting Clouds

It is easy to think of clouds as simply grey and white, but if you look at them carefully, you will be surprised by the variety of colours they contain: the "white" areas may contain hints of pink, yellow, and blue, and the grey areas may appear purplish or brownish.

You will find that your clouds will gain a new vitality and luminosity if painted with delicately "coloured" greys. For a start, reject black and try instead a mixture of ultramarine and burnt umber, or ultramarine and alizarin crimson as your darkening agent. Add water to lighten the colour, and a touch of yellow ochre, raw sienna, or cadmium red for pink or yellow greys. You will find these mixes for greys more lively: adding straight black or white reduces the intensity of the mixture and produces a lacklustre, often muddy grey.

Payne's grey is a very useful ready-mixed grey which is both a yellow and a pink grey. Once you have experimented with mixing greys, you will find that Payne's grey has its place and, like any other colour, there are times when it is suitable to use it straight. Payne's grey, because it is such a delicate mixture of colours, can safely be used for darkening other colours.

Pastel colours come ready-mixed in a choice of tints, which can be very useful for making speedy cloud studies. For example, yellow ochre tint 0 is the very palest tint of yellow, perfect for a sunlit highlight. It will save you from some blending, but it is worth remembering that colours which are not too uniformly combined are often more interesting than those which are efficiently blended.

Highlights are not always found on the tops of clouds – it depends on the position of the sun. In the early evening, when the sun is low, the highlights are underneath the clouds and often tinged pink or yellow. When the sun is high in the sky, the highlights on the tops of the clouds are yellow, reflecting the sun, and the shadows underneath have a bluish tinge, reflecting the sky. Yellow ochre is better than lemon yellow for mixing sunlight highlights.

You will find that if you tint your greys with complementary colours, encouraging minute patches of the pure colour, you will achieve more lively clouds. This means pitting highlights containing warm oranges and yellows against shadows containing cool blues and violets. These colours do not have to be used full strength; even merely tinting your greys with them will produce more vibrant clouds.

Cloud Outlines

Having looked at the different colours of clouds, it is time to study the clouds themselves at first hand. Not just other people's impressions of clouds but real clouds – the ones you find outdoors. In the mid-nineteenth century the painter and art critic John Ruskin (1819–1900) berated the painters of his time (except Turner, whom he eulogized) in his three-volume study *Modern Painters*. Volume I, Section III, is entitled "Of Truth of Skies". Here he moans that contemporary painters make their clouds up from repetitive convex curves, whereas anyone who looks at clouds will know that they are never so monotonous. "First comes a concave line, then a convex one, then an angular jag breaking off into spray, then a downright straight line, then a curve again, then a deep gap, and a place where all is lost and melted away, and so on." This is what clouds are like if you really look at them, and it explains why painting them can become an obsession. Clouds are a constant source of entertainment for the artist – they are never the same, not from any point of view.

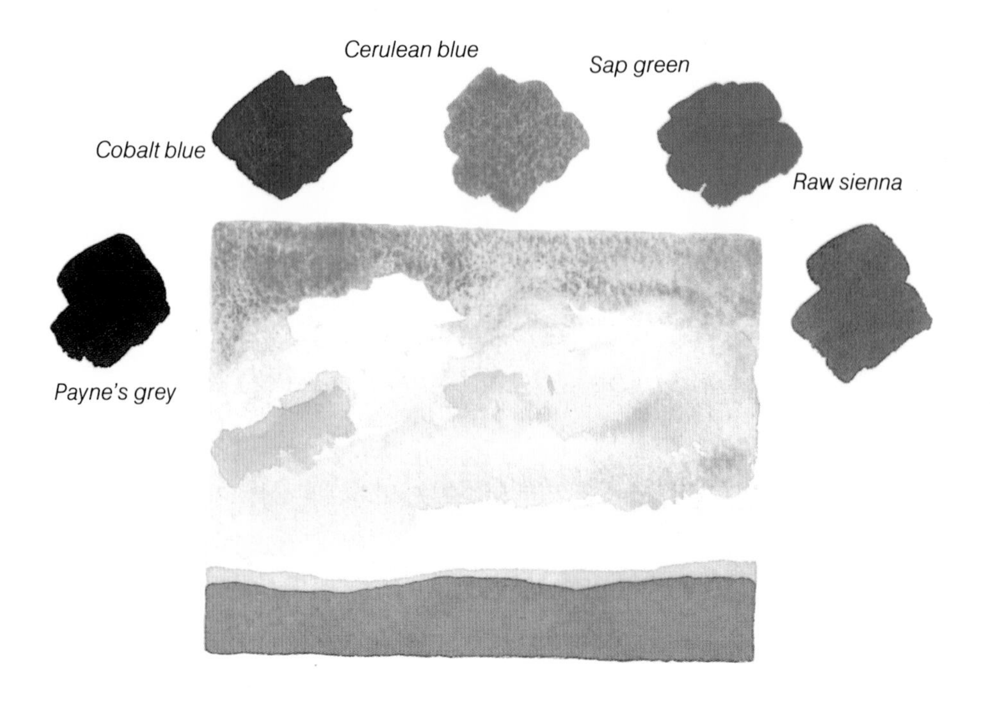

right: Cerulean is a good blue, particularly for a summer sky. The artist has encouraged it to be retained in the dips of the rough paper. Note the sharp edge painted around the highlit top edge of the cloud. The shadows are created by merging coloured grey washes wet-in-wet; touches of raw sienna, Payne's grey, and cobalt blue are visible. Further darker greys are added wet-on-dry.

Step by Step: Lifting Out

1: The artist has to work fast. As soon as the wash is completed, a crumpled piece of tissue is used to gently dab off the blue paint. Slightly more pressure is applied to define the clean edge of the brightly lit top surface of the cloud.

The technique of lifting out produces, with little effort, magic amorphous clouds. In this demonstration, the sky is painted with a thin wash of yellow ochre, overlaid when dry with a thin wash of Antwerp blue. The clouds are created by lifting out the paint before it dries, using a crumpled tissue. (Alternatively you could use a cloth, a sponge, or even a dry brush, depending on the type of cloud you are creating.)

2: Having established the outline, the tissue is reshaped and used to lift off the main body of the cloud. As you work, vary the pressure applied with the tissue to create the irregular shape of the cloud. Take care not to rub the paper or you will destroy the surface; use a press-and-lift motion.

3: Cloud shadows appear, created by the thin layer of blue left by the lifting off process, combining with the yellow ochre wash beneath. To build up these shadows further, washes of grey are applied using the wet-in-wet technique.

Techniques for Painting Clouds

We will now look at useful techniques for painting clouds. Bear in mind, however, that painting is not about slick methods and handy formulas. Formulas are arrived at so that the artist can guard against the unpredictable or the unknown. Yet, as artists, we should seek out the unpredictable and the unknown.

It is always worth taking the trouble to sketch and paint from life, even if you do know one or two tricks and formulas, because the sky is so important in a landscape painting. A slick, mannered, all-too-perfect sky is devoid of any excitement or intensity, whereas a sky painted from direct observation will always reveal something of the artist's emotional response to the subject.

Watercolour lends itself perfectly to reproducing the amorphous, translucent nature of clouds. Keep your colours as fresh and transparent as possible by not constantly reworking them – too much mixing makes them look lifeless. If you find an area is becoming overworked, it is better to start again. Similarly, make your brushstrokes as unlaboured as possible, and don't be afraid to load your brush with plenty of colour – remember that watercolour is much lighter dry than wet.

Many cloudy skies will start with the laying of a background colour wash. It may seem a simple enough technique, but if you want to develop confidence in producing an even wash, you will first need to practice.

With watercolour it is possible to leave the highlights as unpainted white paper. As described above, the lit edge of a cumulus cloud often has a crisp, well-defined edge, while the shadows are soft and diffuse. You will need to plan your image beforehand to work out where the hard edges will fall, so that you can wash the background colour around them. The soft, ragged parts of the cloud can then be allowed to fuse wet-in-wet with the background wash, making a soft edge. Knowing when to take this step – that is, when the receiving wash has dried enough to prevent the second colour from running out of control, but not so dry that ugly streaks and hard edges form – takes experience. But with watercolour, even the highly experienced artist is still caught out.

Another method of creating highlights is to dab the wet paint with a piece of crumpled tissue to reveal the paper beneath. This technique, known as "lifting out", can also be used to soften edges and lighten colour. For example, use it to create soft, misty clouds or streaked wind clouds in a blue background wash. Experiment with the technique, using crumpled tissue, a natural sponge, or a cloth wrapped around your brush to produce different shapes and effects.

above: Arthur Maderson, *Towards Fresh Woods,* mixed media. Between sunset and dusk at the end of a hot August day, the sky appears white, bleached of all colour by the power of the light. The shadowy creek is painted with shimmering blues, complementary to the warm yellow sunlight glimpsed behind the trees.

right: A warm, luminous sky is created with a wash of cobalt blue with a hint of cadmium red, adding a little yellow toward the horizon. Note how the texture of the paper helps to break up the wash, giving it a granulated texture. The tree shadows are made with superimposed flat washes of sap green mixed with touches of yellow, blue and red to vary the colour and shade.

Painting a Vibrant Blue Sky

Inexperienced artists often find it difficult to capture the intensity of blue, and the light which emanates from it, of a high summer sky. On a clear day, the sky positively pulsates with light, but it is impossible to translate this into paint because pigment is opaque and absorbs light. The artist must therefore resort to artifice and create an *impression* of shimmering light by mixing colours optically – in the eye rather than on the paper or canvas. Optical mixes, as we all know, were used to great effect by the Impressionists in capturing the elusive nature of light. The principle is based on the fact that our eyes are unable to focus properly on small areas of colour which are the same shade. The colours resonate on the retina, in effect "dazzling" us, just as light dazzles. For example, green can be mixed from yellow and blue; but a green composed of small dabs, flecks, or strokes of yellow and blue, left unblended, appears more vibrant because the pure yellow and blue are still discernible, and they resonate on the eye. (It is important to point out, however, that this only works if the constituent colours are of equal or near-equal tone.) Optical mixes also appear more vibrant because the paint is applied in small dabs, strokes, and stipples, which themselves have more energy than a flat colour. The trick with skies is to introduce hints of warm pinks, mauves, and yellows into the blues.

Judging the Tonal Strength of Blue Sky

When you are faced with the intense blue of the sky on a perfect summer's day, the temptation is to paint it with the deepest blue pigment you can conjure up. However, this could lead you into trouble because the shade of the sky can easily become too strong – and the rule is that a blue sky is always tonally lighter than the landscape below.

You may find it easier, particularly if the composition contains only a small area of blue sky, to paint the rest of the picture first and then add the sky in a lighter shade.

If, however, the sky dominates the composition, leaving an expanse of sky until last can impair your judgment of the values in the landscape below. In cases such as these, it is a good idea to block in the sky area with a pale blue wash and then work it up when the rest of the painting is well on its way. Working back and forth between the sky and the land is also a useful exercise; it helps to integrate the two, thus creating a more natural and atmospheric effect.

To help you judge the comparative tonal values in a complex landscape, look at it through almost closed eyes. This helps to take the colours out, leaving you better able to judge the tones.

Cadmium yellow

Cadmium red

Cobalt blue

Sap green

Quality of Light

In order to capture an accurate impression of light in your paintings, you have to be able to judge its quality. This quality can be seen in the colour and strength of the light and the effect it has on our perception of what is before us. There are various factors which affect the quality of the light: the weather, the time of day, the time of year, and of course where exactly you are in the world and how close you are to the equator.

It can be very instructive to record in a series of sketches or paintings the effect that changing light throughout the day has on a particular scene. There are various things you will notice when you compare them.

Shade: The light is weaker in the early morning and evening when the sun is low in the sky, so the tonal values are softer and less intense. Such light reduces the limits of the tonal range, but it plays up the variety of the middle shades. In contrast, the power of the midday sun pushes the tonal range to its extremes, but you will find it bleaches out the subtle middle tones.

Colour: Sunlight can cast a cold, blue light in the early morning and a golden or pink light in the evening which will qualify all colours it falls on. At these times of day, colours are generally softer, graduating from highlight to shadow more gently. In bright sunlight, colours appear more vibrant with few middle shades between highlight and shadow.

Outline: You will notice that the weaker the light, the softer the outline an object has. In the light of dusk, even objects in direct light will have soft outlines, while those in deep shadow will be almost indistinct. Bright sunlight produces clearly defined edges where it shines directly on objects.

Shadows: As the sun travels across the sky, shadows alter in length, position, colour, and value. Strong light produces dark, hard-edged shadows, while soft light produces paler, ill-defined shadows.

It is easy to become obsessive about recording the effects of changing light on a particular scene. Claude Monet (1840–1926) certainly was; between 1890 and 1894 he concentrated on the observation of a single subject in a succession of different lights, which resulted in his famous "series" paintings devoted to haystacks, poplar trees, and to Rouen Cathedral. Although it is easy enough to study these paintings in photographs in books, sadly, you will not get full value from them unless you see them "in the flesh". Such series of Monets are collected by museums all over the world but not everyone has the opportunity to see them.

Whether or not you get an opportunity to study such a series at first hand, there is no reason why you cannot create one of your own. I need hardly say that you will gain enormously from doing so, but I realize that such a project is very demanding on all but the most organized and strong-willed of us. As Monet himself often found, it can be extremely frustrating when you fail to catch a magical but all too fleeting effect – and then the light changes and you lose it.

At the end of a year you will be able to analyze your series. Below are some general points to watch out for – but bear in mind that an artist often has to manipulate the truth. You can paint a sunlit winter landscape with pinks and yellows in the highlights, but if you want to get across the ferocity of the below-zero temperature, you will have to play up the cool colours and play down the warm ones.

Colour: Sunlight in winter is generally weak, with a cool blue cast. Daylight in the heat of summer is stronger and warmer. Look carefully and you will see there are more yellows and pinks.

Tone: Because the sun is not as strong in winter, the tonal variety is narrower than in summer. Sunny autumn landscapes seem vibrant because of nature's complementary colours – the blues and purples of the sky juxtaposed with the oranges and yellows of the leaves.

Shadows: The sun does not rise so high in winter, so shadows on the ground are longer throughout the day. They are even longer and softer in the morning and evening. In midsummer the sun casts dark shadows at noon. The sun then can still be quite strong in the evening, casting well-defined shadows.

above: Ray Evans, *Woman of Galladoro, Sicily*, pen and watercolour. Use sketches to explore the tonal values of a particular time of day. Here, the sky is blue, but the sun is weak.

Coping with Changing Light

Unfortunately, you cannot freeze the sun's relentless progress across the sky, so you have to learn to cope with it. "Work fast," they say – but that is always more easily said than done. You may find it helps to restrict yourself to working on a small scale, using a large brush and few colours. This will certainly discourage time wasted on detail, but you may not want to produce this type of work. If you don't want to be hurried, you could try tackling the shadows first, and building up the painting around them. Still another solution is to paint for only an hour or so at a time, returning at the same time of day, until the painting is completed – if you can rely on the weather to remain constant, that is.

If you have to finish your painting in one sitting, amass at the start as much information as you can. Your visual memory can be improved if you work at it by concentrating hard and exploring every part of the scene as if you were painting it. Study the comparative values, scan the contours, explore the character of the patches of light and shadows. Some artists find that sketching these aspects in any detail tends to impair the power of the memory. But it helps to do both.

Unless you specifically want to paint a scene in bright sunlight, you will be better advised to paint outdoors on a slightly overcast day, when drastic changes in the position and intensity of lights and shadows are less likely to occur.

Painting Shadows

Without shadows, light does not exist. So if you want to paint pictures filled with sunlight, you will need to master the art of painting shadows. You can paint a bright highlight, but without an equally dark shadow to give it emphasis, that highlight will not mean anything. Shadows vary enormously, depending on the quality of light. In bright sunlight, shadows are hard-edged and dark; in more gentle light, they are subtle and indistinct. But more than that, changes in the quality of the light during the day and according to the season affect the shade, colour, and configuration of the shadows cast.

It is a common mistake to regard shadows as negative areas of a painting. Not only do shadows help to strengthen the compositional structure, they can also contribute to the atmosphere of a scene and to the mood you wish to convey. For example, bright, crisp sunlight casts sharply defined areas of light and shadow that will emphasize the bracing atmosphere of a seaside scene. But that same scene, painted in late afternoon when the shadows lengthen and the light is hazy, will have an air of calm and peace.

Shadows are never completely black, and only rarely are they a neutral grey. The colour of a shadow is influenced by the local colour of the object on which the shadow falls, and by the colour of the prevailing light. Also, shadows are often tinged with colours complementary (opposite) to the colour of the object casting the shadow; for instance, a yellow object may throw a shadow with a blue-violet tinge.

Another point to watch out for is that shadows vary in density, becoming lighter in shade the further they are from the object casting them.

Step by Step: Hot Sun

This watercolour painting speaks of the hot Mediterranean sun. The artist was attracted by the geometric pattern created by the strong verticals of the walls, countered by the diagonals of the roof against the sky and the mid-morning shadow cast across the wall. The artist's general plan is to work from cool to warm, starting with blues, through to yellows and finally red. In this painting the artist is working mainly from memory, but with the aid of a sketch supplemented with notes and photographs.

1: Having sketched in the outline of the composition, the artist applies masking fluid over those areas which are to be left white, such as the flowers in the foliage.

2: With a large softhair brush loaded with cerulean blue warmed with a little cobalt, the artist paints in the sky area and then the shadows.

3: A wash of yellow ochre, applied wet-on-dry, runs down further than planned, so the paper is laid flat and a tissue is used to fashion the edge of the step.

4: Now the artist starts to work on the details, starting from the centre of the painting with the foliage. The areas of dried masking fluid mean that a merged wash of dark and light green can be painted in without worrying about the intricate shapes of the flowers and stems.

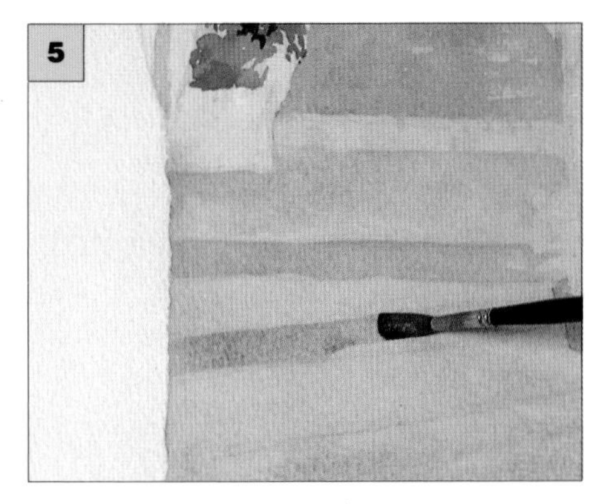

5: Further medium areas of shadow are located with diluted cobalt blue, applied with a smaller round brush to give more detail.

6: When the paint is thoroughly dry, the masking fluid is removed by rubbing with a soft kneaded eraser. Note the delicate, darker shadows which have been added to the window panes.

7: The geranium flowers are painted wet-in-wet. First, a pale pink underwash is applied and allowed to dry. It is then wetted and a spot of alizarin crimson is added and allowed to fuse and spread.

8: The artist decides that the foliage in the centre is too hard-edged, so with a small piece of natural soft sponge she stipples on some green to soften it.

9: To make the painting "sing", a stronger dilution of yellow ochre is taken through the painting, representing reflected light. It is applied on the steps here using the dry brush technique with a flat bristle brush.

10: Finally, the gabled end of the house is knocked back with a gentle scumble of yellow ochre, applied with a dry brush in a circular motion.

above: Hazel Soan, *Spanish Steps*, watercolour. Finally satisfied, the artist declares the painting finished.

Materials Used

SUPPORT: 57 x 77 cm (22 x 30 in) white 300 lb Saunders paper.

COLOURS: cobalt blue, cerulean blue, Hooker's green, sap green, yellow ochre, cadmium yellow, alizarin crimson, Winsor red and burnt sienna.

BRUSHES AND OTHER EQUIPMENT: soft round nos. 3, 7 and 11, bristle flat no. 7 and a small natural sponge for stippling.

Mist and Fog

Mist and fog heighten the effects of atmospheric perspective on the landscape. Foreground, middle ground, and background appear more separate and distinct than normal, and objects only a short distance away seem to melt into a haze. In thick fog, even those forms in the foreground appear almost in silhouette, with few shadows to model their contours. Recession is is achieved through decreasing tonal contrasts, particularly in the background, and by overlapping planes. It's a good idea to start at the horizon with pale, indistinct forms, gradually strengthening the shades as you work toward the foreground – but avoid introducing too much tonal contrast and destroying the illusion of mist. You have to strike a delicate balance.

Fog and mist are characterized by delicate insubstantial effects, muted colours, and indistinct forms, which need to be treated with sensitivity and a certain deftness; the atmospheric nature of a mist will be lost if the medium is overworked.

Watercolours are naturally suited to representing the transient beauty of mist or fog. The translucence of the medium allows the white of the paper to shine through and create a depth of light which exactly captures misty effects. Allow your washes to flow freely, wet-in-wet, to create swirls of moving mist or receding, nebulous planes. Background forms can be reduced in shade by painting their shapes, allowing them to dry, and then using a natural sponge dampened with clean water to lift out some of the colour.

Also with watercolour you can capture the softness of form and colour by applying paint to damp paper and allowing the forms to blur at the edges.

Step by step: Wet-in-wet Mist

This technique shows how watercolour on a white ground can be used to create the atmospheric qualities of mist. Make sure you mix enough of the wash in a saucer beforehand, and tilt the board at an angle so that the colour flows down the paper.

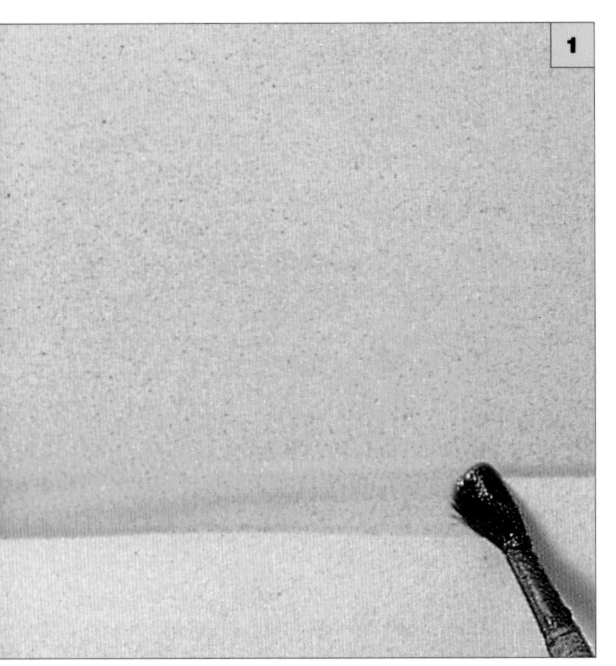

1: On a sheet of dampened paper, pale washes of rose madder are laid in horizontal strokes, starting at the top of the paper.

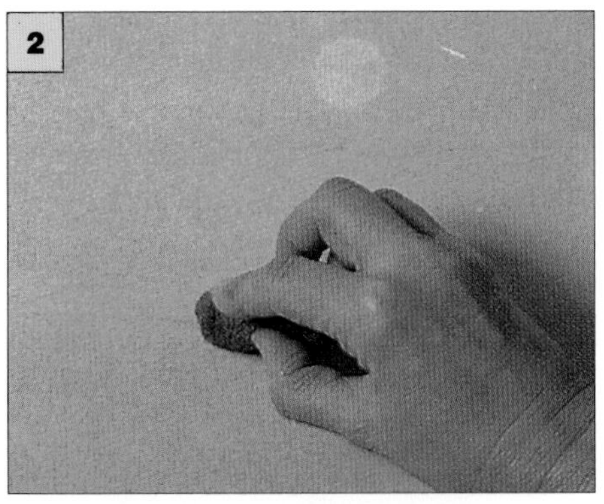

2: While the paint is still wet, patches of colour are lifted out with a small piece of dampened sponge to reveal the white of the paper.

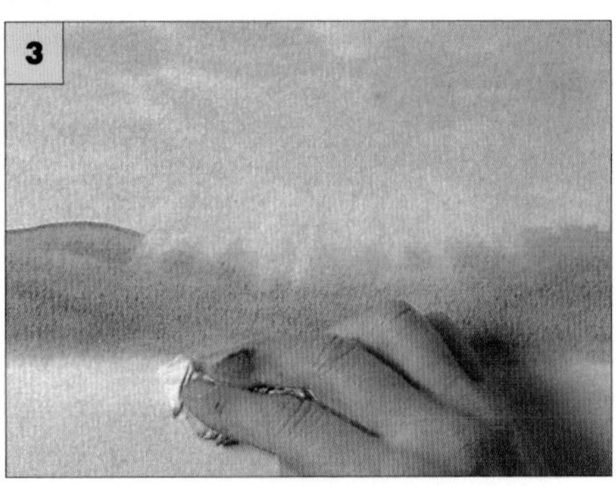

3: The contours of hills are added, using a wash of cobalt blue mixed with light red. The paper is dampened once more to produce the softly dappled colour of the sky and water.

Snow Scenes

For those who rarely see snow and regard it as a treat, it is a sight that brings pleasure and excitement. For others it betides the onset of long weeks or months of cold and discomfort, so they greet it with a less positive attitude. As in all paintings of weather, the artist's emotional response to the subject is at least as important as the presentation of the facts. And it is not only moods that have to be recreated, but sensations such as cold and wet as well.

No wonder there are many who are intimidated by the prospect of painting snow. They feel unable to cope with such an expanse of white, and sub-zero temperatures do not exactly encourage them to take their paints outside to try. But even if you demur from braving the elements in order actually to paint, you can sketch a scene from the inside of a car, or simply take a walk and observe your surroundings with an artist's eye. Certainly it is worth studying at first hand the effect that snow has on the landscape and, particularly, the effect of different kinds of light on the snow itself. Getting closer to your subject in this way, you will soon discover that snow is a fascinating subject to paint.

left: Margaret M. Martin, *Warm Winter Tones,* watercolour. Watercolour is the ideal medium for conveying the feeling of a rapid thaw that is evident in this painting. Notice how the warm stucco colour of the houses is reflected in the pools of water at the edge of the road. The brightness of the scene is defined by well-controlled washes.

above: Doug Lew, *Nicollet Mall at Night,* watercolour. In this night scene, the light emanating from the street lights, tree lights, cars and stores radiates from the centre of the composition. The dark sepia background reveals the stark forms of buildings which are barely perceptible.

If you have ever woken up in bed when there is snow outside, you will know how the room appears bathed in a cool light. This is because snow, being a highly reflective surface, reflects light from the sky in the same way that a body of water does.

For this reason, snow is rarely a blanket of pure white; its colour is affected by the quality of the prevailing light. On a sunny day the sunstruck areas of snow appear dazzlingly white, but the yellow sunlight produces shadows which contain its complementary colour – blue or blue-violet, depending on the warmth or coolness of the sunlight. Warm evening light creates softer highlights, often with a yellowish or pinkish tinge, and deep blue shadows.

In transparent watercolour you have to establish the position of the brightest highlights on the snow in advance and paint around them. Or you could try working on a toned paper and adding body colour (Chinese white) to the colours. The slight chalkiness of Chinese white renders the appropriate powdery effect of snow.

LIGHT ON WATER

The effects of light on water are almost irresistible. Obviously they can seldom be painted on the spot; a shaft of sunlight suddenly breaking through cloud to spotlight an area of water could disappear before you lay out your colours. But you can recapture such effects in the studio as long as you have observed them closely, committed them to memory and made sketches of the general lie of the land.

When you begin to paint, remember that the effect you want to convey is one of transience, so try to make your technique express this quality. This does not mean splashing on the paint with no forethought – this is unlikely to be successful. One of the paradoxes of watercolour painting is that the most seemingly spontaneous effects are in fact the result of careful planning.

Work out the colours and tones in advance so that you do not have to correct them by overlaying wash over wash. It can be helpful to make a series of small preparatory colour sketches to try out various techniques and colour combinations. Knowing exactly what you intend to do enables you to paint freely and without hesitation. If you decide to paint wet-in-wet, first practise controlling the paint by tilting the board. If you prefer to work wet-on-dry, establish exactly where your highlights are to be and then leave them strictly alone or, alternatively, put them in last with opaque white used drily.

above: Francis Bowyer, *It's Freezing!* 38.1 x 53.3 cm (15 x 21 in), watercolour and body colour (gouache white). The effect of the low sun on the choppy water has been beautifully observed and painted rapidly and decisively, with each brushstroke of vivid colour put down and then left alone. In places, such as the more distant waves, the paint is thin enough for the paper to be visible, while in the foreground the shapes of the brush marks have been exploited to give a feeling of movement to the wavelets breaking on the beach.

right: Shirley Felts, *The River Guadalupe,* 53.3 x 73.7 cm (21 x 29 in), watercolour. This lovely painting shows a breathtakingly skilful use of reserved highlights. Each pale reflection, tiny sunlit twig and point of light has been achieved by painting around the area. This can result in tired, overworked paint, but here nothing of the luminosity of the watercolour has been sacrificed and it remains fresh and sparkling.

MOVING WATER

Most people have experienced the disappointment of finding that a photograph of a waterfall or rushing stream has completely failed to capture the movement and excitement of the subject. This is because the camera freezes movement by its insistence on including every tiny detail, and this provides an important lesson for the painter. You can never hope to paint moving water unless you simplify it, so learn to make "less say more" by looking for the main patterns and ruthlessly suppressing the secondary ones.

Rippling water under a strong light shows very distinct contrasts of tone and colour, often with hard edges between the sunlit tops and the shadows caused by broken reflections. Working wet-on-dry is the best way of describing this edgy, jumpy quality, but avoid too much overlaying of washes, as this can quickly muddy the colours. Masking fluid is very helpful here, as you can block out small highlights on the tops of ripples or wavelets while you work freely on the darker tones.

The wax resist method is tailor-made for suggesting the ruffled effect of broken spray on the tops of breakers, while the delicate, lace-like patterns formed when a wave draws back from the beach can be very accurately "painted" by scraping back.

above: Charles Knight RWS, ROI, *Headland,* 27.3 x 37.5 cm (10¾ x 14¾ in), watercolour, pencil and wax. Knight is a committed land- and seascape painter, and a master of the watercolour medium. This wonderfully atmospheric painting provides the perfect illustration of the secondary role played by technique in art. He has made excellent use of wax resist for the waves and given a lovely feeling of movement and drama to the headland with crisp, dark pencil lines, but his techniques, although fascinating to analyse, remain "in their place" as no more than the vehicles which allow him to express his ideas.

Whatever technique or combinations of techniques you decide on, use as few brushstrokes as possible – the more paint you put on the less wet the water will look.

MOONRIVER, ONTARIO

The problems involved in painting water are multiplied about ten times when it comes to painting rapids, waterfalls and fast-moving streams. There's so much action going on, it's difficult to know where to begin.

The painting above demonstrates a number of common errors made by beginners. First, the river appears "frozen", like a cine film that's suddenly stopped, because the student has used his paint too thickly and with far too many fussy brushstrokes. Second, the water appears to be on a flat, vertical plane because there is no reduction in the size of the brushstrokes as the water recedes into the distance. Third, the student has not paid attention to the subtle colours of water: he resorts instead to a stereotyped blue that looks completely unnatural, with thick globs of white paint for foam.

Moonriver, Ontario **by Ronald Jesty demonstrates how a looser, more direct approach can be far more effective in rendering rapid water. In this version the white of the paper does much of the work in conveying an impression of water foaming and churning over the rocks: surprisingly few strokes of colour are needed to complete the image.**

Keep it Simple: Remember that rapid water looks more realistic when it's understated. Concentrate only on the major lines of motion – the ones that capture the essence of the water's movement. Don't allow yourself to be distracted by unimportant details that will clutter up the picture and destroy the illusion of movement.

Confident Brushwork: To paint fast-moving water well requires fast-moving brushstrokes. One deft squiggle can convey far more than any amount of hesitant goings-over, so take your courage in both hands and allow the brush to follow the movements of the water. Notice how Ronald Jesty uses strong, rhythmic brushstrokes to impart a sense of movement and encourage the eye to follow the progress of the water as it rushes over the rocks.

Effective Contrasts: Often the best way to emphasize something is by contrasting it with its opposite. In *Moonriver, Ontario* note the contrast between the water, which is painted with thin paint and very light tones, and the surrounding landscape elements which are painted with more definition and stronger tones. These dark tones and solid shapes make the water appear more fluid and fast-flowing through the confident use of contrast.

above: Ronald Jesty RBA, *Moonriver, Ontario.*

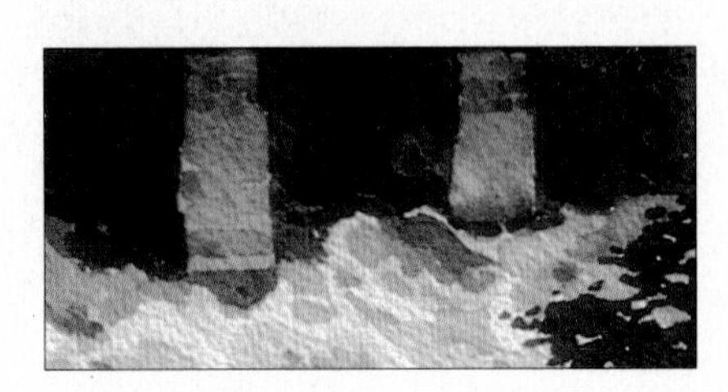

above: Surrounding solid shapes make the water appear more fluid through contrast.

above: Note the water's subtle colour and how the white of the paper is used to represent churning foam. Strong calligraphic brushstrokes capture the churning movement of water.

Still Water

There are few sights more tempting to the painter than the tranquil, mirror-like surface of a lake on a still day or a calm, unruffled sea at dawn or dusk. But although it would be reasonable to believe still water to be an easy subject, particularly in a medium that has such an obvious affinity with it, it is surprising how often such paintings go wrong.

The commonest reason for failure is poor observation. A calm expanse of water is seldom exactly the same colour and tone all over because it is a reflective surface. Even if there are no objects such as boats, rocks or cliffs to provide clearly defined reflections, the water is still mirroring the sky and will show similar variations. These shifts in colour and tone – often very subtle – are also affected by the angle of viewing. Water usually looks darker in the foreground because it is closer to you and thus reflects less light.

It is also important to remember that a lake or area of sea is a horizontal plane. This sounds obvious, but has powerful implications for painting. A horizontal plane painted in an unvaried tone will instantly assume the properties of a vertical one because no recession is implied. It can sometimes be necessary to stress flatness and recession by exaggerating a darker tone or even inventing a ripple or two to bring the foreground forward.

above: Ronald Jesty RBA, *Loch Rannoch, Low Water,* 15.2 x 34.3 cm (6 x 13½ in), watercolour. There is not a single unnecessary brushstroke to disturb the calm tranquility of this scene. The artist has cleverly enhanced the bright surface of the water and its pale, sandy banks by setting up strong contrasts of tone while keeping the colours muted. The crisply painted reflections of the dark trees on the right and the little lines of shadow on the left define the river with perfect accuracy. The water surface is not painted completely flat: a sense of space and recession is created by the slightly darker patch of colour directly in the foreground as well as by the linear perspective that narrows the river banks as it flows towards the lake.

left: Robert Tilling RI, *Noirmont Evening, Jersey,* 40.6 x 58.4 cm (16 x 23 in), watercolour. The magical effects of still water under a setting sun have been achieved by a skilful use of the wet-in-wet technique. Tilling works on paper with a not surface, stretched on large blockboard supports. He mixes paint in considerable quantities in old teacups or small food tins and applies it with large brushes, tilting his board at an angle of 60 degrees or sometimes even more to allow the paint to run. This method, although looking delightfully spontaneous, can easily get out of control, so he watches carefully what happens at every stage, ready to lessen the angle of the board if necessary to halt the flow of the colours. The dark wash for the headland was painted when the first wet-in-wet stage had dried.

REFLECTIONS

Reflections are one of the many bonuses provided free of charge to the painter of water. Not only do they form lovely patterns in themselves, they can also be used as a powerful element in a composition, allowing you to balance solid shapes with their watery images and to repeat colours in one area of a painting in another.

The most exciting effects are seen when small movements of water cause ripples or swells that break up the reflections into separate shapes, with jagged or wavering outlines. Water can, of course, be so still that it becomes literally a mirror, but this does not necessarily make a good painting subject because it loses much of its identity as water.

As in all water subjects, try to simplify reflections and keep the paint fresh and crisp. Let your brush describe the shapes by drawing with it in a calligraphic way (see "Brush Drawing") and never put on more paint than you need. The amount of detail you put into a reflection will depend on how near the front of the picture it is. A distant one will be more generalized because the ripples will decrease in size as they recede from you, so avoid using the same size of brush mark for both near and far reflections or the water will appear to be flowing uphill. You could emphasize foreground reflections by painting wet-on-dry, and give a softer quality to those in the background by using the wet-in-wet or lifting out methods.

above: Michael Cadman RI, ARCA, *Cornish Harbour, Low Tide,* 45.7 x 33 cm (18 x 13 in), acrylic and watercolour on toned paper. Here the artist has exploited the potential of acrylic to the full, using brush marks as an integral part of the painting, so that water, buildings and sky are all broken up into small areas of colour. The reflections are hinted at rather than literally described. Because we cannot be sure where the water ends and the steps and harbour wall begin, the two parts of the picture seem to flow into one another to create a sense of complete unity, reinforced by the overall golden colour key. To help him achieve this, Cadman has painted on a toned ground (oyster-coloured Canson Mi-Teintes paper) and in places has used his paint quite thinly so that the paper stands as a colour in its own right. Although in the main this is a fairly direct painting, in some areas, notably the light on the main building, a dark underpainting of burnt sienna and violet was used and allowed to show through successive coats of overpainted impasto. These were then glazed in places.

right: Ronald Jesty RBA, *Old Harry Rocks,* 48.3 x 30.5 cm (19 x 12 in), watercolour. In this bold composition, the reflection, rather than being an incidental detail, forms part of the painting's focal point. The treatment is stylized to some extent, but nevertheless extremely accurate. There is no unnecessary detail, but there is enough variation in the reflection to suggest both the structure of the rock above and the slightly broken surface of the water. The artist has painted wet-on-dry, and has made clever use of the shape and direction of his brush marks to lead the eye into the centre of the picture.

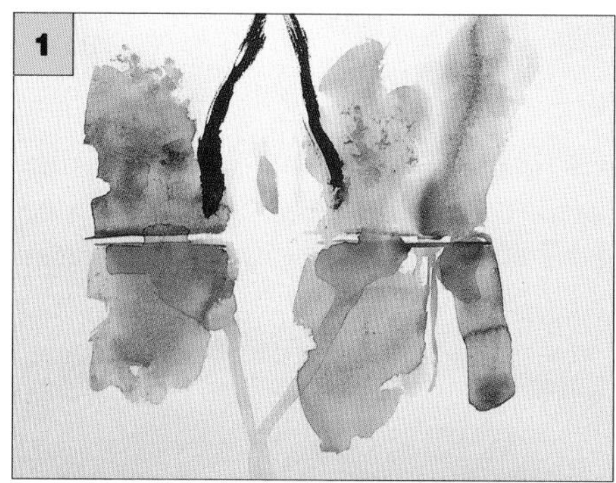

1: Kate Gwynn is an inventive artist who seldom restricts herself to one technique and here she uses various different methods, improvising as she works. First she establishes the main composition, overlaying washes in the water area to create hard edges.

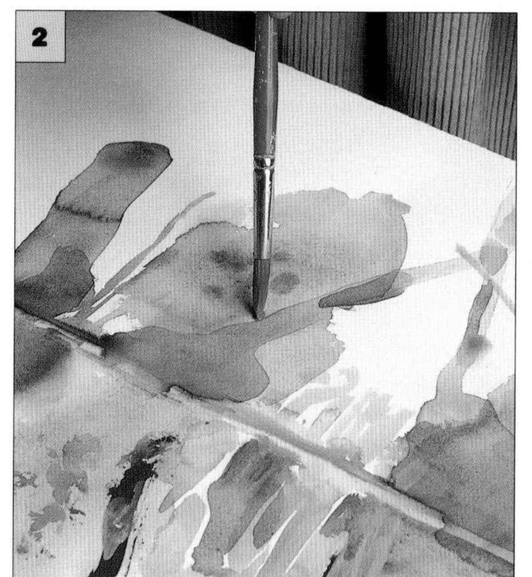

2: Having laid further washes, she now works wet-in-wet with the point of the brush to suggest the effect of the reflected foliage.

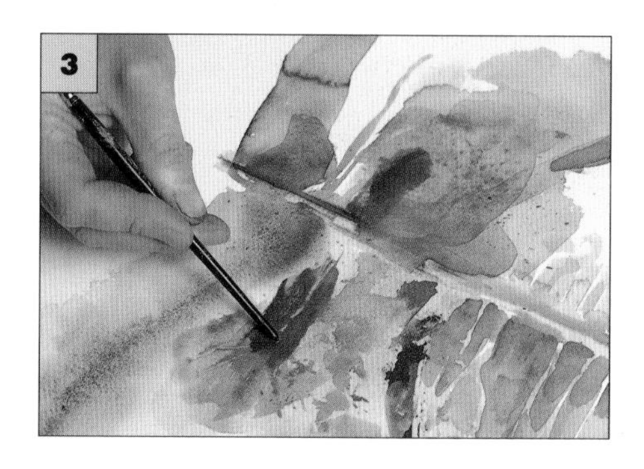

3: The brush marks made in the last stage have now been overlaid with loose, wet washes to achieve a soft, diffused effect. The pale tree trunks seen on the right in this picture have been reserved in the traditional manner, but here the handle of the brush is used to draw into paint slightly thickened with body colour, providing an effective contrast to the loose wash on the right.

4: Sky is suggested with a wet brushstroke of blue, which is allowed to run into the yellow wash below.

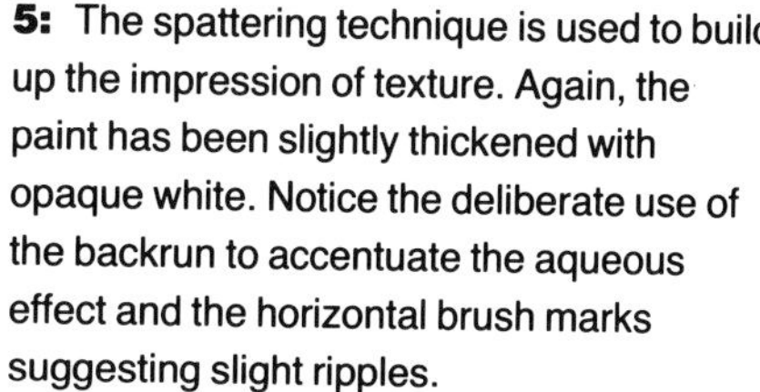

5: The spattering technique is used to build up the impression of texture. Again, the paint has been slightly thickened with opaque white. Notice the deliberate use of the backrun to accentuate the aqueous effect and the horizontal brush marks suggesting slight ripples.

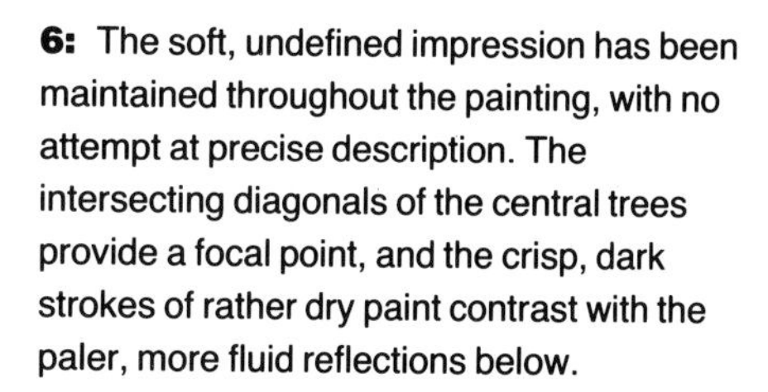

6: The soft, undefined impression has been maintained throughout the painting, with no attempt at precise description. The intersecting diagonals of the central trees provide a focal point, and the crisp, dark strokes of rather dry paint contrast with the paler, more fluid reflections below.

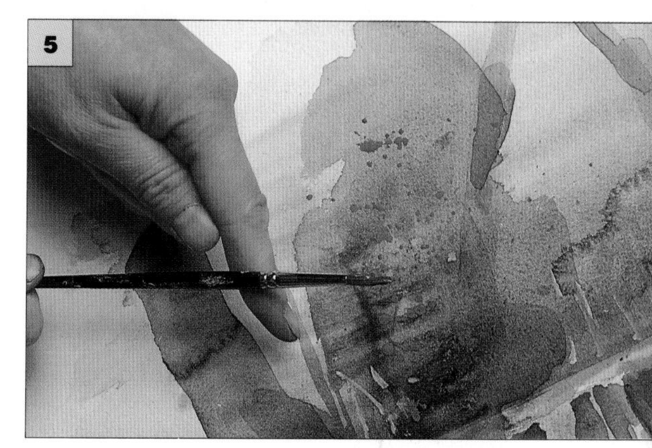

below: Kate Gwynn, *Trees and Water,* 40.6 x 50.8 cm (16 x 20 in), watercolour with some body colour on stretched Bockingford paper.

Linear Perspective

Many people are afraid of drawing and painting buildings because they have guessed that perspective matters a lot. But you will not make the problem go away by avoiding architectural subjects, because perspective matters whatever you are trying to represent – a landscape with a river winding into the distance, a bowl of fruit on a table-top, a chair, a group of figures, or even a single figure.

The feelings of gloom and inadequacy that most people experience at the thought of learning perspective are not surprising. I was recently looking through an encyclopedia article on the subject, and was horrified by the complexity of the diagrams and the impossibility of relating them to anything real, such as a house, or even a table. But it need not be made as difficult as this, and I hope that the drawings and diagrams that you will see in this section of the book will dispel some of the darkness.

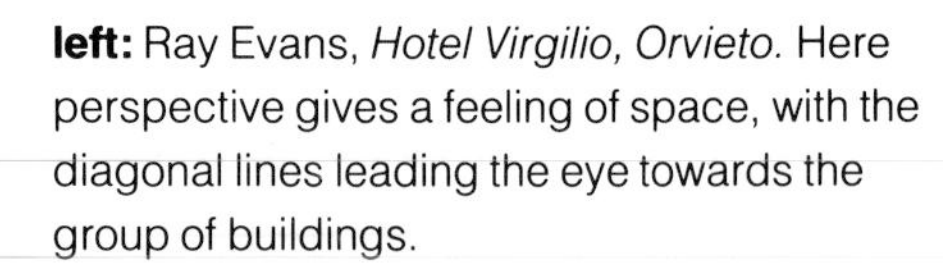

left: Ray Evans, *Hotel Virgilio, Orvieto.* Here perspective gives a feeling of space, with the diagonal lines leading the eye towards the group of buildings.

Optical Trickery

Because the real world is three-dimensional and a painting is a flat surface, artists have over the centuries evolved a series of conventions, or tricks, to translate one into the other. Linear perspective is the most important of these, providing a way of making objects look solid and convincing by suggesting space and volume.

below: Sandra Walker, *Behind Waterloo Station,* watercolour. Again perspective has become a compositional tool, with the gentle curves and arches receding into the distance to create both space and a sense of flowing movement.

There is another kind of perspective, called aerial perspective, which is concerned with tone and colour. This is explained on page 179.

In a way, perspective is the easiest part of painting because it is simply a set of rules that can be learned. The more advanced aspects of art, such as composition or the use of particular colours and shapes to create a specific mood, can involve a long-term personal quest and the conventions adopted are different for every artist, but perspective is the same for everyone. Once you have become familiar with the rules you will find that you can draw with much more confidence because they will have become second nature to you.

The mathematical laws of perspective were invented in Renaissance Italy by the architect Filippo Brunelleschi, and came to exert a great fascination for artists, notably Paolo Uccello. The latter apparently used to work far into the night, producing ever more intricate and complex drawings of multi-faceted objects, and the story goes that when his wife implored him to come to bed he simply sighed, "Oh what a sweet mistress is this perspective".

Although it is unlikely that many of us will share his passion, it is not hard to grasp why he felt so strongly. The newly formulated rules set him free to develop as a painter, and they can do the same for you. You may choose to ignore or distort perspective in the interests of a different kind of truth to the subject – rules, after all, are made to be broken. But in order to break them you must first learn them, so read on.

SIMPLE PERSPECTIVE

If you have a mathematical bent you could probably devote much of your life to the study of perspective, but this section is about buildings, so it makes sense to follow the "need to know" principle and keep matters as simple as possible. The whole system of perspective is founded on one basic tenet, which can be readily observed by eye – the apparent decrease in the size of objects as they recede towards the horizon. Suppose the objects in question are a series of simple cubes – then it follows that the side planes will appear smaller the further away they are. And to make this happen the parallel lines have to become closer together (a geometrical impossibility but an optical fact) until they meet on the horizon line.

The Vanishing Point

This brings us to the golden rule that all receding parallel lines meet at a vanishing point, which is on the horizon. This sounds simple, as indeed it is, but where, you may ask yourself, is the horizon? It is easy enough when you are looking at an expanse of sea or a flat landscape – the horizon is where the land or sea meets the sky – but where is it located when you are in the middle of a city and can see nothing but houses? The answer is that the horizon is exactly at your own eye level, and this is what determines where the lines will converge. Normally, when you are sitting sketching or simply walking about, your eye level (horizon) will be lower than the tops of the buildings, so the horizontal lines of roofs and high windows will appear to slope down, but if you choose a high eye level, for example looking down on a group of houses from the top of a hill, the horizontal lines will slope upwards.

above: *One-point perspective* is the term for the simplest kind of perspective, in which all the receding horizontal lines meet at the same vanishing point (called VP in this and all subsequent diagrams). In this case the artist has drawn from the middle of the street, so the vanishing point is in the centre of the picture. If he had been further over to the right it would have been somewhere on the left. Often it is outside the picture, so you have to estimate its position.

Establishing the vanishing point is the essential first step when drawing and painting buildings, because it gives you a definite framework on which to work – the angle of every horizontal, from the top of a roof to the bottom of a door, is determined by it.

If you are in the middle of a street, with a row of houses on either side, nothing could be easier – the vanishing point is directly in front of you and at your eye level. First mark in the horizon line and then lightly rule as many lines as you need to establish the diagonals of rooftops, window lines and so on.

If you are viewing at an angle, however, the vanishing point will no longer be in front of you and you will have to work out its position. Mark in the horizon as before, draw in the nearest vertical to the required height and then assess the angle of the rooftop by holding up a pencil or ruler in front of you. Extend this line to the horizon, and you have your vanishing point.

Sometimes the vanishing point will be outside the picture area, in which case a certain amount of guesswork is involved, combined with careful observation. If you are making preliminary studies for a painting, or perhaps just drawing for practice, it helps to work on a piece of paper considerably larger than the picture area, so that you can mark in the vanishing point or points.

I have used the plural deliberately because, of course, there is often more than one, so read on for some advice on coping with more complex perspective.

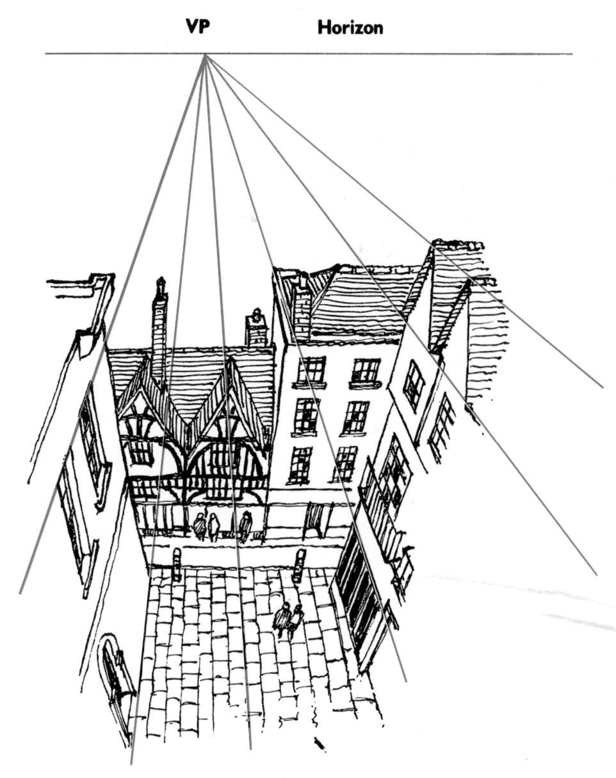

above: *High viewpoint* is still one-point perspective, but because the scene has been viewed from above, the receding lines slope upwards to the vanishing point instead of down, as in the drawing on the left. When you are working on location it is very important not to change your viewpoint, as this immediately alters the perspective. Try this out by holding up a ruler in front of you and then moving your head, or even shutting one eye.

Complex Perspective

Once you have grasped the principle of one-point perspective, two-point – which is what you have when you look at a building from an angle – presents no problems. The rules are the same, and it is an easy matter to plot another set of receding parallels. But you can't always do this when you have a multiplicity of vanishing points, which is often the case if you are painting a street scene, particularly in an old town. Houses are bound to be at different angles because streets will twist and turn, intersecting one another at seemingly random angles.

Moreover, they will sometimes run up or down hill. Although the rules for multiple vanishing points are the same for any horizontal planes, inclined surfaces are rather different: their vanishing point will be *above* the horizon, as shown in the drawing opposite. It is important to remember this because roofs are inclined planes, and if you try to treat them like flat ones you will be in trouble.

Trying to plot every single vanishing point would be a laborious waste of time, and in any case no piece of paper would be large enough, as so many would be far outside the picture area. But this doesn't mean that you can afford to forget about perspective, and you will need to make a careful drawing. The best course is to choose a key building, perhaps the one nearest to you or that in the centre of the composition. Plot the perspective for this carefully and then draw in all the other roofs, walls and details with reference to the verticals and angles of your key.

Take your time, and keep checking your drawing against the subject, making sure that all lines intersect in the right place. Make careful measurements as you work. You can do this by holding a pencil up in front of you and sliding your thumb up and down it, or you can use a ruler.

The advantage of the latter is that you can take exact measurements, and you can also, of course, use the ruler to draw lines and to make sure that verticals are true. To do the latter, measure the distance from the edge of your picture at the top and bottom edge. You might also find the drawing frame illustrated on page 88 a helpful tool.

Don't feel ashamed of using these so-called mechanical aids. All artists employ some form of measuring system, whatever they are drawing, and there is no good reason why all drawing should be freehand. In the case of buildings, one crooked vertical can lead to a distortion of the perspective over the whole drawing. Once you start to paint, you can be as free as you like, secure in the knowledge that you know exactly where to place the colours, and any ruled lines will quickly be obscured.

If you intend to finish a picture on the spot, it is a good idea to make the drawing on one day and paint on another. The drawing will not be much affected by changing light, but the painting will.

above: *Multiple vanishing points:* with a complex subject like this it can be difficult to know where to start. The first step, as always, is to establish the horizon line. Then mark in the vanishing points for the main buildings and draw them as carefully as possible so that you can use them as points of reference for the others.

below: *Two-point perspective:* when a building is viewed from an angle there are two vanishing points. If your eye level (horizon) is low – or you are drawing a tall building – the rooflines will slope downwards very steeply. If the horizon is higher and the building is low, the slope will be much gentler. Always begin by marking in the horizon line, and then assess the degree of angle of the roofline by holding up a pencil or ruler at arm's length.

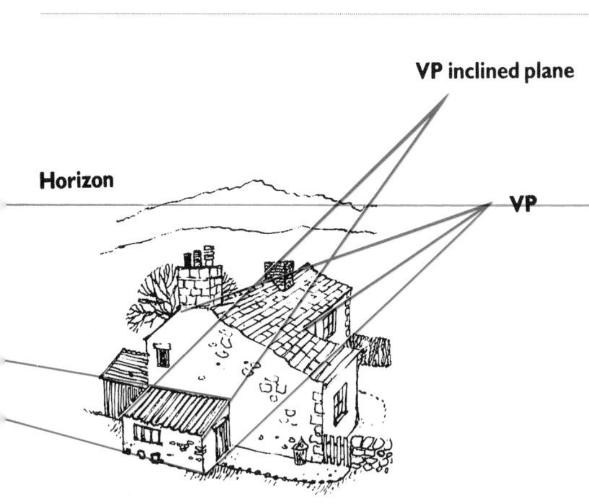

above: *Sloping roofs:* a common mistake in drawing is to use the same vanishing point for both horizontal and inclined planes, often with bizarre results. The parallels that form the sides of inclined planes meet at a point *above* the horizon.

above: Moira Clinch, *Coca-cola Stall, Mexico,* watercolour. Two-point perspective has provided a lively composition of verticals and diagonals, and created a feeling of solidity.

left: Martin Taylor, *View of Florence,* watercolour. Complex subjects such as townscapes are simplified by distance and it is easier to see the main perspective lines. In this case the central houses follow the line of the river, and these, the bridges and the dome and towers have been treated in most detail.

left: John Newbury, *The Sheldonian, Oxford,* watercolour. This building is also seen in two-point perspective, but the horizon (eye level) is considerably lower. The diagonals thus slope at a more acute angle, increasing the sense of height.

above: John Lidzey, *Interior with Desk and Chair,* watercolour. The houses outside have been deliberately "held back", with the minimum of detail and tonal contrast so that they do not compete with the interior.

Inside Looking Out

The way in which you approach a view through a window depends very much on the aim of your painting. Window views, or glimpses of the outside world seen through open doors, have always fascinated artists, as they provide an intriguing and challenging set of pictorial possibilities. But like all good subjects, they have their attendant problems.

The main difficulties are those of creating a sense of space and emphasizing the different qualities of inside and outside without losing the unity of the picture. Of course, not everyone sees things in terms of space – some artists will deliberately ignore it, treating interior walls, windows and the outside landscape as a more-or-less flat area of colour and pattern. If you want to do this, fine, but if your approach is more literal, the following advice may be helpful.

Framing a View

First decide how much of the picture area is to be devoted to the view out of the window or door. Suppose this view is an exciting cityscape and you want to make it the main subject of the painting, with the window itself acting as little more than a frame around the edges. In this case, you can treat the scene just as you would if you were painting it outdoors. But you will have to give extra emphasis to the window in terms of tone or colour – or both – because objects nearer to you always have brighter colour and more tonal contrast (a more obvious division between light and dark) than those in the middle and far distance. This is a neat way of giving a feeling of space and recession to the view itself, because the window will immediately come forward to the front of the picture – known as the picture plane.

Inside/Outside

But you may be as interested in the interior of the room as you are in the view, and herein lies a treble danger. First, you may find that the painting begins to divide into two separate pieces – a landscape and an interior – which do not relate to one another. Secondly, the landscape may start to crowd into the room instead of occupying its proper place in space. And thirdly, if you have been over-zealous in space-creating, the landscape may recede so much that it no longer forms an important part of the picture.

The first and third of these potential problems can be overcome by creating a series of pictorial links between inside and out. For example, if there is bright sunshine outside, make the most of any patches of sunlight that come into the room. If your outside scene includes trees or plants, echo them inside by inventing a foliate wallpaper or curtain, or even a touch or two of green in a shadow. If the landscape has a preponderance of one colour, use some of the same colour or a related one in the foreground as well. Try to limit your palette so that you do not use one set of colours for the outside and another for the inside; nothing could be better calculated to destroy the unity of a picture.

The second hazard, that of an encroaching view, is easily avoided by keeping the tonal contrast stronger in the foreground, as described above. You might also include a brightly coloured object in front of the window, such as a patterned curtain or a vase of

flowers on the sill, which will help to push the landscape back. Or you can exploit the contrast between cool and warm colours, one of the most interesting features of outside/inside subjects, using warm reds, yellows and browns, which tend to come towards the picture plane, in the foreground, and cooler blues, greys and blue-greens for the landscape.

Holding Back

Finally, you may find that the picture you want to paint is the interior itself, but the window is fortuitously present, and you must decide how to deal with it. You may choose to ignore the view altogether, and simply paint the window as a bright area representing sunshine, or an overall neutral which does not draw attention to the outside world. This can be successful, but it sometimes makes a painting look curiously blank and unfinished, like a mirror with nothing reflected in it. If you want to suggest the view without letting it take over the picture and compete with your centre of interest, treat it with the minimum of detail, as little tonal contrast as possible and no bright colours. For obvious reasons, this is known as "holding it back".

below: John Newbury, *Keble College, Oxford,* watercolour. A low viewpoint was the perfect choice for this famous Gothic-revival building, stressing its angular height and outlining the pointed pinnacles against the sky. The artist has placed the building uncompromisingly in the centre of the composition and leaving the sky as a pale monochrome wash of grey. The line of cars and dark figures in the street below give an indication of scale, while the single dark tree enhances the feeling of brooding strength.

right: Sandra Walker, *Brad Street II,* 55.9 x 76.2 cm (22 x 30 in), watercolour. Walker is fascinated by the atmosphere and textures of buildings and has painted a series of large watercolours of London's crumbling East End, of which this is one. Her draughtsmanship is superb and her paintings are remarkable for their accuracy of detail. She has built up texture by a combination of spattering, dry brush and scraping with a razor blade.

The animal kingdom presents the commonest of all problems to the would-be recorder of its glories: none of its members stay still long enough to be painted. One can usually bribe a friend to sit reasonably still for a portrait, but you cannot expect the same co-operation from a dog, cat or horse. If movement is the essence of a subject, however, why not learn to make a virtue of it?

Watch an animal carefully and you will notice that the movements it makes, although they may be rapid, are not random – they have certain patterns. If you train yourself to make quick sketches whenever possible and also take sequences of photographs as an aid to understanding their movement, you will find that painting a moving animal is far from impossible – and it is also deeply rewarding.

We in the twentieth century are lucky, because we benefit from the studies and observations of past generations. We know, for instance, that a horse moves its legs in a certain way in each of its four paces – walking, trotting, cantering and galloping – but when Edgar Degas (1834–1917) began to paint his marvellous racing scenes he did not fully understand these movements. He painted horses galloping with all four legs outstretched, as they had appeared in English sporting prints. It was only when Eadweard Muybridge (1830–1904) published his series of photographs of animals in motion in 1888 that Degas saw his error and was quick to incorporate the new-found knowledge into his paintings. This points up the values of the camera as a source of reference, but photographs should never be slavishly copied, as this will result in a static, unconvincing image – photographs have a tendency to flatten and distort form and "freeze" movement.

Understanding the Basics

Painters and illustrators who specialize in natural history gain their knowledge in a wide variety of ways. Many take powerful binoculars and cameras into remote parts of the countryside to watch and record birds and animals in their natural habitats, but they also rely on illustrations and photographs in books and magazines or study stuffed creatures in museums. All this research helps them to understand basic structures, such as the way a bird's wing and tail feathers lie or how a horse or cow's legs are jointed. In the past, artists were taught that a detailed study of anatomy was necessary before they could even begin to draw or paint any living creature. Some wildlife painters, whose prime concern is accuracy, still do this, but for most this depth of study is unnecessary.

Sketching from Life

Although background knowledge is helpful because it will enable you to paint with more confidence, books and magazines are never a substitute for direct observation. When you are working outdoors, whether in a zoo or on a farm, try to keep your sketches simple, concentrating on the main lines and shapes without worrying about details such as texture and colouring. If the animal moves while you are in mid sketch, leave it and start another one – several small drawings on the same page can provide a surprising amount of information. You may find it difficult at first, but quick sketches are a knack and you really will get better with practice, partly because you will be unconsciously teaching yourself to really look at your subject in an analytical and selective way.

below: Laura Wade, *Macaws,* watercolour, gouache and coloured pencils. The artist has made good use of mixed media to build up the birds' vivid colours and delicate textures. Like many professional illustrators, she used photographs as well as drawings from life for her reference; this is the original of a printed illustration in a guide brochure.

top left, above and right: David Boys, Sketchbook Studies. Boys is a professional wildlife artist, whose studies are used by the London Zoo as part of the information labels outside their aviaries and animal cages. The free and spontaneous appearance of his sketches should not blind us to the fact that they are extremely accurate, and each one is the end-product of several days of careful observation and constant drawing. However, they provide an excellent example of the use of watercolour as a medium for recording rapid impressions.

above: Paul Dawson, *Snowy Owl*, 27.9 x 22.2 cm (11 x 8¾ in), watercolour and gouache. Although the paint has been used thickly in places, this is surprisingly not the case on the bird itself, which was protected with masking fluid throughout the process of building up the background and foreground. The artist wanted the white to be that of the paper (in this case a smooth-surfaced one), which stands out far more brilliantly than opaque white paint.

To achieve the depth of tone in the trees, foliage and grass, Dawson began by laying dark watercolour base washes, over which he worked in gouache. The stones in the foreground are watercolour with a little gouache, stippled on with an old brush with splayed bristles – never throw such brushes away, as they may come in useful.

The feathers of the bird were then built up carefully with small delicate brushstrokes, with care taken not to destroy the effect of the white against the deep browns and greens.

Birds

Birds are a perennially appealing subject, but they are also a complex one. The fur of a smooth-haired animal does not obscure the structure beneath, but the feathers of a bird do – if you look at a skeleton in a museum you may find it hard to relate it to the living, feathered reality. To portray a bird convincingly it is important to understand the framework around which it is "built", and the way the small feathers follow the contours of the body while those of the wing and tail extend beyond it. Never be ashamed to draw on the store of knowledge built up by others: look through natural history books and photographs in wildlife magazines as well as sketching birds whenever you can.

If you are painting birds in their natural habitat, you will need to concentrate on shape and movement rather than detail. Both the line and wash and the brush drawing methods are well suited to this kind of broad impression, but the two most exciting features of birds, particularly exotic ones, are colour and texture, and many bird painters employ a more detailed technique to show these in their full glory.

You can practise painting feathers and discover ways of building up texture by working initially from a photograph or another artist's work or even by painting a stuffed bird. If you find that watercolour is hard to control or becomes overworked, you could try gouache, acrylic or one of the many mixed media techniques.

Domestic and Farm Animals

All the best paintings are of subjects that the artist is deeply familiar with. Rembrandt (1606–69) painted himself, his wife and his children, while much of John Constable's (1776–1837) artistic output was inspired by his native Suffolk. So if you want to paint animals and have a captive subject, such as your own dog, cat or pet rabbit, why not start at home?

One of the great advantages of pets is that they are always around and you can make studies of them sleeping (cats are particularly good at this), running, eating or simply sitting in contemplation. If you live in the country, on or near a farm, sheep, cows and goats are also willing models, as they tend to stand still for long periods when grazing. One of the commonest mistakes in painting an animal is to pay insufficient attention to its environment, so that it appears to be floating in mid-air. Whether you are painting a cat lying on a windowsill or a cow in a field, always try to integrate the animal with the background and foreground, blurring the edges in places to avoid a cut-out effect.

The techniques you use are entirely a matter of personal preference and will be dictated by your particular interests, but it is worth saying that if you opt for a very precise method, using small brushstrokes to build up the texture of an animal's fur or wool, you must use the same approach throughout the painting or the picture will look disjointed and unreal.

above: Ronald Jesty RBA, *Shandie,* 27.9 cm (11 in) diameter, watercolour. Although this is not a particularly small picture, the artist has chosen a circular format reminiscent of a miniature for his delightful dog portrait and has adapted his technique to suit the idea. His usual style, illustrated elsewhere in this book, is a precise yet bold use of wet-on-dry, but here, although still working wet-on-dry, he has used very fine, linear brushstrokes to build up the texture of the fur. The buildings behind are treated in equal detail, but with the tones and colours carefully controlled so that they recede into the background.

right: Lucy Willis, *Lefteri Milking,* 28.6 x 38.5 cm (11¼ x 15⅛ in), watercolour. Willis works directly from life, using a heavy paper that does not need to be stretched, a limited palette and usually only one brush. She says that her aim is simply to translate to paper a selected chunk of what she sees, but she always spends some time looking at her subject before she starts to paint, in order to impress upon herself exactly what it is she is aiming for. Her most frequent preoccupations are with colour and light, beautifully conveyed here, as in most of her watercolours. Notice the attractive sparkle given by the little patches of white paper left uncovered between brushstrokes.

left: Richard Wills, *White Horse,* 76.2 x 50.8 cm (30 x 20 in), watercolour and acrylic. Wills's control of watercolour is quite breathtaking, and here he has used the most delicate of colours to build up a complex series of forms. Where each pale wash overlaps another, a hard line is formed and these have been used with absolute precision to define the bony structure of the head and sinewy strength of the neck. This crispness contrasts with the softer areas worked wet-in-wet, with a light spattering of acrylic into wet watercolour blurring the forms and shadows.

Step by Step: Horse's Head

1: Open, loose washes of blue-grey over a light pencil sketch create the initial light and shade.

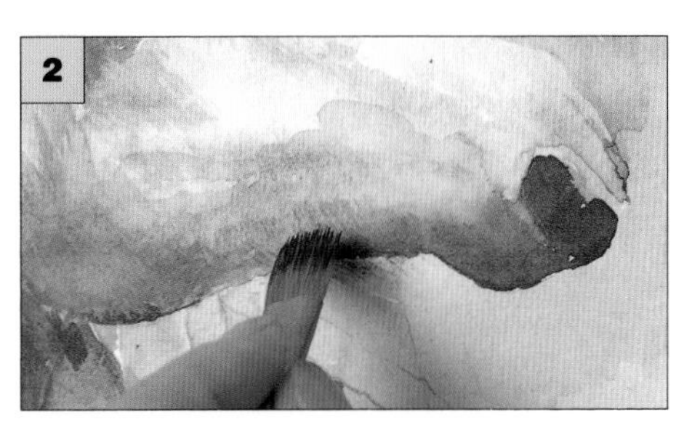

2: Further transparent washes painted wet-on-dry complete the modelling of the head, and are left to dry before the fine hairs over the jaw are suggested with dry brush work.

3: A pencil is then used for added definition in the mane.

4: With any watercolour, too much fiddling around can lose the freshness of the initial washes, so the dry brush and pencil work has been kept to a minimum.

Wild Animals

Painting wild creatures in their natural habitats is becoming an increasingly specialized branch of art, mainly because it involves so much more than simply painting. Professional wildlife artists devote their lives to watching and studying birds and animals in the field, often using sophisticated equipment such as powerful binoculars and cameras with telephoto lenses. However, this does not mean that wild animals are beyond the reach of the ordinary artist. Wildlife is the bread and butter of these specialist painters, and their patrons often require a high standard of accuracy, but not all those who want to paint animals need be so constrained.

There is no need, either, to choose inaccessible subjects. Deer, for example, are eminently paintable and will often come quite close to the viewer in country parks, while shyer, more exotic creatures can be sketched at zoos. A zoo, of course, is not a true habitat for a lion, tiger or monkey, so if you want to use such sketches for a painting of a tiger in a forest you may have to resort to books and magazines for a suitable setting. There is nothing wrong with this – after all, not everyone has the opportunity to paint the forests of Asia and Africa from first hand experience.

above: Sally Michel, *Ring-tailed Lemur,* watercolour and gouache. Michel trained as an illustrator, but began to exhibit paintings when her book illustration work decreased. She became a wildlife artist more or less by accident and is also well known as a painter of cat and dog portraits. She works in both pastel and watercolour and always from life, although she sometimes takes photographs to record a particular pose.

left: David Boys, *Chia-Chia,* sketchbook page, watercolour and pencil. These studies of the giant panda Chia-Chia are the work of the London Zoo artist whose bird sketches are shown on page 205. Although he is a professional wildlife artist, drawing and painting primarily to record precise information, he takes an obvious delight in the watercolour medium, which he uses with great fluency. Notice how the colours have run into one another on the legs of the right-hand panda. This is the result of working on highly sized paper, which can produce interesting results.

right: John Wilder, *Brown Hare,* 38.1 x 50.8 cm (15 x 20 in), gouache. It may seem surprising that this delicate painting was done in gouache, but it provides an excellent demonstration of the versatility of the medium. Although usually associated with bright, bold work, it can be used as effectively for thin, pastel-coloured washes as for vivid, rich impastos. One of its problems is that it dries out very quickly on the palette, but Wilder solves this by using a version of the special stay-wet palette sold for acrylic, a simple device consisting of wet blotting paper under a layer of greaseproof paper.

Wilder started by transferring the main outlines from a working drawing and then laying several very pale overall base washes before beginning to build up the head and body of the hare. Because he likes to leave the outline vague and the brushwork blurred until the final stages, his working process is one of continual painting, blurring, re-defining, over-painting and removing excess paint by sponging or scraping.

Step by Step: Squirrel

1: A series of loose watercolour washes are laid, and then a coloured pencil is brought in to define the details.

2: For the soft grey fur, the artist uses a graphite pencil, making use of the slight grain of the paper to give a broken texture.

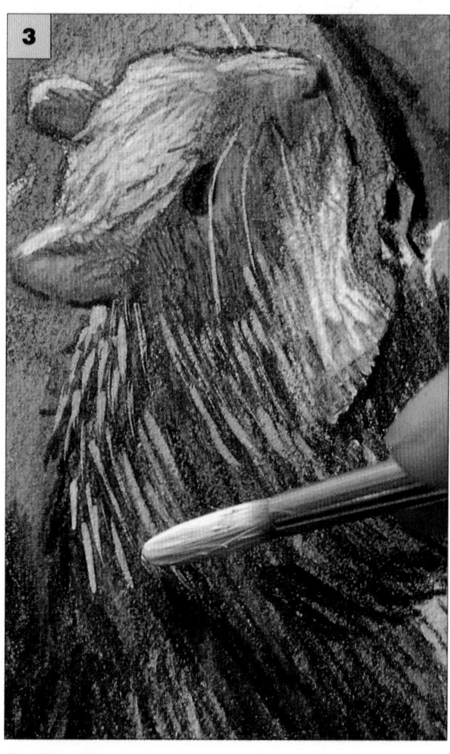

3: Fine lines are then added on top with white gouache to indicate the silvery shimmer so characteristic of a squirrel's fur.

MOVEMENT

When we watch an animal in movement, such as a horse galloping, our eyes take in an overall impression of shape and colour but no precise details – these become blurred and generalized in direct ratio to the speed of the animal's movement. The best way of capturing the essence of movement is to choose a technique that in itself suggests it, so try to keep your work unfussy, applying the paint fluidly and letting your brush follow the direction of the main lines. Alternatively, you could try watercolour pastels or crayons, which can provide an exciting combination of linear qualities and washes. A sketchy treatment, perhaps with areas of paper left uncovered, will suggest motion much more vividly than a highly finished one – the surest way to "freeze" a moving animal is to include too much detail. This is exactly what the camera does: a photograph taken at a fast shutter speed gives a false impression because it registers much more than the human eye can. Photographs, though, are enormously useful for helping you to gain an understanding of the way an animal moves and there is no harm in taking snapshots to use as a "sketchbook" in combination with direct observation and on-the-spot studies.

above: Lucy Willis, *Dog with a Stick III,* 55.9 x 38.4 cm (22 x 15 in), watercolour. Willis has painted rapidly without waiting for washes to dry, so that some brushstrokes have run together. This is offset by crisp brushwork on the muzzle and front paws.

TEXTURES

The fur of an animal or the feathers of a bird are among their most attractive features, but they do present certain problems.

One is that too much attention to texture, the animal's "outer covering", can obscure the underlying form and structure, so you must be careful to paint textures in a way that hints at the body beneath. Perspective makes all objects appear smaller as they recede into the distance, and in the same way the brushstrokes you make to represent fur must vary in size, becoming smaller as the form recedes away from you.

The other problem is the more technical one of how to represent soft fur or stiff, bristly hair with an aqueous medium. Take heart – this is not a real problem at all, but only in the mind, springing from the widely held belief that watercolour can only be used in a broad and fluid manner. In fact, the medium is an extremely versatile one, as can be seen from the illustrations throughout the book.

Fine, linear brushstrokes are an excellent way of painting fur or feathers and, if necessary, the paint can be thickened with opaque white to give it extra body. Another useful technique is dry brush, which can be worked over a preliminary wash or straight onto white paper, while the perfect method for highlighting tiny details, such as whiskers catching the light, is scraping back with the point of a knife, which gives an infinitely finer line than can be achieved with a brush.

right: Kate Gwynn, *Mackerel,* 40.6 x 50.8 cm (16 x 20 in), watercolour.

Step by Step: Mackerel

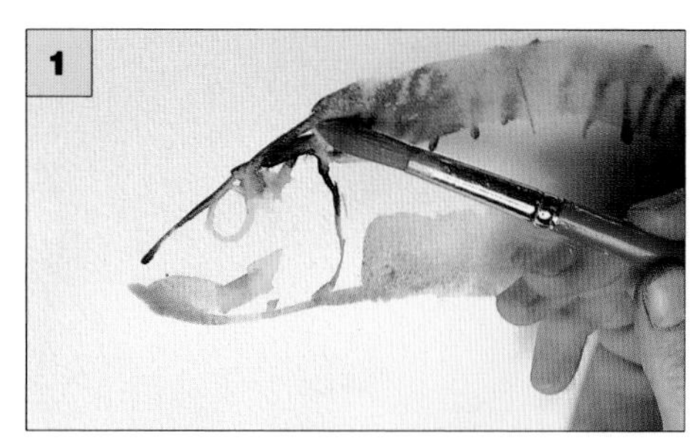

1: The artist begins by working wet-in-wet, allowing slightly opaque yellow paint to merge into the blue-grey.

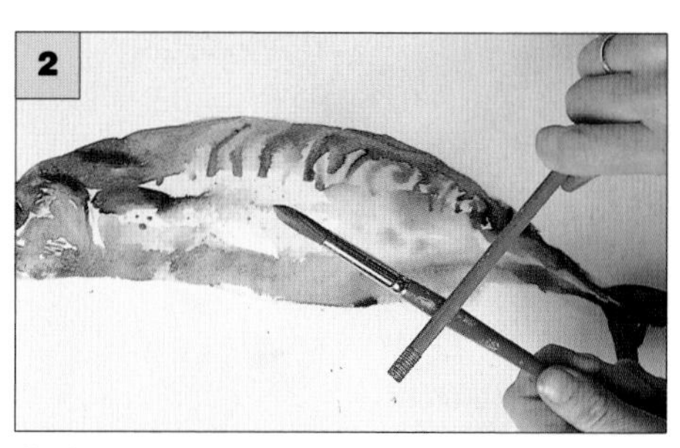

2: Having laid the first washes to establish the main colours and tones, she now spatters paint lightly on to the body.

3: This detail of the finished painting shows a skilful use of overlaid wet washes to describe the soft, glowing colours, with the white paper forming the silvery highlights.

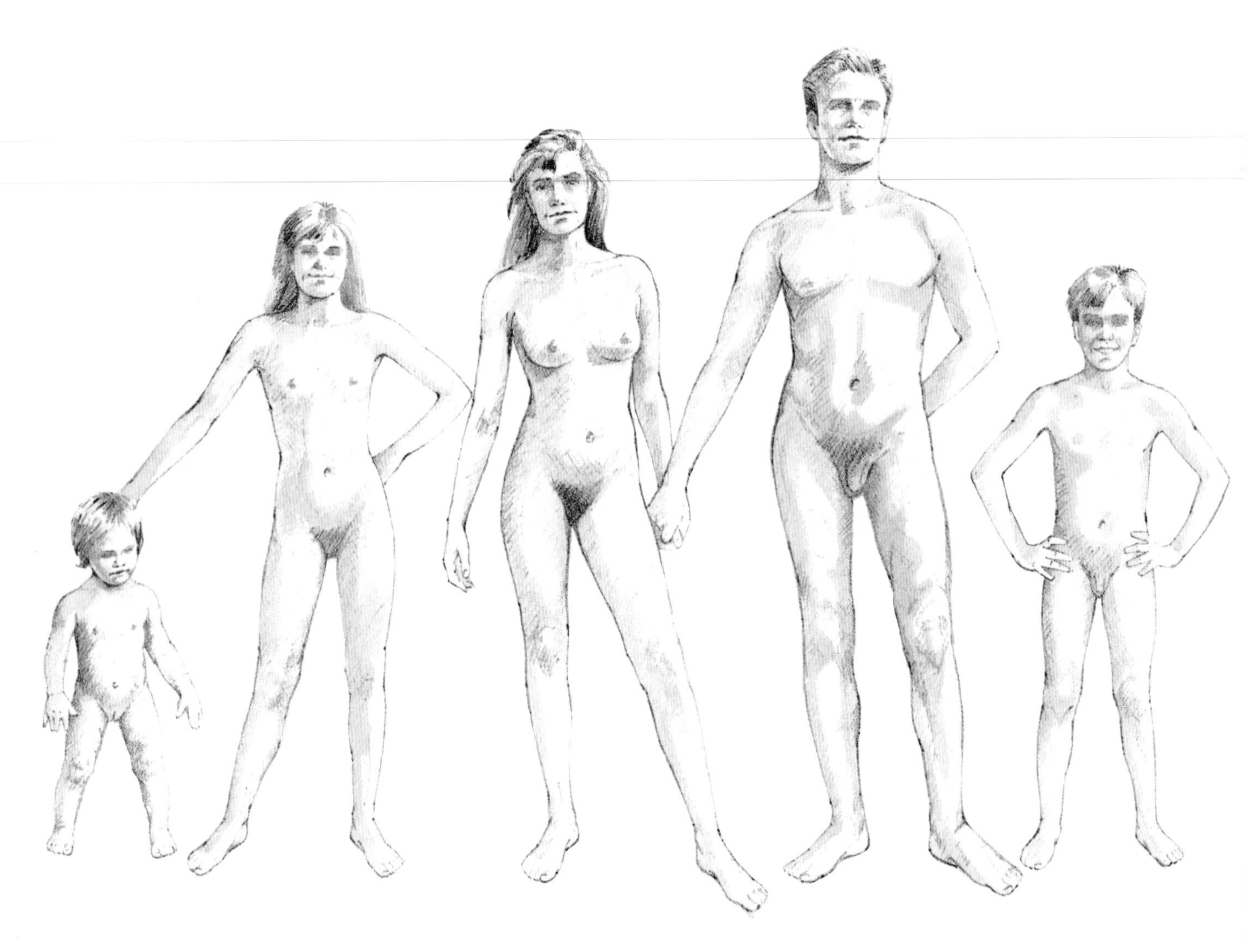

Proportions of The Figure

The key to successful figure drawing is to get the various parts of the body in their correct proportions. This is easier said than done, since our eyes tend to mislead us into seeing some parts as larger or smaller than they really are. The hands and feet, for example, are frequently drawn too small.

Most artists gauge body proportions by taking the head as their unit of measurement. Allowing for slight differences from one person to another, the adult human figure measures seven to seven-and-a-half heads from top to bottom. Although no two people are exactly alike, it is helpful to memorize the proportions of the "ideal" figure and keep these in mind as you draw.

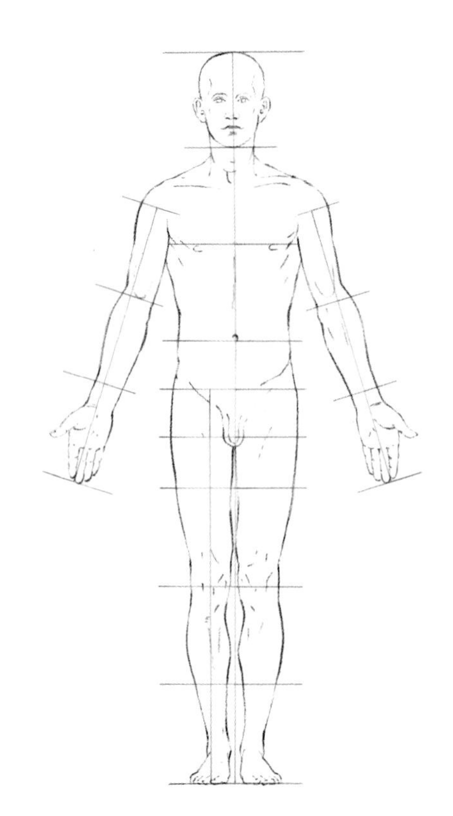

above: These illustrations show the pattern of physical growth from birth to maturity. The average adult body is about seven or eight heads tall; a child's body is about five heads tall; in babies, the body is about three heads tall, and the legs are proportionately shorter.

left: The proportions of the body have preoccupied artists since antiquity. The diagram shows how the French anatomist Richer divided the body into 7½ head lengths. The middle section in the pelvis area is where he added his extra half a head. These ideas of proportion are useful for the beginner, but remember that no system of measurement can replace sensitive observation.

PROPORTIONS OF THE HEAD

Inexperienced artists frequently pay too much attention to the individual features of the face, often drawing them too large in proportion to the head as a whole. The positioning of the features may also be confused, the most common error being that the eyes are placed too high up on the head. When drawing a portrait head, it is important to get the basic proportions correct, because it is these which help to produce a good likeness. While recognizing that it is partly the differences in proportion which distinguish one head from another, it is useful to start by getting the basic, or "normal", head proportions firmly fixed in your mind.

The task of drawing the human head becomes much easier if you break it down into manageable portions: first, draw an outline of the head, then sketch guidelines to enable you roughly to position the features, and finally adjust the position of the features according to the individual face before you.

The easiest way of visualizing the shape of the head is to think of it as an egg sitting on top of the cylinder of the neck. Seen from the front, the egg is upright, while from the side it is tilted at roughly 45 degrees. Having established the shape of the head, you can position the features, and here the "rule of halves" is useful. Lightly sketch a horizontal line halfway down the head; this marks the position of the eyes, and from here it is easy to gauge the eyebrow line. Sketch a line midway between the eyebrow line and the base of the chin in order to find the position of the base of the nose; then draw a line midway between the base of the nose and the chin to find the line of the lower lip. Finally, draw a vertical line down the centre of the head to guide you when positioning the features on either side.

Remember that variations in proportion do occur, and that they distinguish one head from another. The rule of halves is intended only as a guide, so do not follow it rigidly or you will end up with unlifelike portraits. It is, however, a useful basis from which to start. Once your guidelines are drawn in, you can use them as a means of checking and comparing the positions of the features of the actual head you are drawing, making adjustments accordingly.

below: The average shape of the head is enclosed frontally in a rectangle. The same head in profile fits into a square with sides equal to the height of the frontal rectangle. As a general guide, the head comprises two equal ellipses – one positioned vertically and one horizontally. Use the rule of halves to find the correct positions of the features; sketch guidelines to help you, and then draw in the features around them. Remember, though, that the proportions will vary slightly from one individual to another.

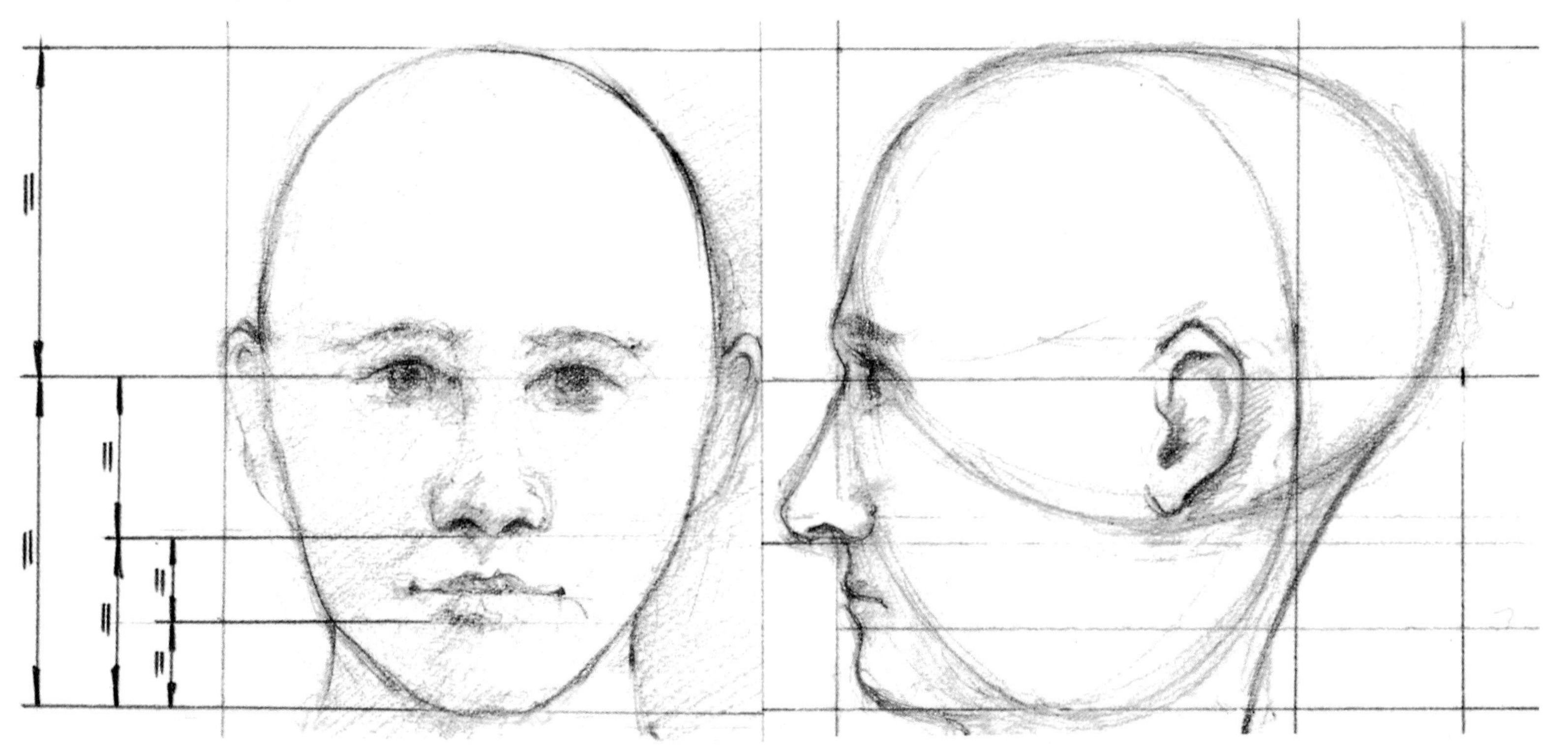

Head From an Angle

One of the most difficult things when drawing a head is to apply the "rules" of proportion if the head is seen in semi-profile, or is tipped back or forward. From these angles, the eyes, nose and mouth may appear compressed together or distorted, because they are seen from a foreshortened viewpoint. Because our mind finds it difficult to accept these distortions, and therefore tries to recreate the head-on measurements, the proportions of the head and the positioning of the features have a tendency to go awry.

Drawing the head from an angle involves careful observation and some precise measuring. As you draw, use your pencil as a tool to measure the distance between, say, the nose and the back of the ear and then compare that with the distance from, say, eyebrow to chin. By constantly measuring and comparing in this way you should arrive at an accurate result.

below and right: When the head is cast downward or tilted back the features appear compressed towards the top or bottom of the face. Note also how the position of the ear alters, appearing higher than the eyes when the head is tipped down, and lower than the eyes when the head is tipped back.

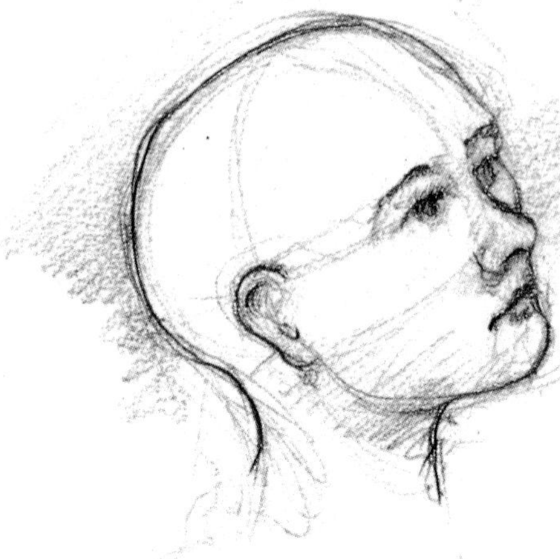

above: Seen from the front, the head is longer than it is wide, but as it is turned to the side, more of the back of the head is revealed. Whereas from the front, the eyes are normally about one eye-width apart, from a three-quarter view that distance may vary, and the eyes are noticeably different from each other in size and shape. As you draw, make sure that the slope of the eyes and mouth is consistent with the tilt of the head; a common mistake is to place the eyes level with each other when the head itself is tilted upwards or downwards.

left: Jan Kunz, *Young Girl,* watercolour. Although more difficult to draw, a three-quarter turned face can often make a more expressive portrait than a face viewed full on. In this portrait, for example, light striking the face from an angle creates interesting highlights and shadows. These not only define the modelling of the features, but also lend life and atmosphere to the portrait.

Flesh Tones

There is no single, all-embracing formula for painting skin tones, because they vary enormously, even within the same sex and racial group – and even between one part of the body and another.

Commercially available flesh tint colours are very useful – for painting clouds at evening. Do not rely on them for painting skin, though, because they are dull, dull, dull! With suitable mixing, you can create hues that are infinitely changeable, enabling you to capture all the warmth and subtlety of human flesh. For example, a suitable mixture for "white" skin might comprise roughly equal quantities of white, alizarin crimson and yellow ochre, with a touch of cadmium red. Mixing these colours in different proportions gives you a good base from which to start. Red, umbers and siennas can be added to warm up the prominent, light-struck areas, while blues, violets and greens can be added in the shadow areas and receding places.

The colours that you choose to mix will, of course, depend on the particular skin type of your sitter. Decide first whether it is generally a warm ivory colour, pale and sallow, ruddy or olive. Mix a mid-tone accordingly and apply it, well diluted, as a base colour. Paint quickly and freely, wet-in-wet. Working from this base colour, start to place the lightest and darkest tones, and then work on the mid-tones – those transitional areas between light and shadow. Remember that the colours in the sitter's clothing and the background will affect the colours of the flesh tones, so develop these along with the face. As you work, it helps to step back from the painting from time to time to check that the combination of colours and tones is creating the desired effect.

Gamboge + a touch of madder lake

Yellow ochre + madder lake

Yellow ochre + madder lake + a touch of cobalt blue

Viridian + gamboge + burnt sienna

Yellow ochre + madder lake, very diluted

Gamboge + burnt sienna + a touch of viridian

above: There is no set formula for mixing flesh tones: your best plan is to experiment with different combinations of colour and see which ones work best. Some suggestions are offered here.

Step by Step: Young Skin

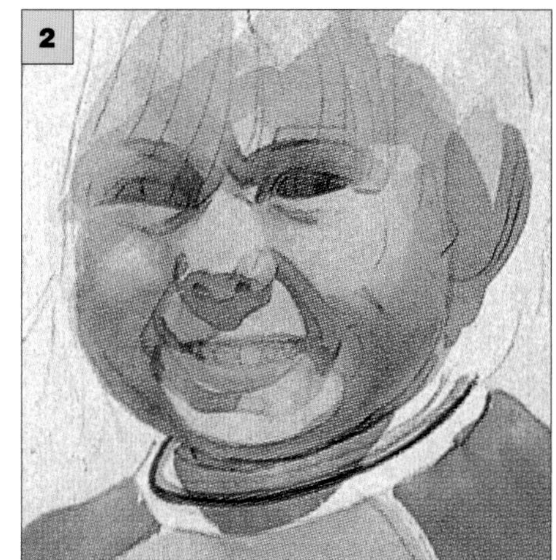

1: When painting the smooth skin of children it is essential to avoid too many hard edges. Here they are used only for the distinct shadow areas, such as the brows, while the colours for the rounded cheeks are blended wet-in-wet.

2: Further washes are introduced, with the artist still paying special attention to the balance of hard and soft edges.

3: The hair acts as a frame to the face, but the artist is careful not to treat it in too much detail as this might draw the eye away from the features. The mass of the hair is painted loosely, wet-in-wet, with crisper wet-on-dry brushstrokes over the forehead.

Burnt sienna + yellow ochre + a touch of madder lake deep

Burnt sienna + a touch of cobalt blue

Yellow ochre + burnt sienna

Viridian + yellow ochre + burnt sienna

Burnt umber + Rembrandt blue

Burnt sienna + a touch of cobalt blue

Burnt umber + burnt sienna + Rembrandt blue

Burnt umber + a touch of madder lake + Rembrandt blue

above: Here are some suggested colour mixtures for painting dark skin tones.

When it comes to painting dark skin tones, you might assume that you would use straightforward mixtures of browns and greys, with a high proportion of black. On the contrary you should follow the same procedures as when painting a white-skinned subject. First, determine whether his or her complexion tends towards the warm or the cool side. Mix a colour that most closely approximates the overall impression and use it for the initial block-in. After this, establish the lightest and darkest tones before introducing the mid-tones. Dark skin looks warmest in the shadows and coolest in the highlights, which have a bluish tinge.

No matter how dark your sitter, resist the temptation to use black in your flesh tone mixtures, as this will kill the portrait. Deeper, richer skin tones can be achieved by working with dark umbers, siennas, ochres, violets and blues. Dark skins generally have more of a sheen to them than Caucasian skins, and thus the contrast between the highlights and the darker areas surrounding them can appear quite strong.

Shadows and Highlights

It is impossible to analyze closely the colour of shadows and highlights on the skin. They are not simply a lightened or darkened version of the basic skin colour, so if you add white to create highlights or black to create shadows, you will find that this is a less than adequate solution.

Highlights and shadows on the skin are fascinating because they often contain quite unexpected colours. If you have the courage to put down the colours you see, rather than those you *expect* to see, you will find that your portraits will come alive. You will notice, for example, that the skin on the prominent, light-struck parts, such as the forehead, nose, cheeks and chin, may contain warm reds and yellows, while the receding planes, such as the eye sockets, the shadow side of the nose and the area under the chin, contain cool blues, browns, violets and green-greys. However, this is by no means an absolute rule; skin is basically warm in colour, so a shadow cast by one area of skin on to another will retail a degree of warmth. You will notice this particularly in folds in the skin, on wrinkles, and in the shadow under the lip.

The use of warm and cool colours in skin tones serves another important purpose: because warm colours appear to advance and cool colours to recede, you can use warm/cool contrasts to model the advancing and receding planes of the face and figure, thereby giving your portraits a strong sense of three-dimensional form and solidity.

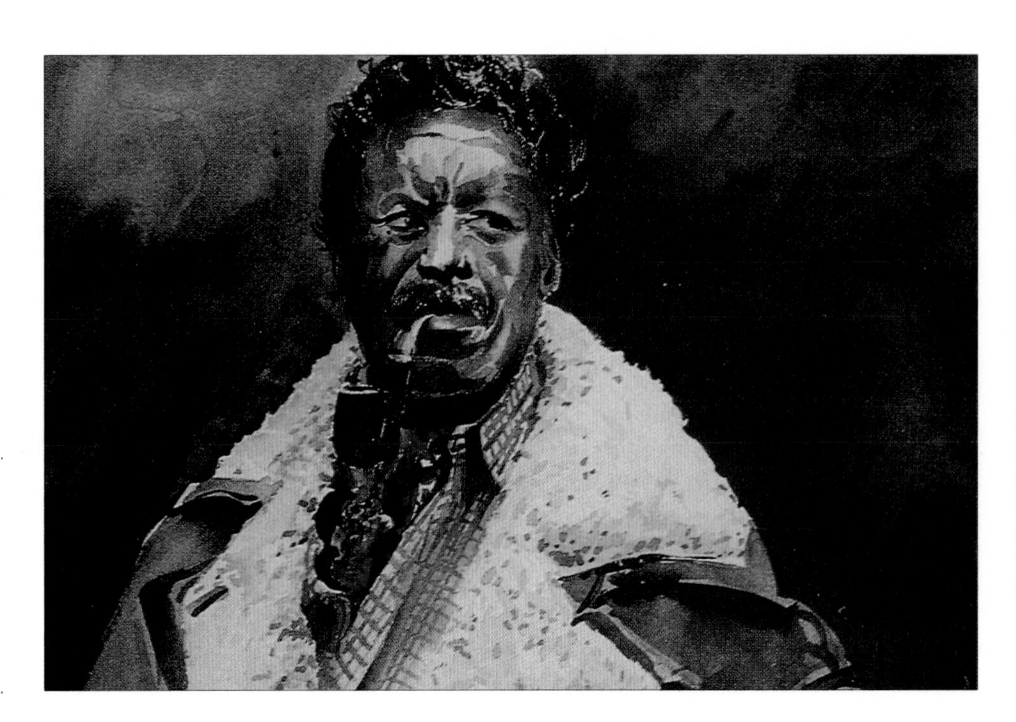

right: Douglas Lew, *Portrait of Gordon Parks,* watercolour. Dark skins generally have more of a sheen than Caucasian skins, and thus the contrast between the highlights and the darker areas surrounding them can appear quite strong.

HAIR

There is such a range of textures and styles seen on the human head that it is impossible to generalize about them, but there are some points to bear in mind when you are drawing or painting. The most important is to ensure that you relate the hair to the head itself. This sounds obvious, but if your subject has an elaborate hairstyle it is only too easy to become so involved in the intricacies of curls and waves that you forget about the shape of the skull beneath and the way the hair relates to the face. Start by blocking in the main masses and then pay careful attention to the rhythms of the hair.

The way hair flows and falls into a series of gentle waves was a source of particular fascination to Leonardo da Vinci, who saw it as analogous to the movement of water as it eddied and twisted past obstacles: you can see this idea at work in a painting such as *The Virgin of the Rocks* in the National Gallery in London. Starting off as gentle undulations, the tumbling hair of the Virgin then begins to form waves and finally breaks up into those characteristic plaiting forms which Leonardo loved to use in so many of his drawings of water. These analogies can be extremely helpful because they tend to reinforce central ideas such as rhythm and flow which are so essential to being able to paint hair convincingly.

Look for the weight of the hair, too, as this is important in giving shape to the style, even in the case of short hair. All hairstylists know that thick, heavy hair holds its shape better than thin, wispy hair, and the more shape it has the easier it is to paint – you can simplify the forms, using long sweeping brushstrokes that follow the flow of the hair. Thin, frizzy or "flyaway" hair does not always follow the shape of the head very precisely, and is in general more demanding in terms of technique.

The final quality to look out for is the sheen of the hair. For the painter this is the most important characteristic of all, the highlight giving the vital textural clues. Dark oily hair will have very pronounced highlights, thick, dry hair diffused ones, and thin, dry or frizzy hair almost no recognizable highlight.

Step by Step: Painting Hair

1: After making a light preliminary pencil drawing, broad, loose washes are laid over the whole of the hair. These are allowed to dry before crisper definition is added.

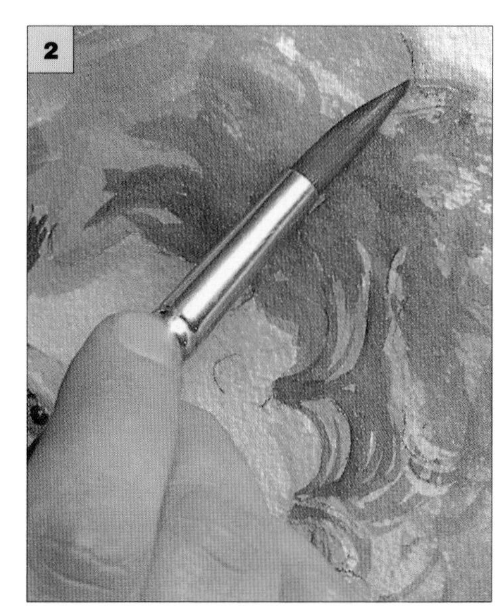

2: The artist is aiming at a hard-edged effect, so he works wet-on-dry to give distinct edges to each wash. He also uses masking fluid to reserve the clearer highlights.

3: In the final stage the effect of the masking fluid can be clearly seen, giving the effect of "negative" brushstrokes in the area above the forehead.

–ARTISTS' HINTS–

- When drawing or painting curly or "flyaway" hair, be careful to avoid hard outlines at the edges.
- A dry brush technique would be suitable for depicting a short beard, or perhaps try a mixture of watercolour and pencil.
- A complex, elaborate texture such as that of very long, curly hair can often be simplified by using indirect lighting on the subject.
- To describe large sweeping waves of hair, allow your brush to follow the main rhythms – don't get caught up in the details.
- With dark hair, where you can't see a great deal of detail, the main mass can be depicted as a simple shape, but be sure to soften the edges to suggest the texture, and perhaps pick out a few individual strands.

Painting Fabrics

Fabrics play an important part in three major branches of painting – portraiture, still-life and interiors – so the only artists who do not have to think about how best to depict them are those who paint nothing but landscape. Fabrics have always represented a considerable challenge to the skill of the artist, and over the centuries you can see the way in which still-life and portrait painters have "showed off" and vied with one another to produce sumptuous and minutely observed renderings of silks, satins, brocades, velvets and Oriental carpets.

On occasion the costume of a sitter became more important than the face: in some of the paintings of Queen Elizabeth I a wooden unnatural-looking head surmounts a jewelled gown of breathtaking intricacy.

In general, artists' interests in the texture of fabrics is less apparent than in the past, but there are exceptions, among the most notable being the modern British painter Lucian Freud (b. 1922), who takes great delight in painting decayed fabrics, with old, battered sofas and frayed cloths providing a fascinating counterpoint to the flesh of his naked figures.

When you start to draw or paint fabrics, whether you are depicting the sitter's clothing in a portrait, curtains or soft furnishings in an interior, or drapery as a background in a still-life, look out for three main characteristics. The first characteristic is the way light is reflected from the material; the second is the arrangement of folds or creases; and the third is the nature of the shadow areas.

Reflected Light

Perhaps the most important of these is the highlight because it will immediately indicate the material's smoothness or roughness. Highlights for a smooth, shiny material such as silk or satin will be sharp and bright, while those for a matt-surfaced, coarse-woven or knitted one will be more diffuse and comparatively duller – they may not even be recognizable as highlights in the true sense of the word.

Another characteristic to look out for is the "speed" of the highlights. In silk you will find that they seem to zip across the material, activating the whole garment, whereas for softer materials such as wool they will be flatter and more static. When painting these characteristic highlights look out for the way they interconnect. A common mistake is to see them as somehow isolated from the rest of the garment, and this leads to a patchy effect. Instead see if you can get a rhythm of highlight areas that passes across the material, uniting all the different parts.

Folds

The folds in a fabric will indicate how thick or thin it is. Thick fabrics will fall into a small number of large folds, while thin materials will have many more folds which are smaller and multi-directional. For the figure and portrait painter these thinner materials such as cottons and silks can present a number of tricky problems, so it is always a good idea to try to minimize them before starting to

Step by Step: Ribbed Sweater

1, 2: You can acquire valuable practice in painting garments by treating them initially as a form of still-life, as in this case, where the sweater has been carefully arranged to create an interesting composition. The artist begins by laying light washes, ignoring the ribbed texture at this stage.

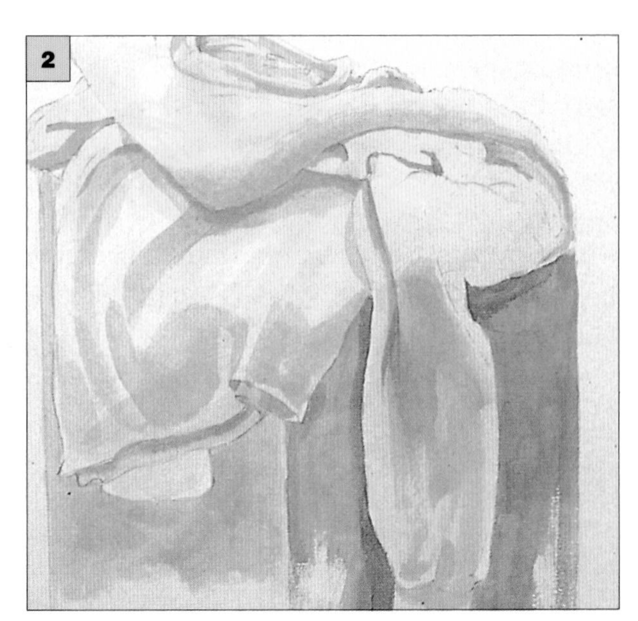

paint. If the subject of the painting is a clothed figure, try and make the arrangement of the clothes as simple as possible. If you have to reorganize clothing by pulling the fabric and letting it fall again, make sure that the new arrangement fits in with the rest of the composition and also helps express the forms beneath. There is nothing more confusing to the eye than a bunch of isolated folds – in a sleeve, for example – or the creasing in a pair of trousers which, although they might have been true to life, do not describe either the flow of the garment or the forms beneath. If you can, be ruthless, and select only the major folds and creases in the garment to draw or paint, ignoring the rest.

Shadow Areas

The final characteristic of fabrics, the nature of the shadows, is a vital indicator of the sheen or shininess of the material. A material such as silk or satin reflects so much light even in the shadows that you will find it difficult to locate a really dark tone except in the sharpest fold. Pay special attention, therefore, to the contrast between the highlight and the tone of the surrounding material. With materials such as velvet the opposite applies – you will find that the deepest folds will be very dark because the rougher surface will not reflect light, and the highlights will be much less noticeable than on a silky fabric for the same reason. Black velvet is one of the few fabrics that does look really black, regardless of lighting.

Pattern and Texture

Pattern can also be a strong indicator of the texture of a fabric, being more sharply defined on a thin one than on a thick, coarse one. This is worth remembering if you want to include a patterned carpet in an interior – often the best way to suggest the texture is to pay careful attention to the design.

However, there are occasions when you might want to make more of the texture of something like a fine oriental rug in a painting, or even make its colour and texture the focal point of the picture. In such cases, the best general rule, whichever medium you are using, is to let the brushwork do the description for you.

Drapery

Drapery, usually in the form of a white napkin or cloth, has been a standard element in still-life paintings for hundreds of years. It is mostly employed as a means of assisting in a composition, with the folds and soft lines of the cloth helping to direct the eye across and around the picture, or breaking up the strong line of the edge of a table, but it can also be extremely useful as a foil to other textures. You will find white tablecloths used in this role in many artists' compositions, the cloth uniting the arrangement of objects.

Curtains can also be employed as a background to the composition. Cézanne (1839–1906), in many of his later still-lifes, used a heavy decorated material as a backdrop for arrangements of pots and fruit, organizing the composition so that the fruit found an echo in the pattern of the material.

3: A fine brush is then used to paint the lines of ribbing, with the pressure varied to produce an uneven line.

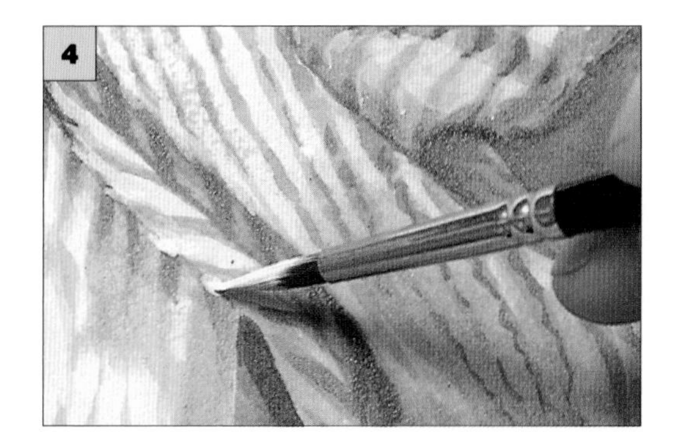

4: White gouache is brought in to soften some of the edges and clarify the lines.

5: Some areas have been described very precisely, while others are suggested; loose washes with the minimum of definition are sufficient for some of the shadow areas.

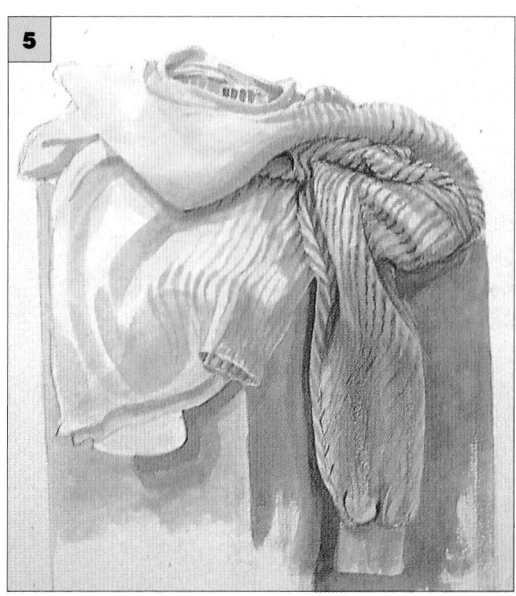

Capturing a Likeness

Capturing a likeness of your subject is not just a question of making an accurate reproduction of the physical features. It is also about getting under the skin of the person and revealing something about their personality and their inner feelings. When these two aspects – sound observational drawing and an emotional empathy with the subject – work in tandem, the result is a portrait that is alive and meaningful.

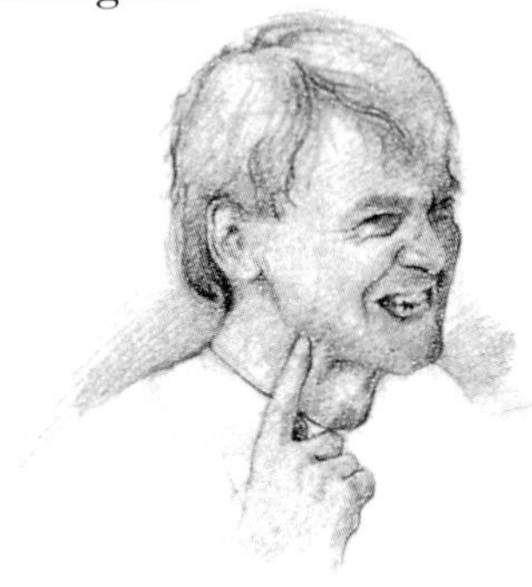

above: To familarize yourself with the range of human facial expressions, make sketches from live models, or from photographs in magazines and newspapers.

above: Getting the features in correct relation to each other is important in capturing an individual likeness. Use your pencil or brush to check angles and distances between points of importance on the face.

Assessing personality will present few problems if your sitter is someone you know well. But even if your sitter is a total stranger, you will find that most people reveal something of their personality as soon as they enter a room. The way in which a person dresses and speaks, and the gestures and mannerisms that they habitually adopt, all give important clues to personality.

Before you even put pencil to paper, try to absorb a general impression of your subject. Is the person confident and outgoing, or shy and sensitive? Does the face have the innocence and bloom of youth, or is it etched with the lines that come from decades of laughter and sadness? Look out for repeated gestures and mannerisms, the tilt of the head, the set of the jaw, the pose adopted when sitting or standing. All of these things are part of an individual's "personal imprint", and every bit as important as their physical features in distinguishing them from other individuals.

As you work, talk to your sitter and do not be put off if he moves slightly or if his expression alters.

above: Douglas Lew, *Duke,* watercolour. In a sense, a good portrait contains an element of caricature. In order to inject life into your portrayal, you need to get to the essence of your subject, to seek out and emphasize those distinguishing features and mannerisms that make this person unique. Here, Douglas Lew has captured John Wayne as we all know and love him – in "cowboy" mode.

If you require the model to sit like a dummy, it will hardly be surprising if the finished portrait looks like one.

Sketch out the framework of the head and shoulders, looking for the dominant angles, masses and shapes. Once these are right you can get down to the finer details. When drawing the facial features, keep checking against the model to see that each is correctly positioned in relation to the other. Does the inner corner of the eye line up with the corner of the mouth? How wide is the mouth in relation to the width of the face? What is the distance between the base of the nose and the upper lip?

Moving Figures

Before starting to draw a moving figure, it is important to spend

some time simply observing your model. Try to feel the overall rhythm of the figure's movement and to understand how it works. Mimic the motion yourself in order to experience the way in which the balance of the body changes at different stages of the action. When you feel ready, make some quick sketches. Try to capture the main actions in just a few lines. Do not worry about detail, but be loose in your sketching, using fluid arm movements rather than working tightly. As you sketch, you will find that you develop your own shorthand of quick strokes and lines that "catch the movement".

While watching your subject, you will notice that certain phases or positions within the movement are more active than others. In a walking figure, for example, the point at which the leading foot is about to hit the ground and the other foot is about to lift is the peak moment of the action. If you can capture this peak moment in a stride, a kick, a swing or a reach, your figures will always have energy and life.

When sketching the figure, use the restating method. A single mark outlining a leg will make it look static, but a series of lines will give the impression of change. When painting, apply washes freely to create the "blurred" impression associated with movement.

The composition of a picture is another important factor in accentuating movement. For example, in capturing the exciting atmosphere of a group of athletes racing towards the finishing line, you might choose a head-on viewpoint that propels the viewer straight into the action.

right: Julia Cassels, *The Coconut Beat,* watercolour. When depicting a moving figure, try to "freeze" the action at or just after its peak. In this study, Cassels depicts the figure at the point just after the stick has reached the point of rest between swinging back and coming forward. This position gives the greatest feeling of energy and motion because it implies forward movement.

below: Julia Cassels, *Zanzibar Women,* watercolour. Using swift calligraphic brushstrokes, Cassels captures the languid elegance of these African women walking across the desert. Watercolour's fluidity and immediacy make it an ideal medium for targeting a moving subject.

below: Douglas Lew, *The Green Cyclist,* watercolour. When we watch a subject moving at speed, our eyes do not register precise details but a blurred impression of shape and colour. Douglas Lew harnessed the fluidity of watercolour for this impressionistic study of a racing cyclist. He worked rapidly wet-in-wet, keeping the surface damp almost to the end and avoiding sharp edges; the sense of speed is enhanced by the streaks and blurs of the paint.

INDEX

Page numbers in italic refer to picture captions

ACKNOWLEDGEMENTS

Quintet would like to thank the following for permission to reproduce copyright material. We apologize for any omissions that may have been made.

John Lidzey 26, 135, 156, 202; Robert Tilling 28, 195; Charles Knight 30, 51, 177, 193; Colin Paynton 30; William Tillyer 34; Paul Riley 35; Christopher Baker 42, 43; Jacqueline Rizvi 42, 51, 113, 114; John Tookey 44, 124; Ronald Jesty 44, 95, 160, 166, 176, 194, 195, 196; Donald Pass 44; Juliette Palmer 45, 108; Michael Warr 46; Hazel Harrison 47; Moira Huntly 50, 72, 158; Robert Dodd 50, 177; John McPake 54; Michael Cadman 54, 75, 196; Lucy Willis 55, 116, 117, 121, 171, 206, 210; Jean Canter 62; Doreen Osbourne 66; Edward Piper 66; Audrey Macleod 67, 169; Cathy Johnson 68; Richard Bolton 73; Rosalind Cuthbert 76, 90; Ian Sidaway 82; Ian Simpson 78, 85; Lesley Gilles 85; Stan Perrott 96, 112; Charles Longbotham 99; Charles Harrington 107; David Hutter 109, 117, 118, 122, 123, 129, 130; Frederick Walker 110; Charles Inge 111; Trevor Chamberlain 115; Ken Howard 119; Moira Clinch 119, 128, 133, 176, 201; Keith Andrew 120; David Curtis 134; Richard Akerman 137; Roy Sparkes 148; Francis Towne 175; Carolyne Moran 156, 166; Martin Taylor 156, 157; Shirley Felts 159, 164; Geraldine Girvan 159, 167; Mary Tempest 165, 167; Muriel Pemberton 165; Jean Canter 168; Sharon Beeden 168; Norma Jameson 169; Michael Chaplin 178; Arthur Maderson 186; Ray Evans 187, 198; Margaret M. Martin 191; Douglas Lew 191, 216, 220; Francis Bowyer 192; Sandra Walker 198, 203; John Newberry 201, 203; Laura Wade 204; Paul Dawson 205; Richard Wills 207; David Boys 208; Sally Michel 208; John Wilder 209; Jan Kunz 214; Julia Cassels 221.